Leaving

Science

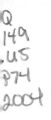

Leaving *Science*

Occupational Exit from Scientific Careers

Anne E. Preston

Russell Sage Foundation

New York

The Russell Sage Foundation

The Russell Sage Foundation, one of the oldest of America's general purpose foundations, was established in 1907 by Mrs. Margaret Olivia Sage for "the improvement of social and living conditions in the United States." The Foundation seeks to fulfill this mandate by fostering the development and dissemination of knowledge about the country's political, social, and economic problems. While the Foundation endeavors to assure the accuracy and objectivity of each book it publishes, the conclusions and interpretations in Russell Sage Foundation publications are those of the authors and not of the Foundation, its Trustees, or its staff. Publication by Russell Sage, therefore, does not imply Foundation endorsement.

Library of Congress Cataloging-in-Publication Data

Preston, Anne Elizabeth.
    Leaving science : occupational exit from scientific careers / Anne E. Preston.
      p. cm.
    Includes bibliographical references and index.
    ISBN 0-87154-694-9
      1. Scientists—Employment—United States—History—20th century.
    2. Sex discrimination in employment—United States—History—20th century.
    3. Discrimination in employment—United States—History—20th century.
    I. Russell Sage Foundation. II. Title.

Q149.U5P74 2004
331.12'615'0973—dc22

2003065968

Text design by Genna Patacsil.

RUSSELL SAGE FOUNDATION
112 East 64th Street, New York, New York 10021
10 9 8 7 6 5 4 3 2 1

To Casey

CONTENTS

ABOUT THE AUTHOR

ANNE E. PRESTON is associate professor of economics at Haverford College.

INTRODUCTION

With the reduction in the percentage of U.S.-born men choosing science and engineering majors over the last thirty years, national attention has turned to recruiting and retaining women and minorities in science. In the 1980s, pipeline issues were prominent as it became clear that the educational conduit through which career scientists must travel was leaking, especially at critical junctures. Research into these phenomena created a host of explanations behind the leakage and has been the impetus behind the implementation of a number of seemingly effective policy proposals. But as the educational system graduates a growing number of women and minorities with a strong scientific education, researchers need to understand that although the pipeline, as defined, ends when a scientific degree is earned, the problem of attrition continues. This book examines attrition from scientific careers for both men and women. This study estimates the rate of occupational exit from science during the period roughly between 1965 and 1995, identifies the differing factors behind exit for male and female scientists, and discusses the consequences for them of leaving science.

Over the last thirty-five years, high school students have become better prepared for careers in science and mathematics at the same time that the percentages of bachelor's degrees awarded in these fields have declined. Since the early 1980s, the average number of high school mathematics courses completed has increased from 2.6 to 3.4, and the average number of science courses completed has increased from 2.2 to 3.1 (U.S. Department of Education, National Center for Educational Statistics [NCES] 2002). The percentages of high school graduates taking calculus, physics, and chemistry have roughly doubled over the same period (National Science Board 2002). As the number of bachelor's degrees awarded has increased by almost 50 percent since 1970, the percentages of these degrees awarded in engineering, the physical sciences, and mathematics have declined. Only biological sciences and computer sciences have experienced relative increases, together increasing from 4.6 percent of all degrees in 1970 to 8 percent in 2000. In fact, the absolute number of mathematics and physical science degrees fell over the period. Similarly, although total Ph.D.s awarded have increased more than 50 percent during the same period, the percentage of doctoral degrees awarded in the natural sciences has declined from 40.6 percent to 32.9 percent and there were absolute declines in mathematics and physical science Ph.D.s (U.S. Department of Education 2002). Only computer science Ph.D.s have increased in relative terms.

This relative decline in science-oriented bachelor's and doctoral degrees over the last thirty years has been especially prominent for U.S.-born nonminority white men. These men are receiving absolutely fewer bachelor's and doctoral degrees than they did in 1976 (U.S. Department of Education 2002). These declines are especially evident in the natural sciences, where there has been a large influx of foreign students. For example, from 1992 to 2001, the absolute number of white male U.S. citizens earning a Ph.D. in the natural sciences or engineering declined by 13.6 percent (U.S. Department of Education 2002). Science policymakers have turned to women and minorities, who had traditionally been underrepresented in science and engineering, to fill the gap. Starting in the early 1980s, governmental organizations such as the National Science Foundation (NSF) and private organizations, including the Alfred P. Sloan Foundation, began financing research programs into the causes of underrepresentation and educational programs at the elementary, secondary, and collegiate level to attract and retain young women and minorities. Although failure to persist is still greater for women and minorities than for white men and certain fields are better at attracting and retaining women and minorities than others, if one judges these programs according to growth in degree recipients, they have been very effective. Since 1970, the percentage of natural science and engineering bachelor's degrees awarded to women has increased from 12 percent to 38 percent; smaller but still significant is the increase from 9.4 percent to 15.8 percent of the portion of Ph.D.s in these areas earned by women. The number of doctoral recipients who are American Indian, African American, or Hispanic has increased from 3.3 percent to 6.7 percent in engineering, from 2.9 percent to 8.1 percent in biological sciences, and from 2.3 percent to 6.3 percent in physical sciences. These same minorities currently make up more than 13 percent of the bachelor's degree recipients in the natural sciences and engineering (U.S. Department of Education 2002).

Although larger numbers of women and minorities are graduating from the science pipeline, little attention has been paid to survival in the workplace for science graduates, regardless of race or gender. But the numbers are striking. Data collected by the Bureau of the Census in the 1980s (Survey of Natural and Social Scientists and Engineers [SSE], 1982–1989) reveal that approximately 8.6 percent of men and 17.4 percent of women left natural science and engineering jobs between 1982 and 1989. In the study, which is the basis for this book and which follows the careers of men and women who graduated with science degrees from a large public university between 1965 and 1990, this two-to-one ratio persists. For science graduates with an average work experience of twelve and a half years, 31.5 percent of the women and 15.5 percent of the men who had started science careers were not employed in science at the time of the survey. The data from the more recent NSF surveys (Division of Science Resource Statistics 1999) allow examination of the younger cohorts of scientists whose degrees were received in the late 1980s through the mid-1990s. In 1999, focusing on individuals under the age of thirty whose highest degree was a B.S. and individuals under the age of thirty-four whose highest degree was either an M.S. or a science Ph.D., women were one and a half times as likely as men to have left science. The statistics are not wholly comparable to the earlier data, since we do not know if these exiting graduates ever entered science careers after the degree was earned, and these individuals are relatively young and inexperienced. Comparably constructed statistics from the public university data reveal that, over the period in which careers were analyzed, 1965 to 1995, female exit rates from science for all science graduates, not just those who start a scientific career, were roughly one and a half times as high as male exit rates five years into the career. Therefore, the more recent statistics show no improvements in retention. Furthermore, they show real problems when compared to attrition of social scientists; in 1999, women under the age of thirty-four with Ph.D.s in the social sciences were half as likely to engage in occupational exit (5.5 percent) as women in the same age cohort with Ph.D.s in the natural sciences and engineering (12.3 percent).

This book is an analysis of the phenomenon of occupational exit from science during the period from 1965 to 1995, giving at least partial answers to the following questions. Why do men and women who have invested extensive time and money on a rigorous science education leave the field? Are the factors contributing to exit related to predictors of success and failure within the field of science? Do these factors differ for men and women? What directions do men and women take after leaving science? What are the consequences, in terms of career and well being, for these leavers?

Exit from the scientific workplace is often wasteful and inefficient for the actors involved. Individuals who have used personal funds to finance a scientific education often turn to occupations for which their learned skills are not nearly as valuable. The social return on educational investments by the federal government is likely to fall, and employing institutions that lose scientific employees cannot benefit from their often extensive training investments.

A better understanding of exit from scientific careers should lead ultimately to changes in the science education process and in the scientific workplace: modifications that will reduce attrition both by improving the information flow to potential scientific workers and by making the scientific workplace more hospitable to career men and women. But such a body of knowledge is also likely to result in workplace enhancements that make science careers more attractive to high-performing educated men and women. Understanding exit is not only a good defense against attrition but also a valuable component of the strategy to increase the attraction and desirability of careers in science.

The primary data set used in the study was collected for the purpose of better understanding attrition of scientists. The 1,688 individuals studied all received either a bachelor's, master's, or Ph.D. degree in natural sciences or engineering from a public university in the northeast between 1965 and 1990. Work histories of these individuals give information on career choices and outcomes from the date of last science degree earned until the survey date, which was roughly 1994. As of that time, only 51 percent of the 1,688 were still working in science. In addition, 103 of the survey respondents—52 men and 51 women—were interviewed between 1994 and 1996 to understand more fully the causes and consequences of exit from scientific employment. The result is a blend of statistical and qualitative analyses of careers of men and women who have earned science degrees. Of those still working in science, some are stars in the scientific community, but most make up the bread-and-butter personnel of our scientific workforce. Their collective stories give a rich and detailed picture of the ultimate product of science education in the United States.

The book begins with a discussion of the period and the people studied, a chapter that describes trends in science and the workplace over the period, blending both statistics and impressions of interviewed scientists. It concludes with a more complete description of the data sets used in the analyses. Chapter 2 continues with a complete examination of the magnitude and character of exit, giving estimates of rates of attrition, identifying demographics of those most likely to leave, and pinpointing major reasons for exit. Chapters 3 through 6 explore the four major reasons for exit identified by interviewees: inadequate salary and opportunity, lack of mentoring, difficulties shouldering family- and career-related responsibilities, and a mismatch between the individual's interests and the requirements of the scientific profession. Chapters 7 and 8 discuss the two important issues in the scientific workplace that were identified as having indirect effects on exit: rapidly growing knowledge within science and perceived discriminatory treatment of women. Finally, chapter 9 discusses policy prescriptions.

CHAPTER 1

Science: The Period and the People

*The scientific discovery process is always peeling away layers of an onion with-
out ever knowing how many you have to peel before you find the core.*
                                                    —Anonymous interviewee[1]

The focus of this study is the workplace experiences of men and
women trained in the sciences between the mid-1960s and the
mid-1990s. As a field of study and work, science has been influenced by four important changes over this period. First, and maybe
most important, federal research funds, which made up two-thirds of
research and development (R&D) spending at the beginning of the
thirty-year period, fell to just over one-third of R&D funds by its end,
as shown in figure 1.1. Second, fields of study that were most successful at attracting public attention, research funds, and new students
changed dramatically during this period. Third, especially in the latter
half of this period, there was an enormous influx of foreign-born scientists into Ph.D. programs and into the scientific workforce. Finally,
women became a nontrivial and an increasing portion of the student
body as well as the workforce in science. All of these changes had important effects on the workplace and careers of scientifically trained
individuals.

Figure 1.1   Federal and Nonfederal Research and
               Development Expenditures

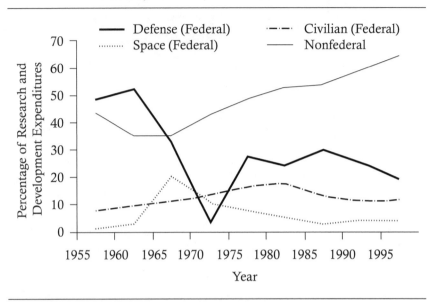

Source: Based on National Science Board 2002, table C-14.

Implications of the Changing
Sources and Destinations of R&D Funding

Scientists interviewed agree that science, as a field, has lost some of the luster that it seemed to enjoy in the 1960s and 1970s. During that time, the United States was engaged in a race to explore the moon and in building a defense system to protect against threats of military action during the Cold War. Jacques Cousteau's undersea explorations were televised to adoring audiences. The environmental movement was born during the late 1960s, and this, along with the high prices and uncertain supplies of oil in the 1970s, turned the public's attention toward the possibility of alternative energy sources. Federal funding of R&D as a percentage of gross domestic product (GDP) peaked in 1964 at 1.93 percent. Approximately 65 percent of all R&D spending originated in the federal government, and over 80 percent of federal fund-

Figure 1.2   *Research and Development Expenditures 1995*
              (Percentages)

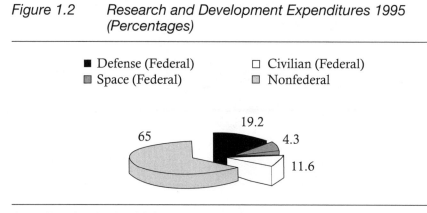

■ Defense (Federal)   □ Civilian (Federal)
▨ Space (Federal)   ▨ Nonfederal

Source: Based on National Science Board 2002, table C-14.

ing of research and development was related to space exploration or defense development.

But during the 1980s and 1990s, public interest changed: the Berlin Wall fell, the fears of escalating oil prices diminished with increasingly stable supplies, the space race took a backseat to more pragmatic public issues, and concern for the environment waned. Federal funding for R&D, while increasing in absolute terms, fell to 0.89 percent of GDP, its lowest level since the mid-1950s. At the same time, nongovernment or private R&D funding, primarily financed by private corporations, increased disproportionately. Private funding, which made up little more than half of government funding in the 1960s, surpassed and nearly doubled government funding of R&D by 1994, as shown in figures 1.2 and 1.3. The federal government remained the spending leader only in basic research, the area that attracts the smallest amount of research funds. With this change in the source of R&D funds, the direction of scientific research has become increasingly dictated by market forces and by the ability to transfer knowledge to those technological advancements with a profitmaking potential.

The relatively slow growth in government funding of scientific research has had the greatest impact on careers of Ph.D. scientists as the traditional academic career path has become more difficult to realize and sustain. In the past, a scientist graduating from a university Ph.D.

Figure 1.3   Research and Development Performance by Sector

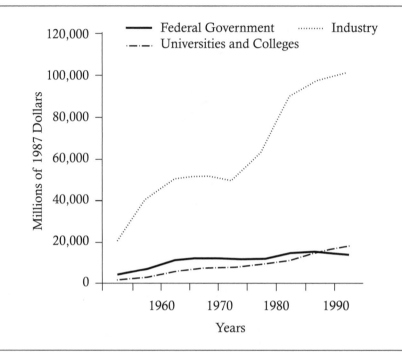

Source: Based on National Science Board 2002, table C-14.

program might possibly take on a two- to three-year postdoctoral position at another institution to get more research experience, land a junior academic position, and apply for grants to set up his or her own laboratory. Throughout his or her career, laboratory research would be funded by government grants from federal agencies such as the NSF, the National Institutes of Health (NIH), or the Department of Defense.

During the period from the mid-1960s to the mid-1990s, R&D funds received by colleges and universities more than tripled while the number of new Ph.D.s increased threefold. But with increasingly sophisticated and expensive equipment, competition for funds grew more intense. Labs were growing in size, and with more subordinates per grant-generating laboratory, the organizations were getting in-

creasingly bottom heavy. Adams and associates (2003) show that between 1981 and 1999, authors per scientific paper increased from 2.8 to
4.4. New Ph.D.s were finding it harder to set up their own laboratories
and increasingly took several consecutive postdoctoral positions before
having the opportunity to settle into a permanent job. The proportion
of new Ph.D.s who take on postdoctoral positions increased from 20
percent in 1970 to 39.4 percent in 1993. In 1993, 20 percent of life science Ph.D.s were still in a postdoctoral position four years after graduation. A young assistant professor in microbiology describes the situation: "the field of microbiology kind of grew like a cancer and one
good lab gave rise to ten good post-docs who set up their own labs." After a while there was no money for new labs, but there was still demand
for postdoctorals to run the existing laboratories. Graduates of Ph.D.
programs moved from one laboratory to another until they got the "big
break" (first authorship of a paper accepted in a high-impact journal)
or they opted for another career path outside of academia. This academic career path has become especially unattractive for individuals
with working spouses who may have problems finding jobs in the temporary locations of the postdoctoral appointments. Family responsibilities also take away from the "tunnel vision" and heavy time commitments that many scientists see as necessary in order to win the
contest for grant money. Because women were more likely than men to
have relatively immobile spouses and were less inclined to request
compromises in either spouse's career or family life to accommodate
job requirements, they were finding the academic career path increasingly inhospitable at the same time that equal opportunity law was
opening more doors for them.

Doctoral Ph.D. students who did land permanent academic jobs
found it progressively harder to survive in science careers as periodic
grant renewals were no longer automatic. One Ph.D. in microbiology
asserted that, during the period from the mid-1980s to the early 1990s,
the percentage of grant applications being funded in her field fell from
one-third to 5 percent. While this assertion may be an exaggeration,
data on NIH grant-making shows that, by the mid-1990s, the success
rates for both new and renewal grants were half the levels of the early
1980s. In addition, only a third of renewal grants were being funded

(Mandel 1995). A Ph.D. physicist at an Ivy League institution who began his career in the early 1970s with plentiful government funds was barely scraping by in the early 1990s. He explained, "It has a real impact on your overall productivity—because of the very large reductions [in funding] and in the people [funding agencies] we used to count on for support. So, in short, we can't help [but] be discouraged psychologically . . . you feel let down."

With R&D funds increasingly originating in private firms, industry grants and opportunities became more attractive to scientists. From 1973 to 1995, the percentage of the full-time doctoral labor force employed in the industrial sector increased from 24 percent to 35 percent (Long 2001). Because the emphasis in industry jobs is more on development and applied marketable research, they have been looked down on historically by academic scientists. As a Ph.D. chemist pointed out, one implicit measure of a professor's success is still "the number of his or her students that have gone on to become professors at big hot shot universities." He continued, "if you go off and do research at a federal laboratory or in industry, you've given in or given up." More recently there seems to be increased acceptance of jobs in industry, possibly because these workplaces are offering desirable perks, such as higher pay and more time for family life, that are not always available in academia.

Although the percentage of industry funds allocated across basic research, applied research, and development did not change, there was a real feeling by scientists that the character of research was changing. A Ph.D. in chemistry working for a successful pharmaceutical company explained:

> The pharmaceutical marketplace has changed more in the past decade [1985 to 1995] than it has ever changed before. . . . In order to be profitable in the pharmaceutical industry you have to approach research with a very different perspective than what you would have done ten years ago. The first question that is asked before committing money to a research program is "is the market there?"

He went on to describe a product that mimics the human growth hormone and that helps young children without natural growth hormones grow into normal, fully developed adults. Although the product is successful, he was confident that it would never have been developed in the environment of the 1990s because the small patient pool, children deficient in human growth hormone, guaranteed low profits. Even with the Orphan Drug Law passed in 1983, which allows firms that develop drugs for rare diseases both to have exclusive rights and to charge high mark-ups, the large pharmaceuticals have tended to stay away from these small markets. He conceded that, even in basic research, firm profits determine direction and focus.

Because science was the foundation of many government initiatives in the 1960s and early 1970s, the discipline was revered, and scientists were perceived as working for the public good. A Ph.D. physicist who grew up in the 1960s reading *Scientific American,* tried to describe the environment: "It was the time of the big space program in the sixties and there was a lot of interest in science in general in the country. . . . And a lot of technology came out of the space race—whole industries grew up from that." Another Ph.D. recipient in the mid-1970s recounted his experience in a NSF summer program for high school juniors in the early 1960s. Marveling at how active the government was in recruiting bright young people to science in the post-Sputnik period, he described a program in which sixty students from all over the country convened at a university campus for an eight-week program in chemistry, physics, and mathematics. He concluded, "I had never been around such smart people . . . and it was just glorious."

In stark contrast to the 1960s, the 1990s were a time when scientists felt neither well respected nor well rewarded. A professor of engineering recounted, "I never found any glamour in telling anyone that I was an engineer. It's much more satisfying and I get a much different response when I tell people that I'm a professor. There's not a lot of value placed on engineering in this society." A career engineer employed in industry had a similar concern: "When I go to a social gathering and they say 'What do you do?' I say 'Well, I'm an engineer.' 'Where?' they say, 'On the Long Island Railroad?' People have no idea what I'm talking about." A woman with a master's in biology lamented the differential respect afforded M.D.s and Ph.D. scientists: "Even the Ph.D. I worked for at the hospital was very envious of the M.D.s because we would be doing all the work . . . we would give them the data, and they would get all the glory." A biology graduate who worked in a laboratory before moving into business pointed out, "I don't think that our society puts enough value on research. Oh, if you find a cure you're wonderful, but [what about] the eight million other people [who] sweat and suffer?" She was disturbed that scientists put in tremendously long hours working on experiments that do not follow a time clock and get compensated by government grants with no overtime pay. Similarly, Ph.D. scientists have had to question the respect afforded them as they spend increasing number of years living on postdoctoral stipends.

The lack of financial reward was an ever-present concern for many of the scientists and engineers who saw research as driven by profit potential. As one engineer commented, "You know we're outside the flow of money in most businesses, we're usually an overhead and a necessary evil." Pay of scientists and engineers may have been low relative to other successful professionals such as lawyers and doctors. However, the scientists more often compared their own salaries to those of their managers. Many corporations have two different promotion and salary tracks: one for management and one for technical personnel. The opportunities and salaries of the technical personnel fall behind the management personnel before midcareer. A large majority of the male scientists left science for management and finance-related jobs with the hope of making more money.

The movement to market-driven R&D funding has occurred at the same time that changing national and world priorities have altered the focus of attention within science. As noted earlier, space exploration, political attention to defending against Cold War threats, developing alternative energy sources, and preserving the environment fueled the prominence of physics, astronomy, and geology in the 1960s and 1970s. By the early 1990s, these issues had receded in the public's consciousness. Over the same period there were remarkable changes in the biological sciences. The discovery of the chemical structure of DNA by Watson and Crick in 1953 created the field of molecular biology and propelled an explosion of basic research, which is having enormous impacts on contemporary medicine. Subsequent work on recombinant DNA paved the way for the biotech industry, which uses genetic engineering to create innovative products with wide ranges of uses. Meanwhile, computer technology exploded, allowing personal computers and the internet to change the structure of jobs in almost every field.

With a changing focus of public attention over the period, general funds for scientific research were reallocated toward these more popular fields, and students entering science were lured to these cutting-edge areas. During the period 1975 to 1995, the number of doctoral degrees awarded in physics increased by 20 percent, but the number of Ph.D.s awarded in math did not change. However, the number awarded in biological and agricultural sciences increased by 38 percent, and the number awarded in computer science increased a staggering 312 percent. As might be predicted by the increasing portion of R&D funds coming from industry, the number of doctoral degrees awarded in engineering also increased 89 percent (Long 2001).

Increasing Presence of Foreign-Born Students and Scientists

Since the late 1970s, there has been a marked increase in foreign-born science and engineering students and workers. Except for a period in the mid-1990s following the Tiananmen Massacre and the Chinese Student Protection Act, there was a steady increase in foreign-born students enrolling in master's and doctoral programs in the sciences and engineering. In 1999, foreign-born students made up 50 percent of all graduate students in engineering, mathematics, and computer science, an increase from roughly a third in the early 1980s. Across all scientific fields, one-third of all doctoral recipients were foreign born (National Science Board 2002). In 1980, foreign-born college graduates made up 11 percent of the scientific workforce; by 2000 this percentage had increased to 19 percent (National Science Board 2002). Sharon Levin and Paula Stephan (1999) find that in 1990 one in four doctoral scientists employed in the science and engineering workforce was foreign born, an increase from one in five ten years earlier. The impact of these foreign-born scientists on the labor market and on the workplace is bound to be significant. However, the focus of the present study is the exit of U.S.-born scientists. From the work histories and the interviews, the influx of foreign scientists seemed to have no direct impact on exit. However, if the influx of these scientists increased the supply of scientists looking for work relative to demand, there would have been downward pressure on earnings, a factor influencing exit. Also likely, the attrition of U.S.-born scientists and the increasing reluctance of domestic men, in particular, to follow a science career have made room for the influx of the foreign-born scientists into graduate programs and laboratories that were trying to grow at a faster rate than the domestic science workforce. While a correlation between influx and attrition may exist, the direction of causation is unclear.

Increasing Presence of Women in Science Degree Programs and in the Scientific Workplace

The thirty-year period from the 1960s to the 1990s was also a time of increasing education and employment opportunities for women, facilitated, at least partially, by public initiatives. The passage of Title VII of the Civil Rights Act in 1964 prohibited sex discrimination in employment, and in 1972, Title IX of the educational amendments of the Civil Rights Act barred sex discrimination in any educational program receiving federal assistance. Over this period, labor-force participation of women increased from 38 percent to 59 percent, the percentage of bachelor's and master's degrees awarded to women increased to more than 50 percent, and the previously stagnant female-to-male weekly earnings ratio rose from 0.63 to 0.75. The science field, which for all practical purposes was a "male" field in 1960, was not immune to the female demand for better and more inclusive education and employment opportunities. Women's entry into scientific fields was facilitated as well by the increasing public attention to and the growing research support of biology and life sciences, fields to which women were disproportionately drawn. Over the twenty-year period from 1975 to 1995, the percentage of bachelor's, master's, and doctoral degrees in science and engineering awarded to women all increased by roughly twelve percentage points.

With the increasing number of women in science, the character of the workplace changed. Prejudices, based on deep-rooted stereotypes that marked women as less capable in conducting science, have created gender conflicts. In the workplace, challenges of attracting women to science have broadened to challenges of retention. In a field in which occupational exit was already disproportionately high compared to other nonscience fields, women were twice as likely to leave scientific employment as men. Institutions were turning their attention to programs that alleviate the conflicts between family and work, which so often burden working women, and to policies that make science a more welcoming field to women in general.

DATA FOR THE STUDY

The remainder of this book studies careers of a group of scientifically trained individuals in an attempt to understand the character of occupational exit from science. Using statistical analysis and interview data, it explores a series of related questions: Who leaves science and who stays? What are the factors influencing attrition decisions? Are these factors different for different groups of scientists? Where do exiting scientists go, and what do they do? What are the consequences of exit and how do career paths of leavers and stayers diverge? What policy actions might improve retention and quality of life of science personnel?

The focus of the analysis is the career paths of men and women with science degrees, including life sciences, physical sciences, mathematics, and engineering. The career paths studied come from three complementary data sets. The first data set, the SSE, 1982 to 1989, was collected by the NSF and gives background data on exit for a national sample of working scientists. The survey, which asks questions concerning job, demographic, educational, and personal characteristics, was sent in 1982 to a stratified systematic sample of more than 100,000 1980 Census respondents. The full sample included a potential science sample of individuals who worked in a set of targeted science-related occupations and who had four or more years of college education, and a potential engineering sample of individuals who worked in occupations targeted as engineering and who had two or more years of college education. All respondents were resurveyed in 1984, 1986, and 1989. Only

69.7 percent of the initial respondents actually worked in science and engineering jobs and identified their occupation as in the natural sciences or engineering. These respondents contributed data on national patterns of exit from science. Table 1.1 outlines their general demographics.

The greatest differences between men and women in this sample are the discrepancies in age, marriage, and children. The men are older, more likely to be married, and more likely to have dependents. Because only a handful of women successfully entered the science and engineering professions before equal employment opportunity laws came into effect in the 1960s, the older cohorts in this national sample are almost exclusively male. Furthermore, engineering was slower in attracting women than even the natural sciences, so the female engineers in the sample are especially young. The difference in age of men and women most likely contributes to the difference in family characteristics. However, multivariate analysis of the data show that, after controlling for age, female engineers are 4 percent more likely not to have been married and 25 percent less likely to have had children than male engineers. Similarly, female natural scientists are 13 percent more likely to never have been married and 20 percent less likely to have had children than their male counterparts. Working women may choose not to marry or have children since the woman is the partner in the dual-career marriage most likely to shoulder the double responsibilities of family and outside employment. The biggest difference in the educational distributions across the sexes occurs for natural scientists seeking Ph.D.s, with the percentage of men earning Ph.D.s about ten points higher than the percentage of women. The percentage of both scientists and engineers who finish their education with a bachelor's degree is about six points higher for women than for men. Because the working engineer, in contrast to other scientists, needs only an associate's degree, educational cells do not sum to one for the engineering columns.

Although analysis of the national data set is particularly helpful in establishing national patterns of exit during a specified time period, the survey has several limitations. First, because it observes the scientific workforce at one point in time, there is a sample selection bias since the workforce includes only those individuals who identify their occupation as a science or engineering field and survived in the workforce un-

Table 1.1   *Descriptive Statistics for National Sample of*
Employed Scientists and Engineers, 1982
(Standard Deviations in Parentheses)

	Natural Scientists		Engineers	
	Women	Men	Women	Men
Age in years	36.6	41.5*	32.3	42.8*
	(9.7)	(10.9)	(8.7)	(11.2)
Percentage never married	29.5	10.6*	31.1	9.2*
Percentage with children	33.4	54.0*	25.8	53.6*
Percentage with bachelor's degree	46.5	40.9*	63.0	57.7*
Percentage with master's degree	33.9	30.2*	19.7	21.8
Percentage with Ph.D.	18.9	28.2*	2.2	3.6*
Sample size	2913	8915	1839	24292

Source: Author's compilation.
*The male mean is significantly different from the female mean at the .01 level.

til the time of the survey. Many eligible workforce participants have already left the science and engineering workforce. Although all the individuals have a college degree, that degree is not necessarily in science or engineering, so it has attracted a group of individuals without formal training in science and engineering. Second, the survey observes each individual four times during the period between 1982 and 1988. These snapshots only give information on labor market and personal characteristics at the time of the observation without providing any information on the individual during the periods between surveys. Finally, information on each individual is limited by the scope of the survey.

In response to these limitations, the university database that contains in-depth information on careers of a set of relatively homogeneous individuals was developed. These data are the result of a work history survey sent to the population of active female alumnae and a random sample of active male alumni who received degrees in science, math, or engineering from a large public university in the northeast from the time of its establishment in the mid-1960s until 1991.[2] The survey asks questions with the goal of describing the complete educational, personal, and workforce histories of the respondents. It also collects information on factors affecting the respondents' career decisions. Of the 5,200 surveys mailed, roughly 400 were returned due to out-of-date addresses, and 1,688 were completed, for a response rate of 35 percent.[3] The survey is unique because it tracks each respondent's complete career progression since college graduation. Other researchers have successfully followed the careers of a set of scientists. For example, J. Scott Long and associates (Long 1978; Long, Allison, and McGinnis 1979; Long and McGinnis 1985) analyze career productivity and progression of male biochemists who earned Ph.D.s during a four-year period in the late 1950s and early 1960s. The present survey allows a more complete examination of attrition because it begins each observation at graduation from college, and it analyzes men and women in a host of different scientific fields. Extensive information is collected for each job. Every separation from the labor force and from a job is documented, and the explicit reasons for exit are identified. The individual's family history is also tracked to identify when in the career marriages, births, and divorces take place.

Demographic characteristics displayed in table 1.2 paint a different scientific portrait from the national sample largely because of the differing populations. Since this particular public university opened its doors in the 1960s, the university data set does not include the cohort of older, largely male scientists and engineers. Therefore, even though many of the characteristics are statistically different for men and women in the university sample, the magnitude of differences is smaller than in the national sample. On average, men are less than a year older than women; the difference in male and female labor-market experience is only slightly more than a year for respondents with a science degree but increases to three years for respondents with engineering degrees. Roughly the same proportion of men and women are married, however a larger percentage of men than women have children. For respondents with degrees in science, women are slightly less educated

Table 1.2   *Characteristics of Respondents to University Survey, 1992 to 1994 (Standard Deviations Are in Parentheses)*

	Natural Scientists		Engineers	
	Women	Men	Women	Men
Age in years	35.4	36.4*	33.5	34.8
	(7.2)	(6.6)	(7.6)	(6.5)
Experience in	9.4	10.7*	7.1	10.3*
years	(6.0)	(5.8)	(4.2)	(6.4)
Time at current	5.8	6.6	4.8	6.1
job in years	(5.0)	(5.1)	(3.4)	(5.6)
Percentage highest science degree: bachelor's	72.7	59.6	47.3	60.5*
Percentage highest science degree: master's	19.4	16.9	47.3	34.2*
Percentage highest science degree: Ph.D.	12.9	23.5*	4.8	5.2
Percentage never married	33.3	29.0	36.9	36.8
Percentage with children	47.5	54.2	42.2	49.1
Sample size	782	421	185	290

Source: Author's compilation.
*Female statistic is significantly different from the male statistic at the .01 level.

than men, with a higher percentage of women earning bachelor's and master's degrees and a higher percentage of men earning Ph.D.s; these findings are similar to those in the national sample. For engineers, there is a larger percentage of respondents with master's degrees in the present sample than in the national sample, possibly because the university has a large engineering master's program, and perhaps surprisingly, women are more likely than men to have earned master's degrees in engineering. The 1980s national data show that men in engineering were slightly more likely to earn master's degrees than women in engineering.

The third data set, containing information from interviews, was designed to understand more fully the factors behind occupational exit of men and women in the sciences. Twenty-six pairs of women from the original university sample were selected to participate in interviews concerning both their education and career experiences. In the original survey, respondents were asked if they would be willing to give an interview; 71 percent responded positively. From the willing respondents, the 52 women were initially selected to mirror the age, education, and family distribution of the respondents to the original survey.[4] The subsample was altered slightly after initial interviews revealed that career concerns varied by degree level, family status, and whether the woman was an engineer. The women in the interview sample, therefore, are slightly more likely to have Ph.D.s, to have studied engineering, and to be married with children than the full sample of women. Within each pair, the two women are similar in age, degree level, field of degree, and family circumstances. The difference between the two women in each pair is that one of the women has left science and one has stayed. The purpose of this pairing process is to help isolate the important factors behind exiting or continuing scientific careers that cannot be identified using standard statistical techniques. Twenty-six pairs of men were also identified and interviewed. The male pairs are matched to the female pairs so that individuals in the two pairs have the same age, family characteristics, level of degree, and subject of degree.[5] Because the occupational exit rate is lower for men than for women, it was not possible to have a stayer and a leaver in each pair. However, approximately 80 percent of the male pairs include both an individual still employed in the sciences and one who has left.

For the purposes of this book, the interview data are especially enlightening. In particular, the interviews identified the major topics to be explored. They also fill in the details, allowing us a deeper understanding of these topics than could have been obtained through statistical analysis. Finally, the interviews bring the topic of working in science to life, as the quotes give us a glimpse of the insights, concerns, humor, and general humanity of the scientists themselves.

CHAPTER 2

The Magnitude and Character of Exit

E xit from science is a slippery concept since "in science" and "out of science" are not easily defined terms. Science encompasses a large number of fields, and scientific skills are used in countless jobs. The boundaries separating "science" from "nonscience" jobs are porous and shifting as, over time, science and technology find their ways into and out of various activities in the workplace. Furthermore, the interfaces between science and management, science and medicine, and science and education are complex and heavily populated "no man's lands" in the attempt to define an "in" and "out" of science.

The definition of "in" and "out" of science that the National Science Foundation (NSF) uses in its surveys is used throughout the current study. Benefits of this definition are that it is easy to replicate and that estimates of attrition can be compared across data sets. In most cases, the scientist defines whether he or she is working in science; exit from science is self-reported. For example, in the 1989 post-Census survey, all employed individuals are asked "During the week of Feb. 5, 1989, were you working at (or temporarily absent from) a position related to the natural sciences, social sciences, or engineering?" to which the respondent can answer yes or no. In the master survey sent to the university scientists, a similar question is posed: "Is your current job related to natural sciences or engineering?" Letting the scientists decide for themselves whether their work is science related circumvents many issues. In particular, because current experts in the scientific field are best equipped to determine whether a job is science related at a particular point in time, respondents' own expertise is employed to help define exit from science.

The self-reported responses are altered somewhat to deal with the interfaces with medicine and education. Following the lead of the NSF, medical doctors and other health professionals whose primary work activity is clinical diagnosis are not classified as working in science; medical doctors whose primary activity is research are working in science. For the purposes of the study and again as dictated by NSF, science educators at the junior college, secondary school and elementary school levels are not considered working in science, but science educators at the four-year college, university, or medical school levels are considered working in science.[1] Survey questions related to primary work activity and employing institution give information to make these alterations.

MAGNITUDE OF EXIT

Occupational exit or departure from a particular field is not the kind of labor-market statistics often reported. However, in 1987, a national survey sponsored by the Census Bureau posed the following question to persons employed in January 1986 and January 1987: "You told me that . . . is now working as. . . ." Then, "was . . . doing the same kind of work a year ago, in January 1986?" A negative answer to the question was interpreted as an occupational exit. According to the data, over the one-year period, 2.6 percent of engineers had exited engineering, a high rate of exit when compared to other professional occupations. In particular, 2.0 percent of college and university teachers, 0.6 percent of health-diagnosing professionals, 2.3 percent of health-assessment professionals, and 0.7 percent of lawyers and judges left their occupation during the same period (Markey and Parks 1989). These alternative occupations are possibly ones that require greater amounts of education, but still the difference in exit rates is startling. Engineers were four times as likely to engage in occupational exit as doctors and three and a half times as likely to exit their occupation as lawyers and judges. Compared to less well-paid occupations such as nursing and college teaching, engineers were still 15 percent to 30 percent more likely to leave their occupations. And as discussed later, scientists leave science to a greater extent than do engineers.

The NSF data was used to derive national estimates of exit from the scientific workforce. As noted earlier, the 1982 sample was originally selected from respondents to the 1980 Census who were in a set of targeted occupations and who had achieved a minimum level of education. Of those surveyed in 1982, only respondents who were employed, who answered yes to the question on employment in science or engineering, and whose stated occupation was in the natural sciences or engineering were tracked over time. This group was followed over the seven-year period to estimate exit rates. By 1989, 90.3 percent of the original respondents were still working in science.[2] The 9.7 percent who had left had either taken jobs unrelated to science, left the labor force, or become unemployed.[3] Even more striking is the fact that women left science at twice the rate as men: 17.4 percent, almost a fifth, of the scientifically employed women left science, and only 8.6 percent of the men left science (see figure 2.1). In the university data

Figure 2.1   *Percentage Leaving Science by Gender, National Sample and University Sample*

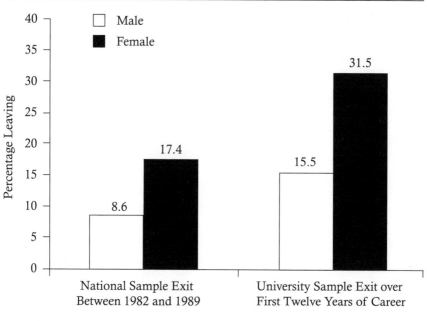

Source: Author's compilation.

set, this two-to-one ratio holds as well, even though the construction of the sample and the characteristics of the population are different. Of all the university-trained scientists who started a job in science, 15.5 percent of the men and 31.5 percent of the women had left scientific employment by the survey date, a period that averages twelve years across all respondents.

The university data set gives us a rare opportunity to examine exit from science by scientists because it allows us to follow these people's careers from the time they graduate from a university with their highest science degree. As expected, many of the scientifically educated college graduates never worked in science: 36.5 percent of the female graduates and 27.4 percent of the male graduates left science before they entered the labor market. Of those graduates who persisted in science, 16 percent of the women and 6 percent of the men had left science temporarily at one time or another, usually to spend some time out of the labor force.[4] Figure 2.2 gives the survival estimates of men and women in science for the university sample. The initial dropoff

Figure 2.2   *Kaplan–Meier Survival Estimates, by Sex*

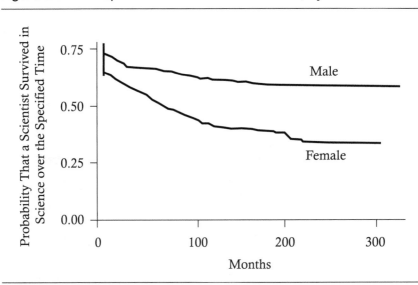

Source: Author's compilation.

from 100 percent is the result of science graduates who immediately started work in nonscience jobs. The female survival curve is well below the male survival curve. Focusing on the ten-year (120 months) mark, roughly 37 percent of the women and 63 percent of the men remained working in science for ten years.

WHERE DO EXITING SCIENTISTS GO, AND WHAT DO THEY DO?

Scientifically trained personnel who leave science can take a variety of paths, directed by choices along the way. The first choice on leaving science is whether to continue to work outside of science or whether to leave employment altogether. If the individual decides to work outside of science, as the majority of leavers do, then he or she has a series of interrelated decisions to make. They include: whether to invest in further education for potentially better positioning in the nonscience labor market, what work activity to undertake, and in which industry to locate.

Exiting Employment Versus Finding a Nonscience Job

Both men and women are more likely to leave science for nonscience employment than to leave employment altogether. Depending on the individual, the route to nonscience employment may include a stint of time not working. Exiting employment is often a temporary situation that commonly ends for men when they find new jobs and for women as their young children grow up. Returning to science after an employment exit, however, becomes more difficult as time passes and skills become more obsolete. Temporary labor-force departure that was intended to end with reentry to science may in fact end with entry into a nonscience job and thus result in permanent exit from science.

Figure 2.3 plots percentage of the respondents to the initial sample who had exited by destination, where destination is nonemployment or work outside of science. For the purposes of the figure, destination is considered a static concept, identified for each worker at the point at which he or she was last observed. In the case of the national survey,

Figure 2.3   *Percentage Exiting by Destination*

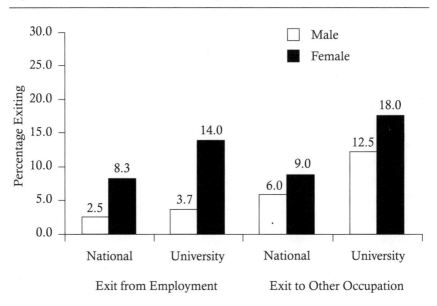

Source: Author's compilation.

the last observation was 1989; in the case of the university survey, the last observation was the survey date, 1992 or 1994. Because women traditionally take on the role of caretaker of the family, they are much more likely than men to exit employment. In the national sample, 8.3 percent of the women working in science in 1982 were not working at any job by 1989, with about 45 percent of these women caring for family. However, 2.5 percent of the men were not working in any job by 1989, but only 5 of the more than 20,000 men were caring for family. These differences are reflected in the university sample as well, where 14 percent of the women and 3.7 percent of the men who started work in science were not working in any job at the time of the survey. Of the seven hundred men whose work histories were documented in the university sample, not one left the labor force to care for his family.

Women are also more likely than men to take on work outside of science. By the time the university survey was conducted, 18 percent of the women and 12.5 percent of the men who had once worked in science were currently working in a field outside of science. In the national sample, 6 percent of the men and 9 percent of the women who were working in science in 1982 had left for another field by 1989. Therefore, putting aside differences in nonemployment, women still are 50 percent more likely than men to leave science for work in nonscience fields.

Education Investment

Investments in further nonscience education are common for scientifically trained men and women who leave science. According to table 2.1 (columns three and four), which reports educational investments of the 1,700 men and women in the university sample, 59 percent of the men and 54 percent of the women who never worked in scientific careers earned advanced degrees outside of science.[5] An M.D. degree was the most sought-after advanced degree for scientifically trained

Table 2.1   *Nonscience Degrees Earned by Scientifically Trained Individuals Who Leave Science and Become Employed Outside of Science*

	Began Science Career		Never Began Science Career	
Percentage Earning	Male (n = 83)	Female (n = 203)	Male (n = 191)	Female (n = 353)
Master's degrees	13.6	15.1	10.3	22.6
Ph.D. degrees	1.5	0.9	0.0	2.7
M.B.A degrees	15.2	13.4	5.1	3.8
M.D. degrees	13.6	16.1	42.3	27.1
J.D. degrees	6.1	3.6	3.4	2.4
Total[a]	42.4	45.5	59.4	54.1

Source: Author's compilation.
[a]Some respondents earned more than one degree, so the individual rows add up to a sum that is greater than the total.

college graduates who did not take science jobs. Because completion of a set of science-oriented courses is a prerequisite for medical school, typically pre-med students majored in a science field. The big difference in type of degree by sex is in the area of medical degree and generic master's degrees. More than one and a half times as many men (42 percent) as women (27 percent) got degrees equivalent to an M.D., and more than twice as many women (23 percent) as men (10 percent) earned nonprofessional master's degrees, and a large number of these master's degrees were related to teaching. Furthermore, 86 percent of the degrees earned by men, as compared to 61 percent of the degrees earned by women, were in the high-paying professional fields of law, business, or medicine.

Investment in further nonscience education by male and female leavers who began careers in science (columns one and two) is surprisingly similar. Approximately 45 percent of these leavers invested in some type of postscience degree. In contrast with the men and women who never started a science degree, the medical degree was not the dominant degree sought. Approximately equal proportions of men and women leaving science work (15 percent) invested in M.B.A degrees, M.D. degrees, and in further master's degrees.

WHAT DO THEY DO, AND WHERE DO THEY DO IT?

Table 2.2 presents information on the four work activities and industries most frequently cited by scientists or engineers working outside of science and engineering. The data are separated by sex and by whether the scientifically educated respondents ever worked in science. As predicted by their educational investments, men who never worked in science were most likely to go into health-related work, with 32 percent having clinical diagnosis as their primary work activity and 13 percent having physician-related health services as their primary activity.[6] Women who never worked in science occupations were most likely to cite teaching and training as their primary work activity (33.9 percent), with clinical diagnosis identified second (21.6 percent) most frequently.

Men who left science after a spell of employment in science jobs were most likely to go into management, with substantially fewer go-

*Table 2.2   Most Common Work Activities and Industries of
Leavers (Percentages Are Given in Parentheses)*

	Began Science Career		Never Began Science Career	
	Male (n = 83)	Female (n = 203)	Male (n = 191)	Female (n = 353)
Work activities				
Most common	Management (28.8)	Management (17.1)	Clinical diagnosis (32.4)	Teaching and training (33.9)
Second most common	Clinical diagnosis (10.6)	Clinical diagnosis (16.2)	Teaching and training (14.5)	Clinical diagnosis (21.6)
Third most common	Distribution and sales (9.1)	Teaching and training (13.5)	Management (13.3)	Physician-related health care (9.9)
Fourth most common	Teaching and training (7.6)	Computer applications (6.3)	Physician-related health care (12.7)	Management (9.6)
Industry				
Most common	Finance, insurance, and real estate (21.5)	Hospital or clinic (12.7)	Hospital or clinic (26.6)	Elementary and secondary school (24.0)
Second most common	Hospital or clinic (12.3)	Other health-related (11.8)	Other health-related (15.0)	Hospital or clinic (21.3)
Third most common	Other services (7.7)	Elementary and secondary school (10.9)	Elementary and secondary school (11.6)	Finance, insurance, and real estate (12.0)
Fourth most common	Elementary and secondary school (6.2)	Finance, insurance, and real estate (10.9)	Finance, insurance, and real estate (8.1)	Other health-related (10.0)

Source: Author's compilation.

ing into clinical diagnosis, distribution and sales, and teaching. For women who left science after working in science, clinical diagnosis and management were the most common work activities, but teaching and training were also prominent.

The industries that leavers entered mirrored the work activities that they took on, with hospitals or clinics, elementary or secondary schools, and finance, real estate, and insurance companies as the most frequently cited. However, for both men and women, the four most common work activities and four most common industries accounted for less than 50 percent of the locations of leavers. Focusing on these prominent industries and work activities, therefore, does not capture the variety of positions taken by leavers.

WHO LEAVES AND WHY?

This question is not an easy one to answer with the available data. Several methods are used for analysis. First, univariate and multivariate statistical analyses of the national and university data are conducted to determine workplace or worker characteristics that increase or decrease the probability of exit. Then, responses to the questions concerning reasons for exit in the work history survey are tabulated. Finally, the interviews of the paired men and women are examined to understand what employment or personal factor made one scientist choose to stay in science and one choose to leave.

Statistical Analyses

Statistical analyses of the probability of leaving science using the national and university data are helpful in identifying correlations between individual or work characteristics and the probability of leaving science. Group differences in probability of leaving are tested first by analyzing differences in proportions and then with multivariate hazard functions estimating the probability of leaving science, conditional on surviving a specified time period, as a function of educational, job, and personal attributes. The results of the analyses, which are consistent across both data sets, identify which scientists are more likely to leave, fueling hypotheses on what factors lead to exit and why.

Most noticeable is the effect that level of education and type of education have on the probability of exit. Exit rates vary by major of degree and by level of degree, most likely because of differences in the extent to which different educational degrees train recipients for a job or a career. In this context, the distinction between engineering degrees and science degrees is important. For example, a bachelor's degree in science is a broad-based degree that develops a body of knowledge and a way of thinking that can be helpful in a variety of careers. However, there are very few jobs, and even fewer careers, that use these skills explicitly. A chemistry major might use the skills learned in college as a laboratory technician at a pharmaceutical company, but most graduates interviewed perceived this type of a job as a "dead end." However, chemical knowledge may prove useful to a graduate hired in sales at a pharmaceutical company. But, as the worker develops his career in sales, the job will probably shift away from chemistry and move more toward sales. Alternatively, an engineering degree, regardless of level, is a narrower professional degree, one that prepares the graduate for a job and a career specifically in engineering. Of the graduates who never spent a day working in science, 90 percent were science majors, while only 10 percent studied engineering. Likewise, the exit rate of engineering majors was approximately half the exit rate of science majors. Finally, according to the university data, although women composed a much smaller percentage of the engineering workforce (7 percent in 1982) than the scientific workforce (25 percent in 1982), the ratio of female-to-male exit remained two-to-one in both subfields.

Doctoral degrees prepare a student for research and teaching, and the skills learned in a Ph.D. program, regardless of whether they are in a science or engineering field, are directly transferable to the jobs and career paths expected of this elite group of scientists. Furthermore, there is a selection mechanism ensuring that students who spend the time and energy to earn a Ph.D. are the same men and women who are both talented in and excited about these fields. Both forces tend to discourage exit. According to both the national and the university data sets, Ph.D. recipients were half as likely to exit science as science students who had only earned a bachelor's degree. Probably even more striking was the differential effect for men and women. Comparing Ph.D. recipients in these two surveys, women were equally as likely as men to leave science. Therefore, women who had made the commitment to the doctoral degree had made the commitment to science. But among master's recipients and bachelor's recipients, the percentage of women leaving was roughly twenty points higher than the percentage of men leaving scientific employment (see figure 2.4).

The characteristics associated with the scientific field from which the worker graduated influence exit. Multivariate analysis of the national data show that the probability of exit decreases in fields in which salaries are increasing. Increasing salaries in a field imply that demand for its scientists is increasing, making opportunities and salaries more attractive both in an absolute sense and in relation to alternatives outside of science. As shown in chapter 7, the rates of growth of knowledge vary across fields and across time. In fields where the rates of growth of knowledge are accelerating, scientists are more likely to leave, possibly to avoid the increasing amounts of retraining and skill update that such a fast-changing field requires.

Characteristics of the worker's situation also affect exit. A scientist whose salary is below average for scientists with his or her characteristics, is more likely to leave than one with an average or above-average salary. Low-level earnings signal a mismatch between the individual's interests and abilities and the requirements of the job. If the mismatch is the result of the particular job's requirements, a scientist may relocate to a better fitting job, but remain in science. But if the mismatch is between the scientist's interests and the general knowledge within the field, the scientist is likely to leave science altogether. Part-time workers are more likely to leave science than those on a full-time schedule. Instead of being a stable long-run employment situation, part-time work tends to be a stopping point, a kind of "half-way house" on one's way to permanent exit from the field.

According to the statistical analysis of the national data, being married significantly reduces the probability of exit for all reasons for men and has no significant effects on the probability of exit for

Figure 2.4   *Percentage Leaving by Gender and Level of Science Degree, University Sample*

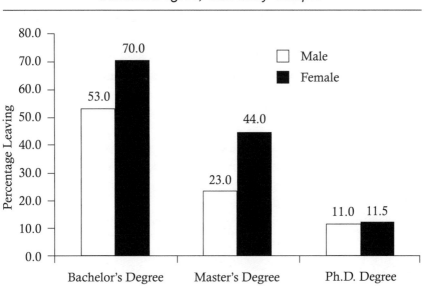

Source: Author's compilation.

women, except in the instance of exit from the labor force where marriage increases that probability significantly. Having children increases the probability of exit to other occupations for both men and women. However, women with children are more likely to leave the labor force than their childless counterparts, while the opposite is true for men. (For a more complete description of the results of multivariate hazard analysis on the national data, see Preston 1994.) In the university data, having children and being married decreases the probability of permanent exit for both men and women, holding percentage of chores and childcare fixed. However, the more chores and childcare taken on, the more likely the individual is to exit science. Because women take on a majority of household chores and childcare, the true impact of marriage and parenting on the average woman is not likely to decrease the likelihood of exit. (Results of hazard analyses on the university data are further summarized in the appendix to chapter 7.)

These statistical patterns give insight into the types of people who are most likely to leave science; they show how differences in circumstances affect the probability of leaving in a marginal manner—tip the scales a little bit one way or another. Although these statistics can support or refute hypotheses as to why some groups are more likely to leave than others, they cannot pinpoint the major reason for exit. This information is really best uncovered by asking the scientists themselves.

Responses to Survey Questions

In the retrospective work histories, those individuals employed outside of science at the time of the survey were asked specifically why they had left science. Each respondent had the opportunity to cite, at most, three reasons for exit from the sciences. The results, presented in table 2.3, show that men overwhelmingly focused on the low pay in science jobs (68 percent) and the lack of opportunities for advancement (64 percent). However, in decreasing order of importance, they also cited other fields being more interesting (36 percent), the lack of science and engineering positions (34 percent), a preference for nonscience positions (23 percent), and promotion out of science and engineering (18

Table 2.3   Reasons Why Men and Women Left Science

Percentage Who Cited:	Men	Women
Pay better in nonscience and engineering positions	68.0%	33.0%
Career opportunities lacking	64.0	34.0
Other fields more interesting	36.0	30.0
Science and engineering positions not available	34.0	21.4
Preferred other positions	23.0	35.0
Promoted out of science	18.0	2.9
Impossible to have a family and work in science and engineering	4.5	21.4
Demands of the career are too severe	4.5	2.9
Hours required are too long	0	20.0
Science and engineering unfriendly to women	0	19.0

Source: Author's compilation.
Note: Work history sample: n = 1,688.

percent). Although low pay and lack of science opportunities were also important to women, with roughly a third of the women citing each of these reasons, a large number of women also identified a preference for other positions (35 percent), other fields are more interesting (30 percent), a lack of science and engineering positions (21 percent), the difficulty of having a family and working in science and engineering (21 percent), length of hours required of a science and engineering position (20 percent), and unfriendliness of the science and engineering field to women (19 percent). Thus, while men exit science primarily because of a lack of opportunities and low pay, women leave for multiple reasons.

Interview Data

Interview data focus even more specifically on the overriding reason behind exit. As noted earlier, the interview sample of 103 men and women chosen from the 1,688 respondents to the work history survey was constructed as a set of pairs in which individuals within each pair were very similar along the dimensions of level and field of scientific degree, age, and family status. The difference between the two individuals was that one had persisted in science and the other had left. The purpose of the pairing process was to help isolate the important factors behind exiting or continuing scientific careers that could not be identified using standard statistical techniques. Within each pair there was an attempt to find the main difference between the two people that leads to the divergence in labor-market outcomes. The process was not foolproof. The interviews uncovered several pairs where both subjects were still in science or where the subjects were so different that identifying a single or a primary and secondary reason for exit was impossible. While an overriding reason for exit for these pairs could not be pinpointed, their interviews still gave important information on forces affecting success in science.

The results from the interviews are very similar to the results from the survey responses. Table 2.4 gives a summary of the results. The men left science primarily to find better career options in terms of higher pay and better advancement opportunities. Of the nineteen

Table 2.4   *Factors Differentiating Leaver from Stayer in Interview Pairs*

	Men	Women
Discontent with income and opportunity in science		
Primary factor	15	1
Secondary factor	0	1
Looking for more interesting work outside of science		
Primary factor	3	8
Secondary factor	6	1
Lack of mentor or guidance		
Primary factor	0	7
Secondary factor	0	1
Difficulty shouldering familial and career responsibilities		
Primary factor	1	6
Secondary factor	0	1
Number of pairs for which a factor differentiating leaver from stayer could be identified	19	22

Source: Author's compilation.

pairs of men for whom a primary (and sometimes secondary) factor differentiating the pairs could be identified, fifteen (79 percent) of the men left in response to salary or career opportunity. In four of these pairs, the leaver was responding to insufficient demand for his skills, and the man who stayed did not have to grope with layoffs or declining work. In the remaining eleven pairs, the exiting man voluntarily left science for a career that he felt offered some combination of higher salaries and expanding responsibilities and prestige, and all but one of these exiting men went to work in management-related work with substantial responsibility and pay. Of the ten men who were looking for better opportunities, six mentioned that they were also looking for more interesting work, which they found in management and business. In contrast, in only one pair of women was the desire for greater pay and more promising career opportunities the major differentiating factor behind the leaver and the stayer.

For women, the reasons behind their decisions to exit were more varied, and three important reasons for exit surfaced. In eight of the twenty-two pairs of women for whom a primary factor differentiating the stayer from the leaver could be identified, the reason for exit was a mismatch of interests. The woman who stayed found the scientific field interesting relative to other opportunities; the women who left did not. For three of the eight leavers, this mismatch was clearly characterized by a pull from another field rather than by distaste for the scientific career. These women left science to go back to school in law, theology, and architecture. For three other female subjects, the mismatch of interests was typified by unhappiness with the scientific career. None of these women have gone back to school but are all working: in administrative work, in finance, and in science education. The last two women experienced both the dissatisfaction of a scientific career and the lure of a new career. Both returned to school: one to a clinical psychology Ph.D. program and the other to law school.

A mismatch of interests was also a primary or secondary factor differentiating the men in nine of the pairs. In three of the pairs, interest in science relative to other occupations was the primary factor behind exit. Of these three exiting men, two were drawn to other occupations, one as a fiction writer and the other as a professor of English whose specialty was technical writing. The third was simply disillusioned with the narrowness of science. In six of the pairs, interest was mentioned as secondary to opportunity and pay. All of these six men left science for management-related jobs.

In seven of the twenty-two pairs of women, the positive guidance of a strong mentor was the primary difference between the women who stayed and those who left. Six of the seven exiting women left in response to a lack of support and guidance in college or graduate school. The seven women have established diverse careers in other sectors in the economy: one became a graphic artist specializing in animal illustration, two began careers in computer science, one runs a daycare center and works part time as a mediator, one works in insurance and is studying to be an actuary, one studied theology and is raising her children, and one is the president of a local chapter of the American Civil Liberties Union. In none of the male pairs was lack of mentoring a primary or secondary determinant of the divergence of career paths.

Finally, family responsibilities were the major factor behind occupational exit in six (less than a third) of the twenty-two pairs of women. Within the six pairs, the ways in which family responsibilities fed into the decision to leave science were somewhat different. For three of the pairs, the two women within each pair had very different ideas about the role of the mother in childrearing. The women who left felt that a stay-at-home mother was necessary for care of the infant and toddler. In one pair, both women felt that a stay-at-home parent was necessary for childcare, but the difference between the paired women was their income-earning potential in relation to their husbands'. The woman who remained in science made a substantially higher and more stable income than her husband, who was a carpenter. Therefore, she continued to work while he cared for their child. In a fourth pair, both women felt that being home with children was important, but the timing of the children was different. The woman who had children immediately after college never developed workforce skills to help her reenter science, while the woman who waited until she was stable in her career to have children was able to reenter and continue employment in science. In the final pair, both women were happy to be working mothers, but one woman was employed in a corporation that she perceived to be inflexible and whose managers were unwilling to let her create a work schedule to meet her family responsibilities. In only one of the male pairs was family commitment the reason for exit. A tenured professor gave up his job so that his wife, also a professor, could accept a position in a different region of the country. Although this man had not been employed permanently for several years at the time of the survey, during this period of voluntary labor force exit, he had several temporary, and sometimes unpaid, appointments in positions related to his field of science.

The construction of the interview sample, which was designed to identify a factor differentiating the leaver from the stayer, necessarily downplays some important issues that affect careers of scientists regardless of whether they stay or leave. In particular, to conclude that men leave science because of financial concerns and women leave because of lack of support, a mismatch of interests, and family concerns is too simplistic. For example, family issues are not absent from a man's decision making. In particular, men's preoccupation with financial concerns is closely tied to desires to provide for their families, and family considerations are sometimes the basis of decisions to forgo risky career moves that might ultimately take the scientist away from science. In addition, the small number of female pairs in which difficulties shouldering family responsibilities differentiated the partners occurred not because conflicts between work and family were not present but because they were so prevalent; there were very few married women with children who did not feel these stresses. Similarly, women's perceptions of sex discrimination and double standards were not absent from the interview dialogues; in fact, they were quite persistent. However, sex discrimination and double standards were only secondary factors in exit decisions as they contributed to low levels of mentoring, a mismatch of interests, and difficulties in shouldering the double burdens of family and career. The following chapters explore in depth the factors most important to success and survival in science.

CHAPTER 3

Leaving Science for Income and Opportunity

The topic of financial success and career growth was the issue on which the male and female interviews deviated most dramatically. In more than three-fourths of the male pairs, the desire for greater income and more promising career opportunities was the primary determinant of exit; a majority of these men left for management jobs. For many of the men remaining in science, career decisions were also dictated by monetary concerns. Even those who did not make decisions with salary in mind often pointed out that science was not a lucrative field. Women, however, rarely mentioned the lack of monetary rewards or career opportunities associated with science. While roughly a third of the women in the surveys pointed to salary and lack of opportunity as a reason for exit, these factors were identified in only one interview as a primary reason and in one other as a secondary reason for exit. This chapter begins with an analysis of the interview data to understand the respondents' concerns about salary and career growth and then reviews some of the economic explanations for occupational change and their associated predictions concerning salary growth. Finally, the work history data is analyzed to estimate the actual impact of occupational exit on earnings and earnings growth.

INTERVIEW DATA

The in-depth, personal interviews reveal that men left science not because of salaries that were low in absolute terms but more often because of salaries that were low relative to perceived alternatives. One of the most calculating of the men interviewed graduated as the valedictorian of his college class and entered a Ph.D. program in chemistry at a prestigious private university. Before finishing a semester of work on his Ph.D., he opted for an M.B.A. program instead. He explained, "It was the work quotient, work divided by income. I didn't want that to be too high . . . the amount of studying that you do in six to eight years to get your Ph.D. and then what? I was thinking if you are going to put in that much work, the reward has to be there." He continued, "Leaving science was the smartest thing I ever did. I retired at age twenty-nine to start my own business."

A graduate of a master's program in marine science who worked in an environmental consulting firm described an eye-opening experience.

> I was making 25K a year. The guy who owned the company, his son was nine years old and he had told his dad, "I want to be a truck driver." This guy had the office next to mine, and his whisper was like your shout. He was on the phone with his wife talking about his son. He said "I can't believe he tells me he wants to be a truck driver. How the hell is he ever going to survive on 30K a year?" All of a sudden I realized he's not stupid; he knows I'm not making a lot of money. He knows that he's paying me less than a truck driver.

Within a few months the young man was working in finance and computer services at a Wall Street firm.

Except for the well-known fact that doctors are well paid, knowledge about salary discrepancies between fields was generally incomplete for undergraduates. An understanding of salary differences only started to emerge as students began graduate programs or entered the labor market. For example, a biochemistry major who worked in a cancer laboratory right after school noted, "Somebody at the university . . . should have turned to me and said, 'hey this is a lovely degree but what the heck are you going to do with it when you get out of school? Don't be naive, lab jobs only pay 13K a year.' Nobody ever said that to me until I went out there and said 'hey . . . here I am, what are you going to pay me?'" Having earned an M.B.A., at the time of the interview this young man was working in information systems and finance in a large financial institution. An exception was this financially savvy engineering graduate who explained the motivations behind his job search:

> As I got closer to the end of [undergraduate] schooling I realized there was a natural [salary] curve for engineers and nonengineers. And the engineering curve is, you get out of school, you get a very nice salary, [but it] hits a plateau very quickly and then what are you going to do? You are stuck in a niche. Nonengineering starts out very low but then opens up to a lot of different fields. So I decided to try and combine the two. And I decided to look . . . for something engineering related but in the business end, in the sales end.

Perceptions of relatively low salaries and limited opportunities in science motivated career decisions within the field as well as decisions to exit. A young man who initially had planned to get a B.S. in chemistry looked back:

> In the middle of my junior year I realized that if I just graduated with a bachelor's in chemistry that I would end up being a waste water technician someplace, you know making some small amount of money that wouldn't be able to support me. And I mean maybe that's kind of a narrow point of view but I realized that, if I was going to go anywhere with this, it would have to be at the master's or Ph.D. level, and I wasn't sure that I really wanted to get into that.

He switched to material sciences, earning a B.E. and then an M.E. four years later. His career has remained in science, but over time, his work activities have switched toward statistical analysis and product or process engineering.

Another man who decided to forgo his plans to get a Ph.D. in mathematics and do research explained his reasoning:

> Basically, at the time you saw that some people were graduating with Ph.D.'s [and] taking about a year or two to get jobs teaching but there was a glut of teachers so they were going to Okay Ponokey Swamp University. Whereas with a master's it was taking [graduates] about two months to find a job, and definitely making more money than the people with Ph.D.s. . . . I was initially going to get a Ph.D. and I thought do research. But that changed, and I decided that I'd like to try industry. That was where the money was.

With his master's in mathematics, this young man began a successful career in computer science.

Equipped with a Ph.D. in physics from a prominent private university in the early 1970s, a young man decided to take an industrial position rather than the expected academic job: "I just didn't see a career path for myself in academia. I think I'm a good scientist but I'm not a great scientist, and you know, if you were a good scientist back in those days, really you could get a job as a post doc for a long time, but you were never going to go any where. So part of it was recognition of my own ability and recognizing that maybe there's a better path for me." This man's decision to take an industry job eventually led him into management, and he became president of a small instrumentation company.

Having left his Ph.D. program in marine sciences, a research scientist at a large oil company explained:

> I wanted to get some real experience, go out and work for a while, and at that time in the early eighties the oil industry was just booming, going wild, and I had an interview with a major oil company. I was seduced away; it was that simple. I mean they waved all sorts of dollars in front of you. You start sitting there, saying to yourself, "I could live like a graduate

student or I can have a real job" I worked much harder as a graduate student than when I first got a job. My starting salary back then was $23,000, and I was living [as a student] on a stipend of $3,100. [My advisor] said, "Why don't you do that for a year, get some experience and then come back." And I told him, "Sure," and never did.

This man, who moved up the ranks of the company to become a high-level scientific manager, understood the costs associated with the move. "I am bought, owned, and controlled by the company. Whatever I do belongs to the company, so I don't have the academic freedom, and I might also add that I don't have the freedom to pursue anything that I want. I have to recommend and propose, and I have to tie it to the bottom line of the company, whether we make it up or not."

The lack of financial rewards in science was also a complaint voiced by many of the men who stayed in science. For these respondents, the absence of a connection between performance and rewards was especially frustrating. The chief engineer of a small electronics company complained, "So that's the extent of my career. After all this time I'm basically not anywhere career-wise. Chief engineer at the defense division of [electronics company X]. Yeah, still not in the money stream. Where I am, there's no cash relationship to what I do or how I do it or how fast I do it." A highly successful engineer at an established aerospace company explained, "I'll be leaving; I sort of have already. I'm at my last step in engineering. I'm called an engineering product manager, but I'm about to go over the fence into program management. Engineers don't get bonuses; engineers don't get stock options; and engineers basically get cost-of-living raises plus anywhere from 1 to 3 percent, based on how good you are."

The notion of two tracks, a management track and a technical track, is prevalent in corporate jobs. A man with a Ph.D. in operations research described the differences, "Advancement comes easier in management than it does in research, so if you choose a management career path you get acceleration in terms of promotion and salary faster than if you stay in research. Although I enjoyed managing, . . . I was probably more suited for doing research." Another man, who after earning a Ph.D. in applied math entered the aerospace industry, gave a tangible example of the differences in treatment of engineers and managers. "One of the things that was a shock to me was when I went to [industry], I had to sit at a desk in a sea of . . . a hundred other people where even . . . as a graduate student I had an office. But they don't do that in the aerospace industry. The only reason they give you an office is if you need one for privacy and confidentiality, i.e., if you're a manager and you have to talk to your subordinates and you have to keep confidential records and stuff like that."

There was recognition by many of the men that the two-tier system resulted in the loss of many talented technical people to management positions. One man described with pride a technical excellence program that his company had started to reward the very productive scientists in ways similar to the rewards of the high-level executives. Unfortunately, this attempt to reward technical expertise seemed exceptional in the world of industry. There were several men who had the opportunity to move to management but decided to remain in the technical track or returned to technical work after a temporary stint in management. One man's reminiscence of his managerial experience echoed a common theme.

> I wanted to get into [management], make a little bit more money and that type of thing, so they made me a product manager of this product group. And it was a year of hell. I had two supervisors and about fifty people reporting to me. When you're schooled in engineering, everything's cut and dry more or less. You get into production and you're dealing with people. . . . When the year was up, you know I sat down with the v.p. 'cause that's who I was working for at the time and he said, "so what do you want to do?" I said "I want out." I just couldn't deal with all the people issues . . . the constant little stuff that drives you crazy. I said I wanted to get back into engineering.

Although the need to develop a secure and often lucrative career was a dominant theme among the men interviewed, there were some exceptions. A young man who earned a Ph.D. in biology but never worked in the field described his motivations:

> I really had very little thought for practical matters, like how I was going to earn my living or anything like that. I sort of treated life as a hobby and it was just following what interested me in an intellectual way without caring very much how it applied to the future. . . . We [the man, his wife, and two children] have sort of muddled along financially, sometimes taking advantage of socialist redistribution of wealth.

More often, for those who stayed in science, the need for income took a backseat to the passion for the discipline. A highly accomplished aerospace engineer, who was active in the space program, estimated that an industry job would increase his paycheck by at least 30 percent. However, this man pointed out, "if you love what you're doing, money is the least of it."

To separate a secure income stream from the need to care for family would be a disservice to these men. Most of the men who talked about income and career growth were family men who perceived themselves as primary breadwinners, working to provide for their families. A man who left marine sciences to work in industry, and who has worked himself up to a high-level position in a large national oil company, explained the impact of marriage on his career: "Being married, and going through that process made me much more focused on money than I otherwise would have been. If I had stayed single I would have . . . [been more likely to go] the 'naturalist' route or the 'pursue the science for the sake of the science' [route] rather than 'if I do this will I be able to earn a living for the family?' [route]." An engineer, frustrated at his inability to break into management, was unapologetic in placing such a high priority on money:

> You know people talk about career all the time. At least to me career is not as important, or at least at this point in my life it's not as important as compensation. I mean my position is, I've got a lot of bills. . . . I've got four children. I've got a house. . . .

[I live in] one of the most expensive areas in the country if not the world. And someone says "Johnny, I want you to sweep the floor but we're going to pay you twice what we're paying you now." Hey . . . I'll find other ways to get satisfaction in my field of interest.

Another man with a master's in mathematics and working in computing echoed the sentiment, "My goal is to earn money, period. I've got children in college, so I'm going to have to pay for that. I mean as far as a career goal, no, there isn't one. My goal is to make as much money as possible."

The male scientist's preoccupation with income stands in stark contrast to the female scientist's seemingly conscious neglect of this topic. As mentioned earlier, only one woman left science because of opportunity and income. This woman had an M.S. in marine sciences and had worked for several years in a government laboratory where she presented and published her work. She was unwilling to go back to get a Ph.D. because she felt that the postdoctoral positions, which most Ph.D.s entered after graduate school, paid incomes well below her current level. Without the Ph.D., however, she was frustrated with her inability to get promoted or to gain the respect of her supervisors at the government laboratory. As a result she left to start a program in physical therapy.

Of the fifty-one other women, only eleven mentioned displeasure with money and opportunity in science, and usually the frustration was associated with an isolated job as opposed to the field more generally. The discrepancy in concern about money and career growth between scientifically trained men and women may be the result of two factors. First, because of the lack of access that women have had historically to high income and prestigious careers, the types of incomes and opportunities available in science for women may be attractive relative to more traditional female labor-market outcomes. Second, the difference in preoccupation with money between men and women may be the result of the different roles that they traditionally play in the family. The male is most often the primary wage earner and is concerned with supporting the family; the woman, if she works outside of the home, is more likely a secondary earner whose income is only supplemental, although it may be necessary to the support of the family. Interview comments by the eleven women who did mention money and opportunity give support for both factors.

When speaking of job choices and transitions, of the eleven women who spoke of displeasure with money or opportunity, six had either turned down or left a low-paying opportunity. All six of these women remained in science in a job with a more acceptable salary, and all the jobs that they left were entry level, four in the nonprofit sector. A seventh woman, with a M.S. in biology and who was working in a nonprofit laboratory, expected to leave her job for a more lucrative science job in the future. She described her thinking, "I'll do this as long as I can and then when I need to make money or really decide to have a family I'll go look for something else." An eighth woman, with a Ph.D. in ecology, was working as an adjunct at a community college, a position identified as outside of science because the institution is not a four-year college or university. She became frustrated at the low pay, especially in relation to the earnings of full-time professors. She left her position when she was pregnant with her third child, spent time with her children, and returned to the labor force several years later in a nonscience job. For all of these women, salary was an important issue, and, while some science salaries were unacceptable, there were jobs in science that could satisfy their monetary needs. They did not see the science sector as being generally characterized as low pay and low opportunity.

Two women who spoke of the lack of money and opportunity in their current jobs felt that childcare responsibilities rather than science were the determining factors for low pay and stalled careers. However, both women felt comfortable with the choices they had made. A computer scientist explained, "I haven't had a promotion since I've come back, which is two years now, which doesn't surprise me. But then in my own mind, I'm thinking I'm not working fifty and sixty hours like the other people in the department are. So, I've come to terms with that myself, because I thought I can't do it all. I can't be at the office working fifty and sixty hours and be fair to my children." The other woman highlighted how the choice to take on day care responsibilities had helped her husband's career.

> I feel marriage and family definitely hurt my career . . . I have so many other responsibilities outside of work. My son is now a year old, and I'm really responsible for getting up in the morning, getting him out to a sitter. Then coming home and feeding him and taking care of him—all the responsibilities [are] really with him now. So it's good, it enables my husband to keep his career and not to have to really sacrifice at his job. But, yeah, it does hurt me.

ECONOMIC ANALYSIS OF OCCUPATIONAL MOBILITY AND ASSOCIATED SALARY GROWTH

The large number of men leaving science in search of higher salaries and more attractive career opportunities makes one wonder whether these men are really achieving their goals. Because economics, more than any other social science, focuses on monetary returns as a motivator, economic theories of occupational mobility speak directly to the resulting earnings consequences.

Occupational mobility has been analyzed in two different frameworks: as a human capital investment strategy and as an extension of the literature on job matches and imperfect information. Human capital theory (Becker 1993; Mincer 1962; Schultz 1960) has long been used by economists to explain occupational decisions and outcomes. In this theory, just as managers of firms make investments in physical capital, plants, and machinery to increase production and profits, individuals can invest in their own human capital. The stock of human capital for any worker is his or her set of skills and know-how that determines productivity in the workplace. That stock can be rented to employers in return for job opportunities and associated wages. Therefore, an individual, often with family input, makes postsecondary educational decisions that have important impacts on potential human capital. Investments in college and graduate school education determine the human capital stock at labor-market entry, which is characterized by, among other factors, educational degree earned and field of major. Having finished formal education, an individual can continue to invest in human capital creation through countless activities, including on-the-job training, seminars, and informal skill update.

The model of human capital states that an individual decides whether to take on a particular investment in much the same way a businessman decides whether to buy a new machine: by comparing the present value of benefits to the present value of costs. For the individual, the costs are likely to be fairly immediate and will include the direct costs of program and supplies, the opportunity costs of time spent in other endeavors, and possibly nonpecuniary costs associated with the investment, such as unpleasant feelings toward study or an ignored spouse's scorn. Because of the relative immediacy of these costs, they may be easy to predict. Benefits, the increase in potential earnings, and the more satisfying job opportunities, however, are not likely to be realized until a future date and will be more long lasting. At the same time, since benefits are pushed into the future, there may be more error in predicting them. Most human capital models assume perfect information on the part of potential investors.

In addition to activities that increase the stock of skill and expertise, the theory also models actions that increase the value of a given stock as human capital investments. Therefore, job search activities designed to improve the match between a given stock of human capital and a potential job or migration activities to geographical regions where a particular type of human capital is more highly valued have been analyzed as investment strategies in this framework. Along the same vein, Kathryn Shaw (1987) considers the process of occupational change as an investment in human capital—a premeditated move in a well-planned career path. Human capital accumulated within an occupation through on-the-job training or other direct investments will have varying levels of value in other occupations depending on the degree of transferability. Opportunities for human capital development and salary growth vary across different occupations. As a result, in a world free from uncertainty, workers choose occupations to chart an occupational career path that maximizes the present discounted value of the earnings stream. Shaw finds strong evidence that occupational change is positively related to the transferability of skills and the declining opportunity for occupational investment in the initial occupation. Therefore, in this scenario, workers plan an occupational strategy where persistence in an occupation will continue as long as there are sufficient opportunities for profitable skill development and salary growth. Once these opportunities dry up, there is a preplanned exit to a new occupation that will value the skills already developed and offer superior opportunities for further skill development and salary growth.

Alternative theories of job and occupational mobility focus on career decisions in a world of uncertainty. Boyan Jovanovic (1979), who first developed the literature on job matches, job-specific human capital, and turnover, has posited that occupational mobility is the result of worker-employer mismatch. Because of imperfect information surrounding the employment transaction, the quality of a potential match between a job and an employee is not known with certainty ex ante. The employee evaluates a potential job based on expected salary, salary growth, and job characteristics. Predictions of earnings are likely to rest on knowledge of average earnings for employees with varying levels of seniority within an occupation. In such a scenario, unmet salary expectations may arise for two reasons. First, person-to-person differences in salaries within an occupation will depend on the quality of the occupational match, the extent to which the requirements of the occupation match the traits of the individual, or the extent to which the individual can be productive in the chosen occupation. Second, knowledge concerning occupational wage structures at the time of labor-market entry may be incomplete, and unforeseen supply-and-demand forces may alter relative salaries across occupations, making salaries in the selected occupation generally less attractive. Nonwage characteristics, such as hours, work conditions, or flexibility, of an occupation are also likely to be predicted with error for two reasons. First, nonwage attributes will differ within an occupation, and often the full set of nonwage attributes of a job are impossible to appreciate without experience within that workplace. Second, all individuals will not agree on the valuation of a particular nonwage attribute. For example, a working parent may see flexibility as a positive and frequent overseas travel as a negative in a job, while a young single employee may be more likely to rate these features in the opposite manner.

Once the employee takes the job and information is revealed over time, mismatches may lead to exit. The mismatch may take the form of lower than expected salary or lower than expected utility, the economist's catch-all term for happiness. As soon as expected salary or utility in the current job falls below some threshold value, exit will result. The more severe the mismatch, the increased likelihood of occupational exit. There is considerable empirical support for the theory relating mobility to job mismatches. In his analysis of job mobility patterns of young men, Henry Farber (1994) finds that the monthly probability of a job ending increases with tenure at the job for tenure levels between zero and three months and then decreases monotonically with further tenure. This probability pattern is predicted by the job-matching theory if information on the quality of the job match is not revealed fully once the job is taken but instead reveals itself over time. In an empirical test of the theory's application to occupational movement, Jovanovic and Robert Moffitt (1990) estimate a model of occupational mobility that tests the validity of two competing explanations: sectoral shock versus employee-employer mismatch. They conclude that a majority of the mobility between occupations is the result of employee-employer mismatches.

Both explanations of occupational mobility imply that the worker is better off after the move. The human capital explanation of occupational mobility predicts that the exiting worker will enjoy higher future discounted earnings after the move than he would have experienced had he stayed in the initial occupation. Although the job-matching literature does not deal explicitly with postexit outcomes, the implication is that the worker leaves in anticipation of a better match and thus higher utility, which may or may not mean higher earnings. More specifically, if exit is the result of unmet salary expectations, the worker will be searching for a new job with higher earnings; if the employee is unsatisfied with nonwage characteristics of the job, he will be looking for a position with more favorable work conditions, probably at the expense of earnings. There is strong empirical support for the relationship between job change and salary increase. For example,

Robert Topel and Michael Ward (1992) find that job mobility in the early career, which need not be occupational mobility, is the source of at least a third of early career wage growth.

The human capital explanation goes even further, predicting that the lifetime earnings profile of the switcher is always above the profile that would have been experienced with another occupational course. In the context of scientists leaving science, at time of labor-market entry, they believe that the present value of the salary profile associated with their chosen path of a stint in science followed by nonscience work will be greater than the present values of the salary profiles of career scientists or career nonscientists. These workers not only anticipate higher future returns outside of science than inside science after exit, but they also anticipate higher returns within science than outside science before exit. Therefore, the explanations for occupational mobility differ in their implicit evaluation of the job experience in the initial occupation from which the worker is exiting. While the human capital explanation argues that time in any occupation is a profitable stepping-stone along an optimal career path, the job-mismatch explanation argues that the initial job or occupation is a mistake; time could have been spent more profitably in an alternative situation.

In the context of occupational exit from science, the fact that individuals who are leaving have high levels of scientific human capital raises two important issues. First, having at least invested in a bachelor's degree in science, these workers should be entering scientific jobs with a good amount of occupation-specific information. Second, high levels of scientific human capital make the monetary returns of scientific exit questionable unless human capital is transferable to the destination occupations. Although exiting scientists may expect to transfer skills, the transferability of science knowledge to nonscience jobs is an empirical question that can only be addressed through data analysis. In analyses of the salary repercussions of occupational exit, it may be helpful to separate those who leave for salary reasons, labeled income seekers, and those who leave in search of more favorable job conditions, labeled amenity seekers, since there is no reason to anticipate salary gains for the latter group. Furthermore, in these empirical analyses, income seekers, who are exiting science as a part of a planned career path, may differentiate themselves from income seekers leaving due to imperfect information because their salary profiles up to and including time of entry into nonscience occupations will be above salary profiles for people who never enter science during the same period.

DO NONSCIENCE CAREERS PAY MORE THAN SCIENCE CAREERS?

The results of an empirical analysis of salaries within and outside of science will necessarily depend on the qualifications of the workers whose salaries are being compared. Given the nature of this study, the focus is on men and women who have earned at least an undergraduate science or engineering degree. Differences in earnings patterns arise among people leaving science according to how much science education they have accumulated, the fields in which they have earned their degrees, how much time they have spent working in science, and how much and what type of education they invest in after leaving science.

Salary Changes Associated with Leaving Science

The first comparison of salaries of science-educated individuals who have left science to salaries of those who have remained uses the 1982 to 1989 NSF data. Using a national sample of respondents who worked in science in 1982, the data chart salary and labor-market characteristics for each of these individuals in 1984, 1986, and 1989. Regression analysis then allows the estimation of the wage gain or loss accompanied by movement from a job within science to a job outside of science.[1] These analyses, as displayed in table 3.1, estimate that men who left science experienced a 4 percent loss in salary, and women leaving science experienced a 10 percent salary loss. These losses represent an average loss for all scientists leaving over this period, regardless of level of education and experience in the labor market. However, further analysis shows that the earnings loss is slightly greater for individuals who have been in the labor market longer, and for men, the loss is more severe for those with science Ph.D.s than with lower level degrees; the opposite is true for women.

The unambiguous salary loss might be surprising except that exiting individuals have not been differentiated according to reason for exit. As noted in the earlier section on economic models of mobility, leaving to improve nonpecuniary attributes, such as work hours, geographical location, or flexibility, is likely to result in reduced earnings. To deal with this problem, leavers are differentiated according to responses to a survey question asking about reasons for exit. Income seekers are respondents who identify better pay or promotion opportunities as their motivation behind exit, and amenity seekers are respondents who report leaving because of locational preferences or desires for a nonscience position. The salary change on exit is then reestimated for these two groups of leavers.

The results of the new analysis are presented in rows two and three of table 3.1. Male income seekers benefited from a 4 percent salary gain on exit from science, while male amenity-seekers experienced a 12 percent salary loss. Similarly, female income seekers experienced no change in earnings on exit, and female amenity seekers experienced a 13 percent salary loss. Clearly, income-seeking leavers earned higher salaries on exit than amenity-seeking leavers. But because of the short window of time in which the respondents are observed, these data do not allow an estimation of the long-term salary effects of leaving science. Alternatively, the work histories of the uni-

Table 3.1   Percentage Change in Salary for Men and Women Leaving Science

	Male	Female
1. All leavers	4 percent salary loss*	10 percent salary loss*
2. Income-seeking leavers	4 percent salary gain*	No change
3. Amenity-seeking leavers	12 percent salary loss*	13 percent salary loss*

Source: Author's compilation.
*Change in salary is statistically significant at the 0.01 level.

versity data can be used to compare longer run salary profiles of career scientists, career nonscientists, and science leavers.

Salary Profiles of Career Scientists Versus Career Nonscientists

The career scientist is a person graduating with a degree in science who lands his or her first job in the science labor market and remains in this area for his or her full labor-market career. The career nonscientist also graduates with a degree in science but lands his or her first job in nonscience work and, either consciously or through the luck of the draw, develops a career solely in nonscience work. Career nonscientists may choose many different paths. As pointed out in chapter 2, a large number of these students, especially the men, use the science degree to help them get into medical school, and they begin careers six to seven years later as doctors. Graduates may also invest in other professional degrees in law or business or even master's or Ph.D. degrees in other fields. Salary comparisons must account for these educational differences.

Figures 3.1A and 3.1B trace the relation between the percentage changes in salary of the average worker and months of experience in the labor force for career scientists and career nonscientists. As noted in the figures, the average starting salary of noncareer scientists without postscience degrees is normalized at one and thus becomes the standard of comparison. All changes from this standard of comparison can be thought of as percentage changes. The comparisons within the samples of men and women are made using statistical analyses that, by holding worker characteristics such as marital status, science education, or time outside the labor market constant, attempt to compare otherwise identical employees. Figure 3.1A focuses on men, and salary profiles are charted separately for men who left science without a postscience graduate degree, men who remained in science, men who left science and invested in a medical degree (M.D.), men who left science and invested in a law degree (J.D.), and men who left science and invested in a business degree (M.B.A.).

Focusing first on men who did not get a professional degree after

Figure 3.1   Career Scientists Versus Career Nonscientists

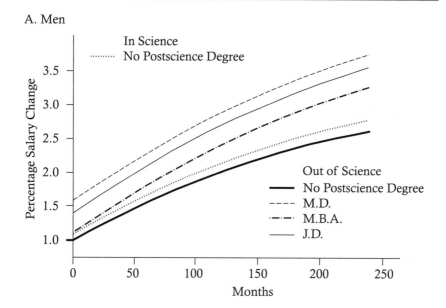

A. Men

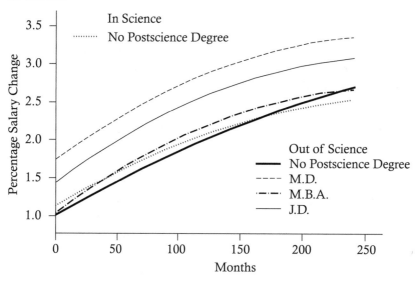

B. Women

Source: Author's compilation.
Note: The average starting salary of respondents who are out of science without a postscience degree is normalized at one with percentage salary changes measured on the vertical axis. 1.5 on the vertical axis corresponds to a salary that is 50 percent above the starting salary of a respondent who is out of science and has no postscience degree.

exit, men in science earned starting salaries 9 percent higher than men in careers outside of science. Salary growth was slightly higher inside science than outside of science, ensuring that salary profiles of career scientists remained above salary profiles of career nonscientists who did not invest in further education. The salary profiles of men who earned professional degrees in medicine, law, or business reveal that these professionals experienced much higher rates of salary growth than career scientists or career nonscientists with no further education. With the exception of short-term internships or clerkships, initial salaries in law and medicine were 30 percent and 50 percent, respectively, higher than initial salaries in science, making these careers clearly much more lucrative than science. Although the initial salary in business was comparable to that in science, the higher salary growth in business ensured that the salary of M.B.A. recipients remained above the salary of science graduates working in science. The true return to each of these professional degrees can only be calculated by weighing the salary returns against the costs of obtaining the degree in terms of forgone earnings and direct costs. The most expensive professional degree is probably the M.D. since medical school is the longest program and the one least likely to be accomplished part-time while holding down a full-time job. At the same time, this degree has the highest salary profile.[2]

This same comparison of salaries for women is given in figure 3.1B. Comparing first those women who did not invest in a postscience degree, women working in science received starting salaries about 13 percent higher than salaries of women working outside of science. But science salary profiles reached a plateau before nonscience profiles, and nonscience salaries rose above science salaries fourteen years into the career. As with the men, women who invested in an M.D. or a J.D. experienced much higher salary profiles than women without a postscience degree. Women doctors had starting salaries about 60 percent higher than women in science, and the starting differential between lawyers and scientists was about 30 percent. Furthermore, salary growth was higher for these women with professional degrees. Women who earned an M.B.A. had starting salaries below salaries of women in science, but the higher salary growth pulled salaries of women with

M.B.A.s above salaries of women in science about three and a half years into the career.

These high estimated returns to nonscience professional degrees and comments in the interviews about high engineering salaries early in the career call for a comparison of salary profiles of career scientists (with a nonengineering degree) and career engineers. Using regression analysis to compare scientists with similar individual and workplace characteristics, the NSF data estimate a 20 percent salary premium for engineers at labor-market entry while the university data estimate a 22 percent salary premium. Although these premiums are below the law and medical school premiums, they are above the salary gains for an M.B.A., and in contrast to the other professions, engineering does not require a postcollege degree. Both the NSF and the university data estimate lower returns to experience for engineering majors than for science majors, but the higher salary growth for science majors never makes up for the higher initial salaries of engineers. In both data sets, the average career salary profile of engineering majors is always above the average career salary profile of science majors.

Figures 3.1A and 3.1B give a consistent picture of salary profiles for graduates with a degree in science. Career nonscientists without a professional degree earned lower salaries than career scientists, regardless of sex. Within the groups of career scientists, engineering majors earned higher salaries throughout the career than pure science majors, even though salary growth was slightly lower. Earning a nonscience professional degree, particularly an M.D. or J.D., increased salary levels as well as salary growth relative to remaining a scientist. This pattern calls into question the wisdom of leaving science for money. Men leaving science in search of higher salaries may find their goal elusive if they do not invest further in a professional degree.

Salary Profiles of Leavers Versus Career Scientists

A comparison of salary profiles of leavers and career scientists is instructive for a number of reasons. First, it is helpful to know how leavers compare to career scientists while both groups are in science. Are they as successful as stayers or is their exit possibly a result of low salaries earned while in science? Who leaves is likely to have an impact on estimates of salary consequences of exit. Also, people who have worked in science have developed skills through these labor-market experiences that may or may not be transferable to nonscience jobs. The amount of time that a leaver has worked in science may affect the initial salary that the leaver can command in nonscience work and even the amount of training investment the new employer is willing to make. The first issue is addressed with an empirical technique called first differencing that estimates the average within-person salary change for leavers as they move from the science to the nonscience job rather than an average salary differential between similar individuals who are within and outside of science. These salary changes are estimated for all leavers and then separately for income-seeking and amenity-seeking leavers because their differences in reasons for exit imply different experiences within science and varied salary consequences on exit. In order to account for the effects of preexit scientific skill accumulation on postexit salaries, the regression model includes an interaction term that allows the salary change to differ according to the amount of science-related experience. As with the comparison of career scientists and nonscientists, the statistical analysis holds constant other potentially important characteristics. Because the earlier analysis clearly shows that investing in a postscience professional degree shifts the salary profile upwards, this analysis only focuses on graduates who did not invest in such degrees. Furthermore, salary changes are estimated solely for individuals who voluntarily left their nonscience jobs.[3] Figure 3.2A gives the salary profiles of men who start careers in science, separating men who stayed in science from men who left. Leavers started out with salaries approximately 12 percent lower than stayers implying that, as hypothesized in Jovanovic's (1979) job-matching model, exit might have been the result of discontent with one's own earnings relative to science norms. Salary growth was similar for leavers and stayers while the leavers were in science. After an average of twenty-seven months, the median duration of time in science for leavers, the leaver switched to a nonscience job, and male leavers experienced a 6 percent salary gain on exit. The change in salary was dependent on the amount of time spent in science before

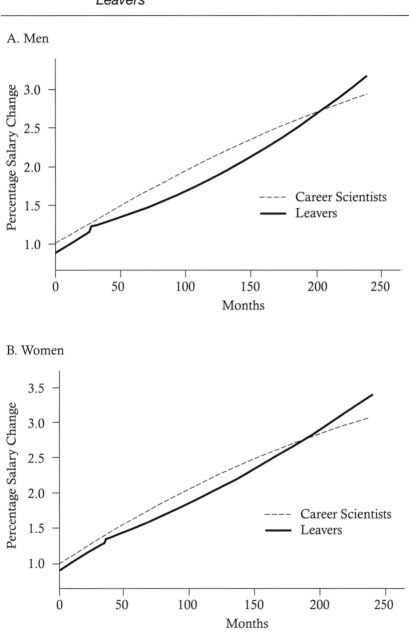

Figure 3.2   Comparison of Salaries of Career Scientists and Leavers

A. Men

B. Women

Source: Author's compilation.
Note: Starting salary of the male career scientist is normalized at one with all changes interpreted as percentage changes: 1.5 on the vertical axis corresponds to a salary that is 50 percent above the starting salary of male career scientists.

exit. Since time in science is not as highly valued outside of science as within, the salary change on exit fell with more time spent in science. For example, a man who left after six years in science experienced a 9 percent salary loss at time of exit rather than the 6 percent gain mentioned previously. Earnings growth immediately after exit was slower than earnings growth within science, possibly as leavers were learning new skills outside science. However, as the career progressed, the salaries career scientists earned in science generally reached a plateau while salary growth for leavers started to accelerate. By seventeen years into the career, male leavers were experiencing both higher salaries and higher salary growth than career scientists. However, it is not clear that lifetime earnings of leavers were above that of career scientists. The relative valuation of these earnings streams depends on the length of the career and the rate at which individuals discounted future income. For men with long, uninterrupted careers who have very low discount rates, exit may have increased lifetime earnings. But these are strong qualifications, and ex ante knowledge of these salary comparisons are not likely to have lured men out of science.

The salary profiles of female leavers and career scientists shown in figure 3.2B look very similar to the male profiles. Female leavers started out earning about 10 percent lower salaries than career scientists while in science. After an average of thirty-five months, the female leavers exited science and experienced a 9 percent salary increase that again depended on duration in science. Earnings growth outside of science started slowly, but after a period accelerated at about the same time that earnings growth of career scientists was slowing. At about sixteen years into their career, female leavers started to benefit from both higher salaries and higher salary growth than their peers who remained in science. However, because of temporary labor market departures motivated by familial responsibilities, many women do not have the long uninterrupted career that is necessary to ensure the returns of a career move to a nonscience occupation.

Comparisons of the salary effects of leaving for engineering majors and pure science majors reveals that the skills of engineers may not be as highly valued outside of science as the skills of less applied scientists. Wage loss on occupational exit is lower and subsequent wage growth is higher for science majors than for engineering majors. However, these differences are still small relative to the large initial salary differences earned by science and engineering majors. Again, figures 3.2A and 3.2B give a consistent story. The financial returns to leaving science are neither immediate nor automatic. Only individuals with long careers and low discount rates will prefer the salary profile of leavers to that of stayers. Therefore, the obvious question becomes: Are men and women who leave science in search of more lucrative careers chasing windmills or are they the lucky ones, the ones who do find unambiguous financial success?

In an attempt to determine whether income-seeking leavers were more successful at earning financial rewards, the analysis is restructured to allow salary profiles to differ for leavers who claim they left for money and career growth versus leavers who left for other reasons, such as improvement in amenities and nonmonetary work conditions.[4] Figures 3.3A and 3.3B present the salary profiles of stayers, income seekers who left for higher salaries and greater opportunities, and amenity seekers who left for better work conditions. For both men and women, income seekers left science after a shorter amount of time in science than amenity seekers, possibly because they were aware that experience in science is not well rewarded in nonscience jobs. In addition, income seekers experienced higher financial rewards in their new positions than amenity seekers, most likely because amenity seekers were trading off income for more favorable job characteristics, such as flexible hours or more enjoyable work.

Focusing first on men, income-seeking men were earning slightly higher salaries than career scientists while in science, and on exit benefited from a 9 percent salary jump. Again, salary growth was slow immediately after the move, causing salaries of leavers to dip below those of career scientists very slightly at about five years into the career. However, by eleven years into the career, these men were enjoying higher salaries and salary growth. By twenty years into the career, leavers were making almost 50 percent more money than career scientists.

In contrast to the male income seekers, female income seekers' earnings were about 10 percent lower than career scientists' while they

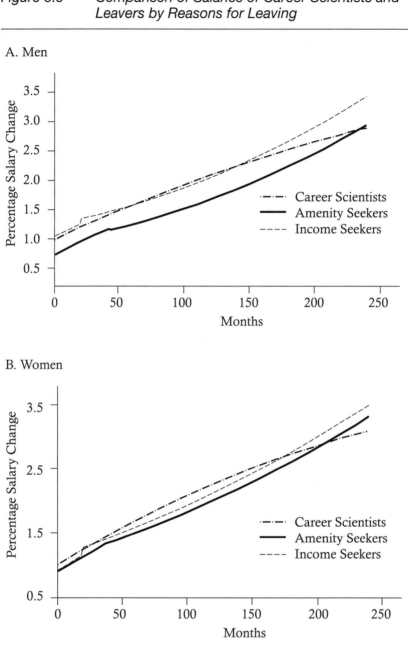

Figure 3.3   Comparison of Salaries of Career Scientists and
             Leavers by Reasons for Leaving

A. Men

B. Women

Source: Author's compilation.
Note: Starting salary of the male career scientist is normalized at one with all changes interpreted as percentage changes: 1.5 on the vertical axis corresponds to a salary that is 50 percent above the starting salary of male career scientists.

were in science, further reinforcing the idea that these women were leaving in response to unmet expectations about their own salaries within science. On exit, female income seekers enjoyed a 14 percent increase in salary, but again the slow salary growth early on outside of science kept the leavers' salaries below salaries of career scientists until about fifteen years into the career. Although it is possible that these women stay in the labor market long enough to reap the returns from leaving science, one has to question whether the salary profile documented is the salary profile that these women expected when they left science.

Both female and male amenity seekers started out with relatively low salaries within science, and their salary profiles remained well below salary profiles of career scientists until nearly twenty years into the career. Even for individuals with long uninterrupted careers and a low discount rate of future income, it is unlikely that the lifetime income of amenity seekers lies above the lifetime income of career scientists. But the amenity seekers were not seeking wealth as they exited science; rather, they were seeking more comfortable working conditions, which often come at the expense of income.

Salary Profiles of Leavers Versus Career Nonscientists

The final question becomes: Do leavers have higher salary profiles than career nonscientists, or would they have been better off never entering science? As in the earlier analysis, the question is only really relevant for people who do not go on to get a postscience advanced degree. Similar to the previous analyses, the comparison is between otherwise similar individuals and separated by sex and by reasons for exit. Assuming that experience profiles are similar, the analysis produces estimates of the difference in the level of salaries of career nonscientists and of leavers while the latter are still in science and estimates of the difference in salary levels of career nonscientists and of leavers once the latter have entered the nonscience career.

Using transitive reasoning, income-seeking men must have higher earnings than career nonscientists since they earned more than career scientists who, according to figure 3.1A, enjoyed higher salary profiles than career nonscientists. According to the statistical analysis, during their time in science, income-seeking men benefited from salary profiles about 13 percent higher than career nonscientists. Once they entered the nonscience occupations, their salaries were 10 percent higher than career nonscientists. Therefore, it seems reasonable that for these men, the career path that began in science and ended outside of science may have been a well-considered plan to maximize lifetime income.

The results are less clear for income-seeking women who earned salaries below career scientists for much of the early and middle career. These women earned similar salaries to career nonscientists both while they were working in science and while they were working outside of science, implying that with respect to lifetime earnings, it does not matter whether or not they started their careers in science. Neither amenity-seeking men nor women benefited from a temporary stint in science relative to career nonscientists. Male amenity seekers earned salaries below career nonscientists while they were employed both within science and outside of science. Female amenity seekers earned salaries comparable to the noncareer scientists while working in science. Once they left science, however, their salaries fell below the noncareer scientists.

Returning to our original question of whether science leavers gain financially, the answer is uncertain. Investing in a professional degree is a ticket to higher salary levels and higher salary growth, but there is a cost in terms of forgone income and tuition. For leavers without postscience degrees, the empirical results substantiate the interviewees' claims that salary growth outside of science begins to accelerate in mid-career when science salaries commonly plateau. In general, exiting science without a professional degree will not improve lifetime earnings. Only income-seeking men and women, who are savvy about finding nonscience work that rewards their scientific skills and who have long careers, potentially increase lifetime income by leaving science. But the deferred salary gains from exit may be another factor contributing to why women did not mention salary as a reason for exit. Many women do not anticipate the long, uninterrupted career necessary to reap these gains.

With respect to the theoretical arguments, only income-seeking men seem to have the high relative salary profiles predicted by the human capital theory, implying that there may be a group of men that is well informed about job opportunities and earnings within and outside of science and is acting on that information. Income-seeking women, however, have low incomes while they are in science and seem to be leaving due to a mismatch of their own talents and those required of science work. Similarly, male and female amenity seekers are experiencing unfavorable job attributes and relatively low salaries while in science, implying imperfect occupational matches along more than one dimension. Since imperfect matches are often a result of a lack of information on occupational opportunities, these results call for improved and more widely disseminated career and salary information for scientifically trained individuals.

CHAPTER 4

Family Responsibilities and Their Effects on a Scientific Career

F amily responsibilities affect career outcomes in very different ways for men and women. Responsibilities associated with a spouse and children commonly result in the reallocation of the woman's time away from work and toward the family. However, family responsibilities for a man lead to a reallocation of time toward work to increase the size and stability of his income. While the shift in time commitment for the woman leads to career compromise in a majority of cases, the reallocation of a man's time can have a similar effect as short-term income and stability cannot be sacrificed for long-term advancement. This chapter explores the intricacies of the relationship between work and family for these scientifically educated individuals. After a short account of some of the more prominent economic and sociological work done on this topic, the chapter continues with a blending of the work history and interview data to create a deeper understanding of the often complex conflicts and struggles for both men and women as they try to combine career and family. Finally, the chapter ends with an empirical analysis estimating the quantitative effects of marriage and parenting on continuation in science and on earnings and earnings growth.

ECONOMIC EXPLANATIONS FOR FAMILY EFFECTS ON CAREERS

Economists use knowledge of traditional gender roles in the family to explain how differences in behavior and perceptions of employees and employers result in differing impacts on careers of men and women. Even before marriage or parenting, men and women may make human capital investment decisions in compliance with their expected family life. Anticipating the role of "breadwinner," men may invest in high levels of formal education as well as informal learning that may help to enhance their careers. Women, however, anticipating a role as a secondary and often intermittent earner, may invest in less education and, when investing, may seek skills that are geographically mobile and not prone to decay when not in use. These different patterns of human capital accumulation are likely to result in real differences in earnings.

For those men and women who enter the workplace with similar educational investments, as is the case for many of the men and women in this sample, employer perceptions of future careers may result in differences in training opportunities. Because of well-known differences in housework generally, and childcare in particular, performed by men and women, employers may allocate development resources toward men and away from women because they expect higher levels of career commitment from men. Career progress, seemingly similar at entry, may then diverge with time at work.

Once marriage and parenting occur, economists predict changes in behavior. In order to reap the gains from specialization within marriage and family, men will concentrate on work and career while their wives will take care of household tasks. Not only will this specialization result in a reallocation of time but also one of attention. Women will reallocate time away from market work and toward housework or childcare to varying extents: from leaving the labor force altogether, to working part-time, to reducing overtime hours. For those mothers who remain in the labor market full-time, economists have argued that they will have less energy to apply to work if their home time involves childcare (Becker 1985). With women spending less time at work and placing family concerns above those at the job, they may be less productive. On the other hand, men, free from family responsibilities and having more dependents to satisfy, may be especially industrious. Therefore, careers will move further apart with family formation.

With the women's movement's message of independence and Title IX's doorway to enhanced educational opportunities, traditional gender roles are being challenged, and there are women whose career aspirations and educational investments match those of the most ambitious men. Many of the theoretical assumptions and predictions of the standard human capital models do not do not hold for these women. Recent declines in the marriage premium for men (Blackburn and Korenman 1994), while not fully understood, have been attributed to declining specialization as women have entered the labor market and their husbands have had to take on more family responsibilities (Gray 1997). Gary Becker's (1985) theory that women who care for children have reduced energy for career pursuits has been challenged as men have taken on increasing childcare responsibilities with no evidence to date of resulting negative earnings consequences.

The persistent negative impact of family on careers of high-achieving women has been explained theoretically with models that focus on solutions to informational problems when employers cannot judge future productivity of employees. For example, statistical discrimination in which employers use outdated perceptions of traditional gender roles to guide training and funding opportunities for male and female workers, regardless of their true commitment to work (Preston 2001), can create divergences in the career progress of men and women and can alter career decisions of women. Similarly, institutionalized workplace structures, designed to weed out all but the most dedicated employees, may force tough choices on women who are trying to balance family and work. Renee M. Landers, James B. Rebitzer, and Lowell J. Taylor (1997) cite the work practices of large law firms as an example of a rat-race equilibrium in a historically male-dominated professional labor market where hours of work are signals of commitment. Only those lawyers who work the excessively long hours will make partner since profit sharing among partners ensures that one person's slacking impacts everyone's earnings. Citing statistics from a large law firm where 96 percent of associates and 89 percent of partners feel that "willingness to work long hours when required" is very important for promotion to partnership, they acknowledge that these norms of work hours are incompatible with success of women who are starting families. Academic labor markets may be another example of a rat-race equilibrium. Similar to law firms, academic departments give a junior member several years to prove his or her worth. While there is no monetary surplus shared by tenured faculty members, there are shared prestige benefits attached to the reputation of the senior faculty. Tenured members will only vote to accept a new member if that person has shown high commitment to the field. Again, because the years during which academics earn tenure are the same period during which families are being formed, the excessively high signals of commitment necessary for promotion may come at too high a price for many women.

RESULTS OF PREVIOUS EMPIRICAL RESEARCH ON FAMILY AND CAREER

Empirical economists and sociologists have documented the differing impact of family on men's and women's labor-market success. Earnings studies of large national data sets have shown that marriage is associated with a wage premium for men and at best a negligible effect on wages of women (Korenman and Neumark 1992; Kilbourne, England, and Beron 1994). The positive effect on male wages has been relatively stable over time (Goldin 1990), and most economists attribute the marriage premium to increased specialization in the family, thus a change in behavior of husband and wife once they marry.

Average earnings effects of children are even more dissimilar for men and women as fatherhood is coupled with a significant wage premium and motherhood is linked to a significant wage loss (Korenman and Neumark 1992; Waldfogel 1997). During the period of this study, the "family gap," the difference in earnings between mothers and non-mothers, increased at the same time that the gender gap declined (Waldfogel 1998). Several studies estimate more specifically the wage and salary effects of time spent working in the home. Evidence of the larger burden of household chores borne by the woman of the household than by the man is widespread (Biernat and Wortman 1991; Coverman 1983; Hersch and Stratton 1997; Shelton and Firestone 1988), and estimated income reductions resulting from time spent at home, while sizable for women, are small and usually insignificant for men (Coverman 1983; Hersch 1991; Hersch and Stratton 1997; Shelton and Firestone 1988).

The literature on career outcomes of college-educated women has invariably focused on the fact that women with families have a hard time succeeding in a professional, predominantly male workforce. For example, Claudia Goldin (1997) shows that, in the twentieth century, there has been no cohort of women that has successfully combined work with family. The most recent cohort that she analyzes is women who graduated from college in 1972, a group who, unlike any of their female predecessors, were given wide access to traditionally male professions such as law, medicine, and business. Only 13 percent to 17 percent of these female college graduates had both a career and a family by the age of forty. In a study of graduates of the University of Michigan Law School, where variation in ability and education is relatively small, Robert Wood, Mary Corcoran, and Paul Courant (1993) find that in the tenth year after graduation, salaries of women are only 60 percent of the salaries of their male classmates. Forty-four percent of the gap is due to fewer hours, greater part-time work, or more time out of the labor force for women than for men, which the authors attribute to greater childcare responsibilities.

Literature on the effects of marriage and children on careers of scientific women has concentrated on academic women, and outcome variables analyzed have been rank and productivity rather than earnings. While most scientists encounter the belief that marriage and motherhood do not mix with a scientific career (Cole and Zuckerman 1987), in general, the empirical results are not conclusive. In particular, Jonathan Cole (1979) and J. Scott Long (1990) have shown a positive effect of marriage on productivity, while Robert Helmreich and associates (1980) show no effect. Long, Paul D. Allison, and Robert McGinnis's (1993) work on biochemists estimates a positive effect of marriage on promotion from assistant to associate professor, but no effect on promotion to full professor. Gerald Marwell, Rachel Rosenfeld, and Seymour Spilerman (1979) conclude that, relative to their male peers, married academic women are geographically constrained in job search, are more likely to locate in large labor markets, and tend not to be as mobile as their male counterparts. Long's (1978) work on the effect of work setting on publication rates implies that any compromise in job location by women in dual-career marriages is likely to lead to reductions in productivity.

Estimated effects of children on productivity are also not conclusive. In a study of seventy-three women, Cole and Harriet Zuckerman (1987) find no evidence that these women's publication rates decline after bearing children. They do find that having children does impact careers, however, by reducing flexibility to conduct time-consuming projects and reduced time for informal discussions and socializing with colleagues. Long (1990) does not find direct effects of children on productivity, but he does find that the probability of collaborating with one's advisor is lower for mothers of young children than for childless women, although having young children does not affect the probability of collaboration for male scientists. With collaboration an important determinant of predoctoral and postdoctoral productivity, mothers may be at a disadvantage.

DATA FROM WORK HISTORIES AND INTERVIEWS

Family responsibility data from the work history survey reveal that traditional roles of women continue to exist even in the most educated segment of our society. First, women are more likely than men to be constrained by the career aspirations of their spouses. Second, regardless of the couple's career situation, women tend to take on a larger share of family responsibilities than men. Table 4.1 gives data concerning these issues for men and women. According to rows one and two, 56 percent of women and 34 percent of men were married to spouses with advanced degrees. Women were almost twice as likely as men to have spouses who worked full-time. Similarly, according to rows three and four, women were approximately twice as likely as men to have altered residential localities and sacrificed career opportunities to satisfy their spouses' careers.

With regard to household and childcare chores, the women and

Table 4.1   Impact of Spouse's Career and Family
Responsibilities

	Women	Men
Number of respondents with spouses	703	507
1. Percentage of respondents whose spouses earned an advanced degree	56.8*	34.4
2. Percentage of respondents whose spouses predominantly worked full-time during the marriage	95.7*	56.6
3. Percentage of respondents who altered location decisions to satisfy spouse's career	44.6*	23.4
4. Percentage of respondents who sacrificed career opportunities and work effort to satisfy spouse's career	24.6*	11.6
5. Percentage of household chores spouse is responsible for	34.8* (17.8)	65.1 (16.4)
Number of respondents with children	449	363
6. Percentage of childcare spouse is responsible for	15.1* (13.9)	67.0 (26.3)
7. Percentage of childcare individual is responsible for	60.2* (27.9)	17.6 (15.4)
8. Percentage of respondents who took time off from work to care for children	36.3	0.0

Source: Author's compilation.
*Percentage for women is significantly different than percentage for men at the .01 level.

men in the sample give very similar answers concerning the share of these activities that both the female and the male of the household assume. Such consistency is striking given that these respondents are not married to each other. In these highly educated households, the woman performs twice as much of the household work and up to four times as much of the childcare as the man. These figures are similar to those reported in studies using time-use data (Hersch and Stratton 1997; Shelton and Firestone 1988), although time spent caring for children often is not separated from time spent performing other household chores. In previous studies in which childcare is analyzed separately, the ratio of female-to-male time with children is higher than the same ratio for time doing household chores (Coverman 1983). Even when constraining the set of women to those who worked full-time and never took leave from work to provide childcare, the women in the current study still accounted for 50 percent of the childcare, and their husbands performed no more than 15 percent, the same as reported previously. As women worked longer hours, their reduced participation in childcare was picked up by outside caregivers rather than by their husbands. Finally, according to row eight, 36 percent of the 454 mothers in the university data took leave from their careers, beyond the standard maternity leave, to care for their children. Of the 371 fathers, none reported career interruptions to care for their children.[1]

The interview sample confirms the importance of family responsibilities as a factor responsible for exit of women but not of men. Family responsibilities comprised the major factor behind occupational exit in six of the pairs of women and only one pair of men. In three female pairs, the difference between the two paired women was their opinions concerning the role of the mother in childrearing. The women who left their careers felt that a stay-at-home mother was necessary for care of the infant and toddler. In the fourth and fifth pairs, the four women all agreed that a parent should stay at home with a preschool child. The difference between the women in the fourth pair was in their income earning potential in relation to their husbands' potential. The woman who remained in science made a substantially higher and more stable income than her husband, who was a carpenter; therefore, she went to work while he cared for their child. She also was aware that a stint at home would be more damaging to her career growth than to his. The fifth pair of women, who were both in their early sixties at the time of the interview, had children at different stages of their careers. The woman who had children immediately after college never developed workforce skills to help her reenter science; the woman who waited until she had developed a career to have children was able to reenter and continue employment in science. In the final pair, both women were happy to be working mothers. However, one of the pair was employed in an inflexible corporation whose managers were unwilling to let her work part-time to meet her family responsibilities. She was forced to work full-time or quit.

The sole male pair in which family responsibilities led to exit highlights the difficulties in accommodating the dual-career marriage for men and women with Ph.D.s. Both men got Ph.D.s from excellent institutions and have strong long-lasting marriages, but their wives chose very different educational trajectories. The first man gave up tenure at a university to follow his wife to a tenure-track job as a professor after she had spent more than a decade as an adjunct instructor at his institution. While not permanently employed at the time of the interview, he still worked in science in a temporary, and sometimes volunteer, nature. The second man developed his career in science as his wife, who stopped her education after receiving a bachelor's degree, raised their children and managed the family.

The interviews also give a more complete understanding of the complex interaction between career and family that men and women in different careers must manage. For women, exit was not a common response to the difficulties of shouldering family and career responsibilities. A much more common response was a lower level career compromise: limiting job search to a specific location, working part-time, or forgoing promotions that require travel. In all but one circumstance, career compromise was directly related to family responsibilities coming from the respondent's marital family. The exception was a middle-aged woman who left the labor market to care for her ailing parents, a behavioral pattern that may potentially become more prominent as the respondents age. Of the thirty-four women married with children, 80 percent mention at least one lost career opportunity forgone to accommodate husband or children. Of the ten women married without children, 50 percent mention similar career sacrifices, and all relate these compromises to accommodating their husband's career. Not one of these women felt that they had made a conscious decision that would advance their careers at the expense of their families. In retrospect, one woman felt that the problems her preschool child developed might have been related to having a working mother. Of the seven women who were single and childless, six had not yet faced the conflicting pulls from family and work. One woman confessed that she had sacrificed a relationship that could have led to marriage to advance her career.

Of the thirty-five married men with children 54 percent felt that their families had had no negative effect on their careers, and many men talked about the flexibility that their wives' careers, or lack thereof, afforded them in pursuing their own. Thirty-one percent of the men felt that the need to provide income and security for their wives and children limited the extent to which they could invest in their own career growth. In particular, many men felt that they could not return to school for an advanced degree or look for opportunities in different locations. Lost income and the risk of an unsuccessful move prohibited such a change. In addition, as their children aged, many men found that new job searches in response to unexpected layoffs, plant closings, or firings had to be geographically constrained to assure stability for their children's educational and social development.

FAMILY AND CAREER CONFLICTS FOR THE DOCTORAL RECIPIENT

From the interview data, we can identify when the balance between family and career becomes most difficult. The most trying periods occur at different stages of family development for men and women with different levels of education and career aspirations. For women with Ph.D.s who are aspiring to academic jobs, the biggest hurdle occurs early in the career, which is often early in the marriage as well. The typical career for Ph.D. recipients in a scientific field requires a high degree of geographic mobility during this period. Those individuals earning Ph.D.s typically work at two or three postdoctoral appointments before taking a permanent position. Such a career path may require up to four geographical moves after the Ph.D. is completed in order to find a permanent position. Additionally, these first jobs themselves may last only six years, until the time of a tenure decision. Early geographic mobility and then subsequent location of two rewarding jobs within close geographical proximity are challenges that may lead to career or relationship compromises for a dual-career couple. Confirming Marwell and associates' (1979) results, in these situations, married academic women of the study felt geographically constrained in early job searches and subsequently relatively immobile throughout the career.

Women in scientific fields typically have professional spouses (table 4.1) and many are married to scientists (Cole and Zuckerman 1984). These women find it very hard to continue their career paths as Ph.D. scientists when it requires their husbands to switch geographical locations often. Generally, professional women marry men who are older and more established in their careers.[2] The husbands tend to earn more money than their wives for these reasons. Therefore, the costs of relocation are high. Of the twelve married women with Ph.D.s, six were married to men who also had Ph.D.s. The other six all spoke about the geographical constraints that their husbands' careers put on their own careers. While men may also encounter these difficulties, they are less likely to have spouses who have severe occupational constraints. In cases where there are conflicts, because the man is usually older, he has the advantage of establishing himself first, with his wife restricting her job search to accommodate his initial location. Of the sixteen married men with Ph.D.s in the interview sample, four had wives with Ph.D.s, but only two of these four women were pursuing academic careers. However, two other men of the sixteen did have early marriages with women who were also pursuing Ph.D.s; in both cases the marriages dissolved because of the stresses of the dual career. Of the remaining ten, all but two were married to women who worked in flexible, female-oriented occupations, such as nursing, teaching, home management, or childrearing.

The difficulties of the dual-career marriage in which one or both of the spouses have a science Ph.D. are best explained by the scientists themselves. One woman, who was finishing a postdoctoral position in microbiology explained:

> My husband moved with me from New York to Boston when I got this job, and if I got a job in Boston or Chicago or Los Angeles or another major city, I think my husband would be willing to move with me again; but unfortunately a lot of faculty positions, especially first ones, are not in Chicago or L.A. Those positions are really tough to get. At this point, he's

pretty far along in his career, and he's got a really good job so I just can't pick up and leave and not go to another major city.

In addition, many women felt that they did not have the right to ask their husbands and families to move. They did not want to shoulder that added responsibility. For example, a world-renowned woman in her field who remained an adjunct professor for her complete professional career described her decision not to take a tenure-track position in a university hundreds of miles away from her home and family:

I didn't want to take the responsibility . . . my husband didn't want to move and I didn't want to take him away from a job, to ask him to redefine his career. That was it. I was afraid of that emotional burden. He said he was willing to do it but I wasn't willing to take the responsibility for his emotional health. I couldn't do it. That's why I never looked for another job.

The outcome of these stresses is not always career compromise; marriages dissolve as well. A mid-career geologist employed in a senior technical position at a large private company remembered his situation as he graduated with his Ph.D.

My career goal was teaching. I applied for a few teaching positions and I interviewed for two of them but I was not offered a position. Now appreciate at this time in geology, these jobs were getting 100, 150 applicants. It was also a time when affirmative action was having an affect on the hiring practices. For a number of years, through the eighties really, many, many of these available jobs went to women or minorities and rightfully so. But for those of us who were not either, it was very, very difficult unless you were completely outstanding which I wasn't. So I came to [company X] with the thought of not staying and with the acknowledgment that this was not a part of the country that I wanted to live in. My wife was much more adamant about that at the time. She'd grown up in northern California and her goal, our goal, was to get to a nicer living environment. To make a long story short, about two years after we got here, she went back to school to get a Ph.D. [on the West Coast] and . . . that was pretty much the beginning of the end of our marriage. We divorced three or four years after that. . . . It was a situation where I had no opportunities that were nearly as attractive as the one that I had here . . . so I stayed here. And she followed her own career in science and we have both done quite well, but not together.

He continued somewhat philosophically,

I seem to have had to face a decision between a technical career, one in which I was very comfortable and challenged, and rendering my career second to keeping the marriage together, to my personal life. As things evolved, I let the career take precedence. Now, there's no control group right? I can't say what would have happened if I had made the other decision, but there's certainly, certainly a significant amount of baggage that comes along with it.

Every married woman with a Ph.D. in my interview sample narrowed the geographical scope of her job search to accommodate her husband. In the few geographical areas densely populated by universities, women have been successful in landing academic jobs. A woman with a Ph.D. in molecular biology found her job search constrained to the New York City metropolitan area. After two postdoctoral positions in private laboratories on Long Island, she got a tenure-track position in one of the colleges in New York City. She has developed a well-equipped laboratory with grant money and is a highly productive scientist. However, she explains that the geographical constraint made the initial development of her career difficult. "I needed to stay here, based on whatever circumstances. I went to a place where they didn't have the funds that other places might have had, and I started at ground zero with practically no money at all."

More often, the geographical constraints on job searching cause women to look outside of academia for job prospects. A woman with a Ph.D. in oceanography commended her husband for following her to her second postdoctoral position, which she was just finishing at the time of the interview. But he had gotten a good job, and instead of dragging him away once again, she was looking into job openings in foundations and government—jobs that require as much managerial expertise as scientific expertise. Many women also looked to industry jobs to solve the problems associated with dual-career marriages. Another woman finishing a postdoctoral fellowship in molecular biology at a prestigious East Coast university was considering jobs in the biotechnology industry. Although she felt that such a job choice would compromise her career, she was not sure how she could fit her husband and future children into academia.

Many of the men in the interview sample spoke of the importance of having a spouse who accepted the flexibility that is necessary to accommodate the geographical mobility of a science career, an advantage few women have. A Ph.D. in a tenure-track position in computer science at a midwestern university pointed out that his career had benefited from, as well as impacted, the work activities his wife had chosen. "We made six moves, New York to Berkeley and back, Los Angeles, Australia, Berkeley again and then the Midwest, all because of my career. You may have noticed she had a few different jobs—working with mentally retarded adults to property management to administrative work in Australia to retail sales and now payroll." Few men would be satisfied with such a patchwork set of work activities.

Once the early postdoctoral years are over, finding two jobs within the same city is not easy for an academically employed couple. A microbiologist whose early career benefited from having a wife with transferable skills described the problem from the other side of the issue as he tried to recruit young scientists to his university in the Washington-Baltimore area. "A lot of people in my field are scientific couples and most of the candidates have a scientific spouse and they need a position. It's tough. I mean there are worse places than here . . . the best places are Boston and San Francisco where there's plenty of opportunity." In many instances, however, the man is older than the woman and is already established in a job; therefore, the wife has to find the job to accommodate his initial location. As a result, the only instance in which a Ph.D. scientist gave up tenure for a spouse's academic career is the case of a male chemist. He explained,

> that was a very nice job for me, but the academic couple is not happy unless both have good situations. And it was not such a good situation for my wife because she came without a job, and she was seven months pregnant and she didn't work for a year and then she wanted to go back. . . . She took part-time work in the English department as an instructor, and these big state universities depend on exploiting various kinds of people to teach their lower division courses. She got roundly exploited over the space of twelve years. After eleven years we decided we would leave, and we would go to the place where she could find the best job.

Even though the structure of the academic scientific career discourages participation by women with interests in a family, most of the women acknowledge the importance of this early career mobility. A molecular biologist clarified, "It's very important in my field when you do a Ph.D. in one place that you move somewhere else to do a post-doc and then you move somewhere else to get a job. Most of this has to do with different kinds of experiences making a better scientist." A marine scientist described a similar rationale for mobility.

> I got my degree here. They don't want me to stay. They think it would be better for my career to go somewhere else and learn from somebody else. I did do that in Maryland for a while but I came back. . . . but to them they would think well, hey, maybe you should go to Florida. Stay there for a while and go to Washington and then to California. There's truth to that because you learn from different people.

This model of the production of cutting-edge science is deeply rooted in the scientific culture. The costs in terms of lost staffing, and occasional harm to personal relationships, are high. Therefore, it is important to consider whether this mobility is necessary for the advancement of science, or whether there are alternative models that do not compromise quality yet are more embracing of family needs. With today's increasingly sophisticated communication and transportation technologies, there may be alternative ways to have young scientists learn from other more experienced scientists or engineers in other locations.

The issue of family and children surfaced again when women Ph.D. recipients talked about the need to secure grants early in their careers in order to establish a laboratory and succeed in the academic environment. With increasingly sophisticated and expensive equipment and larger numbers of grant applications, these scientists reported increased competition for grant funds, which translated into more of their time allocated to research activities and less to families and nonwork activities in general. With an increasingly uncertain success rate, they were often not sure whether they wanted to make this added sacrifice. The solution of many women was to find jobs in industry where research money was provided, albeit at the expense of autonomy.

A woman finishing her postdoctorate in molecular biology at a prestigious university and pondering her choices noted, "there is a tremendous feeling among scientists both men and women that . . . in order to be a good, productive scientist, a federally funded scientist, you have to put in a lot of hours, and if you can't put those hours in you won't get the grant money, and if you do put those hours in you are doing it to the detriment of your marriage and children." She felt that women, more than men, were passing up the academic career to increase the quality of family life. She lamented that the most successful of the scientists are those who forgo outside interests, thus reinforcing the stereotype of the nerdy scientist.

Another woman with a Ph.D. in geology, who left science, as I formally define it, to engage in teaching and training, described her professors in graduate school.

> They were dedicated to their families but they weren't spending the time with their families, doing the things that their wives were doing. They felt very strongly about going home in the evening. They would work from eight in the morning until six at night, which is a very long day, and then spend time

with their kids at night, but sometimes they would come back after their kids went to sleep. If their wives were taking the kids some place in the evening they would go to work. [Work] was the only thing they had and it was very obvious to me they weren't cooking and they weren't cleaning and . . . they weren't going to the kids' plays—the things that somebody's got to do and usually the woman ends up doing. Most of their wives either weren't working or they were only working part-time . . . in very nondemanding professions.

Although the voices questioning the "tunnel vision" required to succeed in academia were predominantly female, there were some male echoes. A chemistry Ph.D. concluding his postdoctorate at the time of the interview was discouraged by the immense amount of time that his advisor put in to ensure grant funding; he anticipated looking for a job at a teaching college. "I've pretty much decided that I don't want to go for the big Domo type jobs that are out there and that apparently my advisor thinks I could have been headed for. . . . [I am] just realizing that I don't want to be doing work for eighty hours a week basically until I get tenure. I'd much rather be trying to raise my son or doing stuff with him in the community."

Stressing the difficulty underlying the dual-career marriage is not meant to overlook the troubles encountered while balancing children and scientific work of Ph.D. recipients, a stress felt primarily by women. Many of the women spoke of feeling the need to hide pregnancies as long as possible because of the negative connotations related to work commitment that they might evoke; one prominent scientist, a mother herself, admitted to reducing her opinion of her own female colleagues once they started having children. Having children was not a deal breaker for these women, however. In response to the dual-career conflicts, some of these women had found or were seeking a work situation, possibly outside of science, that could accommodate both marriage and childcare. Others persevered and entered the work-intensive environment of academia and grant proposal writing. These women recounted late nights at the lab, chaotic scheduling, and heavy reliance on relatives and daycare providers, an exhausting balancing act with uncertain success. But the level of commitment to career that had gotten them to that point kept them working through the challenges.

FAMILY AND CAREER CONFLICTS FOR THE SCIENTIST WITH A BACHELOR OF SCIENCE OR MASTER OF SCIENCE

Women who terminated their education with a bachelor's or master's degree and worked in private industry found the greatest difficulty balancing the conflicting demands of young children and companies that were often inflexible to their needs. Generally, these women were trying to establish scientific careers in business, government, or nonacademic nonprofit organizations. Although dual careers can be complicated to balance, jobs in these sectors are not as tied to a specific geographic area as they are in academia. In addition, individuals with a B.S. or M.S. degree often qualify for a broader set of jobs than do Ph.D. recipients with narrow and specialized training. For these women, finding jobs for two professionals was not the overwhelming barrier that it was for Ph.D. scientists. Many of these women, however, found that the most challenging problems arose when the couple started a family. Some women felt the need for one parent to stay at home during the early years of a child's life, and other women were looking for job situations that allowed a comfortable shouldering of the double burden of work and family. Many of the women were looking for jobs with opportunities for part-time work, flexible hours, minimal travel and overtime hours, and no relocation requirements—all characteristics that reduce the potential for increased earnings and promotions. These women often took on the family responsibilities and looked for these workable situations either because the husband was more established and his participation would generate large financial sacrifices, or because the woman felt that it was her responsibility to do so and was something she wanted to do.

The difficulties that women in science careers have balancing children and work are echoed in interviews with men. An electrical engineer working at a large defense firm and married to a woman with a

B.S. in electrical engineering who worked at the same firm described how family impacted her career. "She was doing fine and everything until we decided to start having kids . . . she went back part-time after the first one, and after the second one she retired."

In the business field, there was often a lack of flexibility in meeting the demands of working mothers. Part-time and flex-time work, while increasing at the beginning of the twenty-first century, were rare in science and engineering jobs during the 1980s and early 1990s. Eighteen percent of the women working outside of science and engineering worked part-time while only 8.5 percent of the women working in scientific jobs were part-time. For women in science and engineering, part-time work during childrearing may be an important way to keep skills current so that reentry to a full-time science- or engineering-related job is possible once the children enter school. Companies were also often inflexible concerning time off for sick children, and many women left in response to this conflict. Leaving the labor force during their children's preschool years, these women invariably reentered the job market in a position unrelated to science.

This pattern was apparent in one interview with a successful technical sales employee who had more than ten years of experience at a large, well-established computer company and was denied part-time work after her first child. She left the workforce and does not feel able to return to the same field since so much has changed in the ensuing five years. Similarly, a successful software developer in a large pharmaceutical company described her company:

> This company calls itself a family company, but indeed they are kind of hostile to working mothers in time off and the type of situations that arise when you are a working parent. Supposedly the company has a high divorce rate. . . . You need to take vacation time when the child is sick. In other companies, you get personal days; you can take time without pay if you have to. In this company that's not an option. . . . There is no part-time work; you have to resign.

At the time of the interview, she was hoping to leave the company once she had accumulated the financial resources necessary for investment in further education in order to change careers.

The interviews did uncover positive situations in which companies or their employees worked with women to craft opportunities that would ensure the flexibility needed by these women. One female respondent with a Ph.D. in math and computer science education went to work for a company that developed mathematical software for schools. The president of the company supported her efforts to have a family and a career.

> When I was going to have a baby, he's the one who said "just put him in your office" and I took him up [on it]. I brought my little one to work every day. . . . By the time he was about a year, he was getting too big—it just wasn't appropriate. I needed to work at home. So, instead of coming into the office every day, maybe I'd stay six hours or so and then come home and work. . . . That was always encouraged, and once in awhile I wouldn't go in; I would work at home.

After working for this company for six years, she left to start work toward a law degree. The president of the company who had supported her efforts to blend family and career had sold the company to a large business that did not offer her the sort of flexibility to which she had grown accustomed. Among other reasons, she said that she left because she was looking for the kind of flexible work environment she had under the company's original founder.

Many of the women who were frustrated by the lack of job flexibility questioned the rationale behind their companies' policies. A computer science graduate working in the research and development department of a private company explained. "It just seems very stupid to me—economically stupid—for a company to train somebody and then force her out. That has to cost the company money. They invest money and everybody invests time. So why just lose that because people want to have children? They make it a very hard issue. If they were a little more flexible, I would be infinitely loyal and I would stay with this company—I think I would work harder, really."

All of the women in the interview sample were highly motivated career-oriented women. They had overcome the social pressures discouraging them from studying math and science in junior high and high school. They had succeeded again in a somewhat more alienating science or mathematics curriculum in college and had landed a science-oriented job. Except for a few women who had always planned to stay at home with their children, none of the women anticipated the difficulties they would face balancing career and family. Some women became aware of the struggle during the pregnancy when they saw their responsibilities at work diminished. Others first felt the conflicting demands with the birth of their first baby. Still others first understood the conflicting pressures as they returned to work and attempted to compete for responsibilities and raises with other men and women who did not have the same family responsibilities.

Women respondents who remained employed after motherhood, regardless of education, pointed out that the balancing act was a persistent and ongoing struggle. Some of the persistence of this struggle is due to the natural changes that children and families undergo as they grow. A computer software developer explained. "I'm thinking ahead to see what happens when he [my son] wants to visit friends or he wants to play sports or be a boy scout or whatever—these things are done after school and that is four, five o'clock. I don't want to penalize him—I don't want to say to him 'you can't do it because I have to work.'"

However, other aspects of the persistence of this struggle are due to the nature of science itself. Science is a continually evolving field of study, and often individuals working in science need to work on updating their skills on their own time. Married women with children are immediately at a disadvantage in this respect if they are taking on more of the family responsibilities than their male counterparts. As one woman explained, "The one thing they [the company] seem to highlight now is outside reading, which is not unusual. They want their technical people to read as much as they can to get new ideas and things like that. I understand that and that's great, but I don't have a lot of time for outside reading."

The impact of starting a family is very different for men. Most of the male interviewees talked about their early careers, when they worked long hours to gain higher salaries and better promotion opportunities for the sake of their families. A young mechanical engineer who was moving into management at a large construction company talked about opportunities for advancement, "[I] definitely see an opportunity to move up, but this environment requires pretty intense dedication of your own personal time. So there's no such thing as nine to five or anything even close to that." And when asked whether having children would impact his career, he continued, "I don't think it will impact it immediately . . . [it depends on] whether I can keep this pace up and sort of miss the early years of my child's life. I think the reality is that I work ten- or twelve-hour days, so I'm not really going to see my children except on the weekends."

A man with a Ph.D. in operations research and working in industry described his early career: "I was working a lot of extra overtime hours and I wasn't getting home much. My wife was supportive of that because I was making good money and I was trying to get into a position to buy a home and do other things. We needed more money, but at the same time the extra hours and not having much time at home to spend with the kids and having her burdened with almost all the time at home . . . all was kind of rough."

As many of the men aged, however, family stresses started to put constraints on their careers. A man with a B.S. in computer science who started a family soon after finishing his degree explained. "Early on I had the desire to go to school but I saw the people around me who were doing that and saw what it took and I basically had to make a decision, 'what was I valuing?' And I decided that I wanted to value my family. At some point it may impact how far I can go in my career, but I'm willing to live with that because I place my family above my career." A male respondent who left a Ph.D. program in math after obtaining a master's degree, entered industry and developed a successful career in computer science. With changes in the industry, he found himself laid off in midcareer with a wife and two children. He explained, "My wife and I made an agreement that I wouldn't go pursuing jobs out of state, and we sort of said we're going to stay here and raise the kids. In other words, we're not going to uproot the kids and the family." This man found a good job and felt that the layoff, along with some good luck, had a positive impact on his career. A man with a B.S. in geology who entered the electronics field because of limited opportunities in geology, felt that he could not take any risks to look for new opportunities because of the responsibilities of providing for his five children. "I have to have a job, and I have to make sure I have a decent job with enough pay so that I can support my family. That's a consideration for moving or for taking another job."

At some point, many men just decide the family sacrifices are not worth the income. The operations research Ph.D. who worked such long hours early in his career, was struck down with a life-threatening illness in midcareer. Back in good health and in a good job, he talked about his new position:

> I'm sure there will be opportunities for advancement if I want to try and be aggressive and go for it because of the growth of the company. But I'm getting to the point where I've got a lot of responsibilities at home with my family. A lot of what you do to get ahead is to do a lot of traveling and a lot of hard pressure things, being on the go and all. So it's kind of a trade off for me there—as long as I'm making a good living and I'm enjoying my work and I'm able to keep my wife and kids happy.

FROM INTERVIEWS BACK TO WORK HISTORIES

The interview data highlight the importance of family responsibilities in defining both a man and a woman's career. They also underline the complexity of the interaction between family and career. However, three consistent patterns seem to emerge, which can be tested with the larger university data set. First, with respect to Ph.D.s, the career compromise for women comes early. Marriage to a professional man often requires female Ph.D. scientists to compromise their career goals, possibly through movement to a nonacademic or a nonscience position. Second, women with a master's or bachelor's degree find that the career compromise comes with children. Third, both men and women point out that time with children reduces the time spent developing a successful, well-paid career.

Turning to the 1,688 work histories, statistical analysis is used to determine whether these patterns hold for the full sample. First, the analysis estimates the probability of working in a science job as a function of the amount of previous experience in science jobs, the amount of previous experience in work outside of science, the time spent out of work, and then the variables identifying whether the scientist is married and whether the scientist has children. The samples are separated by level of degree and by sex. The results are presented in table 4.2.

The results confirm the interviewees' impressions. Married women with Ph.D.s are 11 percent less likely to be employed in a science job than female Ph.D.s who are single. However, having children, once the woman is married, does not affect the probability of being employed in science. Interestingly, male Ph.D.s are 12 percent more likely to be employed in science if they are married than if they are single, probably because men marry women with transferable skills and careers who are

Table 4.2   Effect of Marriage and Children on Employment in Science

	Marriage	Children
Women with Ph.D.s (n = 113)	11 percent less likely to work in science if married*	No effect
Men with Ph.D.s (n = 118)	12 percent more likely to work in science if married*	No effect
Women without Ph.D.s (n = 862)	No effect	17 percent less likely to work in science if with children*
Men without Ph.D.s (n = 591)	No effect	No effect

Source: Author's compilation.
*Effects are significantly different from zero at the .01 level.

willing to take on the full share of family responsibilities. Although the scientific employment of women with master's or bachelor's degrees in science is not impacted by marriage, women with children are 17 percent less likely to work in science than women who are childless. Family considerations have no impact on the employment of men with bachelor's or master's degrees in science. For women, family formation is strongly and negatively correlated with persistence in science, yet the stage of family formation that creates difficulties differs according to career track. Women with Ph.D.s have trouble merging the dual-career marriage with a scientific career, while women with B.S. or M.S. degrees have trouble accommodating children.

Regression analysis is used to estimate salary profiles over time for men and women with different family situations. These profiles reveal estimated salary growth for men and women while they are single, married but childless, and parents. Each parent in the work history survey was asked to estimate the percentage of childcare that they took on while their children were preschool age. Using their responses, salary levels and salary growth can be estimated for parents with differing amounts of childcare responsibility taken on during their children's preschool years. For both men and women, the percentage of childcare has large, statistically significant negative effects on salary levels. While the effect of childcare on women's earnings mirrors results of Shelley Coverman (1983), Joni Hersch and Leslie S. Stratton (1997), and Beth Anne Shelton and Juanita Firestone (1988), the significant negative effect on male earnings is unprecedented.[3] Also unique to this study's sample of parents, the childcare variable explains the full earnings differential between men and women. Comparing male and female science-educated parents, mothers and fathers who take on the same amount of childcare earn, on average, identical salaries. These large and significant negative effects of childcare on earnings as well as their power to explain gender-based earnings differentials hold up under considerable statistical testing (Preston 2001).

Figure 4.1 presents the estimated salary profiles as the average respondent moves through the stages of family development. The natural logarithm of salary is measured on the vertical axis, which allows all changes to be interpreted as percentage changes. For example, the

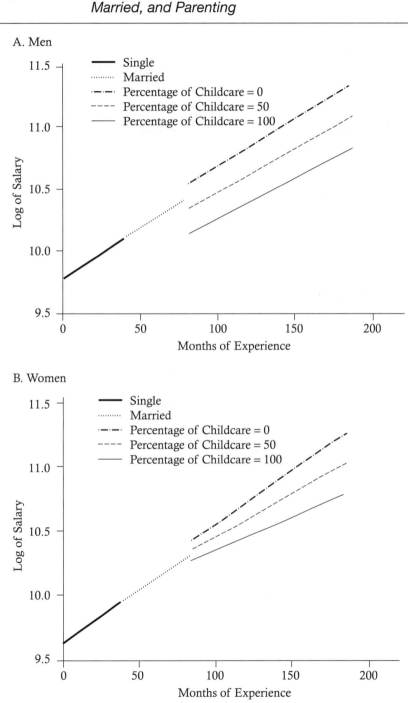

Figure 4.1　Salary Experience Profiles While Single, Married, and Parenting

A. Men

Single
Married
Percentage of Childcare = 0
Percentage of Childcare = 50
Percentage of Childcare = 100

Log of Salary

Months of Experience

B. Women

Single
Married
Percentage of Childcare = 0
Percentage of Childcare = 50
Percentage of Childcare = 100

Log of Salary

Months of Experience

Source: Author's compilation.

increase from 9.75 to 10.0 on the vertical axis corresponds to a 25 percent increase in earnings. With respect to levels, 9.75 corresponds to annual earnings of $17,154. Once the individual becomes a parent, the graph traces out three hypothetical salary profiles: one for the parent who takes on 100 percent of childcare, one for the parent who takes on 50 percent of childcare, and one for the parent who takes on 0 percent of childcare.[4]

The salary profiles again confirm the interviewees' comments. Looking first at figure 4.1A, men who take on 100 percent of childcare, of whom there are very few, experience a 28 percent salary loss relative to salary immediately preceding childbirth. Men who take on none of the childcare experience a 12 percent salary gain, possibly as they work harder to provide for the child. Men who take on 50 percent of childcare, still a large percentage relative to the average man, experience an 8 percent loss in salary. After childbirth, salary growth does not vary according to the amount of childcare taken on, but the large differences in salaries persist.

The salary profiles for women are qualitatively very similar. Women who take on no childcare also benefit from an 11 percent jump in earnings after childbirth. Women who take on full childcare responsibilities experience a drop in earnings of 4 percent. And women who take on 50 percent of childcare, a figure slightly below the average, enjoy a 4 percent increase in salary. After childbirth, however, salary growth also varies by the amount of childcare taken on, with women who take on no childcare experiencing the fastest salary growth and women who take on 100 percent of childcare experiencing the slowest salary growth. As a result, the earnings differences between women with differing childcare obligations increase with time, and ten years after childbirth, the dispersion in salary according to childcare obligations for women is as wide as the dispersion observed for men. The results are consistent and strong; time spent with children has a negative effect on one's career, and this effect can be observed through lower salary and salary growth. These results hold for men as well as women.

Analysis of the survey and interview data both support previous conclusions and give evidence for new conclusions concerning the effects of family on professional men's and women's careers. For scientific women, family formation reduces the probability of persisting in a scientific career. The geographical constraints imposed by dual-career marriages are correlated with attrition for female Ph.D. scientists, and the burdens of caring for children and working in science are often unmanageable for women whose science education ended with a B.S. or an M.S. For those scientists who do try to shoulder the double burden, the percentage of childcare responsibility taken on has large negative effects on earnings for both men and women. Comments by mothers did not support Becker's (1985) hypothesis that these women have less energy for work, but more that, similar to Cole and Zuckerman's findings (1987), they cut back on the nonessentials, like eating lunch with colleagues, overtime hours, traveling to conferences, and outside reading—all activities that contribute to career growth. Rather surprisingly, for the parents in the sample, the gender gap in earnings was fully explained by differences in time spent on childcare.

CHAPTER 5

Mentoring

Mentoring stands out as an extremely important factor influencing career decisions and dictating career outcomes of science-educated women in the university sample. Mentoring early in the science career has an immediate impact on the woman's probability of continuation and success in science. Although more prevalent, mentoring of men, especially in the academic arena, has a less pronounced effect on short-term career outcomes. The apparent differences in the extent and impact of mentoring for men and women is not surprising since science is a male-dominated field. Mentoring relationships may develop naturally for men because a large majority of the potential mentors in science are men, but the guidance may be knowledge that the men could gather from interactions with peers. However, female scientists are likely to feel isolated and even stigmatized for violating traditional social patterns, and the science workplace is likely to resemble a foreign landscape. Any guidance for women, while hard to find, may be especially helpful. This chapter analyzes the role of mentoring in scientific careers beginning with an explanation of how mentoring fits into economic explanations of skill development. This is followed by a review of the research on mentoring generally, and in science more specifically. The chapter moves on to an examination of the presence and effects of mentoring for individuals in the interview sample and then relates perceptions of the interviewees themselves on the value of a mentor.

MENTORING AND HUMAN CAPITAL ACQUISITION

The theory of human capital in economics posits that each individual has a stock of human capital, skills, and know-how, which he or she can rent to an employer for a wage. Higher levels of human capital imply higher productivity levels in a workplace and thus higher earnings. An individual builds his or her own human capital through investments in education and postschool training. The decision about whether or not to invest in any strategy is made by comparing the present value of costs and long-term benefits. Susan Athey, Christopher Avery, and Peter Zemsky (2000) have pointed out that mentoring is a process through which a student, or mentee, augments his or her human capital stock. As articulated by scholars of science, the enhancement of the human capital may take varied forms, such as more scientific know-how, better research techniques, improved scholarly connections, and higher self confidence. But each form should lead to increased productivity as a scientist. The magnitude of the benefits to the student depends on the extent and time frame of increased productivity, while costs are primarily opportunity costs of time spent developing and participating in the relationship. Human capital theory also acknowledges that there are possibly nonpecuniary benefits and costs associated with the investment decision, which might also enter into the calculation.

Analyzing the mentoring process as a human capital investment results in three important conclusions. First, because students will be more likely to enter into a mentoring relationship the greater the potential benefits, all else equal, students will prefer a mentor who is more eminent and more productive. Second, the degree of comfort between the student and mentor will translate into nonpecuniary characteristics of the relationship, which may alter investment decisions. Thus, women may prefer female mentors and men may prefer male mentors. Finally, because women are a minority in science and may be naturally excluded from informal interactions through which human capital is shared, a formal mentoring process may have a greater impact on a woman's productivity than on her male peers' productivity.

Therefore, women may be more likely than men to seek out a mentoring relationship.

The theory of human capital assumes perfect markets and no barriers to investment. However, we cannot assume such perfection in the case of mentoring. The mentor has to agree to engage in a mentoring relationship, and as with the students, such a decision hinges on a comparison of costs and benefits. The costs of mentoring are again the opportunity costs of time spent developing and maintaining the relationship, and the more eminent the professor, the higher the opportunity costs. The benefits can be quite varied but might come in the form of research assistance, creative collaboration, and enhanced reputation in the field. All of these benefits will be greater the more productive the student becomes. As a result, the mentor is likely to select only the students who are most able and whose futures are most promising. In such a situation, mentors may steer clear of female students. Jonathan Cole and Burton Singer (1991) maintain that there are no early screening devices to show who among a cohort in a given discipline with similar educational credentials will be the most important producer of science. Cole (1979) further argues that irrelevant characteristics such as race or sex will be predictors of outcomes when there is little other information with which to judge an individual's contributions or when the processes through which rewards are allocated are nonstandard and secretive. Therefore, the practice by which a mentor chooses a student is potentially ripe for biases against women. In addition, practical reasons for passing over a female student for a male student are well documented. Empirical studies show that, on average, female scientists are less productive than male scientists (Cole and Zuckerman 1984; Long 1992), and women are more likely to bear the burdens of family than their male peers (chapter 4).

The mentoring process is different than other human capital investment decisions because there is a matching process between two individuals who are both looking to benefit from the relationship. Neither student nor mentor will engage in a relationship if the expected costs exceed the benefits. Although it is likely that women will benefit more than men from a mentoring relationship, there are two important reasons why women may be less likely to be in mentoring relationships. First, if female students place a large premium on having a female mentor, they may be disappointed, especially in those departments such as mathematics, physics, and engineering where female faculty are scarce. Second, because mentors are also calculating the costs and benefits of the relationship, they may prefer to mentor men over women because of historical differences in success within science.

PREVIOUS RESEARCH ON MENTORING

The role of the mentor in science careers has been analyzed in much of the literature on Ph.D. scientists, and the potential and varied benefits to the student have been well articulated. Studying Nobel laureates in science, Zuckerman (1977) maintains that the mentor educates the student in "what matters" in science and science research. Ann Gibbons (1992) credits the mentor with connecting the student to meeting organizers and to journal editors, helping the student develop a "style," and encouragement. J. Scott Long and Robert McGinnis (1985) hypothesize that the mentor plays three crucial roles: as sponsor, teacher, and collaborator. Concrete effects on the academic's career have also been estimated. In a study of Ph.D. chemists, Barbara Reskin (1978) finds that the productivity of one's dissertation advisor, as measured by publications, is positively associated with predoctoral productivity; the eminence of one's advisor, as measured by awards, is positively associated with placement in a university tenure-track position. In a similar study of male biochemist Ph.D.s, Long and McGinnis (1985) find that the performance and the eminence of a dissertation advisor is positively correlated with predoctoral productivity, the probability of a postdoctoral appointment, the prestige of the first faculty appointment, and postdoctoral productivity. Although the strengths of these positive relations between productivity, eminence, and student outcome vary by outcome, in general, the positive correlation is stronger and the effect is larger in magnitude if the student and the advisor collaborate and coauthor. While the authors equate advisor with mentor, they do point out that the development of a mentoring relationship is more likely if the advisor and student work on joint research projects.

The role of mentor to female scientists has not been as extensively researched. Reskin (1978, 1979) has argued that collegial exchange, a likely by-product of a mentoring relationship, may be even more important for women than men since it may relieve the stresses of role conflicts. Because of societal gender roles, women may feel pressure from their families and their employing organizations to reallocate time from research to more traditional work, such as mothering and teaching. In an empirical study of male and female biochemist Ph.D.s, Long (1990) finds that female students are more likely than male students to have a female advisor, and for women, having a female advisor increases the probability of collaboration. For this same group of biochemists, having young children reduces the odds of collaborating with an advisor for women but not for men. It is well known that female Ph.D. scientists are less likely to have children than their male counterparts (Cole and Zuckerman 1987; Long 1990), so this finding does not give evidence on differences in the extent of mentoring for men and women. In fact, Long finds that men and women are equally likely to collaborate with their advisors. However, the productivity and eminence of advisors to female students are significantly lower than the productivity and eminence of advisors to male students.

The empirical results that show positive correlations between performance of mentor and student outcomes lead to questions about the matching process between mentor and student in science. Do the most esteemed mentors only take on the most able students, as measured by productivity during graduate school, or do the students taken on by the most respected mentors become more able because of the mentor's teachings? An intermediate position may be that the most eminent scientists take on the students they expect to be most productive and then, through mentoring, enable these students to succeed. Although Long and McGinnis (1985) conclude that in mentoring relationships where collaboration occurs, the student's productivity is enhanced through teaching, they do not dismiss selectivity as an additional factor behind the positive correlation between student success and prestige of mentor. Long's (1990) result showing the reduced probability of coauthorship between advisors and female students with small children, further fuels questions surrounding the matching process. One interpretation of the result is that women with small children have little time to coauthor; another is that the professor's impression of the female student is diminished with the advent of motherhood. Suzanna Rose's (1985) study of approximately ninety assistant professors of psychology raises questions about when a mentoring relationship actually occurs. She finds that the networks created by young female professors are less likely to have ties to their doctoral institutions, implying weaker ties to the dissertation advisor. Therefore, assuming a mentoring relationship between dissertation advisor and female students may not be appropriate.

Generally, research on mentoring of minorities has focused on senior minority professionals mentoring younger minority members. In a theoretical piece, Athey, Avery, and Zemsky (2000) analyze firms where there is majority representation at the senior level and a mixed "type" junior workforce, where each senior member only mentors individuals of his or her type and where increased mentoring increases human capital of the young worker. Firm promotion policy that maximizes long-term profits is more likely to perpetuate majority representation at the senior level the more important mentoring is to human capital formation and productivity, since junior minority "types" will lose in the race to accumulate human capital. Only when the short-term costs of promoting less able minority personnel are offset by the longer term advantages of increased mentoring of the most able minorities will firms become more diverse at the senior levels. In addition, affirmative action policies that result in promotion of minorities to senior levels will have long-ranging positive effects on diversity because of increased mentoring of minorities. Translating the model to practice results in the conclusion that mentoring may be one of the forces that perpetuates segregation in the workplace, and because real-life firms are more short-sighted than their theoretical peers, they are not likely to alter the status quo without government-mandated programs.

Empirical work on women mentoring women has had little success identifying any benefits, possibly because the mentoring relationship is not well established or the benefits are not well defined. For example, Brandice Canes and Harvey Rosen (1995) find no evidence that increasing the number of female faculty members in science and engineering departments increases the number of undergraduate women choosing to major in those fields. David Neumark and Rosella

Gardecki (1998) examine the effects of the gender of the dissertation advisor and the female representation in the graduate department on the career progress of women in economics Ph.D. programs. Although not a natural science discipline, economics is the social science discipline that has the lowest representation of women with only 26.6 percent of economics Ph.D.s awarded to women in 2000 (U.S. Department of Education 2002). They find that the women with female dissertation advisors and women in departments with higher percentages of female faculty do not get more prestigious jobs than their female peers with male dissertation advisors or in departments with lower female representation. However, they do find that women with female advisors and women in departments with more females do finish more quickly and are less likely to drop out of graduate school than their peers with fewer female contacts. Using these results to downplay the value of mentoring relationships between women seems misdirected. First, the study never establishes a mentoring relationship for any of the women studied. Second, even if there were a mentoring relationship between two women, its effect on prestige of first job is likely to be insignificant or negative if the student is being compared to other female students who are mentored by men, the majority group in the economics profession. Finally, the positive effects on persistence—if they are indeed the result of mentoring of women by women—are important in a field where Ph.D. dropout rates of women are more than twice the dropout rates of men (Kahn 1995).

INTERVIEWS

In seven of the twenty-one pairs of women for whom conclusions about exit could be drawn, the positive guidance of a strong mentor was the primary difference between the women who stayed and those who left. Six of the seven exiting women left in response to a lack of support and guidance in college or graduate school. All seven women have established diverse careers in other sectors in the economy: one became a graphic artist specializing in animal illustration, two began careers in computer science, one runs a daycare center and works part-time as a mediator, one works in insurance and is studying to be an actuary, one studied theology and is raising her children, and one is the president of a local chapter of the American Civil Liberties Union.

Many interviewed women, outside of this group of seven pairs, felt that positive mentoring was an important prerequisite for career success in science. Seventy-three percent of the women interviewed described situations where either positive mentors advanced their careers or the indifference, and even hostility, of potential mentors impeded their careers. Especially at the educational institutions, mentoring of women was rare. Of the fifty women interviewed, 13.5 percent had guidance as an undergraduate, and of the thirty-three women who were in a graduate program at some time, 20.5 percent were assisted by senior scientists. The presence of a mentor was extremely influential in determining success in graduate school, increasing the probability of finishing the graduate program from 0.6 to 1.0. Similarly, mentoring by supervisors or colleagues in the early stages of the career was important to the success of women in the scientific workforce. Of the forty-four early employment situations described by interviewed women, mentoring relationships were present in only twenty-three. However, having a mentor increased the probability of a successful employment situation from 0.52 to 1.00.[1]

Mentoring proved less important in career development for men. First, in the eighteen pairs of men for whom a primary reason for exit could be identified, mentoring was never identified as the factor differentiating the scientist who stayed and the scientist who left. In general, men did not speak of the importance of mentors as frequently as did women. Second, men were more likely than women to have mentors in college and graduate programs, but their success in graduate programs was not dependent on mentoring. Forty percent of the men had mentors as undergraduates, and 65.7 percent of the men had mentors in graduate programs. The probability of completing the intended plan of study at the time of entry to graduate school was 0.75 for men without mentors and 0.74 for men with mentors. Finally, although men were equally as likely as women to have mentors in early employment situations, success in employment was not as closely tied to these relationships. 51 percent of the men cited having mentors in early employment, but the probability of a successful employment experience for mentored men (0.83) was not much higher than the probability of success for men without this guidance (0.70). While the estimated short-term career impact was not large, it becomes clear from the comments about mentoring that follow, the relationship offered long-term personal and professional benefits for many men.

The role of mentor in both men's and women's careers was less as a role model or inspiration but more as a teacher or guide. In productive mentoring relationships, there was a transfer of human capital in the form of knowledge and skill from mentor to student. In the case of young scientists working to complete a master's degree or a Ph.D., the mentor was most often the advisor or another departmental professor who worked closely with the student, introducing them to research questions, methods, and presentation, or even helping them to network with other professionals. Often the mentor helped the young scientist to get his or her first grant or first job. As a result, the mentor may have had long-term impacts on the student's research career and teaching, both in terms of style as well as substance.

The importance of the role of advisor was not lost on these students. A midcareer Ph.D. chemist, who at the time of the interview was working in a start-up company, described his Ph.D. advisor as "the first person that stood out as a pivotal element in my life. . . . He changed my life in a very real way, ways that I can still think back to . . . [and] really affected the way I look at certain things professionally, if not personally as well." He continued to describe the laboratory situation that his advisor created:

> We had a reasonably small group: I think three or four graduate students, one post-doc. . . . There was a lot of intimacy in the group. And he [the advisor] was not aloof in any way. . . . He was in the lab every single day working side by side with us and very involved with the attention to detail, understanding that he had to be participating on the levels that involve details as opposed to just giving the bigger picture. . . . I think that these principles, that on some level I internalized at the age of twenty-three or twenty-four, are still with me twenty years later.

A young woman who received her Ph.D. in molecular biology and is now a successful young scientist with tenure at a college in New York City, gave a similarly enthusiastic depiction of her advisor whose style, while very different, was also successful: "My mentor was very supportive and was an excellent scientist. I think that part of being able to pursue a Ph.D. depends a lot on who your mentor is. He was really very good as a person and also in terms of just guiding you." More specifically, she continued, "It's just the kind of science that he does. The atmosphere of his lab was very conducive for creativity—a big lab, a lot of discussion. There were maybe twenty-five people in the lab and there was a lot of opportunity to talk with other people—not just with him, but with other people in the lab which is a very good environment." Another woman who got a Ph.D. in math education at a prestigious university recalled her Ph.D. experience: "I truly had a mentor there and she's a woman involved in math. . . . She was my advisor; it was ideal. I had the best doctoral experience of anybody I know."

Even though the importance of a positive relationship between mentor and students was well known, there were many instances, especially for women, of advisors who were indifferent or even antagonistic toward their students. I call these latter advisors "anti-mentors." A woman who left science to go to art school after earning a master's in zoology in the 1980s recalled her graduate school advisor. "I didn't get much feedback from this professor at all on how I was doing. Only when I was leaving and decided to go back to art school, did he tell me, 'It was too bad. You were a good scientist or you're going to be a good scientist.' I thought, 'really? I didn't know that. You never told me that.' . . . If I had had an advisor who was more nurturing or just a little more sensitive, maybe I would have stayed in the field."

Men who had indifferent advisors were less likely to find fault with this approach. A man who earned an M.S. in oceanography depicted his graduate advisor, "He wasn't one of those professors that got involved with you a lot. He let you do a lot on your own, which kind of suited my style of peaceful coexistence. But I probably could have benefited more from a mentor . . . [gotten] more insight into what it's all about. One of the problems I had in graduate school was a sense of isolation." These comments were in spite of his initial assertion, "I had a great advisor. I liked him a lot." Another man, who was an identical twin and earned his master's degree under a professor who was raising identical twins, acknowledged that their relationship was not what he expected a mentoring relationship would be:

> I always wanted him to be the kind of mentor that I had heard about. You know, they invite you over to their home. They take you under their wing, that kind of stuff. . . . I was ready to give him all sorts of advice about how to raise twins. . . . And he didn't 'cause he was really introverted and was never around. So I took independent study with him, but it wasn't that he really guided me. If anything he taught me how to be self-sufficient, because . . . [he said] "okay here's your study and now you just have to go out and do it. I'll review it and I'll tell you what things need work but I'm not going to be here every day." So it was a different kind of mentor, but I trace everything back to him.

Examples of anti-mentors for women were plentiful, and without exception, each woman scientist felt that a contributing factor to the antagonistic relationship was her sex. For example, the woman who earned a Ph.D. in freshwater ecology in the late 1970s and then went to work at the American Civil Liberties Union, described her advisor's input into her thesis. "I think my major professor thought I was doing some sort of game, and whatever I did was all right because it really didn't count. I think if he were more supportive he would have been more careful to make sure that I did a thesis that I could apply to a position somewhere. My thesis was extremely esoteric and had no practical application." When asked if he helped her get a job, she related, "I think his attitude toward me was that I wasn't a serious student, that I was doing this before I had a kid, and that I was just kind of a cute little thing to have around. . . . A sweet little young thing to have around probably was how he wrote the references, and I'm sure they did not help." This woman never received a tenure-track position at a college or university and, after several years as an adjunct professor in a community college, left science for her current job.

The relationship between student and advisor often became so adversarial that it jeopardized the completion of the Ph.D. A young woman recounted her relationship with her advisor while she was working for a Ph.D. in chemistry: "We got along for a little bit. . . . The whole thing started out because he started doubting my chemistry. Things weren't working so he said 'you must be doing it wrong.' As it turned out, I wasn't doing it wrong. We had very different thought processes and personality conflicts—it would get to the point that I would come home in tears. In the mornings I would come in on the train, and I would be nauseous because I didn't want to go see him. I said 'enough of this' and started looking for a job." This woman quit school with a master's degree in chemistry and joined the research department of a private firm.

Another woman who eventually earned a Ph.D. in physics remembered her experience in graduate school in the 1960s:

> When I got to graduate school there was no mentor that I attached to until finally when I passed the prelims, I had to sit down and kind of pick somebody. I worked with this guy. . . . I thought maybe I'd do research with him, but he assigned me to this . . . old-fashioned kind [of work] when in fact he was flying things in space and designing things to fly in space, and he trained all his men students to do that. But I was put in a closet to work a dull type of data. I never, never complained.

Ultimately she dropped out of the program.

In the small number of instances where men were part of an antagonistic advising situation, the men were more likely to attribute the difficult relationship to faults of the advisor, and the impact on the student was less severe. A man who earned a Ph.D. in geology at a prestigious university and has had a successful career in the research department at an oil company describes his advisor: "My advisor when I was in graduate school working for my Ph.D. was a very difficult personality, and he and I communicated very poorly. We had kind of an antagonistic relationship." The man persevered and the relationship did not alter his career plans in any way. In fact, the two men keep up with each other, and the oil company employee has analyzed the problem more specifically, "Since I graduated, he has gotten over what he has since told me were the very worst years of his life—when I was his student. Not because I was his student but because of many other things going on in his life."

Because men and women with bachelor's or master's degrees do not anticipate careers in academia, the influence of professors is generally more limited for them than it is for Ph.D.s. However, once in the workforce, and especially in the first job while the scientist is developing confidence, mentors can be extremely important. The transition from student to employee is often difficult, as the theoretical concepts of the classroom do not transfer easily to the day-to-day hands-on work at the job. Therefore, efforts by a colleague or supervisor to take the scientist under his or her wing, to support her efforts, and to help in training reduce the probability of departure and increase the likelihood of career success.

A female chemist at a government agency, whose career has taken on managerial responsibilities, identified factors important to her development of a successful career in the sciences. "Actually one of the things that really helped me along is the person who is above me who is male. He has really helped me a lot. He has probably taught me every single thing that he knows involving working in a laboratory. Some of the attitudes you might find in chemistry about women, I guess he didn't believe in them. . . . He just helped me." A master's degree recipient in computer science who started his employment career in a shipyard recalled what he learned from his mentor: "There was a chief engineer in the nuclear design department that I helped . . . get familiar with some of the programmatic issues that he had when he was responsible for a submarine design. After a few months I just moved directly under him and reported to this fellow and became the staff engineer. I learned a tremendous amount from him on how to manage people in a technical environment. That was probably the best learning experience I've had in my fifteen years working."

Scientists who did not have this type of relationship often felt that they were floundering and having difficulties making a positive impact in their work. Employed in a private defense-related company, a computer science graduate remembered her first job. "In retrospect it wasn't a good place for a college graduate to start. I mean, just thrown into something—I didn't have a mentor, I didn't even have a supervisor, so I was really thrown into projects, like five-year contracts . . . where you kind of spin your wheels for a couple of years to figure out what's going on. Part of it was my fault because I didn't get any guidance at all and so I fell into a 'what do I do?' type syndrome and I think I felt like I was floundering."

The interview data make clear that company culture has much to do with how new employees, and possibly new female employees especially, are incorporated into the work environment. Responding to a question about whether she had a mentor at her first job, a woman who worked for a large oil company explained,

> It's hard for me to identify any one person as being a mentor. I don't really feel like I had that kind of relationship with anybody my first few years at work. The culture at [company X] is good in that everybody is very helpful about teaching new employees so I got a lot of attention and help, but not that different from any new employee because people would just take the time to explain things to you and teach you. That's definitely a company culture. People liked doing that and that is very helpful to new employees.

Another woman found her company very different. "They had no way of bringing me into the group other than to say 'well, if you see somebody going to do something, tag along with them.' I was supposed to listen to this guy get a phone call, say 'we have a problem on the airplane' and I'm supposed to say 'oh, can I go with you?' That was the extent of their training, orientation type of program. That was it. They just made me flounder."

Although small in numbers, the interview data are striking in results. Every woman who identified a period of work with a positive mentor also identified a successful science experience. Since creation of a mentoring relationship involves a matching process, as noted previously, one can argue that mentors choose to help those scientists who they anticipate will succeed, and student success is not necessarily the result of mentoring. The small number of mentored women in the study may be the select few who have the talent and drive to succeed. The interview data, however, give concrete examples in conflict with this explanation. Even with the small numbers there are numerous instances of women who failed in their early graduate education or work experience because of the lack of mentors or even the presence of anti-mentors. These same women, moving on to other science positions with positive mentors, experienced renewed confidence and success.

The same woman who was floundering at the defense-related private company thrived at her second job. In response to an inquiry of whether she had mentors at this new position, she stated,

> Yes, two actually. . . . One was actually my supervisor. He was just smart and real bright, but very down to earth and he just would show me a lot of stuff. He was always open and receptive. . . . [The second was] his supervisor, who's a woman and our manager for the department. She was always taking people under her wing, and you would be able to go into her office and just ask her any type of a question . . . technical questions—labor related, management related, anything like that. . . . She was always pointing people in the right direction.

Similarly, the woman who got nauseated on the train while commuting to her laboratory every day, recalled a very different relationship with her boss in industry. When asked to identify the factors that contributed to her becoming a successful scientist, she responded, "Having a good boss—when I got the job at [the company] he allowed me to develop at my own pace. Industry is very different from academia, and when I first hit industry I was like a fish out of water. He brought me along very nicely. He always encouraged me to do more. It's essentially getting a good mentor."

There were even instances of changes in outcomes with changes in the mentoring relationship for women who had not substantially altered their work or educational environment. A woman who worked for a telecommunications firm since earning her master's in mechanical engineering described her mentoring experiences:

When I first came to [firm X], I had a supervisor that was not very good for me. In talking with other people he was not good for them either. I needed a lot more guidance than he provided. After about three or four years, I changed advisors to a woman . . . she did not do design [work] so that aspect of my work was not brought up. But she mentored me in that she made me more assertive. She gave me projects that gave me more visibility and in that sense she was my mentor.

Later on in the interview, this same woman was asked to identify any obstacles in her career. She noted, "Not having a strong supervisor when I first started working. That was something that I had to overcome because it created an impression of me that was not very good." Similarly, the woman who was assigned dull data work in her physics Ph.D. program eventually started another Ph.D. program in physics, worked with two mentors in theoretical physics, earned her Ph.D., and became a successful research scientist.

While the transfer of human capital is the outcome of the mentoring relationship, it is clear from the men's comments that this conduit only functions if there is a personal connection between the two participants. In one of the most adamant statements, a male Ph.D. in chemistry asserted, "It is my opinion that mentoring relationships basically are, for most people in academia, . . . responsible for what people are. You don't fall in love with a subject matter by and large. You fall in love with a person and this person leads you to the subject matter. I'm really convinced of that." Another scientist who earned a Ph.D. in geology after first spending several years in a physics Ph.D. program related his view on the key to success: "I really feel that having a good personal connection with the advisor is perhaps the single most important requirement for success. If you don't click with your advisor on a personal level, not just on a scientific level, it's very much harder." And the personal connection is not just important for the academic mentor. A midcareer scientist who used his B.S. in biology to become an investigator for the county medical examiner was asked whether he had a mentor. "Definitely my senior partner . . . he's taught me everything about my job that I have to know, and we became personal friends."

Although the women were less likely to comment on the personal nature of the relationship, they did develop mentoring relationships with women, often purposefully, to a greater extent than did men. Of the fifty-two women, twelve, or 23 percent, reported having had a female mentor in science. Of the fifty-two men, only one reported a female mentor in science and one reported a female mentor in English, the field in which he ultimately earned a Ph.D. The personal connections that women feel with other women may help to ignite the mentoring relationship. One woman, who earned a Ph.D. in neuroscience, had two female mentors but found the first relationship unsatisfying. She described this woman as a mentor in a professional status, "but not someone I could relate to on a personal level. When I was with her she was a man in woman's clothes. She was a woman who acted like a man and she hated working with women. All her favorites were men who drank a lot, who bragged a lot, who were chauvinists, not all of them, but many of them were. So I did feel out of place there." But her second female mentor was different. "She was my mentor in the sense that she had more technical expertise, and I would go to her to consult when I had an idea or methodological difficulties. . . . She definitely had an impact on me in terms of allowing my feelings to come through and evaluating what's important in my life . . . [and letting me] acknowledge that my children and my family life are very important."

This theme of finding the mentor, male or female, who understands the woman's familial concerns was prominent among the interviews. The mentoring relationship can be especially valuable in the continuation of the career of a new mother when the mentor is aware of the conflicts between family and career and supports the woman's efforts at balancing these two responsibilities. A woman with a Ph.D. in biology, whose career has been in research, related, "my chief at the Veterans Administration is more of a mentor than other people have been. She has been encouraging, and she's seventy years old so she fits into the category of super-achiever. She went to medical school in 1946. She also delayed having children and regretted it so she was very encouraging and accommodating about my having children."

Several women, both in academia and in industry, pointed out that they sought mentors or supervisors who not only had families but also enjoyed spending time with their families. A molecular biologist who received a postdoctorate at a prestigious university describes the process by which she picked the professor with whom she worked.

I made a conscious decision to go to work for someone who was married and who had children. That wasn't the first thing I looked for but I wrote to about five people, and I interviewed with all of them. The person whom I'm working for now has pictures of his daughter up in his office, and he is married and has a home life. That was very important to me because I felt he wouldn't be someone who would pressure me to work a twenty-hour day and he would allow me to spend time with my family. A lot of scientists are single and don't have any family or home life.

Although women were less likely than men to point out instances where the mentor became a fast friend, clearly the most successful mentoring relationships were the ones where the woman felt a shared connection. This connection seemed more difficult to create between a man and a woman than between two women. In a telling statement, a Ph.D. in biology differentiates between his advisor and his mentor:

The one who definitely stands out, he was one of the professors in the program. . . . He was the one who I enjoyed most and probably learned most from in the short time with him. Obviously I was close to him throughout my whole time in the program although he was not my advisor. He was the one I went to if had a problem and [I liked] his whole approach to everything. . . . my advisor . . . I was very close with him, too. He was a different culture, he was Indian and so he was less of a mentor to me than an advisor.

Exploring the effects of ethnic and racial diversity on mentoring relationships is beyond the scope of this study because a large majority of the respondents are Caucasian. However, it is clear from the preceding quote, and many like it, that the connection made in a mentoring relationship requires a level of comfort that is harder to establish when there are real cultural and experiential differences between the participants.

The interviews give evidence that mentoring has a crucial impact on persistence for women in science. While mentoring does not impact persistence of men to the same extent, many of the men who remained in science felt that the mentoring process had positive long-term impacts on their success within the field. Women in academic settings, however, were less likely than men to be mentored, possibly because of the small number of potential mentors who understand the needs of a woman in science and possibly because of potential mentors' differing expectations about the success of men and women in science. Being a minority in science creates a double jeopardy for women. First, women are less likely than men to develop positive mentoring relationships. Second, for those men and women who never develop a mentoring relationship, the probability of career continuation and success in science is much lower for women than for men.

CHAPTER 6

Leaving Science Because of Discontent with Science Itself

A ccording to the university data set (table 2.3), more than a third of both men and women who exit science relate that they find alternative careers more interesting and rewarding than scientific careers. The interview data (table 2.4), however, reveal that discontent with scientific work is more likely to be a primary reason for exit for women than for men, and many women who remain in science express similar reservations with their own work and the field in general. In this chapter, the interview data identify the forces that initially draw men and women to science and then the characteristics of a scientific career that drive many scientists away. Finally, combining results from analysis of the men's and women's insights with previous research findings gives some understanding of why dissatisfaction with science is more pervasive for women than for men.

WHAT DRAWS YOUNG PEOPLE TO SCIENCE?

According to the interviews, men and women chose science predominantly because they had an aptitude for the field. They discovered, usually in junior high or early high school, that they could shine in science and math. Whether the interest preceded or followed this realization varied by individuals. But their successes in their studies carried them through college and into a career.

What sparked the scientific interest also varied by individual and somewhat by sex. In general, the men were much more likely than the women to talk of hands-on experiences with science as children. These experiences commonly consisted of experimenting with chemistry sets or microscopes, tinkering with lawn mowers or cars, or exploring nature. Approximately one-third of the men and one-tenth of the women identified these types of experiences as their initial motivation to study science. A man who got a Ph.D. in neurosciences and worked for several years in academia before leaving to go to medical school, talked about his early interest in science, "I was about six. I caught butterflies. I collected leaves . . . I was interested in . . . chemistry sets and microscopes to look at things bigger than they were—looking at drops under water and that sort of thing. As far back as I can remember, I enjoyed science and nature and did everything that I could to learn as much about it as I could." Another man who is working as an electrical engineer related, "I was always interested in building and how things worked. . . . In high school I took some remedial electricity-type courses. I wound up becoming the neighborhood handy-boy. The toaster oven would break, I would fix it and stuff like that. . . . By the time I ended high school I was doing full electrical work for people in the neighborhood." The exceptional women who did participate in these types of childhood activities always identified a family member, father or mother, who initiated the experience. Possibly because social custom has labeled these hands-on science activities as "male," young girls were less likely to initiate them on their own.

Women were more likely than men to identify family members as reasons why they chose science. Based on the data, the family member most likely to steer them to science was their father, for both men and women. Of the twenty-one women who cited the influence of a family member, seventeen targeted their father and of the fifteen men, thirteen identified their father. In most cases, the father was working as a scientist or engineer and thus served as a role model. Many of the fathers went further to develop their child's interest in science. A midcareer male scientist with a Ph.D. in an interdisciplinary science program related:

> My father was a mechanical engineer. I guess he was one of
> these intuitive engineers—that is to say he could look at things

and could see how they work. . . . He was also a pilot. He flew in WWII and airplanes entranced him. He was in the air force when I was a kid. So I was around air force bases with all of that technology. In other words, I was just surrounded by airplanes and he flew all day long, and then he came home and talked about flying and then we built model airplanes. So a lot of my earliest experiences associated with the natural world had to do with things that flew—watching birds fly and paying attention to butterflies and bumblebees. He was just a flight crazy sort of person.

Eight of the women and none of the men cited their mother's influence on their choice of study. Only two of these eight mothers had degrees in science—both in chemistry—and only one went to work in science after school. During their elementary and junior high school years, however, the children of these two women accompanied their mothers to their labs and started learning the basics of scientific research. One woman recounted, "she [my mother] used to take me into the lab on weekends when she went in to do extra work or something. She would let me 'help her.' Of course, everything had to be redone, but she had some cute miniature glassware and stuff like that. That's how it evolved. I always liked it. I always wanted to do science." The other mothers wanted to help their daughters succeed in areas where they did not. When asked whether her parents supported her interests in science, an African American woman replied, "my mom especially . . . my mom always felt that the only way that a woman could survive was if she had an education and could fall back on her own self to support the family. My mother never worked outside of the house. I think she felt kind of trapped because of that." She continued, "[she] was always into me exploring . . . the bathtub, it was the perfect place to incubate things. . . . So I was always making all these concoctions . . . I was mixing bleach and ammonia and all kinds of stuff and nearly passing out, but it was fabulous. Salt and pepper and some yogurt or whatever the hell it was back then and mixing it and checking it out and seeing whatever would grow depending on what was in there." Another mother had started college in an aeronautical engineering program but had never graduated. Strikingly, of the eight women who cited their mothers as helping spur their interests in science, five studied for their Ph.D.s and four earned their doctorates.

Prior research relating parental education to children's decisions to study science support the finding that family influences may be greater for women than for men. Judith McIlwee and J. Gregg Robinson (1992) find that female engineers come from more highly educated families than male engineers. The National Academy study on gender differences of doctoral scientists and engineers (Long 2001) reports that in the early 1960s, women with Ph.D.s in science were one and a half times as likely to have a college-educated father and twice as likely to have a college-educated mother than were their male counterparts. Although the gap in parental educational attainment has fallen as the percentage of individuals earning a college degree has risen, female Ph.D. scientists still have better educated parents than male Ph.D. scientists. While the link between parental education and parental influence is implied and not proven, the comments of the interviewed women strongly support this connection.

Publicity of important scientific events has the potential to woo men and women into science with unrealistic expectations. However, relatively few of the scientists identified these types of events as the impetus behind their interest in science. Only two of the men and one of the women spoke of becoming infatuated with marine sciences by watching Jacques Cousteau specials on television. A woman who was a postdoctoral scientist in a prominent marine sciences department at the time of the survey did point out that the reality of a career in marine science took years to sink in.

> I was real naive like a lot of people are today and maybe looked at too much Jacques Cousteau . . . younger people . . . all want to go into marine sciences and work with the dolphins. That's Jacques Cousteau—that's what he does. [But] that's not real marine sciences. That's the glory end of it; very few people do that. If you are going to work in the northeast, you don't go play with dolphins. You worry about pollution; you worry about how excessive nutrients affect Long Island

Sound. You don't play with the whales. You play with blue-fish.

While this woman is looking for a job outside of science, she does not cite an incompatibility with the work as the main reason.

Slightly more influential, the space race was the initial spark that kindled the scientific interest in four of the young men and two of the young women. Three of the men and both women earned undergraduate degrees in fields related to space exploration. However, all but one developed successful scientific careers in other fields. The remaining man earned a master's in astronautics and has worked at NASA in space exploration for many years. Although not an astronaut himself, he was active in the team that developed the Mars Pathfinder.

WHAT ARE THE CHARACTERISTICS OF A SCIENTIFIC CAREER THAT DRIVE SOME SCIENTISTS AWAY?

According to the interview data, in three of the male pairs and eight of the female pairs the primary determinant differentiating the leaving and staying scientists was discontent with the science itself. The one common thread in all the discussions of men and women who leave science because of discontent with the field was the narrowness of science. Many scientists found the work too specialized. In particular, individuals with a broad set of interests, of which science is a subset, were likely to become dissatisfied with a scientific career, even careers afforded to Ph.D. scientists. One woman described her career in computer science, "It's not as rewarding as I thought it would be. It's a nice income; it's a nice environment in some ways but it's not what I want to look back on when I'm seventy years old. I want to have other experiences." A man who left science after earning a Ph.D. in ecology and evolution to work in a museum and write novels, related the main obstacle he encountered in science: "I would say maybe a temperament obstacle because by temperament I am a generalist rather than a specialist. I like doing lots and lots of different things. In the museum where I work, I do blacksmithing and antique woodworking using the methods of the seventeenth century. . . . Outside of that, in the home I've learned electrical wiring, and plumbing and spackling, painting—all the homemaker-type skills, expansive gardening in the backyard. All of these things are distractions from concentrating on a specific career." The individuals who remained in science and engineering were different. They were much more directed early on with narrowly defined interests, and they often decided on a college major well before graduation from high school.

Other exiting scientists, especially those at the Ph.D. level, expressed concern that the scientists themselves have to become very narrow in order to succeed in the field. Because of the intense competition for funding, only those individuals who are extremely focused and limited in their interests can compete. A man who left sciences after earning a Ph.D. in molecular biology explained, "While I was in graduate school it was clear what you did was who you were. . . . Then being back in New York, back in the whole vibrant atmosphere . . . I was living in an apartment building [where] everybody did something different and theaters, authors, business, and real estate, and just everybody had a life, but they had a life outside of what they did. And I kind of realized I wanted to make that kind of distinction too between what I did and who I was. And it seemed to me, at that time, to be successful in the sciences in a pure research environment you couldn't make that separation. You had to be so devoted to what you were doing that it had to be your life. That's not what I wanted."

Another man who left a Ph.D. program in biology to get a Ph.D. in English recounted, "I didn't want to be cooped up in a lab for fifteen hours a day. That was too limiting for the kind [of person] I am, the kind of lifestyle I want." One woman in a biology postdoctoral program lamented that science is likely to become dominated by the stereotypical "nerd" scientists. Scientists with outside interests and families will not be able to compete with those who spend all their time in the laboratory. Upset by the narrowness of the scientists who were succeeding at the higher levels, she expressed concern that eventually science, itself, will suffer.

Many women, in particular, were troubled over the isolation associated with science. They reported becoming dissatisfied with the lack of personal contact or the lack of any connection between science and personal relationships and emotions. These women tended to look for new jobs that were more "people oriented," such as teaching or clinical psychology. For example, a woman who earned a Ph.D. in neurobiology was always interested in understanding individuals' emotions and thought processes. Early in her education, she thought that studying the brain would satisfy these interests. She explained, "Well, it's interesting how people behave and it's particularly interesting why people think the way they do. Those aspects of life interest me and grab my attention, and I thought with my background in science, if I go into neuroscience, possibly I could try to figure out some of the processes underlying that and the relationship to nature." Although there were early signs that she would not be satisfied with a career in science, this woman persevered: "I took a course in neurochemistry and I totally hated it when I was an undergrad. All these subjects I hated [and thought] were boring. I recognized they were challenging and they were fascinating in their own right. I had mazes to go through and logic puzzles to solve, and I liked being part of that, but there was totally no emotional connection. However, it took me a long, long time to accept the fact that I needed emotional connections with my work to make myself happy, and that's one of the reasons why I switched." More than ten years after that first course in neuroscience, she gave up her first grant in neuroscience and started a Ph.D. in clinical psychology. At the time of the interview, she was much more hopeful about creating a productive and meaningful career.

A woman who had early aspirations in religion got hooked on geology as an undergraduate. After a successful undergraduate career, she enrolled in a master's program in geology. She explained her desire to make the study of geology more meaningful: "I really wanted to integrate the geology, because I loved it and still love it, into life. I didn't want to do this sterile thing out there. I wanted it to be relevant in some way, at least to my life." After a semester of study, she dropped out of the master's program. She described her decision to leave science, "I couldn't integrate it on my own; I couldn't find any whole people that were dealing with it, and as a woman I couldn't find any peers that were working in science. . . . I think the biggest [obstacle] for me was that science was not relational. That's a fairly obscure statement but . . . the people, the scientists, didn't relate well and the material was not integrated very well. Both those things. No one was really interested in making connections." This woman returned to her first interest and earned a master's degree in theology. At the time of the interview, she was considering, among potential career moves, going back to school to get a Ph.D. in clinical psychology.

Although respondents of both sexes focused on some aspect of the narrowness of science, there were some interesting differences between the three exiting men and the eight exiting women. The three men had either earned or worked toward a Ph.D. in the biological sciences. The eight women were in a number of different fields and had varying levels of degrees. While the exiting men left science during or immediately following graduate school, the women were not necessarily leaving at the very early stages of the career. For some women, such as the geologist-turned-theologian, the frustration with science and the resulting departure did occur early on. However, five of the eight women left later in their careers. Some of these women, similar to the neuroscientist, persevered in hope that the initial frustration in science would abate and left after amassing several years of experience. Other women found that as they grew and developed as human beings, their interests expanded, and their desire to leave science surfaced after many relatively contented years in the field. Therefore, exit that results from the mismatch between the individual's interests and the nature of a scientific career may occur at any stage of the career. The financial sacrifices of leaving science after substantial work experience, however, are much higher than those associated with leaving early in the career, possibly explaining why women, who may rely on their husband's income to cushion financial losses, are more likely to leave for this reason after substantial work experience.

WHY WERE WOMEN MORE LIKELY THAN MEN TO VOICE DISCONTENT WITH THE PRACTICE OF SCIENCE?

According to the interviews, both women who had left science and those considering exit were more likely than their male counterparts to cite discontent with science. Although there are several hypothetical explanations of this pattern, some or all of which may ring true, this study can give no definitive answers, only insights gained by interview comments. Whatever the answers, there seems to be a link between stated differences in discontent of men and women and their differential priorities concerning income, opportunity, and nonpecuniary conditions of work. There is considerable meta-analytic evidence in the psychology literature that there are significant gender-related differences in social interaction and personality and that these differences conform to gender stereotypes. In particular, women's behaviors tend to be socially sensitive, concerned with others, and friendly; men's behaviors are dominant, controlling, and independent (Eagly 1995). Such differences in attitudes and interactions are likely to affect work decisions. Helen Astin (1979) notes that when students were asked about career interests, women were more likely to answer that their future work would contribute to society, help others, give them the opportunity to work with people and ideas, and to express themselves. Men were much more interested in pay, prestige, and advancement. Analyzing surveys of career aspirations of college freshmen from 1969 to 1984, Stephen Cole and Robert Fiorentine (1991) find that early in the period, status attainment values were much more important to men then women, while nurturance values were more important for women. By the end of the period, the gap in percentage of men and women who felt that being "well off" was very important fell from twenty-two points to nine points, and the status attainment values became as important for women as nurturance values. The fact that many of the women who exited because of discontent with the practice of science established new careers with more of a nurturing component, such as lay minister, high school teacher, and clinical psychologist, supports the hypothesis that gender-based differences in attitudes about work may have contributed to differences in the evaluation of and response to scientific work.

This gender-related difference may also be due to the fact that women are more likely than men to act on this disillusionment. Women acknowledged that the financial security of their husband's income often allowed them the freedom to leave. Social and cultural norms may also give women further freedom. Cole and Fiorentine

(1991) posit that the ties to occupation are weaker for women than for men because there is a culturally defined difference in the importance of occupational success attained by the two sexes. Because women may attain "adult status" through family or career while men are confined to achieving "adult status" solely through occupational success, men may be more persistent in face of difficulties or obstacles. Therefore, even if men do feel the same discontent with a scientific career, they may be less willing to respond to this dissatisfaction with exit. With exit not a real possibility, men may be less willing to articulate the frustration. Interestingly, one similarity that stands out among the three men whose primary reason for exit was a mismatch of interests is that all three men were not driven by career ambition. They uniformly felt free to pursue areas that they enjoyed. This liberation from cultural restraints may liken their incentives to those of women who are often making career decisions in the context of the familial roles of wife, mother, and secondary earner: the status of the occupation receives lower priority than other lifestyle characteristics. The biologist-turned-novelist related, "My career decisions have been motivated by just what I felt like doing." He does point out that there have been financial sacrifices. "Some people wouldn't be satisfied with the neighborhood we live in. Some people wouldn't be satisfied with the house that you have to fix up yourself. Some people wouldn't be satisfied with ten-year-old cars." The young man who switched from a biology to an English Ph.D. program stressed that individuals should make career decisions by following their hearts and worry about employment possibilities later.

Another potential reason why women are more likely to leave due to discontent is that the typical structure of a man's scientific career results in a broadening of responsibilities that satisfies expanding interests while women's careers may remain more narrow because of fewer opportunities and more nonwork obligations. There were several examples of men who had developed careers in science that would have addressed the concerns of many of these exiting women. A man who got his B.S. in earth and planetary sciences was working at the Environmental Protection Agency (EPA) in a job that involved both diverse activities and close interactions with people. He described his job, "I

work a lot with the public trying to make a difference in people's lives
. . . you know how complex it is to try and get these super fund sites
cleaned up. . . . I try to get around the obstacles . . . between all the at-
torneys and all the legal requirements. There are a lot of opportunities
to meet with the public one-on-one as well as in large groups. It's not
uncommon for us to have the media present at different public meetings . . . lots of questions and lots of heated moments also. It gets
pretty exciting sometimes." He also felt that he connected to his colleagues at work and had a life outside of his job, "I work with a great
group of people. Working for the government you get more time to
yourself. So a lot of the people are in similar situations you know as far
as families and kids and like to spend time with them. We're allowed
to work a compressed work schedule. I'm off tomorrow cause it's my
day off. You get off every other Friday. Work a nine-hour day." There
were very few women who spoke so glowingly of their jobs.

Just as some leavers described their frustration with the science career, there were several stayers who were eloquent about their passion
for the field. A male Ph.D. geologist explained, "I became interested in
geology as a historical science and what fascinated me most about it
was the time element, the unfathomable length of time that geology
seems to demonstrate. And that placed mankind and all of his philo-
sophical musings in a perspective, in a position of some insignificance
I guess on the broader scale of the history of the planet. And that's
what really interested me." When asked if he ever thought of leaving
science, he responded, "I'll say almost not at all because I just can't
think of anything else that I can make a living at that I enjoy as much."
The employee at NASA described his job, "I mean it would be nice to
get new shoelaces and a second car and that type of stuff but you know
when I have a three-day weekend I think that's another day I'm not going to work. It's stuff that I really love doing. . . . that really no one has
done before." Enthusiastic about a new project, he continued,

> We have a mission that we're toying with where you would
> send a balloon to Mars and in the daytime it would float
> around and then at night when it gets cold it would sink and
> the gondolier would touch the surface and then analyze the

soil. The next morning when the sun comes up it would float up again to a new site. . . . Can you picture coming into your building where there's a big spiral staircase and you see this big balloon on the basement and then in the afternoon it's up in the ceiling and the next morning it's down on the floor again?

When asked what it is about science that interests him, a man finishing his chemistry Ph.D. responded, "the thing I like most about it is being able to put various pieces together and to form this sort of larger picture in maybe a way that someone else or the field in general has not seen it before. . . . it's [the] discovering aspect I guess."

With a couple of exceptions, female stayers did not convey the excitement and passion for science that was evident in comments of a relatively large subset of the males. Women in science have to find their place in a male-dominated, often unwelcoming, environment in which men find a more natural fit. Women are often left to navigate these potentially treacherous waters without guidance from a mentor or a role model. In addition, they frequently have to shoulder the burdens of both work and family, a double burden that they perceive few male counterparts either share or understand. For some, dealing with all these other pressures may wear the passion thin. For others, the passion may still burn, but a discussion of careers focuses on these other issues first.

CHAPTER 7

Does the Rapidly Changing Knowledge Within Science Affect Exit?

The most important defining characteristic of science as a field or body of knowledge is change. The constancy of change is the direct result of the nature and quantity of scientific research. Assembling building blocks that are dependent on the research that came before, scientific researchers are constantly expanding and reconfiguring the edges of our knowledge. They are conducting experiments, solving systems, and developing proofs to solve the mysteries of our bodies and environment. Although much of scientific research is expensive with highly technical equipment being a prerequisite for successful experiments, funds for scientific research dwarf research funds in all other academic areas. Researchers in science, different from research personnel in other disciplines, find homes in colleges and universities, corporate R&D departments, government laboratories, and nonprofit think tanks. Therefore, the nature of the field and the extensive research activity within the field ensure that the body of knowledge that we term "science" is evolving rapidly both in absolute terms and in relation to the knowledge in other fields.

With rapid scientific development come the often-concrete benefits of technological progress. But change can be stressful to scientists working in the field since there are constant pressures to "keep up," to remain current with all the new developments. For those who are researching at the cutting edge of the field, keeping up might be a part of the day-to-day research activity. For the rest of the employees, however, keeping up may mean using off hours to read journals, going to training seminars, and often learning new techniques. As long as employers pay for the training and it is incorporated into the workday, the monetary costs are relatively low. Invariably skill update impinges on nonwork time. Change also ties employees to their work in ways that are not evident in fields where change is relatively low. A leave of absence to care for an ailing relative or a stint in a charitable enterprise has the normal costs of lost earnings and experience, but also the increased cost of skill depreciation. Time away from work means that skills developed on the job may erode and lose their value as new techniques replace the old. Employees who leave scientific fields for even a short period of time may face difficulties reentering the field, and when reentry is possible, salaries may fall below salaries earned at time of exit. Furthermore, reentering employees may find that they are on a different career track than the one they left, and salary growth may be lower. A study on exit from scientific occupations cannot ignore the effects of rapidly changing fields on decisions to leave. This chapter begins with theoretical explanations for the impact of knowledge growth on career outcomes, continues with a description of the measurement of knowledge growth across fields used in this study, and then uses the work history data to estimate the quantitative effects of knowledge growth on the probability of exit and on salaries after exit.

THEORETICAL EXPLANATIONS RELATING KNOWLEDGE GROWTH TO CAREER OUTCOMES

How do high and differing rates of knowledge growth impact decisions to exit science? Does acceleration or deceleration of knowledge growth impact incentives to stay or leave? Economic theory can be used to give some clarity to these complex issues by focusing on the concept of skill depreciation. Just as physical capital can depreciate and become obsolete, so can human capital, and that process is usually called skill depreciation. When a science-educated man or woman enters the scientific labor market, his or her stock of human capital can be characterized by level of education, field of study, and market value. Over any period, the value of this capital stock can depreciate for two reasons. First, if the scientist is working in a scientific job, he or she maintains mastery of the expertise learned in school: but without further investment, the scientist may fall behind the recent advances in the field and the value of the human capital stock in the labor market will fall. Here the stock has not changed, but its value has diminished. Second, if the scientist takes time off from the scientific job, not only might the existing stock become less valuable in the marketplace, the skills mastered at time of exit are likely to become rusty with disuse and the actual stock of human capital will diminish. Therefore, for both working and nonworking scientists, skill depreciation is potentially a drag on career progress, and the higher the rate of growth of knowledge within a field, the more serious will be the drag.

Human capital theory predicts a number of career outcomes that will vary with skill depreciation of a field. First, following a period of temporary occupational departure, earnings on reentry into a scientific field are likely to be below earnings at time of exit since the stock of human capital as well as its value will have fallen. The earnings loss will increase with more time out of the scientific field and will be higher in fields that achieve higher rates of knowledge growth during the scientist's departure. Because of the potential earnings loss, individuals anticipating episodes of occupational exit during the lifetime are likely to choose fields where the rate of knowledge growth is relatively low. Specifically, women who foresee periods of nonwork while they bear and raise children will be less likely than men, who tend to be freer of time commitments associated with child-raising, to choose science as a career, and once in science, will choose to concentrate in more stagnant fields. In a related prediction, scientists in fields where knowledge is accelerating will be less likely to engage in a temporary exit than those in fields where the growth rate of knowledge is stagnant or decelerating. At the same time, unanticipated acceleration in rates of knowledge growth within a field during periods of departure may force temporary exits to become permanent ones. Finding a new job will become increasingly difficult as the length of time away from science grows. Ultimately, some scientists will not be able to find a new job within science because their skills will have become obsolete. In all fields there is likely to be some threshold level of skills below which reentry becomes impossible, and how fast one's expertise can fall to that level during periods of nonuse will depend on speed of knowledge growth within the field.

For those scientists who remain employed in the scientific workplace where change is a constant, the optimal activity to ensure earnings growth and career progress involves shifting investment in skill development from earlier to later stages of the career as well as potentially increasing lifetime investment in order to combat the continuous loss of human capital. Whereas individuals in completely stagnant fields may invest in an educational degree at the start of the career without any further training over the life cycle, in fields where knowledge growth is increasing, human capital investment profiles will become more constant over time or, in extreme cases, where knowledge growth is accelerating, may even require increasing investment with time in the career. While all scientists are likely to expect some degree of training updates throughout the career, those workers whose skills begin to depreciate at higher than expected levels will be required to engage in higher than anticipated skill update at later and later stages of the career. Because this unexpected level of retraining requires unbudgeted time and resources, it is likely to make inroads on time spent at leisure and on earnings. As a result, some workers will bail out of the field, making a permanent exit to an occupation with fewer demands on training. Unexpected increases in knowledge growth and resulting skill depreciation are likely to increase the probability of permanent exit.

PREVIOUS EMPIRICAL FINDINGS RELATING SKILL DEPRECIATION TO CAREER OUTCOMES

Empirical attempts to test the theoretical predictions associated with skill depreciation have been hindered by data limitations and measurement issues. However, using a large national worker data set to derive depreciation rates from earnings profiles, Sherwin Rosen (1975) estimates lower bounds on depreciation rates for high school graduates (0.15) and college graduates (.10).

As an alternative to estimating depreciation rates directly, many empirical economists have tested for empirical patterns that are predicted by the theory of skill depreciation. The early literature focuses on skill depreciation as an important factor behind differences in male and female labor-market outcomes. In particular, the periods during which women leave the labor force to care for children are when valuable job-related skills depreciate. As a result, women who interrupt their careers will have lower salaries and salary experience profiles than their male counterparts. Jacob Mincer and Haim Ofek (1982) find evidence of skill depreciation in a longitudinal analysis of wage profiles of married women. They find that wages on reentry to the labor market after a time of nonwork are lower than wages at time of exit, and the wage loss is greater the longer the interruption. They also find that there is relatively rapid wage growth after return to work as these women try to restore skills that eroded during nonwork.

Measurement issues associated with knowledge growth and obsolescence were first addressed by sociologists studying science. Derek Price (1965) states that patterns of citations can give important information on research activity within a field. In 1970, he developed an index that uses the percentage of references to works published within the last five years as a proxy for obsolescence. Calculating this index for journals in a variety of fields, he finds that obsolescence rates are higher in fields such as physics and chemistry than in social science fields. In an attempt to measure knowledge growth within a field, Duncan MacRae (1969) estimates a model of age distribution of citations that controls for parameters measuring growth in the amount of literature within a field. He also finds that citations in sociology refer to older articles than citations in the natural sciences. John McDowell (1982) estimates a literature decay rate in seven broad-based academic disciplines (physics, biology, chemistry, psychology, sociology, history, and English) to measure obsolescence of knowledge, or skill depreciation, for Ph.D. recipients. As one would expect, his measure shows that the humanities have more durable knowledge than the sciences. In support of his theoretical predictions, the output profile of scholars is more constant in fields where knowledge is less durable and where investment is more constant than in fields where knowledge is more durable. He also finds that female Ph.D. recipients are more likely than men to locate in fields with more durable knowledge and they are more likely to concentrate on teaching rather than research, potentially because teaching is less affected by obsolescence of knowledge.

James Ragan and Qazi Rehman (1996) also focus on academics in looking at earnings profiles of department heads. They find that department heads experience lower future wage growth after their terms as department chairs than before these spells, and they attribute the reduced wage growth to depreciation of skills during the administrative post. Furthermore, they find that the reduction in wage growth is most severe in the sciences, fields that they assume have the highest rates of skill depreciation.[1]

Only one study has analyzed the effect of knowledge change on permanent labor-market exit. Ann Bartel and Nachum Sicherman (1993) look at the relation between technological change, which leads to skill obsolescence, and retirement decisions of older workers. Using industry-based measures of productivity change as proxies for technological change, they find evidence that older workers are more likely to retire in response to unexpected increases in the rate of technological change. They hypothesize that these retiring men are responding to unanticipated and unwelcome requirements to invest in retraining.

MEASURING KNOWLEDGE GROWTH ACROSS SCIENTIFIC FIELDS

The rate of change of knowledge varies greatly within science, across subfields and across time depending on the nature of the field, what stage it is in its development, the funds allocated to research in the field, and public excitement about the field. Empirical measures of the rate of growth of knowledge, although not commonly constructed, tend to resemble Price's index (1970) and McDowell's literature decay rate (1982) and thus focus on age of citations of academic articles. Specifically, a field with newer citations (that is, lower age) in any given year is a field in which knowledge is changing more rapidly as new research is building on more recent results. McDowell's measure, the percentage of all cited articles within a journal-year that are five years old or less, reveals that literature within physics is decaying and making way for new findings at six times the rate at which literature is decaying in English. The measure of growth of knowledge across time and field created here also uses age of citations in the leading journals in a scientific field. The annual Science Citation Index (Institute for Scientific Information 1975–1992) includes the *Journal Citation Reports,* a volume that identifies journals that publish scholarly articles for each specific scientific field, and then calculates several measures of age of citations and a measure of impact for each journal. The measure of age of citations used in the variable construction is the citing half-life, the median age of all cited articles in the journal during the year. For example, a citing half-life of 3.2 years for *Nature* in 1988 means that 50 percent of the cited articles in *Nature* in 1988 are 3.2 years old or younger. The impact factor is a measure of the frequency with which the average article in a journal over the past two years has been cited in a current year. Journal X's impact factor in 1988, for example, is the ratio of total number of 1988 citations of articles published in Journal X in 1987 and 1986 to total number of citable articles published by Journal X in 1987 and 1986. Therefore an impact factor of five would mean that, on average, an article published in Journal X in 1987 or 1986 was cited five times in 1988.

Within each field-year is calculated an average citing half-life, CITE,[2] which is the weighted average of the citing half-lives of the five highest impact journals where the weights are the impact factors. This average citing half-life is calculated annually for the roughly fifty fields identified by scientists in the survey from 1975 to 1992.[3] While CITE measures growth of knowledge at a particular point in time, it can also be used to determine whether growth in knowledge is decelerating or accelerating over time. The change in knowledge growth over a time period becomes the difference between the citing half-life at the period's beginning and end.

Table 7.1 ranks selected fields according to the percentage change in citing half-life over the period and gives the average citing half-life for these fields for 1975 and 1992. The fields at the top of the chart have the highest percentage change in CITE, and for these fields, the growth of knowledge has been slowing most rapidly. The fields at the

Table 7.1   *Citing Half-Lives in 1975 and 1992 for Selected Fields (Ranked According to Percent Change in CITE)*

Field	Percent Change in CITE–1975 to 1992	CITE–1975	CITE–1992	Percent Female[a]
1. Astronomy	42.0	4.62	6.56	0.097
2. Physics	41.4	4.74	6.70	0.097
3. Operations research	35.7	6.22	8.44	0.112
4. Geology	31.3	6.13	8.05	0.129
5. Mathematics	24.1	7.80	9.68	—
6. Applied mathematics	21.5	6.78	8.24	0.311
7. Environmental biology	18.0	5.89	6.95	—
8. Applied physics	15.2	4.29	4.94	0.156
9. Paleontology	15.2	8.24	9.49	—
10. Computer science	15.2	5.27	6.07	0.293
11. Chemistry	12.4	5.71	6.42	0.292
12. Agronomy	6.6	8.93	9.52	—
13. Microbiology	−1.4	5.57	5.49	—
14. Immunology	−1.6	3.82	3.74	0.382
15. Ecology	−4.7	7.87	7.50	—
16. Marine biology	−8.7	8.95	8.17	—
17. Biochemistry	−13.7	4.22	3.64	0.341
18. Genetics	−14.9	4.30	3.66	—
19. Cell biology	−18.6	4.78	3.89	—
20. Parasitology	−21.7	7.42	5.81	—
21. Neurobiology	−25.3	6.59	4.92	—
22. Biology	−29.5	6.77	4.77	0.281

Source: Author's compilation.
Note: A positive percent change means that knowledge growth has slowed.
[a]Percent female is calculated from working scientists in 1982 in the Survey of Natural and Social Scientists and Engineers.

bottom of the chart, however, have the lowest and most negative percentage change in CITE. For these fields, the growth of knowledge has been increasing most rapidly. The changing values of CITE are consistent with changing national priorities. Over the period, public and government attention has shifted away from space exploration, defense-related research, and alternative energy research, all of which fueled the prominence of physics, astronomy, and geology in the relative rankings of the natural sciences prior to this period. Similarly, the attention to environmental issues has waned. During this same period, however, there has been an explosion of interest in microbiology and the diverse uses of biological discoveries in technology and health, thus the acceleration of knowledge in biology and health-related fields.

The rate of knowledge growth in any year is also informative. In 1975, the fields in which knowledge was growing most rapidly were immunology, biochemistry, genetics, applied physics, astronomy, electrical engineering, and physics. By 1992, the fields where knowledge growth was highest were biochemistry, cell biology, immunology, genetics, neurobiology, and applied physics. Given the fifty fields and the eighteen years analyzed, the fields and years during which knowledge was growing most rapidly were information science in 1988 (CITE = 3.2 years), applied physics in 1989 and 1990 (CITE = 3.3 years), and environmental science in 1982 (CITE = 3.5 years). The fields and years where knowledge was growing most slowly were mathematics in 1990 (CITE = 10 years), paleontology in 1988 (CITE = 9.75 years), and mechanical engineering in 1985 (CITE = 9.7 years).

Column four gives the 1982 percentage of female scientists employed in science-oriented jobs for pay for as many of the fields as was possible using data from the Survey of Natural and Social Scientists and Engineers (NSF, 1982). Surprisingly, the fields in which knowledge growth is slowing generally have a low percentage of women; knowledge growth is accelerating in fields with a high percentage of women. Except for environmental biology and applied math, the nine fields with the greatest deceleration in knowledge growth employ a labor force that is less than 20 percent women. The fields where knowledge growth is accelerating, rows thirteen to twenty-two, are either biology- or health-science-related, all of which have relatively high concentrations of women, close to or in excess of 30 percent.[4]

To determine whether this pattern is replicated in the survey data, table 7.2 presents average citing half-life in field at time of graduation

Table 7.2   *Average Citing Half-Lives of Men and Women at Graduation and at Survey Date*

	CITE at Graduation	CITE at Survey Date	Total Change in CITE	Average Monthly Change in CITE
Men	6.53*	6.48*	−0.056*	−0.003*
	(1.33)	(1.67)	(1.438)	(0.017)
Women	6.75	6.26	−0.481	−0.007
	(1.25)	(1.85)	(1.484)	(0.017)

Source: Author's compilation.
*Male mean is significantly different than female mean at the 0.01 level using a one-tailed test.

(column one) and at time of survey (column two) for men (row one) and women (row two) separately. At the time of graduation with most recent science degree (column one), the scientific fields in which women majored had an average citing half-life of 6.75 years; the scientific fields in which men majored had an average citing half-life of 6.53 years. As predicted by the theory, at time of graduation, women on average were locating in fields with lower growth rates of knowledge than men. However, at the time of the survey, the fields in which women majored had an average citing half-life of 6.26 years, and fields in which men majored had an average citing half-life of 6.48 years. Therefore, over the period of study, the fields in which women majored experienced much higher acceleration in knowledge growth than the fields in which men majored, probably because women are concentrated in biology and health-related fields of science. In fact, growth of knowledge accelerated in the fields of biology and health science and decelerated in the fields still heavily dominated by men.

INTERVIEW DATA

In none of the interviews was growth of knowledge identified as a major determinant of the decision to exit. However, the fast rate of information growth in science was often noted, with some attention to its impact on careers. Many scientists observed that the ability and desire to learn new skills continually were important attributes for success in science. A midcareer man who had earned a Ph.D. in oceanography in the mid-1970s felt that his flexibility and adaptability saved his career when he could not find a good match within oceanography. Employed by an aerospace company at the time of the survey, he recollected, "They brought me in to do optimization . . . not that I knew that much about it but I was capable of learning in the field and always changing. You always have to keep learning."

Having a different take on this same concept, a mechanical engineer stopped just short of identifying the need to update skills as a necessary pursuit to progress in science His viewpoint was colored by the experiences of his father, who was a linotype operator in the printing trade. He recalled, "Early on when I was growing up, my dad was laid off a few times. The linotype machine was actually being phased out as newer technology came in. So having observed that, it was clear that one needs to stay current." He identified the narrowness of some jobs within science as an impediment to this requirement.

> Well I think early on when I was in the design engineering group, I was concerned that I was the design engineer for an eighteen-inch hull valve on a submarine. I was concerned that, if my skills didn't change and develop in a different area, it would be very difficult to stay employed or have any career options because my skills would be pretty much limited. I would have been an expert with this hull valve, but you can only use them on submarines so it would be very difficult to move to another position.

This particular man continued his education while he worked, earning both an M.B.A. and a master's in computer science. He eventually moved into a managerial position within science at his initial company.

As pointed out earlier in the chapter on family responsibilities, the need to update skills constantly and digest new ideas is often more of an impediment to women with families. Since they are, in essence, working a double shift, there is little free time for enrichment and skill update. The female computer scientist who worked in development at a computer software company and identified skill update as a necessary activity for promotion, pointed out that, with her husband working long hours, she is the major caretaker of their two children when she is not at work. She felt like she did not have even an hour to spare for professional reading.

WORK HISTORY DATA

The need to update skills was a common theme that surfaced in the interviews; some respondents saw skill update as an opportunity while others viewed it as an obstacle. Although no one specifically identified this characteristic of their work as a major determinant of exit, some did feel that it put them at a disadvantage, thus contributing to these respondents' decisions to leave science. In order to examine whether differing rates of growth in knowledge had marginal impacts on exit rates, multivariate statistical analysis was performed on the work history data. The first theoretical issue addressed is whether the variation in rates of growth of knowledge across scientific fields affects the salary loss on reentry to science after a temporary exit from the labor force. Because the work history data encompasses several data points on each individual, it allows the estimate of the salary loss for each person leaving the labor force and an analysis of how this loss is related to the length of time off and to the growth of knowledge in the individuals' field. The average duration of labor force exit is relatively short, as one might expect, given the relatively high rates of growth of knowledge. The mean duration of exit is eleven months for men and twelve months for women, and 93 percent of all temporary labor-force exits are concluded within two years.[5]

I estimate salary loss on reentry as a function of time out of the labor force, the average annual rate of knowledge growth of the scientist's field during exit, time spent in science before departure, and a set of demographic characteristics. For both men and women, the longer time out of the labor market, the greater the wage loss on reentry. As predicted, this earning loss varied by rate of growth of knowledge. Figure 7.1 displays the impact of time out of the labor force on the natural logarithm of salary at reentry, in comparison to natural logarithm of salary at exit for individuals in high-, medium-, and low-skill depreciation fields. Salary at exit corresponds to the salary at zero months out of the labor force, and for men, 10.35 corresponds to an average salary of $31,257; for women, 10.11 translates to an average salary of $24,588. Because salaries are transformed to natural logarithms, movements along the vertical axis correspond to percentage changes in salary. For the mean duration of exit, men who had exited fields where the high rates of new knowledge creation was causing rapid depreciation of older knowledge (CITE = 3.5 years), reentered science with earnings 11 percent below their earnings at time of exit eleven months earlier. Men exiting fields where knowledge was growing at the mean rate (CITE = 6.0 years) only experienced a 6.8 percent salary loss, and men leaving fields with low growth rates of knowledge (CITE = 9.5 years) suffered a mere 2 percent loss.

The pattern was similar for women. Women reentering fields with high growth rates of knowledge, medium growth rates, and low growth rates, experienced a 10 percent salary loss, a 3 percent salary loss and a 3.5 percent salary gain, respectively. While the salary gain in fields where knowledge growth is low is surprising, one needs to remember that these fields, such as math and mechanical engineering, are where women are underrepresented, even for science standards. During this period, the increased attention to equal employment opportunities may have pressured employers in these fields to increase female representation possibly prompting increased salaries for women in general. The earnings analyses confirm the human capital prediction that scientists engaging in temporary labor force exit experience earnings losses that are more severe the higher the rate of growth of knowledge in their field of science. Furthermore, they validate the use of age of citation data as measures of knowledge growth.[6]

Models estimating the probability of exit from science were developed differentiating permanent and temporary exit. Temporary exit is defined as any exit that concludes with reentry to science before the survey date. Exit is permanent if the respondent has not returned to science by the survey date. This definition is slightly imprecise in that some of the permanent exit is temporary exit in process. Therefore, the extent of temporary exit is most likely underestimated, and the extent

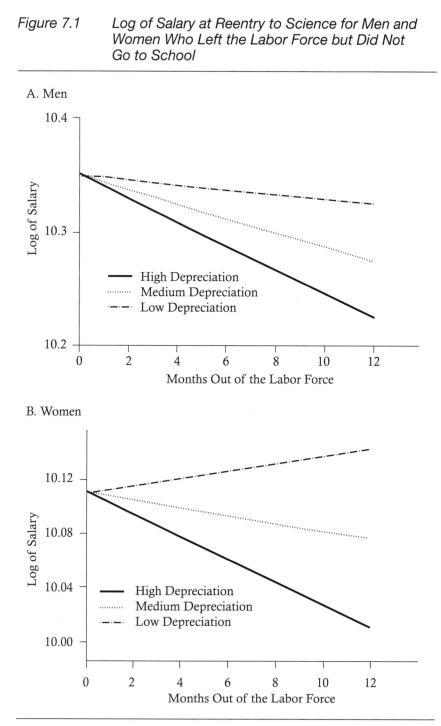

Figure 7.1 Log of Salary at Reentry to Science for Men and Women Who Left the Labor Force but Did Not Go to School

A. Men

Log of Salary

10.4

10.3

10.2

High Depreciation
Medium Depreciation
Low Depreciation

0   2   4   6   8   10   12

Months Out of the Labor Force

B. Women

Log of Salary

10.12

10.08

10.04

10.00

High Depreciation
Medium Depreciation
Low Depreciation

0   2   4   6   8   10   12

Months Out of the Labor Force

Source: Author's compilation.

of permanent exit overestimated. The average probability of permanently exiting science at the end of any science job is 10 percent, while the average probability of exiting science temporarily is closer to 7 percent.[7] As with other measures of exit, these probabilities are roughly twice as high for women as for men.

In order to determine the effects of skill depreciation on decisions to exit science, a competing hazard function where exit can take on two values—permanent or temporary—is estimated. The model estimates the probability of permanent departure from science and temporary departure from science conditional on surviving in science for some specified time period. Covariates predicting departure include months of time out of science, months out of the labor force, and variables representing level of science degree, type of employer (nonprofit, for profit, public), full-time status, marital status, and children, and two variables representing responsibility for household chores and childcare. The skill depreciation variable that is important in predicting exit is the average annual change in CITE from the time of graduation with highest science degree until the point of time at which the individual is considering exit.[8]

The empirical results reveal that increases in citing half-life, corresponding to deceleration in knowledge growth, have significant positive effects on the probability of temporary exit for men and women. For men in fields where knowledge growth is decelerating, the probability of engaging in temporary exit is 5.2 percent while it falls to 3.8 percent for men in fields where the growth of knowledge is accelerating. Similarly for women, the probability of leaving science temporarily is 10.6 percent in fields where knowledge growth is decelerating and 7.3 percent in fields where knowledge growth is accelerating.

Turning to the results for permanent exit, which is more important to the current analysis, for both men and women, decreases in the citing half-life, that is, an acceleration in knowledge growth, result in significant increases in the probability of permanent exit. Women in fields where knowledge growth is slowing have a 10 percent probability of permanent exit while this probability increases to 15 percent in fields with high levels of acceleration. Similarly for men, in fields where knowledge growth is accelerating, the average probability of permanent exit is 8.3 percent while it falls to 5.5 percent in fields where knowledge growth is decelerating.

Although not considered a major determinant in the decision to leave, individuals in fields where knowledge growth is accelerating are statistically more likely to leave science permanently. The requirement of constant skill update may be a frustration to some science personnel, another factor leading them to consider exit. Moreover, temporary exits are more likely to stretch into permanent departures as skills depreciate at increasingly rapid rates. Because women, in this sample specifically and over the time period more generally, were more likely to experience accelerating growth rates of knowledge than men, and because women have family obligations that often preclude skill update during off hours and require temporary exits, rapidly changing knowledge may be more of a factor in their decisions to exit than in men's decisions.

CHAPTER 8

Perceptions of Discriminatory Treatment

While perceptions of discriminatory treatment and unequal opportunities were not a direct cause of exit for any of the interviewed women, a majority of the women recalled instances when they felt that they were not respected or not treated appropriately solely because of their gender. This unequal treatment may have led to fewer connections to potential mentors or less interesting assignments or lower pay that may ultimately have been the reasons for exit. As a result, we cannot rule out discriminatory treatment as an indirect factor behind exit of women. However, proving discrimination is almost impossible since differences in outcomes and opportunities can also be a result of differential choices on the part of women in the labor market. This chapter begins with a partial review of the voluminous sociological and economic literature on gender discrimination generally and in science, and continues by outlining some of the difficulties involved in measuring discrimination. Turning to the data collected for the study, the chapter highlights the types of complaints voiced by women in the interviews and examines the larger data sets to estimate gender differentials in labor-market outcomes in the science workplace.

THEORETICAL AND EMPIRICAL DISCUSSIONS OF GENDER DISCRIMINATION

Gender discrimination occurs when two equally qualified and productive individuals are treated differently solely because of their sex. If gender discrimination occurs in employment relationships, the direct result may be different labor-market outcomes for men and women. In particular, women may earn lower salaries, have less promising job opportunities, face limited occupational choices, and have higher workforce separation rates than do comparable men. Women who perceive discrimination in the labor market and the resulting diminishment of employment outcomes, may make labor market choices based on this information. They may decide to invest in less human capital formation, such as education, training, and job search, because the forecasted returns are not as high as for similarly situated men. They may decide to stay home with children because the opportunities in their career are not as interesting or as lucrative as those offered to their male peers. As a result, there are indirect effects of discrimination as women engage in behaviors that further solidify the less attractive labor-market outcomes.

Economic theories of discrimination attempt to describe how discrimination and the resulting differential outcomes can arise and persist in a market economy. Gary Becker's theory of discrimination (1971) is based on discriminatory preferences on the part of employers, fellow employees, and customers. He posits that there are economic agents who prefer to employ, work with, or buy from one group—in this case men—rather than another, women. These economic agents are willing to sacrifice income to satisfy their own preferences. In all three scenarios, the theory predicts largely segregated workplaces with higher wages paid to the favored group. Customer discrimination also predicts that women will be pushed into less visible and less customer-oriented occupations while men remain the more publicly visible employees. In the long term, the theory predicts that competition between nondiscriminating and discriminating employers will result in expansion of the lower cost, more efficient establishments of the nondiscriminating employers at the expense of discriminating employers, forcing a move toward equalization of labor-market outcomes between men and women. Discriminatory preferences on the part of coworkers or customers are not necessarily incompatible with efficient behavior on the part of employers and may result in ongoing differential outcomes.

Statistical discrimination (Phelps 1972) is an alternative theory that, rather than dwelling on personal prejudices, focuses on profit-making behavior in an uncertain environment. Because employers cannot judge the true productivity of a new job applicant, they look for an observable trait, such as skin color or gender, as a predictor. Using the average historical productivity of a group as a whole to predict the future productivity of a member of that group, the employer makes early employment decisions. Because of fewer opportunities and societal pressures to conform to gender stereotypes, past productivity of women falls well below productivity of men, leading to discriminatory treatment. The impact of statistical discrimination on persistence of differential outcomes is not immediately evident. For those persistent women who experience early labor-market discrimination but continue to work, time at the job will reveal true ability, and women should catch up to equally able men. Furthermore, as women improve performance and persistence in the labor market, productivity distributions of men and women should merge, nullifying the validity of gender as a predictor of productivity. However, feedback effects may occur as women, faced with less attractive early employment opportunities than their training would predict, make decisions that compromise their own labor-market futures as well as those of their female peers. In particular, they may alter their behavior in ways that reinforce gender stereotypes both within the labor market and within the family, and thereby continue to validate discriminatory behavior on the part of the employer.

Occupational crowding models predict that occupational segregation that results in "male" and "female" jobs may also lead to male-female salary gaps (Bergman 1974). If the supply of women for female jobs is high relative to demand, wages will be pushed down. With lower wages in female jobs, employers will find it profitable to use more labor-intensive production techniques keeping female productivity low. With higher wages in male jobs, however, employers will implement more capital-intensive production techniques pushing male productivity up. Occupational crowding models then focus on the factors driving women to continue to crowd into low-paying jobs. Some theorists contend that these jobs offer nonmonetary characteristics especially valuable to women (Killingsworth 1985). Other theorists contend that there are barriers preventing working women from choosing male jobs. These barriers may be created by discriminatory preferences on the part of the employer (Bergman 1974) or by co-worker hostility at the male job (Jacobs 1987). Or they may be the result of socially constructed gender stereotypes that have developed within the family and spread to the workplace. Institutional economists focus on institutional arrangements that perpetuate segregation. Examples include strength requirements or veteran's preferences (Reskin and Hartmann 1986), internal labor markets, which, immune to market forces, establish separate job ladders with differential mobility to men and women in the same firm, or nonstandard employee searches that bias the applicant pool for certain jobs. Such historically embedded practices are likely to continue through organizational inertia or short-run accounting where the costs of changing practices exceed benefits in a short-term perspective.

In contrast to economists, sociologists are more likely to look at the social and organizational contexts that give birth to and perpetuate inequality. Jonathan Cole and Burton Singer's theory of limited differences (1991) was developed initially to understand the web of factors leading to gender inequalities in scientific career attainment. It offers a theoretical explanation of changing dynamics of the relative standings of groups, in this case men and women, over time. Individuals sharing a general career path are likely to encounter a series of similar events as they progress through their professional life. Associated with each event is a kick, the outcome of the event, and a reaction, the individual's response to the outcome. At the individual level, they posit that small and limited differences in reactions to certain events may have lasting consequences on long-term career attainment, and discrimination or unequal treatment may manifest itself in differential kicks across groups. For example, an early event that all science Ph.D.s encounter is admissions to a doctoral program. If women have a lower chance of getting into high-powered programs than men (a differential kick), they may react with a lowering of aspirations. Cole and Singer contend that the accumulation of these responses can result in inequalities that should not be attributed to a single cause, and a deep understanding of these inequalities requires a complete knowledge of the individuals' career histories and the social and organizational networks in which they operate.

Measurement of Inequality

The existence of discrimination and the extent of the inequality are often estimated using regression analysis on large data sets of employees. The conceptual experiment is to compare otherwise identical men and women and estimate average outcome differentials. Regressions are run with a particular outcome, such as income, as the dependent variable and a set of independent variables that encompass all the personal and workplace characteristics that determine income. With sex included as an independent variable, the estimate of discrimination becomes the residual inequality in income between men and women, once all the relevant personal and workplace characteristics are accounted for. Estimating discrimination in this way is problematic. First, it is often impossible to account for all the characteristics affecting the outcome. In the case of income, we want to compare two equally productive individuals, but productivity may be multifaceted, not observable and difficult to measure. Second, if some of the inequality in income is a result of inequality in education, and the inequality in education is itself a result of discrimination, residual estimates of discrimination after differential education is accounted for probably underestimate the extent of discrimination.

Regardless of the problems, the technique of estimating discrimination persists, and, with appropriate qualifications, it gives benchmark estimates that can be compared across workplaces and over time. Francine Blau and Lawrence Kahn (1997) use the Panel Study of Income Dynamics to estimate the changing male female wage differential in the United States during the period from 1979 to 1988. They find that with controls for human capital, education, experience, and part-time status, the female hourly earnings loss for full-time employees in 1988 was −21.7 percent, a reduction from −33.54 percent in 1979. With addition of industrial, occupational, and collective bargaining status variables, the loss in 1988 falls to −12.6 percent, but differential occupation and industrial location and union status, which account for slightly less than half of the original differential, may themselves be direct effects of discrimination.

Occupation specific studies, which take advantage of greater homogeneity of the workers involved, have also estimated differentials in salary and opportunity. Examining promotion rates of a sample of lawyers who entered corporate law firms in the 1970s and 1980s, Stephen Spurr (1990) finds that women were only half as likely to make partner as males. Controlling for background characteristics and productivity, he estimates that the standard for promotion of a woman was 50 percent to 70 percent higher than for a man. Robert Wood, Mary Corcoran, and Paul Courant (1993) estimate salary differentials for 1973 to 1975 graduates of the University of Michigan Law School fifteen years after graduation. Gross male earnings were two-thirds higher than those of their female peers; however, men worked significantly longer hours than the women in the sample. Controlling for personal, work history, and job characteristics, the differential fell but remained significant at 13 percent.

Studies of Ph.D. scientists are especially informative because data on publications give a good measure of productivity. Cole (1979) examines occupational attainment, as opposed to income, for a sample of American Ph.D. scientists in the period from 1965 to 1970. During this period, academic women had significantly fewer publications than their male peers, and, controlling for this difference, the prestige of the academic department was similar for men and women. But there was a 10 percent lower promotion rate between 1965 and 1970 for women than for men, even after differences in productivity and labor-market attachment rates were considered.

In a more recent study of the population of Ph.D. scientists that does analyze salary differentials (Long 2001), the 22 percent gross advantage in median salaries earned by male scientists in 1995 falls to about 7 percent once controls for career age, field, and sector of employment are added to the analysis. Comparing academically employed scientists, the differential falls to between 4 percent and 10 percent with controls for professional age, rank, quality of doctoral institution, quality of employing institution, and number of publications. Comparisons to 1973 show that, while the gross advantage in median salaries of men does not change over the period, the 1995 residual differences (after accounting for relevant factors) are roughly half the magnitude they were in 1973.

Measuring discrimination more directly has been attempted in some creative quasi experiments. In an audit experiment where comparably matched men and women applied for jobs as restaurant waiters, David Neumark, Roy Blank, and Kyle Van Nort (1996) find evidence of substantial discrimination against women in high-priced restaurants where they were 40 percent less likely to be interviewed and 35 percent less likely than their male peers to be offered a job. Claudia Goldin and Cecilia Rouse (2000) compare the success of women auditioning for symphony orchestras in blind versus open auditions. They find that women are significantly more likely to get a callback if auditions are conducted when the performer is hidden behind a screen than if the performer is observed by the judges. Discrimination in hiring practices of scientific institutions is less likely to be the focus of one of these studies because of the complexity and length of the hiring process. However, L. S. Fidell (1970) sent resumes of equally qualified men and women to psychology department heads with a request for an evaluation of each applicant. Male applicants were more likely than female applicants to be appraised favorably and levels of recommended appointments were higher for men than women.

The remainder of this chapter relates the interviewed women's perceptions on discrimination in the scientific workforce and estimates differences in labor-market outcomes using the work histories and the NSF data. The intent is not to prove discrimination but to understand the perceptions of these women and to recognize the interrelation between perceptions, behavior, and outcomes.

INTERVIEW DATA

A large number of the interviewed women perceived that they had been treated unfairly at some point in their career solely because of their sex. This fact stands in stark contrast to interviews conducted by Cole and Harriet Zuckerman in the late 1980s (Cole and Singer 1991) in which most of the women scientists denied ever personally experiencing discrimination. The difference in perceptions may be attributed to two factors. First, the samples interviewed are very different. Cole and Zuckerman interviewed women who had earned Ph.D.s and become academically employed. These women were the success stories, and their success may have been due to the fact that they did not experience discrimination or that they refused to acknowledge unequal treatment and opportunities. The sample for this study is more representative of the American female science major, and only a few of them ever attain university faculty or research jobs. Not being "stars," they may be more susceptible to perceptions of discriminatory treatment. Second, the two groups may have had different definitions of discriminatory treatment. The women in the Cole-Zuckerman sample were older than those interviewed in this study, with two-thirds having earned a Ph.D. before the late 1960s, and definitions of discrimination may have changed over the period from blatant, discreet events to more subtle and pervasive attitudes.

Deliberate illegal acts were not commonly cited by the women in the interview sample, and those that were mentioned occurred exclusively in the earlier half of the period. A young woman with a master's degree in mathematics who worked for a textbook company was forced to resign in 1969 when she became pregnant. Several years later the company was the subject of a class-action lawsuit. A Ph.D. mathematician was denied an assistant professorship at a university in 1969 because her husband was finishing a Ph.D. in English and would probably move her elsewhere. The job was eventually offered to a man who had not even finished his Ph.D. and whose wife was also working toward a Ph.D. in English. Working as a professor at a small college, this same woman describes the early years of her employment: "I was one of two people in the math department. I had a Ph.D., the other person didn't. He was always paid more than I because he was a man, and I was told that. It was open." Even in the mid- to late 1970s, women were still facing rigid barriers. In an interview for graduate school, a woman was discouraged from pursuing her dream to become a veterinarian when she was told that the university only accepted two females to their veterinary school per year.

More common than facing blatant and illegal treatment, many women found that their male counterparts were at a loss as to how to treat them, and the perceived result was inequality in opportunity. Some found themselves working with men who felt that a female colleague's sexuality was a threat to the normalcy of their work and family lives. In such circumstances, the woman was usually excluded from certain work situations. A woman in an engineering master's program in the early 1980s describes how she was denied study in corrosion engineering: "I initially wanted to go and pursue the field of corrosion engineering. However, the professor that was in that area came out and told me that he didn't want to work with a woman doing the research project . . . because he was recently married and he didn't want to have problems with his wife and because he didn't want to have to watch his language around me." One of only a handful of women employed at a large engineering company related her boss's justification for not taking her on business trips in the late 1980s: "When you go on a business trip, there is not much to do and a lot of times we sit down in a hotel bar at night and have a few drinks and, well, you never know what can happen." A woman with a master's in mechanical engineering who worked for an engineering company recalled that her male co-workers purposely excluded her from socializing at lunch. They explained it to her, "Nothing personal, we just want the guys." Finding it impossible to develop friendships with her colleagues at work, another female engineer recounted, "Every time I made a friend of someone, I was accused of having an affair with him." The general attitude of her male colleagues about her socializing at work was, "talk to the secretaries . . . stay with the women." There were also situations when the isolation was self-imposed because the women felt that the work or social environment involved sexually offensive language and, in fewer instances, pictures. The segregation that many of these women faced hampered their career trajectories since a lot of business and networking is conducted in groups or in social situations.

Other women described circumstances where men, unclear on how to treat their female colleagues, fell back on stereotypical sex roles common in patriarchic societies. In the most literal case, a woman who earned a Ph.D. in mathematics describes her relationship with her advisor: "He perceived me as his next wife. . . . I drove his mother to work, I picked him up at the airport when he was out-of-town, I taught his classes." One woman described how, as a graduate student in geology, both her fellow graduate students and professors often commended her good secretarial skills and put more administrative responsibilities on her than on her male colleagues doing identical work. Another woman, who earned a Ph.D. in math education, described an incident where a male professor patted her on the head as he told her how much she would enjoy graduate school. Finally, there were stories about male colleagues being protective of their female coworkers. An engineer describes the results of a study in her company concerned with why female employees were being rated lower than male employees: "They found a lot of it had to do with the assignments that the people were given, and a lot of it was that the supervisors were being very protective towards the women. They weren't giving them the meaty assignments because they didn't want them to fail so they were giving them the safe, easy jobs which they could do but couldn't get any fame and glory for them." Because sexual stereotypes reinforce the subordination of women, women subjected to these attitudes were not likely to advance as quickly in their careers as their male colleagues.

Most prevalent of all were comments about how pregnancy was a condition to be hidden as long as possible because of the negative impressions that it gave male scientists. Even successful Ph.D. scientists were treated differently once pregnancy became an issue. One woman described her female advisor's reaction when she told her that she was pregnant, "she asked me if I knew how to use condoms." Another woman doing her postdoctorate in biology at a prestigious private university describes the situation in her program: "Initially male and female postdocs are treated equally, but I think that, if you become pregnant, there is a definite change in how they will treat you. You are not taken that seriously anymore. Maybe this is unfair for me to say because I have never been pregnant, and to be really frank I'd be a little bit afraid to because it's perceived as such a negative thing. . . . Very often you will get your project taken away from you." A woman, with two successful postdoctorates in biology, felt that it was necessary to wear baggy clothes and to hide her pregnancy as she applied for assis-

tant professorship jobs. Another woman talked of hiding her pregnancy during her master's program in geology: "I didn't tell them I was
pregnant. By the time I started I was six to seven months pregnant—
but I never showed. I always had the impression that a man would say
about himself, 'I am a geologist' but would describe a female colleague
as a 'female geologist' and a pregnant colleague as a 'pregnant female
geologist.' I never wanted people to focus on me like that." A female
engineer working in sales for a computer software company, who was
pregnant at the time of the interview, felt that short-term projects and
rewards would be altered when her bosses discovered her condition:
"Case in point, even now when I'm pregnant, I haven't told them yet.
I don't know if you know about sales—our year starts November 1st
and that's when we get our new quotas, our new assignments, our
raises. I chose not to tell them until after that." Finally, a woman with
a master's in engineering who worked at a prestigious communications
company described the management's response to her pregnancy: "My
projects were taken away from me. . . . I knew I was going to be away,
out. So obviously I had to transfer responsibility but I was told 'you're
transferring responsibility for this project, you're not going to get it
back.' That was hard. Both times they were projects that I had started
from the ground. I had designed them from the very beginning. I'd
come up with the concept for them and I had to let them go before I felt
they were complete."

Often just the potential of a pregnancy closed doors. A woman in
development at a computer software company described the male
management's attitude toward women: "Women are not really treated
very seriously because I think that they feel like 'she's going to have a
baby next week and leave' and that's it. I just get the sense that they
don't invest a whole lot of time with the women in the department—a
case in point—seminars or [outside] training will come up and they
will send some of the men to go do that . . . and they don't do that with
the women."

And it is not just men who treat women in this way. A woman with
a B.S. in chemistry, who has two children and runs a government laboratory, confessed that she was reluctant to hire a pregnant chemist and
looks at a male job applicant more favorably than a female job appli-

cant. A female Ph.D. in physics who encountered tremendous obstacles as she attempted to get her Ph.D. in the 1960s admits, "I have prejudices against women. I see a woman student and I tend to think she is not as serious as the men until proven otherwise." However, there were also women who favored female students and workers because of characteristics unrelated to their reproductive system. A woman with a master's in geology and working for a computer science company, gave her impression of female employees: "I see a lot of women trying harder than a lot of men. I like to have women on my team—I take three or four women on my team—by and large they have a more intense feeling about their work than some of the guys do."

A large majority of the women interviewed felt that they were judged by a different standard than their male peers. There was a small minority of women who had never been in any situations where they felt that they were treated differently. These women tended to be relatively young, less educated, and more likely to be employed in industry. Not only did the younger women have shorter careers over which they might experience discriminatory treatment, but they entered a labor market where equal employment opportunity laws had existed for more than two decades. Additionally, discriminatory treatment in academe seemed to surface in graduate programs with very few women feeling any differential opportunities during their undergraduate years. Finally, perceptions of unequal treatment during employment were quite pervasive and only absent in a small number of organizations where a culture advocating equality had been forcibly put into place by the management hierarchy.

More common were acknowledgments that double standards permeate the field. For some women, the double standards manifested themselves in differing interactions with their male colleagues. A woman with a master's in chemistry talked about different treatment afforded men and women by her advisor: "He tends to be more lenient with the guys. For a girl, he would give you something to do on Friday at six o'clock, come in Monday morning at eight o'clock and ask you if you have it. And he'll rib you about taking time off or not being there, you know, and the guys—they don't ever get asked anything." Similarly, a woman who earned a Ph.D. in biology recalled that in graduate school, the few female students called their male professors by their last names and titles while the male students were all on a first-name basis with their professors. But most insidious was how hard the women felt they had to work to be taken seriously. A woman with a biology Ph.D. related, "I know men who bullshit, and they sound really good, but they know nothing. They are taken seriously by colleagues, whereas women could say anything they want, and they are just not taken seriously." One woman who was a marketing executive in biotechnology found the road to success especially hard for women: "The industry that I've spent most of my career in is so male dominated that if you're not really, really good you're just going to get chewed up and spit out." And not only do these women have to be really good, she continued, "they have to be leaders or they will be 'walked all over' by their male colleagues." A computer scientist in development at a software company described the problem in very plain terms: "In order to be taken seriously, you have to do double what the men in the department are doing." These comments blend into a well-tuned chorus to Evelyn Fox Keller's description (1991) of how women have fit historically into science: "Successful assimilation has thus tended to require not equal ability, but extra ability—the extra ability to compensate for the hidden costs incurred by the denial or suppression of a past history as 'other.'"

Most of these women had been proving themselves since high school, although the different standards often only became evident in graduate school or at entry into the workplace. Many women accepted these reactions from male superiors and colleagues as a way of life, but one with costs. The constant battle became wearing, taking a toll both emotionally and mentally. A woman with an M.S. in mechanical engineer recalled, "I found many women who I had worked with who were successful in the sciences, at least from the exterior, had hardened themselves and become more manlike." Justifying her decision not to continue study for her Ph.D., a female chemist felt the struggle to earn a master's degree had changed her:

> I'm a different person now, I'm more hostile and more abrupt. . . . Writing my thesis, I couldn't focus on things. I

would sit with people and I didn't even want to hear what they said after awhile. I'm not like that—I like people. I always did before and I just thought, "How different would I be after I got my Ph.D.?" Would that grating every day really wear as it's beginning to wear? . . . I'm less likely to be friendly, and I'm more defensive on a daily basis, and I can't see any other reason for it other than I'm working seventy hours a week and tired, and not getting any credit, and not getting any respect.

STATISTICS BEHIND THE PERCEPTIONS

From the interview data one cannot determine the extent to which the reported cases of discrimination are real or only perceived. Regardless of the veracity, perceived discrimination is likely to cause feelings of inadequacy, helplessness, and anger—all emotions that may lower the quality of the female scientist's personal and professional lives. Turning to the survey data, we can document a host of unequal labor-market outcomes between male and female scientists. The extent to which these differences are due to differences in treatment and differences in choices and behaviors is hard to establish, even with sophisticated statistical techniques.

Statistics on attachment for respondents to the university sample, presented in table 8.1, reveal that even after graduating from college, women are dropping out of the scientific pipeline at a faster rate than men. Thirty-two percent of women who start Ph.D. programs never finish, roughly twice the male drop-out rate. Similarly, a much larger percentage of women with degrees in science (36.5 percent) than men (27.4 percent) never step into a science career. At the time of the survey, twice as many women as men who had started science careers had left them permanently. We can blame these differences on choice, but we then have to question why women are consistently making different choices than men. Attributing the different choices to family responsibilities is a possibility, since expectations about future familial roles and responsibilities were certainly a factor even in the early career decisions of many of the interviewed women. But from the analysis of surveys and interviews, family burden is just one of several reasons for

Table 8.1   *Differences in Postgraduate Attachment to Science by Sex (Percentages)*

	Male Science Graduates (n = 711)	Female Science Graduates (n = 977)
Percentage who never start a science career	27.4	36.5
Of those who start a Ph.D. program, percentage who never finish	15.0	32.0
Of those who start a science career, percentage who exit science	15.5	31.5

Source: Author's compilation.

exit. Furthermore, in previous statistical analysis of the NSF data (Preston 1994), that is replicated with the university work histories, the direct impact of family on occupational exit of scientists was not able to explain the male-female differential in exit, and single women were more likely to leave science than single men. However, the indirect effect of "family" in a generic rather than personal sense cannot be ignored if employer and co-worker expectations about the impact of family on women's careers alter opportunities afforded women and the diminished opportunities lead to decisions to exit.

Salary differences between men and women in science careers are also quite significant. Table 8.2 presents female salary differentials estimated using ordinary least squares (OLS) regression analysis conducted on both the NSF data and the university work history data. The dependent variable, the natural logarithm of annual salary for men and women working in science at the time of the survey (1982 to 1989, NSF; 1993 to 1994, university data), allows us to interpret the differential as a percentage difference. Each row of the table presents alternative estimates with different controls included in the analysis. All differentials presented are significantly different from zero at the 99 percent confidence level unless otherwise specified. The initial analysis with no controls (row one) reveals that women in science earned on average 28 percent to 30 percent lower salaries than men. Confining the group to full-time workers, the differential falls to 24 percent to

Table 8.2   Female Salary Differentials (Percentages)

Controls	NSF All Workers[a] (n = 37,959)	NSF Full-Time Workers[a] (n = 37,119)	Work History All Workers[a] (n = 1,503)	Work History Full-Time Workers[a] (n = 1,359)
1. None	−28	−25	−30	−24
2. Age	−22	−18	−27	−21
3. Experience	−21	−17	−25	−19
4. Experience and highest science degree	−22	−18	−26	−20
5. Experience, highest science degree, and engineering degree	−18	−15	−19	-15
6. Experience, highest science degree, engineering degree, and family characteristics	−16	−12	−19	−14
7. Experience, highest science degree, engineering degree, family characteristics, and percent of early child-care responsibilities and percent of household chores taken on		−3*	−6	

Source: Author's compilation.
[a]Worker counts are based on 1982 information for NSF data and time of survey for work history data.
*Differential is not significantly different from zero.

25 percent, a magnitude slightly smaller than economywide estimates of male-female salary differentials. Additionally, while not shown in the table, all the female differentials in both the university and the NSF sample are between five and ten percentage points higher when the sample is not constrained to working scientists, implying that salaries are more equal within than outside of science. Because women are

slightly younger than men in the work history sample and appreciably younger than men in the NSF sample, the differential falls three percentage points in the work history data and six percentage points in the NSF data when controls for age are included (line two). Labor-market experience, more directly related to skill level or productivity, differentiates men and women since women, on average, will have more time out of the labor market than men of the same age. However, controlling for years of experience may undermine attempts to estimate discrimination since differing experience levels of same-aged men and women may be the result of differences in workplace treatment and social norms dictating gender roles in the family. Nevertheless, comparing men and women working in science with the same amount of experience, the female differential falls two percentage points for the work history samples and one percentage point for the NSF samples (line three). Adding controls for a master's degree in science and a Ph.D. in science increases the magnitude of the female differential insignificantly (line four) since, even though these degrees have positive impacts on salaries in science, there is not a marked difference in the percentages of men and women earning them. However, the female differential falls to 18 percent to 19 percent for all workers and 15 percent for full-time workers with a control for engineering degree (line five). Within science careers, engineers earn between 15 percent and 20 percent higher salaries than nonengineers, and women are much less likely to be engineers than men. Controlling for marriage and children makes little further impact on the magnitude of the female salary differential (line six) in the work history data but reduces the differential by two percentage points in the NSF data.

Interestingly for all rows, the differentials estimated with the two data sets are very similar even though the data cover slightly different periods (1980s versus 1990s), and the breadth of the samples are very different. Furthermore, the impact of specific controls on the magnitude of the estimated earning differential is almost identical across the two data sets. These similarities in magnitude and pattern across time and sample signal the stubborn persistence of these earnings differentials.

Because of the common perception that childbearing was a roadblock to career success and that family responsibilities conflicted with work responsibilities, the final analysis (line seven) includes controls for share of household chores and share of childcare for preschool children assumed by the respondent. These measures of family responsibility are only available for the university work histories. Once included in the regressions, the male-female earnings differential falls markedly. For the full sample, the differential becomes an insignificant 3 percent, and for full-time workers the differential is 6 percent. The larger decline of the differential in the full sample, which includes part-time workers, is probably due to the fact that much of the variation in salaries for part-time workers, who are predominantly female, is due to variation in hours, and family responsibilities are likely to be highly correlated with hours for part-time workers. Regardless of the sample analyzed, the results are clear: men and women who take on the same family responsibilities earn similar, although not necessarily equal, salaries. But in fact, as noted in chapter 4, men do not take on the same extent of family burden. On average, women take on more than twice the load of family responsibilities as their spouses, and family responsibilities have large negative effects on earnings. Whether the women choose a less committed career profile once the family responsibilities mount or employers take away opportunities when children and other family responsibilities become evident is unknown, although the comments from the interviewed women imply that both factors may be occurring. The clarity of the results makes a strong statement about career equality. If there were more equality in family responsibility between men and women, equality in career attainment would be likely to follow. Economic theories of discrimination against women need to underline the fact that attitudes and behaviors on the part of employers, co-workers, and the women themselves that lead to differential outcomes of women in the labor market are directly related to the traditional role of wife and mother in the family and the gender stereotypes that those roles imply.

The relevance of the perceptions of the interviewed women and the statistical results to the experiences of current and future female scientists is high, possibly evoking feelings of both hope and resignation. On the one hand, many of the identified patterns of behavior are likely to disappear as women become a larger portion of the scientific workforce. Several of the issues discussed arose because female scientists were oddities—unknown quantities in a traditionally all-male workplace. As men become more used to dealing with female students and colleagues and as women move into powerful positions in science, a growing body of experiences within an integrated workplace will guide individuals on how to interact with scientists of the opposite sex. On the other hand, the issue of childbearing and childrearing will always be a factor. As long as pregnancies are equated to a lack of commitment, all women will be subject to the accusation that they are not as serious as their male counterparts. They will be guilty until proven innocent, and the burden of proof will be placed squarely on the women's shoulders.

CHAPTER 9

Policy Initiatives

The factors leading to occupational exit rates from science are likely to contribute to diminished entry as well. Although the number of women pursuing doctoral degrees in the sciences has been increasing steadily since the 1960s, with female representation increasing from about 5 percent of total recipients in 1960 to 25 percent in 1996, the number of men has not. Estimates of the percentage of men with a B.S. or B.E. who earn a Ph.D. in science within eight years of the undergraduate degree show a reduction from 15 percent in 1970 to 8 percent in 1990. Without the increasing participation by women and foreign-born scientists, our science workforce would likely be shrinking. At the same time, our communication, transportation, and production processes are becoming increasingly technological. Even outside the scientific community there is a growing awareness that a productive and well-trained scientific workforce is essential to maintaining a technologically sophisticated, competitive, and growing economy. The standard of living in the United States depends on this workforce. Understanding these factors is only useful if it leads to policy prescriptions that will enhance the attraction of science as a career.

The four major reasons for exit identified in the preceding chapters can help to organize thoughts on policy, and each reason will be addressed separately in making policy recommendations. It will become obvious fairly quickly that because a lot of the reasons are interrelated, policy to address one factor may be helpful with others as well. Furthermore, while the factors behind exit separate very clearly along gender lines, addressing a factor most commonly cited by one sex is likely to benefit individuals of the other sex as well. Policy prescriptions designed at enhancing the attraction of the scientific career should benefit all who choose to participate in that career.

POLICY TO ADDRESS UNMET SALARY AND CAREER EXPECTATIONS

For many men who have exited, science as a career lost its attraction because of low pay and less promising career opportunities relative to alternative professions. Although medicine was the profession of comparison for men early in the career, as the men aged and the rigors of medical studies ruled it out of consideration, management and finance were almost always the professions of comparison. The attraction to this field and its stature as the basis of comparison is documented by the fact that during the period from 1970 to 2000, the number of Americans earning master's degrees in business increased more than fourfold. The M.B.A., or its equivalent, is second to education as the most highly awarded postgraduate degree. With financial success becoming increasingly attractive over the period and, in the 1990s, increasingly attainable in the management professions, scientific careers naturally were losing their luster. Since a large portion of the scientific labor force is employed by government and nonprofit organizations, it is unlikely that salaries, especially at the high levels, will ever compete with top managerial salaries. In conversations with many of these scientists, certain actions were identified that employing institutions could take to alleviate the problem of unmet salary and career expectations.

First and maybe foremost, the scientific community—especially undergraduate institutions, graduate institutions, and professional associations—must educate potential scientists about the careers they can expect with a given degree. Students can only make good career decisions if they have appropriate information. That information should include the type of jobs and career trajectories that might be available for a graduate with a B.S. in biology, or an M.S. in marine sciences, or a Ph.D. in applied mathematics, as well as starting salaries and salary profiles throughout the career.

Informational problems surrounding career choice of potential scientists are widespread for three reasons. First, there is an asymmetry of access to information, with the educational institutions and professional associations having greater access than the students who need the information for decisionmaking. Second, institutions may also have only partial information on careers, the information relevant to its employees. Obviously, scientists are not interested in conducting labor-market studies, and there is no institution that centralizes the information-collection function. Finally, there is a long period of education and training between career choice and job location, so the information collected at the date of career choice may be out of date by the time the individual starts working as a scientist. While the third issue can never be addressed thoroughly without the powers of a psychic, the first two can be addressed fairly easily with advances in information technology.

Ideally, a government agency such as the National Science Board or a professional association should conduct workforce surveys periodically by field with reports on job options, salaries, and salary growth for scientists with differing levels of education and in varying cohorts. The cost and time of such studies can be drastically reduced by use of Web technology, making such a policy prescription realistic. Reports on the studies should then be disseminated to all institutions of higher education, so that individual departments can post the results of these surveys for their students on well-publicized career websites. Increasing the frequency of updates of the studies can keep students well informed as they progress through their studies.

Once students enter these professions with their eyes open, the match between the individual and the career is more likely to be successful. People choosing science careers will be those who value scientific work enough to forgo income earned elsewhere. Even with perfect information, however, there will still be individuals whose needs and preferences will change over their lifetime so that they may feel the need to leave science for higher-paying occupations. Improving information collection and flow will not solve the problem of unmet salary expectations completely, but it will go a long way to reducing its severity.

Second, and equally important, pay and benefits for postdoctoral positions must be set at acceptable levels. In 2001, the annual salary for a first-year postdoctorate funded through the National Institutes of

Health (NIH) was just over $28,000. Furthermore, outside of NIH there is wide variability in pay across fields and institutions. Most postdoctoral scientists are in their late twenties through their mid-thirties, a time of life when many individuals are starting their adult lives with partners and children. This low pay puts stress on this normal progression of life events. With the increasing dependence on postdoctoral positions for early employment opportunities in the sciences, and the biological sciences especially, low pay at these jobs is discouraging young scientists from pursuing a Ph.D.-level career (Freeman et al. 2001). Since many of the postdoctoral positions are financed by federal grants from the NSF, the NIH, and the Department of Defense, it is up to these organizations and the science community to educate Congress of the importance of acceptable salaries and to budget for them. The situation has improved slightly with the NIH making a commitment to increase annual stipends for entering post-doctorates to $45,000 over a number of years. This one-time increase will not be enough. It is important to the future of scientific research in this country that the issue not recede from the public consciousness and that it be addressed every couple of years to ensure adequate salaries for the scientific elite.

Several of the men interviewed implied a need for more imaginative compensation schemes and career trajectories. One man questioned why there was not more pay-for-performance schemes for scientists. Another spoke with pride of the technical excellence program instituted by his company in which technical fellows, scientists with national and international reputations, are given fancy offices and perks similar to those given top executives. Compensation schemes should attract, motivate, and retain employees. For many of the men interviewed, scientific compensation is not effective in the latter two areas. Compensation-for-performance schemes are notoriously difficult to design in organizations not driven by profits, and for employees who work in group settings and whose satisfaction is not tied solely to income. Interview respondents confirm that many scientists find satisfaction in a host of nonmonetary attributes, which might include prestige, creative accomplishment, intellectual recognition, and responsibility. In this arena, desired performance must be articulated and measured with care, and rewards must be continually reevaluated for relevance to the targeted employees. In order to retain employees, compensation must increase with seniority. Deferred benefits or benefits that grow with seniority encourage a continuing employment relationship. Since career trajectory and opportunity was also a complaint, scientists seem to want not just more money but the promise of a broadening of responsibilities with increased time with an employing institution. Designing compensation schemes for scientists that reward both good performance and longevity might go a long way to quieting complaints about the lack of opportunity in scientific careers. Here the private companies with more flexibility in how they spend their resources should take the lead, but the government and nonprofit organizations will have to follow suit in order to stay competitive in the labor market.

POLICY TO HELP BALANCE CAREER AND FAMILY

Policy to address family issues can come in a number of forms, especially since these concerns seem to arise at different stages of family formation for scientists with different educational levels. Dual-career issues are especially thorny for Ph.D. scientists for a number of reasons. First, training is often highly specialized, resulting in limited job opportunities. Second, the job opportunities that exist are often tied to universities or laboratories that are naturally geographically dispersed. Third, because of large space needs, universities are often built in nonurban areas that do not have vibrant labor markets outside of the university. Fourth, the early Ph.D. career, which coincides with early marriage and partnership, often requires several geographical relocations before the permanent job. Finally, the compromises of the dual-career marriage are disproportionately made by female scientists, who are more likely than their male counterparts to be married to an employed professional, and who are likely to be younger and less established than their spouses. Relocating universities is obviously not an option. Still, especially within out-of-the-way university communities, there can be stronger efforts to employ spouses of desired job candidates. Currently, such efforts are most often observed for "star" candidates, and often the spouse's job offer is a step down in the career trajectory. Increasing the coverage of such efforts and ensuring that the job opportunities to spouses are attractive on their own terms would help ease the problems of the dual-career couple markedly. These programs can only be successful with considerable administrative support, since departments do not usually have the know-how or resources to put together a joint package on their own.

Ph.D. scientists make a number of geographical moves in the early stages of the career as they learn from different scientists in graduate school and postdoctoral appointments. This requirement must be reexamined. With the increasing ease of communicating and traveling, long distance collaboration and short-term collaborative research experiences might substitute for numerous geographical relocations. The extent of this substitution will necessarily differ by discipline, and it is likely to depend on the type of lab work performed and the extent to which researchers are tied physically to their laboratories.

Because scientific career paths are well established and deeply entrenched in the scientific culture, change is not going to come easily. Furthermore, change will not come about at all unless it is supported by leaders of the scientific community. Discipline-based associations, together with the National Academy of Sciences, should commission panels to study alternative ways to teach Ph.D. scientists. In the biological and health sciences, biotechnology firms seem to be offering alternative career paths already. Many firms will hire an employee after graduate school, giving him or her a postdoctoral position that often leads to a permanent position. These relatively permanent employment opportunities in urban settings create solutions to the problems of the dual career. There have also been proposals to create staff-scientist jobs in university laboratories for scientists who are looking for a more permanent and predictable employment situation (Marincola and Solomon 1998). Although both of these options help with dual-career issues, there is concern that since the female scientist is more likely than her male counterpart to find a solution to the dual-career marriage by compromising her career, we risk a two-tier workforce where women take the predictable and permanent jobs and only men choose the riskier and more prestigious academic route. Leaders in the academic community need to address the issues of the academic career path, since experience has shown that such a gender-based allocation of scientific talent has not been conducive to attracting women into scientific pursuits.

According to the interview and work history data, policies that help to balance the demands of childrearing and a scientific profession are likely to be most effective at reducing attrition for scientists working outside of academe where work hours and benefits can be rigid. But these policies are likely to improve the quality of life and the productivity of all scientists who take on both career and family responsibilities. Employing institutions have endless options to improve the quality of life of working parents, including but not limited to maternity or paternity leave, increased flexibility of work hours, telecommuting, unpaid personal days for childhood emergencies, a temporary part-time work option, and on-site day care. These reforms are crucial for the success of working parents in all areas of employment, not just in science workplaces. At the time of the survey, respondents felt that these policies were more likely to be implemented in the academic institutions than in the private sector. These impressions may not be valid in the current workplace where, according to media coverage of workplace benefits, family-friendly work policies have become more prevalent economywide throughout the 1990s.

Although Ph.D. scientists in the academic community often find that the flexibility and autonomy these policies create helps to coordinate childrearing demands, the flexibility is often an illusion in the early years when, working toward tenure, the scientist is putting in sixty- to seventy-hour weeks. For these scientists, these childcare benefits improve the quality of the individual's work-life but do not diminish the work time necessary to attain tenure. Giving a parent extra time on the tenure clock for each child born during its duration, a policy increasingly considered in academia, allows the working parent the opportunity to make up for some of the research time lost to early childhood parenting and to spread the time at research over a larger span of calendar years.

Together these policies will help with the day-to-day strains of working parents—mothers in particular—but they are not enough.

Participants at a discussion of problems facing female Ph.D.s in science at one of the most prestigious science universities in the country almost uniformly agreed that taking extra time off after giving birth and stopping the tenure clock would be the kiss of death to one's career. In addition, while these benefits were offered to both male and female faculty, the discussants could not recall any men who took advantage of them. Similarly, in a discussion with female faculty at a female college, the women pointed out that, according to their collective memories, of all the women who had taken maternity leave before tenure, only one female professor was actually awarded tenure. While there are institutions where maternity and paternity leaves and slowed down tenure clocks are used by male and female scientists as they successfully work toward tenure, they are still not the rule and are not the top-tier research institutions. In general, the women interviewed in the study and at these female faculty forums did not trust that these activities would be viewed neutrally in the tenure decision. The result is that some women delay childbearing until after the tenure decision, a seemingly risky strategy for a woman who wants a family. Others take only a minimal maternity leave and return to work to compete as if they were childless. Still others take advantage of the benefit and hope that the gains of the extra time will outweigh any negative perceptions. The distrust felt by these women highlights the fact that, if such benefits are put into place in a college or university, the administration has to stand by them and make sure that the academics, who largely control tenure decisions, stand by them as well. A special committee should be set up to review each tenure case where the individual has taken advantage of a childcare-related benefit that gave the parent extra time away from teaching or on the tenure clock. Ensuring that such activities are not penalized during promotion decisions is paramount to the success of working parents.

There are two important issues here. The first is that there is a predominant feeling in the scientific community, and in American society more generally, that childrearing and careers are in direct conflict, and one has to be compromised for the other. Second, overwhelmingly, expectations are that women will make this compromise. Since employers assume that women will eventually take time off to care for children, they are likely to give them reduced opportunities early in the career. Once career options are decreased, the decision to put childrearing ahead of work is much easier. Thus the prophecy becomes self-fulfilling. Claudia Goldin's (1997) finding that only 13 percent to 17 percent of the college-educated women who graduated in the late 1960s through the 1970s had both a family and a career by age forty is striking evidence of the fulfillment of these expectations. These two issues are difficult to address because both are based on long-standing cultural norms concerning work, family, and gender roles. The American workplace encourages competition and rewards stars with money, prestige, and opportunity. Technological developments, which have recently increased labor productivity, have had little impact on the childrearing function that offers no acceptable substitute for adult-child personal contact; therefore, childrearing is becoming increasingly expensive to American employers. Because childrearing does take time away from work and career development, even for full-time employees, the stars in the American workplace in fields as diverse as business, science, and the arts are not likely to be men or women who spend a lot of time with children and family.

Both issues will become less problematic when men start taking on an increased share of childcare. Once men assume these responsibilities, childcare will be given higher status, and policies to help balance work and family will be given more attention. Furthermore, men and women will be treated much more equally in the labor market. If, in some ideal world, 50 percent of the childrearing responsibilities were taken on by men, employers would not have differential expectations about the long-term commitment to work of men and women. Women and men would be given the same career opportunities leading up to childbirth and before the childrearing choices have to be made. Although there may have been some change in the gender allocation of childcare over the past thirty years, my data reveal that men still take on only a small portion of the childrearing responsibility. Even men who might be interested in staying home with children for a time often resist taking advantage of policies such as paternity leaves, which they feel send the wrong signals to employers. Therefore, change will occur only if upper-level management in these employing institutions, whether they are corporate, academic, or government, give credible promises that there will be no negative repercussions in response to decisions to take advantage of childcare benefits. Other advanced countries, Sweden most dramatically, have national policies aimed at equalizing male and female participation in both childrearing and work. Sweden's Equal Opportunity Act of 1992 requires employers to achieve a well-balanced sex distribution in many jobs and to facilitate the combination of work and family responsibilities. Paid maternity or paternity care, at 80 percent to 90 percent of the salary, is mandated for twelve months. Sweden falls short of requiring men to take some part of this leave, but statistics show that about 70 percent of fathers take some time off and that these leaves have recently been getting longer. Given the difficulty involved with passing the Family and Medical Leave Act of 1993, it is unlikely that this type of workplace policy will be replicated in the United States. Such a policy would go a long way to easing burdens faced by working parents and to putting women and men on equal footing in both arenas.

POLICIES TO ADDRESS MENTORING

A lack of good mentoring experiences is more problematic for women than men, because women are less likely to be mentored than men and because the effects of mentoring on retention and performance are greater for women. According to the interview data, the sex disparity in mentoring is greatest in academic institutions. Mentoring tends to be quite informal in these institutions and thus arises naturally between male professors and male students. With more female professors, female students may find that developing a mentoring relationship is becoming easier. However, because sex ratios of science professors continue to be highly unbalanced, formal mentoring programs for female science students, which have been growing in number in the last ten years, should continue to be set up and supported in all academic institutions. Women who are having trouble developing a personal relationship with a professor can then be directed to professors or graduate students who are willing to take on the role of mentor. Women in science programs that have arisen in a variety of universities, such as the

Stony Brook University, have used multilevel mentoring where a junior biology major may mentor a freshman and also be mentored by a post-doctoral student. Such a program creates a network of women to whom individuals can turn with questions. Social occasions for participants have also been successful in making the relationships more personal and in developing ties with a whole community of women in science. These activities need not be limited to women although, because of the ease with which men seem to develop these relationships in academe, female mentoring programs may make sense for now.

According to the interview data, men and women in industry were equally likely to be mentored, and generally mentoring relationships developed in organizations where mentoring was the cultural norm or where formal mentoring programs had been put in place. Again, for these institutions, mentoring programs are most likely to take hold when upper-level management puts its weight behind them. Besides being a good way to reduce turnover of female scientists, mentoring programs should further productivity. Mentoring, as described by interviewees, is a sharing of human capital and thus a type of informal training that is likely to improve the performance of all employees.

POLICIES ADDRESSING THE INDIVIDUAL–FIELD MISMATCH

Mismatches between an individual's interests and the requirements of the scientific career are addressed in some of the policies advocated earlier in this chapter. Good career counseling for degree recipients in the different scientific disciplines is likely to ward off bad matches due to uninformed expectations. Mentoring relationships and well-developed networks of scientists with similar interests are likely to increase the personal connections that a given scientist makes with other scientists, thus reducing feelings of isolation. The trend toward interdisciplinary work, which has taken place in the last twenty years, should give the individual scientist the opportunity to choose areas of work where the science itself can be connected to a bigger picture. The National Science Foundation and private foundations such as the Alfred P. Sloan Foundation have taken the lead in funding broad multidisciplinary research efforts. Historically, universities have had fairly rigid disciplinary boundaries. In order for scientists to feel free to participate in these interdisciplinary projects, the rewards and promotions processes of employing institutions may have to be restructured to value this type of research.

POLICIES TO ADDRESS CHANGE

Finally, in response to the finding that permanent exit is higher for men and women who are in fields that are changing at rapid rates, institution-sponsored skill update and training programs will alleviate stresses associated with change. The NSF sponsors programs for women who have left science to help them rebuild skills for entry. These types of programs help temporary exits remain temporary. Training programs and skill updates are especially important in academic institutions where separation is not an option for tenured employees, who feel that their skills have become out of date. Foundations such as the Mellon Foundation have been instrumental in supporting programs of career development for professors at all levels in liberal arts colleges. According to the interview data, private companies in the early 1990s did not engage in wide-scale training of existing employees in new techniques and knowledge. Companies may be comfortable with the attrition of older employees who are not willing to engage in skill update because new employees, fresh out of the university, have the updated skills and are less expensive than older, more senior employees. But if the pool of new hires becomes insufficient to replace this attrition, companies will have to face this issue head-on.

The goal of current federal science personnel policy is to build and maintain a sufficiently large and competent national scientific workforce. In the last twenty years, the focus has been on early pipeline issues, building competency and interest in the kindergarten through twelfth grades, and on engaging and retaining women and minorities in the secondary school and college years. But there has been too little attention given to the workplace. Risks of attrition do not disappear at the conclusion of the educational pipeline. Choosing a science career should not be choosing a career of hardship and sacrifice. In addition to interesting and challenging work, science careers should offer a strong support network, the possibility of having a real family life, an income throughout the career that allows a comfortable family life-style, and possibilities for continuous advancement and development. Students in undergraduate science programs at public universities will make up the core of our future scientific workforce. According to interviews, these individuals are competent, motivated, and often feel a deep passion for the field. Our nation has an obligation to keep this passion alive.

APPENDIX

Selected Analyses by Chapter

CHAPTER 2

A. Kaplan-Meier Survival Estimates of Figure 2.2

Let t_j, $j = 1 \ldots$ denote the times, measured in months, at which permanent exit can occur. Let n_j represent the number of scientifically trained individuals at risk of exit just before t_j, and d_j represent the number who exit at time t_j. The Kaplan-Meier nonparametric maximum likelihood estimate of the survivor function is

$$S(t) = \prod_{t_j < t} ((n_j - d_j) / n_j)$$

The survivor function is estimated only for the university data, which does not have the problems of right-hand censorship exhibited by the national data. The survivor functions are estimated separately for men and women over the twenty-five-year period following graduation, and chi-squared tests confirm that the functions are not equal at the 0.01 significance level.

B. Statistical Analysis

The effects of personal and job characteristics on the probability of leaving science are determined from a set of competing hazard analyses estimated with the university and national data sets separately. In these analyses, each scientist is represented with an observed data vector (T_{ij}, E_{ij}, Z_i^t). T_{ij} is months of experience in science accrued by individual i before jth departure from science. E_{ij} is type of exit that, in the national data, can take on four values, exit to other occupations due to promotion, exit to other occupations for reasons other than promotion, exit from employment, and exit from the labor force. In the university data, E_{ij} takes on two values, permanent or temporary exit. Z_i^t is a set of covariates, some of which will vary with time and which vary somewhat over the two data sets. The model then estimates the probability of a specific type of departure from science conditional on surviving in scientific work for time Tj.

In estimating a competing hazard function, the likelihood factor for each type of exit, k, is assumed to be the likelihood that would be obtained if the other type of exit is considered censored at the time of departure of type k. These assumptions allow standard estimation methods for two state conditional probability functions to be used in the competing risk case. Cox proportional hazards model with time varying covariates are used to estimate the type specific probability function. The conditional probability of leaving for reason k is given by: $\lambda_{ik}(t_{ik}) = \lambda_0 \exp(Z^t \beta_k)$ where λ_0 is the unspecified baseline hazard and Z^t is the set of covariates. Cause-specific probabilities are assumed to be independent of each other, and unobserved heterogeneity is assumed to have no effect on the probability functions.

The analysis allows more than one exit by an individual scientist, a necessary condition for the university data analysis of temporary exit. According to the construction of the data, the analysis uses observations that correspond to the end of an activity in science or to working at science at the survey date. Covariates are specific to the activity that is ending. Future activity, which can either be another job in science, permanent exit, temporary exit, or continuation in the current science job, determines the value of the exit variable. After a temporary exit from science, the individual returns to the analysis with the reentry date being the new date at which the individual becomes at risk for leaving, but Tij represents total months in science from time of graduation with highest science degree.

CHAPTER 3

A. Table 3.1

Fixed effect regression analyses were run on the pooled cross-section of individuals from the national data who were working in science in 1982 and who responded to the national survey in subsequent years. The number of observations on any individual could range from two to four. Only natural scientists and engineers were included in the analysis, and all analyses were separated by gender. The dependent variable is the logarithm of annual salary; independent variables include: calendar year; years of experience; years of experience squared; and dummy variables for nonprofit organizations; government organizations; level of degree; part-time work; married; divorced or widowed; managers; and parents with children under five years of age. The variable of interest for the analysis is a dummy representing employment outside of science. This variable is also interacted with a dummy representing reason for departure to determine whether salary on exit differs by reason for exit. Fixed-effect regression analysis controls for fixed traits of the individual and estimates within-person changes in salary as opposed to across-person differences in salary.

B. Figure 3.1

The graphs are created from ordinary least squares (OLS) regression analysis of the logarithm of annual salary on a sample of respondents to the university survey who spent their full work-life either in science or out of science. Dummy variables are included for working in science, having a postscience medical degree, having a postscience law degree, and having a postscience business degree. Coefficients on these variables determine the vertical axis intercepts for the figures; the difference in salaries for the five different groups (those in science, those outside of science without a postscience degree, and those outside of science with one of the three postscience degrees) at time of labor market entry. Variables representing months of experience and months of experience squared for each group are also included in the analysis to allow for differences in curvatures of salary profiles (table A.1). Con-

Table A.1   *Relevant Coefficients for Ordinary Least Squares Estimates of Salary Equations on University Data— Sample of Career Scientists and Career Nonscientists (Figure 3.1)*

Variable	Men	Women
Working in science	0.090***	0.103***
	(0.028)	(0.026)
Months of experience in science	0.005***	0.005***
	(0.0005)	(0.0006)
Months of experience in science squared	−0.00001***	−0.00002***
	1.83 e-06	2.67 e-06
Months of experience outside of science	0.005***	0.005***
	(0.0007)	(0.0006)
Months of experience outside of science squared	−0.00001***	−9.18 e-06***
	3.21 e-06	(2.24 e-06)
Months of experience outside of science—professional degree	0.0019***	0.0008*
	(0.0005)	(0.0005)
Postscience medical degree	0.464***	0.580***
	(0.040)	(0.039)
Postscience law degree	0.305***	0.296***
	(0.056)	(0.099)
Postscience M.B.A.	0.085*	−0.0066
	(0.050)	(0.083)
Postscience master's	0.057	0.038
	(0.043)	(0.036)
Postscience Ph.D.	−0.196	−0.032
	(0.200)	(0.087)
Master's in science	0.146***	0.095***
	(0.024)	(0.022)
Ph.D. in science	0.101***	0.128***
	(0.027)	(0.028)
Adjusted R squared	0.664	0.564
Sample size (person-observations)	2,175	2,763

Source: Author's compilation.
***Coefficient is significantly different from zero at the 0.01 level using a two-tailed test.
*Coefficient is significantly different from zero at the 0.10 level using a two-tailed test.

trol variables include year of observation, months at current job, months out of the labor force since graduation, percentage of chores and childcare responsibilities taken on, and dummy variables for self-employment, nonprofit employer, government employer, new job, full-time employment, management position, last activity out of the labor market, marital status, and children.

Hypothesis testing revealed that there were no significant differences in the experience profiles of doctors, lawyers, and M.B.A. recipients, so the professional experience variable holds for all three professional groups. While the figure does not include lines for postscience master's degree recipients or postscience Ph.D. recipients, these individuals fare no better in terms of salaries than those who invest in no postscience degree. In addition, having a Ph.D. in science or a master's in science has positive effects on salaries.

C. Figures 3.2 and 3.3

In order to compare salary profiles of science stayers (SP_{sci}) to salary profiles of science leavers ($SP_{sci-nsci}$) fixed effects are used to estimate:

$$
\begin{aligned}
Ln(salary_{it}) = {}& a + b(ED_{it}) + c0(EXP(science)_{it}) + c1(EXP(oosci)_{it}) \\
& + d0(OOSCI_{it} \times amenity_{it}) + d1(OOSCI_{it} \times seekinc_{it}) \\
& + d2\,(OOSCI_{it} \times EXP(science)_{it} \times amenity_{it}) \\
& + d3(OOSCI_{it} \times EXP(science)_{it} \times seekinc_{it}) \\
& + f\,(controls_{it}) + e_{it}
\end{aligned}
\qquad (A.1)
$$

EXP(science) and EXP(oosci) represent months in science and non-science occupations respectively. OOSCI is a dummy variable equal to one if the individual is working outside of science, seekinc is a dummy variable equal to one if the individual left science to seek income, and amenity is a dummy variable equal to one if the individual left science in search of better amenities.

The average earnings effect of leaving science at time of exit for amenity seekers is $(d0 + d2 \times \overline{EXP}(science))$, and the earnings effect for income seekers is $(d1 + d3 \times \overline{EXP}(science))$. Where $\overline{EXP}$ is average experience at exit, these estimates become the salary shifts in figures

3.3A and 3.3B at time of exit. The estimated coefficients d2 and d3 can be used to calculate estimates of the extent of skill transferability to new occupations for income seekers and amenity seekers—how valuable science experience is in the new nonscience job. Earnings growth in science and out of science can be compared by comparing the magnitudes of c0 and c1. Figures 3.2A and 3.2B display the results of a simplified version of equation A.1, where leavers are not separated into amenity and income seekers. Therefore, the estimated equation behind figures 3.2A and 3.2B is:

$$
\begin{aligned}
\mathrm{Ln(salary}_{it}) = {} & a + b(\mathrm{ED}_{it}) + c0(\mathrm{EXP(science)}_{it}) + c1(\mathrm{EXP(oosci)}_{it}) \\
& + d0(\mathrm{OOSCI}_{it}) + d1(\mathrm{OOSCI}_{it} \times \mathrm{EXP(science)}_{it}) \\
& + f(\mathrm{controls}_{it}) \\
& + e_{it}
\end{aligned}
\tag{A.2}
$$

Controls for both equations include year of observation, percentage of childcare and household responsibilities, months on current job, months out of the labor force, and dummy variables for: previous activity out of the labor force; nonprofit status of employer; government status of employer; self-employment; full-time status; marital and family status; starting a new job; and having a managerial job. Results from equation A.1 are presented in table A.2.

Construction of the figures requires knowledge of differences in salaries between leavers and stayers while in science and median duration of time in science. Differences in salaries are estimated using OLS salary regressions on individuals working in science and then estimating residuals for those who leave. The results are presented in table A.3.

D. Salary Profiles of Leavers Versus Career Nonscientists

In comparing salary profiles of leavers ($\mathrm{SP}_{sci\text{-}nsci}$) and salary profiles of those who never worked in science (SP_{nsci}), it becomes most important to compare the salary profile before exit for those who leave the science occupation to the salary profile over the same period for those who never entered science. Therefore, the sample is restricted to science

Table A.2   Relevant Coefficients for Fixed-Effect Estimates of
Salary Equations on University Data—Sample of
Scientifically Educated Workers Who Start Science
Careers (Figure 3.3)

Variable	Men	Women
Out of science × amenity seeker	0.219**	0.087*
	(0.067)	(0.048)
Out of science × income seeker	0.122*	0.228***
	(0.070)	(0.081)
Out of science × months in science	−0.006***	−0.002**
× amenity seeker	(0.002)	(0.001)
Out of science × months in science	−0.002*	-0.004
× income seeker	(0.001)	(0.002)
Months in science	0.011***	0.012***
	(0.003)	(0.002)
Months in science squared	−0.00001***	−0.00001***
	(0.0000)	(0.0000)
Months outside of science	0.0052*	0.0069***
	(0.0032)	(0.0024)
Months outside of science squared	0.00002***	0.00002**
	(0.0000)	(0.0000)
Adjusted R squared	0.801	0.737
Sample size		
(person-observations)	1,597	2,039

Source: Author's compilation.
***Coefficient is significantly different from zero at .01 level using two-tailed test.
**Coefficient is significantly different from zero at .05 level using two-tailed test.
*Coefficient is significantly different from zero at .1 level using two-tailed test.

graduates who never enter science and to science graduates who start science careers but leave, thus excluding the science stayers. Fixed-effects estimation is not possible because the comparison is between early careers of different sets of people rather than before-after comparisons. During the early career years, the leavers are in science and those who never entered science are out of science, so a simple "in science" dummy variable gives us the earnings effect of this choice. Once out of science, experience profiles are similar, but the salary at entry to the nonscience occupation may be different than the salary of those with the same amount of experience who never worked in science.

Table A.3   Characteristics of Amenity Seekers and Income Seekers by Sex

	Male Amenity Seeker	Male Income Seeker	Female Amenity Seeker	Female Income Seeker
Median duration of time in science (in months)	43	20	39	20
Log salary residual in regressions run on workers in science	−0.1828 (p = 0.0)	0.0576 (p = 0.32)	−0.0722 (p = 0.0)	−0.0570 (p = 0.14)

Source: Author's compilation.
Note: Figure in parentheses is p value associated with testing the null hypothesis that the average residual for stayers is equal to the average residuals for leavers.

This difference may be related to experience in science. Therefore, OLS estimates of the following regressions are used to compare $SP_{sci\text{-}nsci}$ and SP_{nsci},

All leavers:

$$Ln(salary_{it}) = a + b(ED_{it}) + c0(EXP_{it}) + d0(INSCI_{it})$$
$$+ d2(OOSCIi_{it} \times EXP(science)_{it})$$
$$+ f(controls_{it}) + e_{it} \qquad (A.3)$$

Income-seeking and amenity-seeking leavers separated:

$$Ln(salary_{it}) = a + b(ED_{it}) + c0(EXP_{it}) + d0(INSCI_{it} \times amenity_{it})$$
$$+ d1(INSCI_{it} \times seekinc_{it})$$
$$+ d2(OOSCI_{it} \times EXP(science)_{it} \times amenity_{it})$$
$$+ d3(OOSCI_{it} \times EXP(science)_{it} \times seekinc_{it})$$
$$+ f(controls_{it}) + e_{it} \qquad (A.4)$$

INSCI is a dummy variable equal to one if the individual is working in science. Therefore, if leavers earn higher salaries in science early

Table A.4   *Relevant Coefficients for Ordinary Least Squares Estimates of Salary Equations on University Data: Sample of Science Leavers and Science Educated Who Never Enter Science*

Variable	Men	Women
In science × income-seeking leavers	0.1356***	0.0208
	(0.0549)	(0.0637)
In science × amenity-seeking leavers	−0.1091**	−0.0077
	(0.0436)	(0.0301)
Out of science × experience in science	0.0058**	0.0019
× income-seeking leavers	(0.0027)	(0.0033)
Out of science × experience in science	−0.00004***	−0.00004
× income-seeking leavers squared	(0.0029)	(0.00003)
Out of science × experience in science	0.0033	−0.0012
× amenity-seeking leavers	(0.0081)	(0.0024)
Out of science × experience in science	−0.0002**	−0.00004
× amenity-seeking leavers squared	(0.0001)	(0.00004)
Adjusted R squared	0.650	0.568
Sample size (person-observations)	576	1,152

Source: Author's compilation.
***Coefficient is significantly different from zero at the 0.01 level using a two-tailed test.
**Coefficient is significantly different from zero at the 0.05 level using a two-tailed test.

in their careers than they would have earned in nonscience occupations, $d0$ in equation A.3 will be greater than zero. If only income seekers earn higher salaries in science early in their careers than they would have earned in nonscience occupations, $d1$ in equation A.4 will be greater than zero, while $d0$ will be less than or equal to zero. If having been in science puts leavers at an advantage over their peers who never entered science once they enter the nonscience occupations, $d2$ in equation A.3 and $d2$ and $d3$ in equation A.4 will be greater than zero. Controls are those included in the analysis for figures 3.2 and 3.3. The relevant results from equation A.4 are presented in table A.4.

CHAPTER 4

A. Table 4.2

In order to estimate the probability of working in a science job, assume a latent variable Insci $\times_{it}$, which gives individual i's preferences for a science job at time t. Although the latent variable is unobservable, orientation of job, $INSCI_{it}$, is observable.

> If Insci $\times_{it} \geq Insci_{threshold}$, $INSCI_{it} = 1$, and individual 1 works in a science job at time t.
>
> If Insci $\times_{it} < Insci_{threshold}$, $INSCI_{it} = 0$, and individual 1 works in a nonscience job at time t.

Assuming $Insci_{it}$ follows a normal distribution and is determined by a vector of explanatory variables X, probit analysis is used to estimate the coefficients B relating X to the latent variable. The vector of explanatory variables include months of experience in science, months of experience outside of science, months out of the labor force for reasons other than school, months out of the labor force for nonscience schooling, and dummy variables for marriage and children. Results of the probit analysis explaining the zero-one variable, work in science, are presented in table A.5.

B. Figure 4.1

To determine the effects of children and childcare on salary profiles, fixed effects are used to estimate the following earnings equation:

$$Ln(salary_{it}) = a + b(Children_{it}) + c(Daycare_{it}) + d(Exp_{it} (single))$$
$$+ e(Exp_{it}(married)) + f(Exp_{it}(parent))$$
$$+ g(Daycare_{it} \times Exp_{it}(parent)) + f(controls_{it}) + e_{it} (A.5)$$

$Children_{it}$ is a dummy variable equal to one if individual i has children in time t and $Daycare_i$ is the percentage of childcare of preschool children individual i is responsible. Three work experience variables include

Table A.5 *Probit Estimates of the Probability of Working in Science—University Data: Table 4.2*

	Women with Ph.D.s	Women Without Ph.D.s	Men with Ph.D.s	Men Without Ph.D.s
Months of science experience	0.004***	0.003***	0.003***	0.003***
	(0.000)	(0.000)	(0.000)	(0.000)
Months of non- science experience	−0.018***	−0.004***	−0.002**	−0.004***
	(0.000)	(0.000)	(0.038)	(0.000)
Months out of labor force— nonscience education	—	−0.010***	−0.017**	−0.003***
		(0.000)	(0.020)	(0.000)
Months out of labor force— other reasons	−0.003*	−0.005***	−0.012***	−0.005***
	(0.051)	(0.000)	(0.000)	(0.000)
Married	−0.108**	0.019	0.120**	0.020
	(0.011)	(0.348)	(0.014)	(0.421)
Children	−0.016	−0.172***	−0.034	−0.011
	(0.728)	(0.000)	(0.475)	(0.711)
Log of likelihood function	−333.28	−2246.03	−295.37	−1433.42
Sample size (person- observations)	626	3,664	596	2,459

Source: Author's compilation.
Note: Coefficients have been translated to $\partial F/\partial x$, where F is the probability of working in science, and p values are given in parentheses.
***Coefficient is significantly different from zero at the 0.01 level using a two-tailed test.
**Coefficient is significantly different from zero at the 0.05 level using a two-tailed test.
*Coefficient is significantly different from zero at the 0.10 level using a two-tailed test.

months of work experience while single ($EXP_{it}(single)$), months of experience while married but childless ($EXP_{it}(married)$), and months of experience with children ($EXP_{it}(parent)$). Controls include human capital characteristics: dummy variables representing highest degree (master's, master's in science, medical degree, Ph.D., and Ph.D. in science) and months at current job; job characteristics that include dummy variables for whether the job is a new job, whether the job involves science and engineering, whether the main work activity is management, and whether the job involves full-time work; and year of observation.

The effect of having children on salary levels is given by $b + c$(percentage of daycare). The returns to a month of experience while a parent is $f + g$(percentage of daycare). As a result, salary profiles can be created for individuals with different levels of childcare responsibility. Relevant coefficients for the fixed-effect equations are presented in table A.6.

Table A.6   Fixed-Effect Estimates of the Effects of Children and Share of Childcare Responsibilities on Salary Profiles—University Data: Figure 4.1

Variable	Men	Women
Children	0.1151***	0.1102**
	(0.0435)	(0.0583)
Percentage of childcare	−0.3954**	−0.1530*
	(0.1810)	(0.0915)
Months of experience, single	0.0080***	0.0080***
	(0.0003)	(0.0003)
Months of experience, married	0.0078***	0.0079***
	(0.0005)	(0.0004)
Months of experience, children	0.0075***	0.0083***
	(0.0004)	(0.0007)
Percentage of childcare × months of experience, children	−0.0010	−0.0032***
	(0.0014)	(0.0010)
Adjusted R squared	0.779	0.731
Sample size (person-observations)	2,857	3,870

Source: Author's compilation.
***Coefficient is significantly different from zero at the 0.01 level using a two-tailed test.
**Coefficient is significantly different from zero at the 0.05 level using a two-tailed test.
*Coefficient is significantly different from zero at the 0.10 level using a two-tailed test.

CHAPTER 7

To test whether temporary departures from science have salary implications that vary with the rate at which knowledge is changing within a field, the following log salary equation is estimated for the sample of men and women working full time in science.

$$\text{Ln(Salary}_{it}) = a + b(\text{Months}_{it}) + c(\text{Months}_{it} \times \text{Dep}_i) + d(\text{controls}_{it}) + e_{it} \tag{A.7}$$

Because of the possibility that there are human capital restoration effects that will mask the effects of temporary exit long in the past, the focus of the analysis is on the salary effects of returning from a temporary exit from science immediately preceding the current science activity. Months_{it} represents months that individual i spent out of the labor force immediately prior to activity at time t, and is equal to zero for those individuals who did not exit the labor force. Months out of the labor force is also interacted with the average citing half-life of the individual's field for the period of absence, DEP_i. Therefore, the monthly salary penalty for exit is $b + c(\text{DEP})$. The coefficient b on the months variable should be negative since real salary should decline with a loss in skills. If the theoretical predictions hold, c, the coefficient on the interaction term, should be positive as the penalty for exit is lower in fields that have lower skill depreciation (higher citing half-life).

Controls include variables measuring months of experience in science, months of science experience squared, total months of time out of the labor force prior to last period, total months out of science prior to last period, year of observation, share of responsibility in home chores if married, share of responsibility in childcare if a parent, and dummy variables representing level of degree, marital status, children, manager, and a new job. In order to determine whether there is a restoration effect, a variable measuring months of tenure at the job immediately following a temporary exit is included. The wage equations are estimated for men and women using fixed effects to control for any selectivity bias on the coefficients measuring returns to the nonscience activities in the case that people who leave science work are systematically different from those who stay. In addition, fixed-effects estimation allows us to make comparisons of salary before exit to salary after exit since the within-person variation in earnings and status of last activity identifies the returns to nonscience activity coefficients. Because a vast majority of temporary labor-force departures are short and the few outliers corresponding to lengthy temporary departures may bias the results, the equations are first estimated with departures under a year in duration (76 percent of all departures) and then with departures under twenty-four months in duration (93 percent of all departures). The results are presented in table A.7.

B. Results from Competing Hazards Analysis

Competing hazard analyses were used to determine how changing rates of skill depreciation in a field influence decisions to leave science temporarily or permanently. These procedures estimate the probability

Table A.7   *Salary Effects of Temporary Labor Force Exit Figure 7.1—University Data*

	Spell of Nonwork Is Less Than or Equal to Twelve Months		Spell of Nonwork Is Less Than or Equal to Twenty-four Months	
	(1) Men	(2) Women	(3) Men	(4) Women
Months out of the labor force	−0.0545*** (0.0178)	−0.0529*** (0.0179)	−0.0301** (0.0131)	−0.0244* (0.0126)
Citing half-life × months out of labor force	0.0066** (0.0026)	0.0069*** (0.0025)	0.0030 (0.0021)	0.0041* (0.0017)
Sample size	1,403	1,599	1,403	1,599

Source: Author's compilation.
*Significantly different from zero at the 0.10 level using a two-tailed test.
**Significantly different from zero at the 0.05 level using a two-tailed test.
***Significantly different from zero at the 0.01 level using a two-tailed test.

Table A.8   *Determinants of Temporary and Permanent Exit from Science: Estimates from Hazard Analysis— University Data*

	Temporary Exit		Permanent Exit	
	Men	Women	Men	Women
Half-life at time of graduation	−0.028 (0.118)	−0.001 (0.079)	—	—
Half-life at time of exit	—	—	−0.024 (0.084)	0.089 (0.058)
Increase in half-life	21.43** (9.78)	27.13*** (5.16)	4.91 (12.51)	25.51*** (5.72)
Decrease in half-life	13.04 (12.06)	11.45 (7.48)	24.97*** (7.51)	24.41*** (4.85)
Experience outside of science	−0.091** (0.045)	−0.010 (0.009)	0.003 (0.005)	−0.007 (0.005)
Ph.D. in science	−0.843*** (0.371)	−0.073 (0.281)	−1.669*** (0.533)	−1.372*** (0.389)
Master's in science	−0.326 (0.369)	−0.346 (0.254)	−0.599* (0.331)	−0.880*** (0.208)
Nonprofit employer	0.874** (0.410)	0.320 (0.287)	0.950*** (0.369)	0.433** (0.224)
Government employer	0.092 (0.354)	0.050 (0.240)	−0.676* (0.399)	−0.052 (0.193)
Full-time	−0.858 (0.854)	−0.880** (0.348)	−0.634 (0.693)	−0.120 (0.358)
Married	−0.777 (0.732)	−1.370*** (0.483)	−0.140 (0.486)	−1.105*** (0.409)
Children	−1.089** (0.504)	−0.365 (0.487)	−1.017*** (0.396)	−0.890** (0.423)
Months out of labor force for family	—	−0.020 (0.016)	—	0.005 (0.006)
Months out of labor force for other reasons	−0.004 (0.021)	0.004 (0.011)	−0.002 (0.018)	0.006 (0.012)
Percentage of childcare taken on	2.020 (1.296)	0.012 (0.817)	1.550 (1.008)	0.911* (0.510)
Percentage of chores taken on	0.939 (1.408)	2.395*** (0.670)	−0.317 (0.995)	2.347*** (0.528)
Log of likelihood function	−583.809	−583.847	−344.411	−855.613
Sample size	883	948	898	1,002

Source: Author's compilation.
***Coefficient is significantly different from zero at the 0.01 level using a two-tailed test.
**Coefficient is significantly different from zero at the 0.05 level using a two-tailed test.
*Coefficient is significantly different from zero at the 0.10 level using a two-tailed test.

of temporary or permanent departure from science, conditional on surviving in science until the time of observation, and were described in detail in the section on chapter 2. The dependent variable is accumulated time in science, and control variables include months of experience outside of science, months out of the labor force, percentage of childcare taken on if a parent, percentage of household chores assumed if married, and dummy variables for level of degree, sector of employer, full-time status, married, and children.

The skill depreciation variables included are half-life at time of graduation, included in models predicting temporary exit, half-life at date preceding potential exit, included in models predicting permanent exit, and measures of average monthly change in half-life from time of graduation until the date preceding potential exit. First, a monthly change variable (CHANGE) is calculated as half-life at end of the science activity minus half-life at graduation divided by months of time between graduation and end of science activity. Then the change variable is divided into an increase in half-life (INCREASE) and a decrease in half-life (DECREASE) variable.

INCREASE = CHANGE   DECREASE = –CHANGE if
  if CHANGE > 0;   CHANGE < 0;
INCREASE = 0   DECREASE = 0 if
  if CHANGE < 0.   CHANGE = 0.

An increase in half-life corresponds to a reduction in skill depreciation, and a decrease in half-life corresponds to an increase in skill depreciation. The results of the competing hazard analysis are presented in table A.8.

NOTES

CHAPTER 1

1. All quotes in the book are from initial survey respondents who were subsequently interviewed.
2. An active alumnus is one whose address is on file with the alumni office. One in three of the active male alumni were surveyed, so that the same number of men and women were surveyed.
3. The response rate was higher for women (40 percent) than for men (30 percent).
4. Only fifty-one women were interviewed. The fifty-second woman had died between the time she filled out a survey and the time of the scheduled interview. This woman had a Ph.D. in physics, and because of the small number of women with Ph.D.s in physics, no similar woman could be found.
5. Because of the differing field distributions of men and women, where men are relatively overrepresented in engineering and women are relatively overrepresented in biological sciences, there are three pairs of men that have different subject areas than their female counterparts.

CHAPTER 2

1. More recently, the National Academy of Sciences and other professional societies have been very adamant that secondary-school teaching in science is an important application of science training.
2. In fact, not all of the original scientists and engineers responded to the 1989 survey. Exit rates are based on the members of the original group in 1982 who also responded to the 1989 survey.
3. Retirees at any point over the seven-year period were excluded from the sample so no individual exiting science was actually retiring. Also, any in-

dividual who left the labor force to go to school, regardless of degree, was labeled as a leaver.

4.   A maternity leave is not included as a labor-force exit unless the woman has explicitly defined the period as a period of nonwork and it lasted for more than three months.

5.   These numbers give the percentage of respondents working in a paying job outside of science at the time of the survey who have earned degrees in nonscience fields. In order to be classified as never entering science, the respondent must have zero years of experience in a science job.

6.   Physician-related healthcare careers might include nursing, medical technician, physical therapist, or nutritionist.

CHAPTER 3

1.   The technique used in this analysis and later analyses supporting figures 3.2 and 3.3 is first differencing regressions, which estimate within-person changes in salary as the individual moves from the science to the nonscience job. In the regressions on the NSF data, I include controls for years of experience, year, type of employing institution, whether the individual is academically employed, whether the individual is a manager, part-time status, and family characteristics.

2.   For presentation purposes, I chose not to represent salary profiles of men and women who get nonscience Ph.D. and master's degrees. Initial salaries for master's recipients are not significantly different, and initial salaries of nonscience Ph.D. recipients are lower than salaries of career nonscientists without a postscience degree. Salary growth is lower for these individuals, making these investments not particularly lucrative. Clearly, science graduates who earn nonscience Ph.D.s choose this route for the love of the field rather than for money.

3.   Empirically, I use two techniques to achieve figures 3.2 and 3.3. For all individuals working in science, I use ordinary least squares regression (OLS) to estimate salary differentials for those who eventually leave. This technique estimates difference in salary levels for the stayers and leavers. Then, using first differencing regression on a sample of workers who start their careers in science, I estimate experience profiles through changes in salaries with changes in months of experience and changes in sector of employment.

4.   I use information from table 2.3 concerning reasons for not working in science to define amenity seekers and income seekers. Individuals looking for pay, promotion, and career opportunities are listed as income seekers. Individuals who give alternative reasons for exit are amenity seekers. Two-thirds of the exiting men and one-third of the exiting women are classified as income seekers.

CHAPTER 4

1. When asked about maternity leave, many of the interviewed men responded that taking a paternity leave would not be a good career move and would signal a lack of job commitment.
2. For the population in general, the average age difference between husband and wife is between two and three years (Goldman and Lord 1983; Smith and Zick 1994).
3. There is always concern that individuals who take on high amounts of childcare are those who are less able in the labor market. However, statistical tests do not support this hypothesis. The percentage of childcare is not related to prechild earnings, and the first difference technique measures the within-person change in earnings over the period in which the child is born (Preston 2001).
4. These are only hypothetical percentages. In the data for men, 90 percent of the distribution is above 50 percent with a mode at 17 percent; there are a small number of male respondents who report taking on 100 percent of childcare. The distribution of childcare responsibilities is more spread out for women, with two modes at 100 percent and 50 percent. However, there are several women who report taking on zero percent of childcare.

CHAPTER 5

1. The success of the early employment situation is self-reported. But a successful early employment situation would be one where the scientist progresses in the job with increased knowledge, confidence, job responsibilities, and earnings. An unsuccessful employment experience is one that might end in firing or layoff, or one where the employee never gains the respect of colleagues and never contributes in a way that he or she feels is necessary.

CHAPTER 7

1. This difference in the slope of the wage profiles before and after administrative duties is contrary to Mincer and Ofek's (1982) finding that even though wages fall with periods of exit, postexit wage profiles are steeper than preexit wage profiles (at least temporarily) as women try to restore human capital.
2. CITE is the name given to the skill depreciation variable created for this study. Since it gives the average citing half-life of articles in a scientific subfield during a given year, lower values of CITE correspond to higher rates of knowledge growth and higher rates of skill depreciation.

3. The citing half-life for any journal is always truncated at ten years. However, there is only one instance in the data set when the field citing half-life, the weighted average of half-lives across five journals, is ten years: mathematics in 1990.

4. I have not included engineering fields in this table because the percentage of women in engineering is markedly below the percentage of women in other science occupations. However, chemical engineering, the field with the highest percentage of women, also had the highest rate of acceleration of knowledge growth over the period.

5. The duration of temporary exit from science to a job in a nonscience field is, on average, longer than temporary exit from the labor market. The mean duration is closer to two years than one.

6. In the regressions estimating effects of exit on earnings at reentry, the effects of exit on salary growth after reentry are also examined. Earnings growth after reentry does not differ by duration of exit or by rate of knowledge growth within the field.

7. These exit measures are less than previous estimates because they give the percentage of all jobs in science that end in an exit, either permanent or temporary, rather than the percentage of individuals who exit science.

8. This analysis allows more than one exit by an individual scientist. According to the construction of the data, the analysis uses observations that correspond to the end of an activity in science or to working at science at the survey date. Covariates are specific to the activity that is ending. Future activity, which can either be another job in science, permanent exit, temporary exit, or continuation in the current science job, determines the value of the exit variable. After a temporary exit from science, the individual returns to the analysis with the reentry date being the new date at which the individual becomes at risk for leaving. T_{ij} represents total months in science from time of graduation with highest science degree.

REFERENCES

Adams, James D., Grant C. Black, Roger Clemmons, and Paula E. Stephan. 2003. "Patterns of Research Collaboration in U.S. Universities, 1981–1999." Paper presented to the American Association for the Advancement of Science meeting. Denver (February 13–18, 2003).

Astin, Helen S. 1979. "Patterns of Women's Occupations." In *The Psychology of Women: Future Directions*, edited by Julia A. Sherman and Florence L. Denmark. New York: Psychological Dimensions.

———. 1991. "Citation Classics: Women's and Men's Perceptions of their Contributions to Science." In *The Outer Circle: Women in the Scientific Community*, edited by Harriet Zuckerman, Jonathan R. Cole, and John T. Bruer. New York: Norton Press.

Athey, Susan, Christopher Avery, and Peter Zemsky. 2000. "Mentoring and Diversity." *American Economic Review* 90(4): 765–86.

Bartel, Ann P., and Nachum Sicherman. 1993. "Technological Change and Retirement Decision of Older Workers." *Journal of Labor Economics* 11(1, part 1): 162–83.

Becker, Gary S. 1971. *The Economics of Discrimination.* 2nd ed. Chicago: University of Chicago Press.

———. 1985. "Human Capital, Effort, and the Sexual Division of Labor." *Journal of Labor Economics* 3(1, part 2): S33–S58.

———. 1993. *Human Capital: A Theoretical and Empirical Analysis, with Special Reference to Education.* 3rd ed. Chicago: University of Chicago Press.

Bergman, Barbara. 1974. "Occupational Segregation, Wages, and Profits When Employers Discriminate by Race or Sex." *Eastern Economics Journal* 1(1–2, April–July): 103–10.

Bielby, William T. 1991. "Sex Differences in Careers: Is Science a Special Case?" In *The Outer Circle: Women in the Scientific Community*, edited by Harriet Zuckerman, Jonathan R. Cole, and John T. Bruer. New York: Norton Press.

Biernat, Monica, and Camille Wortman. 1991. "Sharing of Home Responsibilities Between Professionally Employed Women and Their Husbands." *Journal of Personality and Social Psychology* 60(6): 844–60.

Blackburn, McKinley, and Sanders Korenman. 1994. "The Declining Marital Status Earnings Differential." *Journal of Population Economics* 7(3): 3249–70.

Blau, Francine, and Lawrence M. Kahn. 1997. "Swimming Upstream: Trends in the Gender Wage Differential in the 1980s." *Journal of Labor Economics* 15(1, part 1, January): 1–42.

Canes, Brandice J., and Harvey S. Rosen. 1995. "Following in Her Footsteps? Faculty Gender Composition and Women's Choices of College Majors." *Industrial and Labor Relations Review* 48(3): 486–504.

Cole, Jonathan R. 1979. *Fair Science: Women in the Scientific Community.* New York: The Free Press.

Cole, Jonathan R., and Burton Singer. 1991. "A Theory of Limited Differences: Explaining the Productivity Puzzle in Science." In *The Outer Circle: Women in the Scientific Community*, edited by Harriet Zuckerman, Jonathan R. Cole, and John T. Bruer. New York: Norton Press.

Cole, Jonathan.R., and Harriet Zuckerman. 1984. "The Productivity Puzzle: Persistence and Change in Patterns of Publication Among Men and Women Scientists." In *Advances in Motivation and Achievement*, edited by Martin L. Maehr and Marjorie W. Steinkamp. Greenwich, Conn.: JAI.

———. 1987. "Marriage, Motherhood and Research Performance in Science." *Scientific American* 26(February): 119–25.

Cole, Stephen, and Robert Fiorentine. 1991. "Discrimination Against Women in Science: The Confusion of Outcome with Process." In *The Outer Circle: Women in the Scientific Community*, edited by Harriet Zuckerman, Jonathan R. Cole, and John T. Bruer. New York: Norton Press.

Coverman, Shelley. 1983. "Gender, Domestic Labor Time, and Wage Inequality." *American Sociological Review* 48(5, October): 623–37.

Division of Science Resource Statistics, National Science Foundation. 1999. *Scientists and Engineers Statistical Data System (SESTAT) Public Use File, 1993–1999.* North Arlington, Va.: National Science Foundation.

Eagly, Alice H. 1995. "The Science and Politics of Comparing Women and Men." *American Psychologist* 50(1): 145–58.

Farber, Henry. 1994. "The Analysis of Inter-firm Worker Mobility." *Journal of Labor Economics* 12(4): 554–93.

Fidell, L. S. 1970. "Empirical Verification of Sex Discrimination in Hiring Practices in Psychology." *American Psychologist* 25(12): 1094–98.

Fox, Mary F. 1991. "Gender, Environmental Milieu, and Productivity in Science." In *The Outer Circle: Women in the Scientific Community*, edited by Harriet Zuckerman, Jonathan R. Cole, and John T. Bruer. New York: Norton Press.

———. 1996. "Women, Academia, and Careers in Science and Engineering." In *The Equity Equation: Women in Science, Engineering, and Mathematics*, edited by Cinda-Sue Davis, Angela B. Ginorio, Carol S. Hollenshead, Barbara B. Lazarus, and Paula M. Rayman. San Francisco: Jossey-Bass.

Freeman, Richard B., Eric Weinstein, Elizabeth Marincola, Janet Rosenbaum, and Frank Solomon. 2001. "Careers and Rewards in Bio Sciences:

The Disconnect Between Scientific Progress and Career Progression." Working paper presented to the Sloan Scientific Workforce Meeting. Cambridge, Mass. (January 24–25, 2002).

Gibbons, Ann. 1992. "Key Issue: Mentoring." *Science* 255(5050): 1368–69.

Goldin, Claudia. 1990. *Understanding the Gender Gap: An Economic History of American Women.* New York: Oxford University Press.

———. 1997. "Career and Family: College Women Look to the Past." In *Gender and Family Issues in the Workplace,* edited by Francine D. Blau and Ronald G. Ehrenberg. New York: Russell Sage Foundation.

Goldin, Claudia, and Cecilia Rouse. 2000. "Orchestrating Impartiality: The Impact of Blind Auditions on Female Musicians." *American Economic Review* 90(4): 715–41.

Goldman, Noreen, and Graham Lord. 1983. "Sex Differences in Life Cycle of Widowhood." *Demography* 20(2): 177–95.

Gray, Jeffrey S. 1997. "The Fall in Men's Return to Marriage." *Journal of Human Resources* 32(3): 481–504.

Helmreich, Robert L., Janet T. Spence, William E. Beane, G. William Lucker, and Karen A. Matthews. 1980. "Making It in Academic Psychology: Demographic and Personality Correlates of Attainment." *Journal of Personality and Social Psychology* 39(5): 896–908.

Hersch, Joni. 1991. "The Impact of Non-market Work on Market Wages." *American Economic Associations Papers and Proceedings* 81(2, May): 157–60.

Hersch, Joni, and Leslie S. Stratton. 1997. "Housework, Fixed Effects and Wages of Married Workers." *Journal of Human Resources* 32(2): 285–307.

Hornig, Lilli S. 1987. "Women Graduate Students." In *Women: Their Underrepresentation and Career Differentials in Science and Engineering,* edited by Linda S. Dix. Washington, D.C.: National Research Council.

Institute for Scientific Information. 1975–1992. *Science Citation Index Journal Citation Reports.* Philadelphia: Institute for Scientific Information.

Jacobs, Jerry. 1987. "The Sex Typing of Aspirations and Occupations: Instability During the Careers of Young Women." *Social Science Quarterly* 68: 122–37.

Jovanovic, Boyan. 1979. "Job Matching and the Theory of Turnover." *Journal of Political Economy* 87(5, part 1, October): 972–90.

Jovanovic, Boyan, and Robert Moffitt. 1990. "An Estimate of a Sectoral Model of Labor Mobility." *Journal of Political Economy* 98(4, August): 827–51.

Kahn, Shulamit. 1995. "Women in the Economics Profession." *Journal of Economic Perspectives* 9(4, Fall): 193–206.

Keller, Evelyn Fox. 1991. "The Wo/Man Scientist: Issues of Sex and Gender in the Pursuit of Science." In *The Outer Circle: Women in the Scientific Community,* edited by Harriet Zuckerman, Jonathan R. Cole, and John T. Bruer. New York: Norton Press.

Kilbourne, Barbara, Paula England, and Kurt Beron. 1994. "Effects of Individual, Industrial and Occupational Characteristics on Earnings, Intersections of Race and Gender." *Social Forces* 72(4, June): 1149–76.

Killingsworth, Mark. 1985. "The Economics of Comparable Worth: Analytical, Empirical, and Policy Questions." In *Comparable Worth: New Directions for Research*, edited by Heidi L. Hartmann. Washington, D.C.: National Academy Press.

Korenman, Sanders, and David Neumark. 1992. "Marriage, Motherhood, and Wages." *Journal of Human Resources* 27(2): 233–55.

Landers, Renee M., James B. Rebitzer, and Lowell J. Taylor. 1997. "Work Norms and Professional Labor Markets." In *Gender and Family Issues in the Workplace*, edited by Francine D. Blau and Ronald G. Ehrenberg. New York: Russell Sage Foundation.

Levin, Sharon, and Paula Stephan. 1999. "Are the Foreign Born a Source of Strength for U.S. Science?" *Science* 285(5431, August): 1213–14.

Long, J. Scott. 1978. "Productivity and Academic Position in the Scientific Career." *American Sociological Review* 43(6, December): 889–908.

———. 1990. "The Origins of Sex Differences in Science." *Sociological Forces* 68(4): 1297–1315.

———. 1992. "Measures of Sex Differences in Science Productivity." *Social Forces* 71(1): 159–78.

———, ed. 2001. *From Scarcity to Visibility: Gender Differences in the Careers of Doctoral Scientists and Engineers*. Washington, D.C.: National Academy Press.

Long, J. Scott, Paul D. Allison, and Robert McGinnis. 1979. "Entrance into the Academic Career." *American Sociological Review* 44(5): 816–30.

———. 1993. "Rank Advancement in Academic Careers: Sex Differences and the Effects of Productivity." *American Sociological Review* 58(5): 703–22.

Long, J. Scott, and Mary Frank Fox. 1995. "Scientific Careers: Universalism and Particularism." *Annual Review of Sociology* 21: 45–71.

Long, J. Scott, and Robert McGinnis. 1985. "The Effects of the Mentor on the Academic Career." *Scientometrics* 7(3–6): 255–80.

MacRae, Duncan, Jr. 1969. "Growth and Decay Curves in Scientific Citations. *American Sociological Review* 34(5, October): 631–35.

Mandel, George H. 1995. "Funding of NIH Grant Applications: Update (in Letters)." *Science* 269(5220, July): 13–14.

Marincola, Elizabeth, and Frank Solomon. 1998. "The Career Structure in Bio-Medical Research: Implications for Training and Trainees/ *The American Society for Cell Biology Survey on the State of the Profession*." *Molecular Biology of the Cell* 9(11): 3003–6.

Markey, James P., and William Parks II. 1989. "Occupational Change: Pursuing a Different Kind of Work." *Monthly Labor Review* 112(9, September): 3–12.

Marwell, Gerald R., Rachel A. Rosenfeld, and Seymour Spilerman. 1979. "Geographic Constraints on Women's Careers in Academia." *Science* 205(21, September): 1225–31.

McDowell, John M. 1982. "Obsolescence of Knowledge and Career Publication Profiles: Some Evidence of Difference among Fields in Costs of Interrupted Careers." *American Economic Review* 72(4): 752–68.

McIlwee, Judith Sampson, and J. Gregg Robinson. 1992. *Women in Engineering: Gender, Power, and Workplace Culture.* Albany: State University of New York Press.

Mincer, Jacob. 1962. "On-the-Job Training: Costs, Returns, and Some Implications." *Journal of Political Economy* 70(5, part 2): S50–S79.

Mincer, Jacob, and Haim Ofek. 1982. "Interrupted Work Careers: Depreciation and Restoration of Human Capital." *Journal of Human Resources* 17(1): 3–24.

National Science Board. 2002. *Science and Engineering Indicators.* Washington: U.S. Government Printing Office.

Neumark, David, Roy J. Blank, and Kyle D. Van Nort. 1996. "Sex Discrimination in Restaurant Hiring: An Audit Study." *Quarterly Journal of Economics* 111(3): 915–42.

Neumark, David, and Rosella Gardecki. 1998. "Women Helping Women: Role Models and Mentoring Effects on Female Ph.D. Students in Economics." *Journal of Human Resources* 3(1): 220–27.

Phelps, Edmund S. 1972. "The Statistical Theory of Racism and Sexism." *American Economic Review* 61(4): 659–61.

Preston, Anne E. 1994. "Why Have All the Women Gone? A Study of Exit of Women from the Science and Engineering Professions." *American Economic Review* 84(5, December): 1446.

———. 2001. "Sex, Kids, and Commitment to the Workplace: Employers, Employees and the Mommy Track." Working paper. Haverford, Penn.: Haverford College.

Price, Derek deSolla. 1965. "Networks of Scientific Papers." *Science* 149 (3683, July): 510–15.

———. 1970. "Citation Measures of Hard Science, Soft Science, Technology and Non-science." In *Communication Among Scientists and Engineers*, edited by Carnot E. Nelson and Donald K. Pollack. Lexington, Mass.: D.C. Heath.

Ragan, James F., Jr., and Qazi Najeeb Rehman. 1996. "Earnings Profiles of Department Heads: Comparing Cross-Section and Panel Models." *Industrial and Labor Relations Review* 49(2, January): 256–72.

Reskin, Barbara. 1978. "Sex Differentiation and the Social Organization of Science." *Sociological Inquiry* 48(3–4): 6–37.

———. 1979. "Academic Sponsorship and Scientists' Careers." *Sociology of Education* 52(3): 129–46.

Reskin, Barbara F., and Heidi L. Hartmann, editors. 1986. *Women's Work, Men's Work: Sex Segregation on the Job.* Washington, D.C.: National Academy Press.

Rose, Suzanna M. 1985. "Professional Networks of Junior Faculty in Psychology." *Psychology of Women Quarterly* 9(4): 533–47.

Rosen, Sherwin. 1975. "Knowledge Obsolescence and Income." In *Education,*

Income, and Human Behavior, edited by F. Thomas Juster. Cambridge, Mass.: National Bureau of Economic Research.

Schultz, Theodore W. 1960. "Investment in Human Capital." *American Economic Review* 51(1): 1–17.

Shaw, Kathryn L. 1987. "Occupational Change, Employer Change, and the Transferability of Skills." *Southern Economic Journal* 53(3): 702–19.

Shelton, Beth Anne, and Juanita Firestone. 1988. "An Examination of Household Labor Time as a Factor in Composition and Treatment Effects on the Male-Female Wage Gap." *Sociological Focus* 21(3, August): 265–78.

Smith, Ken R., and Cathleen D. Zick. 1994. "Linked Lives, Dependent Demise? Survival Analysis of Husbands and Wives." *Demography* 31(1): 81–93.

Spurr, Stephen J. 1990. "Sex Discrimination in the Legal Profession: A Study of Promotion." *Industrial and Labor Relations Review* 43(4, April): 406.

Topel, Robert H., and Michael P. Ward. 1992. "Job Mobility and the Careers of Young Men. *The Quarterly Journal of Economics* 107(2, May): 439–79.

U.S. Bureau of the Census, Department of Commerce. *Survey of Natural and Social Scientists and Engineers, 1982–1989.* Washington: U.S. Government Printing Office.

U.S. Department of Education, National Center for Education Statistics (NCES). 2002. *Digest of Education Statistics, 2001.* NCES 2002–130. Washington: U.S. Department of Education. Available at http://nces.ed.gov/pubs2002/2002130.pdf (accessed January 9, 2004).

Waldfogel, Jane. 1997. "The Effects of Children on Women's Wages." *American Sociological Review* 62(2): 209–17.

———. 1998. "The Family Gap for Young Women in the United States and Britain: Can Maternity Leave Make a Difference?" *Journal of Labor Economics* 16(3): 505–45.

Wood, Robert G., Mary E. Corcoran, and Paul N. Courant. 1993. "Pay Differences Among the Highly Paid: The Male-Female Earnings Gap in Lawyers' Salaries." *Journal of Labor Economics* 11(3): 417–44.

Zuckerman, Harriet. 1977. *Scientific Elite: Nobel Laureates in the United States.* New York: The Free Press.

INDEX

ACADEMIC AND PROFESSIONAL IDENTITIES IN HIGHER EDUCATION

The latest volume in the Routledge International Studies in Higher Education Series, *Academic and Professional Identities in Higher Education: The Challenges of a Diversifying Workforce*, reviews the implications of new forms of academic and professional identity, which have emerged largely as a result of a broadening disciplinary base and increasing permeability between higher education and external environments.

The volume addresses the challenges faced by those responsible for the well-being of academic faculty and professional staff. International perspectives examine current practice against a background of rapidly changing policy contexts, focusing on the critical "people dimension" of enhancing academic and professional activity, while also addressing national, socio-economic, and community agendas. Consideration is given to mainstream academic faculty and professional staff, researchers, library and information professionals, people with an interest in teaching and learning, and those involved in individual projects or institutional development.

The following provide the key themes of *Academic and Professional Identities in Higher Education: The Challenges of a Diversifying Workforce*:

- The implications of diversifying academic and professional identities for the functioning of higher education institutions and sectors.
- The pace and nature of such change in different institutional systems and environments.
- The challenges to institutional systems and structures from emergent identities and possible tensions, and how these might be addressed.
- The implications of blurring academic and professional identities, with a shift towards mixed or "blended" roles, for individual careers and institutional development.

Professor George Gordon was the founding Director of the Centre for Academic Practice at the University of Strathclyde. As Emeritus Professor, he retains an association with the Centre, and is currently Chair of the Society for Research into Higher Education.

Dr. Celia Whitchurch is Lecturer in Higher Education at the Centre for Higher Education Studies, Institute of Education, University of London.

International Studies in Higher Education
Series Editors:
David Palfreyman, OxCHEPS
Ted Tapper, OxCHEPS
Scott L. Thomas, Claremont Graduate University

The central purpose of this series of a projected dozen volumes is to see how different national and regional systems of higher education are responding to widely shared pressures for change. The most significant of these are rapid expansion; reducing public funding; the increasing influence of market and global forces; and the widespread political desire to integrate higher education more closely into the wider needs of society and, more especially, the demands of the economic structure. The series commenced with an international overview of structural change in systems of higher education. It has proceeded to examine on a global front the change process in terms of topics that are both traditional (for example, institutional management and system governance) and emerging (for example, the growing influence of international organizations and the blending of academic and professional roles). At its conclusion the series will have presented, through an international perspective, a composite overview of contemporary systems of higher education, along with the competing interpretations of the process of change.

Published titles:

Structuring Mass Higher Education
The Role of Elite Institutions
Edited by David Palfreyman and Ted Tapper

International Perspectives on the Governance of Higher Education
Alternative Frameworks for Coordination
Edited by Jeroen Huisman

International Organizations and Higher Education Policy
Thinking Globally, Acting Locally?
Edited by Roberta Malee Bassett and Alma Maldonado

Academic and Professional Identities in Higher Education
The Challenges of a Diversifying Workforce
Edited by George Gordon and Celia Whitchurch

Academic and Professional Identities in Higher Education

The Challenges of a Diversifying Workforce

Edited by
George Gordon
and Celia Whitchurch

Routledge
Taylor & Francis Group

NEW YORK AND LONDON

First published 2010
by Routledge
270 Madison Ave, New York, NY 10016

Simultaneously published in the UK
by Routledge
2 Park Square, Milton Park, Abingdon, Oxon OX14 4RN

Routledge is an imprint of the Taylor & Francis Group, an informa business

© 2010 Taylor & Francis

Typeset in Minion by
Keystroke, Tettenhall, Wolverhampton
Printed and bound in the United States of America on acid-free paper by
IBT Global

Library of Congress Cataloging-in-Publication Data
Academic and professional identities in higher education : the challenges
of a diversifying workforce / edited by George Gordon and Celia
Whitchurch.
p. cm. – (International studies in higher education)
Includes bibliographical references and index.
1. College teachers–Professional relationships–Cross-cultural studies.
2. Scholars–Professional relationships–Cross-cultural studies. 3. Group
identity–Cross-cultural studies. 4. Diversity in the workplace–Cross-cultural
studies. I. Gordon, George. II. Whitchurch, Celia.
LB1778.A2 2009
378.1'2–dc22
2009021904

ISBN 10: 0–415–99090–4 (hbk)
ISBN 10: 0–203–86525–1 (ebk)

ISBN 13: 978–0–415–99090–5 (hbk)
ISBN 13: 978–0–203–86525–5 (ebk)

Contents

Illustrations

Annexes

Boxes

Series Editors' Introduction

International Studies in Higher Education

This series is constructed around the premise that higher education systems are experiencing common pressures for fundamental change, reinforced by differing national and regional circumstances that also impact upon established institutional structures and procedures. There are four major dynamics for change that are of international significance:

1. Mass higher education is a universal phenomenon.
2. National systems find themselves located in an increasingly global marketplace that has particular significance for their more prestigious institutions.
3. Higher education institutions have acquired (or been obliged to acquire) a wider range of obligations, often under pressure from governments prepared to use state power to secure their policy goals.
4. The balance between the public and private financing of higher education has shifted—markedly in some cases—in favor of the latter.

Although higher education systems in all regions and nation-states face their own particular pressures for change, these are especially severe in some cases: the collapse of the established economic and political structures of the former Soviet Union along with Central and Eastern Europe, the political revolution in South Africa, the pressures for economic development in India and China, and demographic pressure in Latin America.

Each volume in the series examines how systems of higher education are responding to this new and demanding political and socio-economic environment. Although it is easy to overstate the uniqueness of the present situation, it is not an exaggeration to say that higher education is undergoing a fundamental shift in its character, and one that is truly international in scope. We are witnessing a major transition in the relationship of higher education to state and society. What makes the present circumstances particularly interesting is to see how different systems—a product of social, cultural, economic and political contexts that have interacted and evolved over time—respond in their own peculiar ways to the changing environment. There is no assumption that the pressures for change have set in motion the trend toward a converging model of higher education, but we do believe that in the present circumstances no understanding of 'the idea of the university' remains sacrosanct.

Although this is a series with an international focus, it is not expected that each individual volume should cover every national system of higher education. This would be an impossible task. While aiming for a broad range of case studies, with each volume addressing a particular theme, the focus is upon the most important and interesting examples of responses to the pressures for change. Most of the individual volumes bring together a range of comparative quantitative and qualitative information, but the primary aim of each volume is to present differing interpretations of critical developments in key aspects of the experience of higher education. The dominant overarching objective is to explore the conflict of ideas and the political struggles that inevitably surround any significant policy development in higher education.

It is expected that volume editors and their authors will adopt their own interpretations to explain the emerging patterns of development. There will be conflicting theoretical positions drawn from the multidisciplinary, and increasingly interdisciplinary, field of higher education research. Thus, we can expect in most volumes to find an intermarriage of approaches drawn from sociology, economics, history, political science, cultural studies, and the administrative sciences. However, while there are different approaches to understanding the process of change in higher education, each volume editor imposes a framework upon the volume inasmuch as chapter authors are required to address common issues and concerns.

This fourth volume in the series is edited by Professor George Gordon, who is widely recognized as one of the United Kingdom's most experienced practitioners in the enhancement of learning and teaching; and Dr. Celia Whitchurch, who, as a former university administrator and manager, has had a longstanding involvement with the development of professional staff. Their contribution is particularly timely in the context of turbulence in the world's economic systems, with implications for the careers, motivations, and morale of staff in universities. On the one hand, this situation brings greater uncertainty and instability for both institutions and individuals. On the other hand, there is already some evidence—and past recessions bear this out—that in difficult times more people turn to educational establishments to upgrade their qualifications and retrain, albeit this is likely to result in greater pressure on staff in coping with heavier workloads without commensurate additional resources.

Universities are often major local employers, if not *the* major employer in many regions, while also operating in global markets for talented groups of staff and students. As institutions seek to become employers of choice, comparability issues will arise in relation to, for instance, remuneration, facilities, location, and benefit packages, whether staff are recruited locally or internationally. At the same time, however, as key players both in the socioeconomic life of nations and as international trading partners, universities are likely to make a significant contribution to economic and social recovery.

While detail differs between and within higher education systems, the regulatory and policy background of higher education systems has also become more complex, particularly in respect of legislation relating to employee and employer rights and obligations, and equity issues around, for instance, disability, race, and gender. These external pressures are accompanied by changing staff profiles and new institutional dynamics, as distinctions blur between academic and professional activities and groupings. Furthermore, whereas 'management' was once something that was undertaken only by the most senior managers in relation to the majority of 'other' staff, many more people are now likely to have such responsibilities. As a result, new relationships are developing, both in the formal sense and in terms of the "lived environment" (Knight, 2005) of day-to-day interactions. However, these developments have not been well documented, in contrast with, for instance, broader issues around policy and governance. We therefore particularly welcome this volume, which gives some pointers as to movements and directions, continuity and change in developments associated with 'the people dimension'. We consider that it makes a significant and timely contribution to the wider debates in this series.

David Palfreyman
Director of OxCHEPS, New College, University of Oxford

Ted Tapper
Visiting Fellow, OxCHEPS, New College, University of Oxford and CHEMPAS, University of Southampton

Scott L. Thomas
Professor of Educational Studies, Claremont Graduate University, California

References

Knight, P. (2005) "The Contribution of University Human Resource Departments to the Professional Formation of University Teachers." Paper given at the OECD Conference on Trends in the Management of Human Resources, August 25–26, Paris.

Contributors

Editors

George Gordon was the founding Director of the Centre for Academic Practice at the University of Strathclyde in Glasgow. He retains a functioning association with the Centre and the University in the role of Research Professor, in addition to being an Emeritus Professor. He is presently Chair of the Society for Research into Higher Education. He has published widely on aspects of staffing, academic and professional development, leadership and management, and quality assurance and enhancement in higher education. He is a former head of an academic department, and a former Dean of Arts and Social Sciences.

Celia Whitchurch is Lecturer in Higher Education, Centre for Higher Education Studies, Institute of Education, University of London. During a career in university administration and management she was active in the development of professional staff, and was the founding Editor-in-Chief of the journal of the UK Association of University Administrators, *perspectives: policy and practice in higher education*. She has published widely on higher education management, staff development, and institutional policy and planning. Her current research interests include changing professional identities in higher education, the emergence of "blended" roles between professional and academic spheres of activity, and the implications of these changes for professional careers. Celia is currently an Editor of *Higher Education Quarterly*.

Authors

Judith M. Gappa has spent her career as a university administrator and faculty member. She is currently Professor Emerita at Purdue University. She has served as Director of Affirmative Action/Equal Opportunity at Utah State University (1975–1980), Associate Academic Vice President for Faculty at San Francisco State University (1980–1991), and Vice President for Human Relations at Purdue University (1991–1998). From 1998 to 2006 she was Professor of Higher Education Administration in the Department of Educational Studies at Purdue University. Her research and publications have covered equity and faculty employment issues in higher education. She has coauthored two books: *The Invisible Faculty* (Jossey-Bass, 1993), with David Leslie, and *Rethinking Faculty Work: Higher Education's Strategic Imperative* (John Wiley, 2007), with Ann Austin and Andrea Trice.

Mary Henkel is Professor Associate in Politics and History at Brunel University. She has been active, nationally and internationally, in higher education, science policy, and evaluation studies for the past twenty years. Her principal research interests are in the implications of such policies for academic work, academic values, and academic identities. Her main publication in this field is *Academic Identities and Policy Change in Higher Education* (Jessica Kingsley, 2000).

Derek Law has worked in several British universities and has published and lectured extensively. Most of his work has been on the development of networked resources in higher education, and the creation of national information policy. Recently he has worked on the use of technology in developing new methods of teaching and learning. This has been combined with an active professional life in organizations related to librarianship and computing. A committed internationalist, he has been involved in projects and research in over forty countries. He was awarded the Barnard Prize for Contributions to Medical Informatics in 1993, Fellowship of the Royal Society of Edinburgh in 1999, an honorary degree by the Sorbonne in 2000, the International Federation of Library Associations and Institutions (IFLA) Medal in 2003, and Honorary Fellowship of the Chartered Institute of Library and Information Professionals (CILIP) in 2004.

Craig McInnis is Director of PhillipsKPA, consultants to the Australian and international higher education and vocational and training sectors. Prior to that, he was Professorial Fellow at the University of Melbourne and Professor and Director of the Centre for the Study of Higher Education. He has conducted a number of studies of the academic profession, including two national surveys funded by the Australian Research Council and the Commonwealth Government. His most recent projects include a national review of career development services in Australian tertiary education institutions, and a range of strategic reviews of university operations.

Robin Middlehurst is Professor of Higher Education at Kingston University, where she undertakes national and international research and consultancy projects, and contributes to postgraduate teaching and institutional research and development. From 2004 she has been seconded half-time to the UK Leadership Foundation for Higher Education as Director, Strategy, Research, and International. Here she is responsible for commissioning research on leadership, management and governance, and leadership development in higher education, and for developing the Foundation's international strategy. She also co-directs the United Kingdom's Top Management Programme for Higher Education and is a Council member of Roehampton University. Her research interests focus on leadership and governance in higher education, quality assurance and enhancement, and the internationalization of higher education. She is the author of multiple publications on leadership and management, including *Leading Academics* (SRHE/Open University Press, 1993).

Christine Musselin is Director of the Centre de Sociologie des Organisations, a research unit of Sciences Po and the CNRS. She leads comparative studies on university governance, public policies in higher education and research, state–university relationships, and academic labor markets. She has been Chair of the Consortium for Higher Education Research since 2007, and Chair of the Reseau d'Étude sur l'Enseignement Supérieur (RESUP), a French network on higher education research. She was a Deutsche Akademischer Austausch Dienst (DAAD) Fellow in 1984–1985 and a Fulbright and Harvard Fellow in 1998–1999. Recent publications include *The Long March of French Universities* (Routledge, 2004), *Le Marché des universitaires* (Presses de Sciences Po, 2005), and *Les Universitaires* (La Découverte, 2008).

Kingston Nyamapfene is former Deputy Vice-Chancellor at Vista University in South Africa, and is currently Dean of the Center for International Programs at the State University of New York's Empire State College, at Saratoga Springs, New York.

Jun Oba is Associate Professor of the Research Institute for Higher Education (RIHE), Hiroshima University, Japan. His current research centers around changing university governance and staff structures. Recent publications in journals include "Creating World-Class Universities in Japan: Policy and Initiatives," *Policy Futures in Education* 6 (5), 2008; "Developing Professional Staff in Universities under Quality Assurance Systems," *Higher Education Research in Japan* 5, 2008; and "Governance Reform of National Universities in Japan: Transition to Corporate Status and Challenges," *Journal of Comparative Asian Development* 6 (1), Spring 2007.

Gary Rhoades is currently General Secretary of the American Association of University Professors, on leave from the University of Arizona's Center for the Study of Higher Education, where he is a Professor of Higher Education and was Director from 1997 to 2008. His research focuses on the restructuring of higher education and of academic professions. His books are *Managed Professionals: Unionized Faculty and Restructuring Academic Labor* (SUNY Press, 1998) and *Academic Capitalism and the New Economy* (with Sheila Slaughter) (Johns Hopkins University Press, 2004).

Patricia Smit has an interest in leadership in higher education and is currently Head of Research Support at the University of Pretoria, South Africa. She previously worked for the Department of Education in the Higher Education Policy and Development Support Unit. Prior to that, she was engaged for some years in project management in higher education in South Africa and the UK (while completing her Ph.D).

Tony Strike is University Secretary at the University of Southampton, and an Honorary Research Fellow in the Centre for Higher Education Management and Policy at Southampton (CHEMPaS.) He is a co-opted member of the Higher Education Funding Council for England's Workforce Strategy Committee, and the Association of Commonwealth Universities Human Resource Management Network Committee. Formerly he was Director of Human Resources at

Portsmouth Hospitals NHS Trust, and then at the University of Southampton. Tony won a Fellowship from the UK Leadership Foundation for Higher Education in 2006 to research changing academic careers, and has been presenting on this topic internationally while pursuing a Ph.D.

Jane Usherwood has been Secretary General of Universitas 21, the international higher education network, since 2005. Universitas 21 currently has twenty-two members from thirteen different countries, five of whom have joined since 2005 to extend membership into Korea, Japan, India, Ireland, and Mexico. As Secretary General her role is to facilitate collaboration between members, identify strategic opportunities, oversee communications with external agencies, and act as corporate secretary. She was previously Director of Personnel Services at the University of Birmingham, and has worked in personnel in both the public and private sectors. A graduate of the University of Manchester (United Kingdom), Jane has also studied at universities in Münster (Germany) and Newcastle (United Kingdom).

Preface

Traditions of academic freedom, professional autonomy, and allegiance to disciplinary fields continue to characterize what it means to work in higher education. An extensive literature points to the survival of these values as being critical to the future of academic work. It might seem, therefore, that there is little space for another monograph. However, we would contend that while these values remain a vital theme, higher education systems worldwide are undergoing change, partly because of environmental pressures and partly because of the aspirations and approaches of new generations of staff. Not only is their central 'core' of academic faculty diversifying as a result of new entrants to the academy, for instance, from the health and social fields, but also, alongside them, a 'penumbra' of highly qualified professional staff is emerging, contributing in areas as diverse as teaching and learning, information services, institutional research and development, enterprise, and community partnership. The activities of all these groups increasingly overlap, with two-way traffic occurring between them, and this has implications for the identities of a range of staff.

We suggest that a wider lens on professional identities in higher education is further justified by the fact that 'people' responsibilities continue to ripple outwards and downwards in increasingly distributed institutional structures. Close partnerships arise, for instance, between heads of department and professional managers in trying to maximize opportunities for colleagues within what are often severe resource constraints. New responsibilities (which may be lateral, and between peers, as well as hierarchical) are also occurring at an earlier stage of people's careers. While it is a truism to say that staff are an institution's most valuable resource, we would suggest that the 'people dimension', comprising the relationships that are constructed between, for instance, senior management teams, managers such as deans and heads of academic and functional departments, and colleagues who work in mixed teams to contribute different forms of expertise to cross-institutional projects, will continue to be of paramount importance if institutions are to survive and prosper in current environments.

Those working in higher education, including ourselves, continue to feel that the institutions we work in are indeed 'special' and 'different'. While we may take cognizance of practices from other sectors, their wholesale application is unlikely to be appropriate. However, the not insignificant traffic of both academic faculty and professional staff between higher education and other sectors suggests that influences from elsewhere will continue to permeate. The way that such influences might be translated into a university context, and be used to facilitate and enhance the activities of academic faculty and the professional colleagues around them, is what we have tried to capture in this book.

George Gordon
Emeritus Professor, Centre for Academic Practice and Learning Enhancement, University of Strathclyde

Celia Whitchurch
Lecturer in Higher Education, Centre for Higher Education Studies, Institute of Education, University of London

Part I
Contexts and Concepts

1

Introduction
Change and Continuity in Academic and Professional Identities

MARY HENKEL

There has been no shortage of research or scholarly study of the almost seismic changes that have occurred in the world of higher education and academic research during the past forty years, changes in conceptions of these activities, in the institutions through which they are pursued, in their governance and administration, and in the political, economic, social, technological, and ideological contexts within which they work. The past twenty years have seen growing interest in the implications of these developments for academic faculty, the academic profession, academic careers, academic practices, and academic identities. Important as these are, they are, however, only one dimension of the changes that have occurred in the workforces of higher education institutions, the nature and scale of which have, as Gary Rhoades points out in Chapter 3, remained curiously invisible to both researchers and policymakers but also, in a sense, to the institutions themselves. There is evidence that individual researchers and international bodies in the early 1990s (Kogan et al., 1994) were aware of the needs for new policies and new policy frameworks for the staffing of higher education, but the frameworks have been slow to emerge (El-Khawas, 2008), and the primary concern has remained with academic faculty.

This book seeks to help redress that imbalance. The editors have brought together an international group of researchers, managers, and practitioners who between them have already made significant and, in some cases, groundbreaking contributions to the identification of trends in the workforces of higher education and the development of conceptual frameworks within which to analyze them.

The main task of this chapter is to set the context in which the diversification of higher education institutions has occurred during the past forty years, with a view to highlighting the scale, speed, and exponential nature of the changes and, more particularly, of the challenges they present to our understanding of the identities of those who work in higher education, who they are, how they define their professional selves, and from where they find a sense of meaning and worth.

Transformations in Higher Education and Its Contexts

For much of the twentieth century it remained plausible to conceive of higher education in exceptionalist terms, occupying a unique, bounded, and protected space of action in many societies and characterized by substantially self-defined and exclusive forms of knowledge and inquiry, educational ideas, and academic values. Higher education had significant functions in the maintenance of many nation-states, but one grounded in an acceptance by governments of academic authority in the fulfillment of those functions. In short, higher education's 'core' workforce (if such a term had been admitted to this arena) enjoyed optimal conditions for the formation and maintenance of distinct, stable, and legitimizing identities.

The exceptionalist concept of higher education was sustained through various structural and functional divisions in different societies, as its elite purposes began to be diluted—divisions of labor within institutions (Trow, 1970) and between institutions, in binary or stratified systems. The more open, inclusive, and market-based system of the United States was, nevertheless, highly stratified; intense competition for resources between the research universities in the United States helped maintain the values and power of an elite group of institutions. This type of mechanism remains in contemporary global contexts, notably in the competitive struggle to achieve the status of 'world-class university' and thus, again, to belong to a distinct, privileged category of institution. It makes it possible for earlier ideas of academic identity to retain a place in the lives of some academic faculty, and also in the minds of observers and analysts.

However, the contexts in which they do so have been transformed. The forces that have brought about this transformation are multiple and interactive. One of the most important has been the massification of higher education. It was part of wider political, social, and ideological processes of democratization that generated pressures from populations with rising and more varied aspirations; from newer professions, so-called 'semi-professions', and occupational groups seeking recognition and status, as well as greater expertise; and from governments wanting larger and more direct inputs to the economy and society from higher education, notably in applied science and technology, professional training, and management and business studies. The result was enlargement and diversification of academic faculty through the incorporation into higher education of new defining communities, some with strong cultures of their own, and some with forms of knowledge rooted in fields or practices where knowledge was less codified and its validity more contested. Academic faculty became a less exceptional and less cohesive group.

The extension of massification into or toward universalism brought larger transformation. Trow (1970), writing in the wake of the events of 1968 in US universities, conceptualized the shift from elite to mass to universal participation in higher education as one from 'privilege' to 'right' and then to 'obligation', and the consequence as a change in the cultures of the student population. Higher education had come to be seen as a prerequisite for success, even survival, in the labor market. Acceptance of academic authority, values, and even definitions of higher education could not be taken for granted. The further extension of the horizontal concept of universalism into the longitudinal or recurrent concept of lifelong learning meant still more diversification of student cultures, student needs, and student status. It also gave impetus to shifts in higher education from teaching to learning, with new implications for the definitions of expertise and practice expected of faculty.

The impacts of these developments were intensified by and intermeshed with wider changes, economic, ideological, and technological. The crisis in welfare states, the abandonment of Keynesianism, and the advent of neoliberalism meant major recasting of relations between the market and the state in many nations of the world. The restriction of public expenditure became a major goal of governments, at the same time as the demands upon public services such as health and education increased. Privatization became an increasingly important means of expenditure control, along with the imposition upon public-sector bodies of more stringent forms of accountability against criteria of economy, efficiency, and effectiveness.

Marketization and new forms of governance and management were introduced into the public sector, including greater autonomy for public institutions, but within policy frameworks defined increasingly explicitly by government priorities. Higher education institutions, now carrying new burdens of responsibility for their futures, were increasingly impelled into markets and quasi-markets: for more selective and conditional public funding, for new sources of income, including industry, and for new student populations. With the advance of globalization, institutions were increasingly managing different combinations of local, national, regional, international, and global markets. There was a high premium on institutional adaptation and flexible workforces. This meant major extension of fixed-term and part-time employment contracts and of performance-related pay. Some systems saw the abolition of academic tenure.

All of these developments—massification, universalism, neoliberalism, new public management, and globalization—brought with them various forms of external regulation, a new phenomenon for many institutions, and a greatly enhanced burden for others. The value of higher education and research, and of those who pursued them, was no longer taken for granted. Quality assurance, performance measurement, and benchmarking were some of many new forms of expertise with origins in the private sector that higher education had to develop in its workforces.

Globalization, in part driven by technological change, most conspicuous in information and communications, has brought about a dramatic compression of time and space and "a new age of borderlessness" that has "disrupted a variety of nationally organised structures" (Urry, 1998: 5). It has triggered demands for changes in educational and research practices and structures, and, beyond these, new conceptions of higher education and its organization, for example, "borderless education" and "virtual universities", as described by Middlehurst in Chapter 13; international or global networks; and consortia and franchising. They bring with them changes in the balance of power between providers and consumers, and new sources of competition for higher education provision from new parts of the world and new sectors of the economy, business, and industry.

Technological change has also been a key dimension of the emergence of 'knowledge societies' and 'knowledge economies', concepts that have a variety of meanings and implications, some of them conflicting, for higher education and those who comprise its workforce. At a general level they are 'metaphors' characterizing the transformation from industrial to postindustrial societal orders

(Askling et al., 2001). One set of theories emphasizes the critical role of theoretical knowledge, particularly pure science, as the source of new technologies and innovation, now regarded as the key to economic competitiveness in the global economy. One implication is that universities become "axial structures" of societies (Bell, 1973).

However, an increasingly strong theme in theories of the production of knowledge has been the complexity of the relationship between science and technology and the blurring of distinctions between pure and applied research and their exponents. The science–technology relationship has come to be seen "in terms of a *dynamic* [emphasis original] system with many connections and feedback loops" (Martin and Nightingale, 2000: xvi) between multiple parties, including scientists from different disciplines and firms, sometimes from different industries. Similar patterns of interaction feature in the broader formulation by Gibbons et al. (1994) of a new transdisciplinary mode of knowledge production.

Universities and other higher education institutions may be said to have become "axial structures" of knowledge societies, but in doing so they have had to develop increasingly close and complex relationships with other sectors and organizations, managing the value of engagement with that of autonomy. The boundaries and distinctions between universities and other organizations have loosened, sometimes to the extent encapsulated in the 'triple helix' metaphor for relationships in which universities, industries, and governments each take "the role of the other, with universities creating an industrial penumbra or performing a quasi-governmental role as local [or regional] innovation organiser" (Etzkowitz and Leydesdorff, 1997; see also Reichert, 2006).

In short, universities have had to equip themselves to confront complexity, novelty, and instability: to position themselves in a multilevel ("glonacal") (Marginson and Rhoades, 2002) and multidimensional (collaborative/competitive; public/private) environment that offers high risks as well as opportunities. The implications for the composition and structures of their workforces and for career trajectories are profound (Middlehurst, 2004; Rhoades, 2006; Whitchurch, 2004, 2008a).

Institutions need not only draw on a greater variety of professional expertise, but also recruit personnel with the capacity and experience to fulfill new and more sophisticated management functions, to create organizational and policy development roles, and to work in partnership with or leadership of faculty. Some will have academic qualifications equal to those of faculty; some will bring forms of knowledge, values, and practices from other sectors of societies that may compete for equal legitimacy in contemporary higher education settings. Such developments create demands for change from structures based on taken-for-granted hierarchies of authority or esteem, and on binary and traditional expertise-centered assumptions (academic/non-academic; academic/administrative) to structures giving priority to flexibility, pluralism, task, and cross-border negotiation and collaboration (matrices, project teams, "interstitial structures" (Rhoades, 2006: 389)), or new spaces (Whitchurch, 2008a, b).

Other theorists of the knowledge society have developed tangential theses about the democratization of knowledge and the broader threats to academic power: the wide distribution of knowledge in societies erodes distinctions between expert and non-expert actors and organizations and thus the authority of experts and professionals (Delanty, 2001; Nowotny et al., 2001). The revolution in communication technologies means a massive increase in the speed and extent to which knowledge is acquired, exchanged, and recontextualized by individuals and organizations.

Delanty (2001: chap. 10) argues that another set of divisive influences penetrated deep into the university in the 1980s, with implications for the epistemologies of academic curricula and research agendas, and also for the sources of academic and student identities. Some universities "became sites of the culture wars of gender, race, ethnicity and religion". The outcome of many of these wars or struggles in universities has been the "transformation of cultural categories into legal categories". Many identities have come to be "sustained by their capacity to be expressed in . . . legal rights" (Delanty, 2008: 130).

It will be argued later that gender is of particular significance for changing concepts of identity, partly because of the feminization of higher education that has occurred in a number of systems since the 1980s, and partly because of the growing influence of feminist theories in this period.

Implications for Identities in Higher Education

Meanwhile, the story of the transformation of higher education and its institutions can be read in a number of ways, but first as an account of the breakdown of longstanding conditions for strong, stable academic identities, sustained internally by the structures and cultures of academic systems, and beyond them by the nexus of power relations in the nation-states of which they were part but which accorded them, in different degrees, a bounded 'space of action' and self-regulation.

The story is one of the diversification and enlargement of the academic profession. It charts the blurring of the boundaries between academic faculty and other occupational groups within higher education institutions, and challenges previously taken-for-granted status hierarchies. It discredits the idea that academic faculty should be the exclusive focus of studies of identities in higher education.

It raises questions about the differences between higher education institutions and other organizations in knowledge societies. At the very least it makes clear that higher education systems now need organizations and workforces that embody values, forms of knowledge, structures, and relationships that are more varied than, and do not necessarily sit comfortably with, those of academe if they are to meet contemporary demands.

Finally, and perhaps most fundamentally, it signals the need for, and emergence of, new concepts, theories, and frameworks for understanding professional or occupational identities in higher education. The transformation of higher education is enmeshed in more far-reaching changes in societies and the ways in which we understand them, notably those encapsulated in theories of 'late' or 'high' modernity. They are perhaps felt particularly acutely in higher education, where premodern institutions, practices, and self-understandings have retained their influence for so long, and premodern metaphors have abounded in the works of those who research them.

Identity Concepts and Theories Revisited

By the beginning of the twentieth century the concept of profession had become a strong source of identity for many occupational groups. It was, however, contestable in the case of academic faculty (even in the United States and the United Kingdom, where it was most strongly established), for whom "community" long remained a significant normative ideal (Clark, 1987). For most of the century, it was plausible to understand academic identities within communitarian theories in which identities are formed and developed within defining communities (Taylor, 1989) with strong normative power, and individuality is both distinctive and embedded: "what I am is in key part what I inherit" (MacIntyre, 1981). While individual identity and reputation were defining aspirations and values in academe, the choices made by individuals were also significantly shaped by community histories, values, and norms.

A particular kind of community, the discipline, has long been seen as the primary source of academic identities, an epistemic community with a distinctive culture in which there is a powerful dynamic between ways of knowing and "ways of being in the world" (Geertz, 1983; see also Becher, 1989). Clark (1983) noted how academic disciplines "generated a steady flow of symbolic materials about themselves" that enabled their members to build up dominant self-identities.

Clark and Becher saw commitment to the value of disciplines as uniting and dividing academic faculty. Becher's characterization of disciplines as tribes with their own territories in what is sometimes termed a map of knowledge has strong connotations of interdisciplinary rivalry as well as diversity. Within his overarching metaphorical framework, he pays a good deal of attention to disciplinary gatekeeping and territoriality, equating strong boundaries with tightly knit communities.

Boundaries and boundary maintenance are common preoccupations of identity theorists in higher education and more generally. For Bernstein (1996), the strength of the boundaries protecting the space between groups, disciplines, or discourses constitutes the critical factor. Jenkins (1996), drawing on the work of Barth (1969), argues that identity is constructed at and across boundaries between groups, with those outside as well as inside: boundaries are permeable, but processes of boundary maintenance are integral to identity formation and sustenance.

Probably the most powerful and pervasive themes of the story of higher education transformation are those of blurring, loosening, stretching, breakdown, and collapse of different kinds of boundaries and distinctions in higher education itself, and in the societies of which it is a part. Higher education institutions, and those who work in them, are now understood as operating in a world where fixed boundaries or categories, defined 'spaces of action' and established structures, roles, and practices are being overtaken by "the reorganisation of time and space" and "the expansion of disembedding mechanisms, which prise social relations free from the hold of specific locales" (Giddens, 1991: 2; see also p. 20). We have already observed how staff in higher education are finding themselves having to move between local contexts to different levels and dimensions of space across the world, some visible and part of a common geography, others virtual; some of their own construction (networks or new markets), others created by new funding mechanisms or policies.

Meanwhile, it is evident that new definitions of working or projective spaces are being created within higher education institutions themselves. As functional and professional boundaries are loosened or reconstructed, predefined or linear career pathways become less common. New models for career progression are now emerging (see, for example, Strike in Chapter 5), incorporating frameworks that may legitimize new opportunities for choice, changes of direction, and more divergent career trajectories. Also, staff fulfilling new institutional functions and "blended roles" are said to be creating "new forms of space" in between existing professional and academic domains (Whitchurch, 2008a, 2009; Oba in Chapter 6). More visible spaces are being designated in the form of 'incubators' for various forms of external–internal initiatives in for-profit research and development. Firms are coming inside, while academic faculty are being encouraged to move outside, literally and figuratively, by forming spin-out companies.

The combination of transformations of time and space and the expansion of disembedding mechanisms is said to be providing the context for a third major influence on the dynamics of contemporary institutions—that is, reflexivity, or "the susceptibility of most aspects of social activity to chronic revision in the light of new information or knowledge" (Giddens, 1991: 20–21).

Increasingly, identity is conceived as a process or, in Giddens's terms, a "project"—one, moreover, that has no endpoint but, rather, is "continuous and reflexive" (Jenkins, 1996: 20; Taylor, 2008), an interaction between (internal) self-definition and the (external) definitions of oneself offered by others or an "internal–external dialectic of identification" (Jenkins, 1996). The context is increasingly likely to be indeterminate and complex (Taylor, 2008), tending to generate a "process of construction, deconstruction and reconstruction" (Barnett and Di Napoli, 2008) of both individual and collective identities. Coherence and continuity of identity may then become a function (or fiction) of the biographical narratives that individuals create for themselves (Hall, 1992: 277).

In this world, individuals may have more freedom and opportunity to construct new identities and new images of their present and future occupational selves. They are less likely to be confined within one type of institution, as institutional identities are more diverse and less stable and as intersectoral boundaries are less rigid. On the other hand, the processes involved, including deconstruction as well as reconstruction, may be more or less voluntary and involve loss as well as gain of meaning and self-esteem (Ylijoki, 2005). Individuals occupying new roles in new functional areas such as academic development or student support may be vulnerable to uncertainty about the robustness of the knowledge they bring, to hostility from established groups, notably faculty, or to the coercive force of already powerful managerial discourses. In consequence, they will find it hard to develop identities as distinct from subjectivities (Land, 2008).

Identities have become both more provisional and more multidimensional. Whereas in a period of comparative stability it was possible for academic faculty to see identity development as a cumulative process from which identities could be built that were dominant, sometimes not only in their working context, but also in their whole lives, that now seems likely to be a far more rare occurrence. The idea of multiple identities has become more potent, although it may take different forms. As staff in higher education, whatever their formal designation, find themselves moving between different working spaces, tasks, roles, and reference groups, it is more plausible that they will construct and reconstruct how they define their identities over time, and perhaps also simultaneously. Individuals may find that in different contexts with different reference groups, they foreground different values, aspirations, strengths, and sources of self-esteem. Such multiple identities may not be easily reconcilable.

The feminization of higher education may also have reduced the likelihood of one professional identity providing the frame for the individual's whole sense of self. Identities of this level of dominance were observed at a time when most academic faculty were, or were assumed to be, male and in a world in which the significance of (male) public space far outweighed that of the separate and private (female) space of the family. As feminist theories gained more influence over modes of thought, the idea that public and private lives can or should be independent of one another became increasingly discredited. More recently, commitment has grown among both women and men to achieving significant change in the work–life balance, more shared public and private space, and more equality.

Main Conclusions

It seems that in the space of a few decades there have been profound changes in the way in which we think about identities in higher education workforces. Identity development has moved from being seen as a process in which visible continuities in the achievement of professional self-definition and esteem are foregrounded, a function of stable community membership, boundary maintenance, established divisions of labor, and hierarchies of authority. Instead, identity is conceptualized as a project or continuous process of construction, deconstruction, and reconstruction in the context of multiple and shifting collectivities and relationships. Reflexivity has become central to contemporary understandings of identity. Meanwhile, boundary maintenance has become a more provisional and complex undertaking, and the concept of embedded distinctiveness now competes with the more fluid idea of individual positioning in and between spaces.

The workforces of higher education institutions have expanded and diversified. Workforce identities are no longer defined exclusively in terms of academic identities. Rigidly defined boundaries between functions and categories of staff have loosened and structures have become more provisional. Perhaps most importantly, there has been a shift in, and some blurring of, the knowledge boundaries between faculty and other categories of staff. While knowledge-centered endeavors still constitute the defining and driving forces of higher education institutions, the authority of academic knowledge is no longer taken for granted, even in what are still the core activities of education and research. Here, too, there are interstitial spaces, shared and contested with other professional staff.

However, continuities remain alongside the discontinuities. Destabilization of the conditions of professional identity development is widespread, but by no means wholesale. Higher education institutions retain responsibilities, particularly to students, that depend upon due process and predictable systems, and upon sustaining long-established administrative values that underpin them (see Whitchurch, 2008b). Despite the plethora of developments that have undermined the status of the discipline as the primary basic unit of higher education institutions, academic commitment to it remains powerful (Musselin, 2005; Ylijoki, 2005) and its role in academic identity formation is significant (Parry, 2007). Disciplinary organization is still a model that is aspired to and reproduced by newer epistemic communities (Henkel, 2009; cf. Weingart, 1997). At the same time, however, academic faculty with strong disciplinary identities are increasingly comfortable in positioning themselves within a matrix of influences, including Mode 1 and Mode 2 forms of knowledge; academic disciplines and domains; and disciplinary and interdisciplinary groupings. The institutions that have been most successful in responding to change and embracing multiple professional identities are, for the most part, already prestigious and well-resourced universities (Geuna, 1998; Owen-Smith, 2005). Resilience by academic faculty as they adapt to changing disciplinary environments has played a significant role in the success of these institutions.

References

Askling, B., Henkel, M., and Kehm, B. (2001) "Conceptions of Knowledge and Its Organisation in Universities." *European Journal of Education* 36 (3): 341–350.

Barnett, R. and Di Napoli, R. (eds.) (2008) *Changing Identities in Higher Education: Voicing Perspectives.* Abingdon, UK: Routledge.

Barth, F. (1969) "Introduction." In *Ethnic Groups and Boundaries: The Social Organization of Culture Difference*, ed. F. Barth. Oslo: Universitetsforlaget.

Becher, T. (1989) *Academic Tribes and Territories: Intellectual Enquiry and the Cultures of Disciplines.* Buckingham, UK: SRHE/Open University Press.

Bell, D. (1973) *The Coming of Post-industrial Society.* London: Heinemann.

Bernstein, B. (1996) *Pedagogy, Symbolic Control and Identity: Theory, Research, Critique.* London: Taylor & Francis.

Clark, B. R. (1983) *The Higher Education System: Academic Organization in Cross-national Perspective.* Los Angeles: University of California Press.

Clark, B. R. (1987) *The Academic Profession.* Los Angeles: University of California Press.

Delanty, G. (2001) *Challenging Knowledge: The University in the Knowledge Society.* Buckingham, UK: SRHE/Open University Press.

Delanty, G. (2008) "Academic Identities and Institutional Change." In *Changing Identities in Higher Education: Voicing Perspectives*, ed. R. Barnett and R. Di Napoli. Abingdon, UK: Routledge.

El-Khawas, E. (2008) "Emerging Academic Identities: A New Research and Policy Agenda." In *From Governance to Identity*, ed. A. Amaral, I. Bleiklie, and C. Musselin. Dordrecht: Springer.

Etzkowitz, H. and Leydesdorff, L. (eds.) (1997) *Universities and the Global Economy. A Triple Helix of University–Industry–Government Relations.* London: Pinter.

Geertz, C. (1983) *Local Knowledge.* New York: Basic Books.

Geuna, A. (1998) "The Internationalisation of European Universities: A Return to Medieval Roots." *Minerva* 36: 253–270.

Gibbons, M., Limoges, C., Nowotny, H., Schwartzman, S., Scott, P., and Trow, M. (1994) *The New Production of Knowledge: The Dynamics of Science and Research in Contemporary Societies.* London: Sage.

Giddens, A. (1991) *Modernity and Self-Identity*. Cambridge: Polity Press.

Hall, S. (1992) "The Question of Cultural Identity." In *Modernity and Its Futures*, ed. S. Hall, D. Held, and T. McGrew. Cambridge: Polity Press.

Henkel, M. (2009) "Policy Change and the Challenge to Academic Identities." In *The Changing Face of Academic Life: Analytical and Comparative Perspectives*, ed. J. Enders and E. De Weert. Basingstoke, UK: Macmillan.

Jenkins, R. (1996) *Social Identity*. London: Routledge.

Kogan, M., Moses, I., and El-Khawas, E. (1994) *Staffing Higher Education: Meeting New Challenges*. London: Jessica Kingsley.

Land, R. (2008) "Academic Development: Identity and Paradox." In *Changing Identities in Higher Education: Voicing Perspectives*, ed. R. Barnett and R. Di Napoli. Abingdon, UK: Routledge.

MacIntyre, A. (1981) *After Virtue: A Study in Moral Theory*. London: Duckworth.

Marginson, S. and Rhoades, G. (2002) "Beyond National States, Markets and Systems of Higher Education: A Glonacal Agency Heuristic." *Higher Education* 43 (3): 281–309.

Martin, B. and Nightingale, P. (2000) *The Political Economy of Science, Technology and Innovation*. Cheltenham, UK: Edward Elgar.

Middlehurst, R. (2004) "Changing Internal Governance: A Discussion of Leadership Roles and Management Structures in UK Universities." *Higher Education Quarterly* 58 (4): 258–279.

Musselin, C. (2005) "Change or Continuity in Higher Education and Governance? Lessons Drawn from Twenty Years of National Reforms in European Countries." In *Governing Knowledge: A Study of Continuity and Change in Higher Education*, ed. I. Bleiklie and M. Henkel. Dordrecht, the Netherlands: Springer.

Nowotny, H., Scott, P., and Gibbons, M. (2001) *Re-thinking Science: Knowledge and the Public in an Age of Uncertainty*. Cambridge: Polity Press.

Owen-Smith, J. (2005) "Trends and Transitions in the Institutional Environment for Public and Private Science." *Higher Education* 49 (1–2): 91–117.

Parry, S. (2007) *Disciplines and Doctorates*. Dordrecht, The Netherlands: Springer.

Reichert, S. (2006) *The Rise of Knowledge Regions: Emerging Opportunities and Challenges for Universities*. Brussels: European University Association.

Rhoades, G. (2006) "The Higher Education We Choose: A Question of Balance." *Review of Higher Education* 29: 381–404.

Taylor, C. (1989) *Sources of the Self: The Making of the Modern Identity*. Cambridge: Cambridge University Press.

Taylor, P. (2008) "Being an Academic Today." In *Changing Identities in Higher Education: Voicing Perspectives*, ed. R. Barnett and R. Di Napoli. Abingdon, UK: Routledge.

Trow, M. (1970) "Reflections on the Transition from Mass to Universal Higher Education." *Daedalus* 99: 1–44.

Urry, J. (1988) "Contemporary Transformations of Time and Space." In *The Globalization of Higher Education*, ed. P. Scott. Buckingham, UK: SRHE/Open University Press.

Weingart, P. (1997) "From 'Finalization' to 'Mode 2': Old Wine in New Bottles?" *Social Science Information* 36 (4): 591–613.

Whitchurch, C. (2004) "Administrative Managers: A Critical Link." *Higher Education Quarterly* 58 (4): 280–298.

Whitchurch, C. (2008a) *Professional Managers in UK Higher Education: Preparing for Complex Futures*. Final Report. London: Leadership Foundation for Higher Education. Online, available at: www.lfhe.ac.uk/publications/research.html.

Whitchurch, C. (2008b) "Beyond Administration and Management: Changing Professional Identities in Higher Education." In *Changing Identities in Higher Education: Voicing Perspectives*, ed. R. Barnett and R. Di Napoli. Abingdon, UK: Routledge.

Whitchurch, C. (2009) "The Rise of the *Blended Professional* in Higher Education: A Comparison between the UK, Australia and the United States." *Higher Education* 58 (3): 407–418.

Ylijoki, O.-H. (2005) "Academic Nostalgia: A Narrative Approach to Academic Life." *Human Relations* 58: 555–576.

2
Global Contexts

GEORGE GORDON

Introduction

As noted in the Preface, understandings about how institutions relate to their staff, and the expectations each have of the other, are undergoing change. There are significant collective organizational, as well as individual, implications for policies, practices, behaviors, and values. We recognize that the term 'human resource management', or even 'management', may be contested in academic environments. Our approach emphasizes the implications for academic and professional identities, relationships, and careers of a significant and probably accelerating worldwide diversification, albeit from different starting points and differing in detailed nature and pace of change, of those employed in higher education. In this chapter, attention is paid to both organizational and individual issues and perspectives, the complex interplay between them, and the influences of various pressures for change. The chapter builds on earlier work by Gordon and Whitchurch (2007), Gordon (2004), and Whitchurch (2008a, b).

There are significant challenges in obtaining widespread and comparable data on changes to staffing patterns and perceptions in higher education (Musselin, 2007). Even when some sound data are available, care needs to be taken, as Finkelstein (2007) demonstrates in relation to academic employment in the United States, to realize the full scale and future implications of current trends. As other chapters in this volume amply illustrate, there is an extensive scholarly litera-ture on the academic profession, academic identities, and academic perceptions of, and reactions to, changes in higher education in recent decades. There is growing interest in the roles and careers of 'newer' professionals (Whitchurch, 2008a, b) in higher education, and the roles of administrators have also attracted interest (Kogan, 2007). Less attention has been paid to the changing roles, identities, and careers of other substantial groups of employees in higher education institutions such as technical, clerical/secretarial, trades, security, and catering staff. Nor are they the focus of attention in this volume, although reference will be made to a number of issues, challenges, and changes that have affected these groups of staff.

The emphasis in much of the literature is upon the fundamental importance of academic faculty to the health and essence of the university, and of the role of the collegium at the heart of decision making. Administrators, other professionals, and staff are traditionally viewed as applying their particular expertise to support the collegium, advise on procedures and professional matters, and smooth the processes of implementation and operation of academically determined policies.

Legitimacy for such interpretations stems primarily from the view that a key distinctive feature of universities is the creation, testing, and dissemination of knowledge. Conceptually, this view connects with the Humboldtian vision of the role of universities and their relation to society, particularly the importance of associating research and teaching. Kogan (2007) noted that during the first several decades of the twentieth century, the Humboldtian view gradually attained wider influence in higher education. It never achieved universal adherence. Several higher education systems, such as those in France, Eastern Europe, and China, followed the Napoleonic model of a parallel structure of separate prestigious research institutes or academies of sciences with varying degrees of connection to, and impact upon, the work of universities. Indeed, many systems developed some national research institutes or centers, mostly, but not exclusively, in scientific fields. The other notable complication follows from the growth and diversification of higher education systems worldwide and the associated differences in the centrality of research for institutional mission, certainly of relative balance of pure versus applied research and scholarship, or more broadly of the respective weight attached to Boyer's (1990) four forms of scholarship (discovery, teaching, application, engagement), and the implications for reward (O'Meara and Rice, 2005).

Hughes has written in *Reshaping the University* of the mythology of research and teaching relationships in universities. That leads to a plea for myths to be laid aside so that "a wide variety of relationships between the key activities of the university may be feasible, and even new activities or existing ones reshaped so as to open new spaces, new configurations" (2005: 26). Historical perceptions and models need not be cast as myths. However, they are often generalizations, necessarily so in order to enable some order to be depicted, interpreted, and interrogated from complex, multidimensional (and increasingly so) realities. Moreover, the generalizations tend to be shaped by conceptual and positional dominant discourses, such as sociological analysis of the nature of, and threat to, the academic profession, academic freedom, and the role of the collegium. Other interpretations coexist, but may offer a different perspective from the prevailing paradigm. For example, Bergquist (1992), a psychologist and institutional leader, speaks of the four distinctive cultures of the academy (collegial, managerial, developmental, negotiating), of their importance to organizational cultures, and of the fact that academic faculty frequently have to function simultaneously in two or more of these cultures.

Leading researchers are often acutely conscious of the limitations of generalizations which can be drawn from such research, and surround their observations with caveats and notes of caution. Occasionally they sense that a paradigmatic shift may be needed. Thus, Kogan et al. (1994), distilling key messages from an international study of staffing in higher education, commented that a new model might be needed. That has still to materialize, but a wider range of dimensions, challenges, and responses have been published since that work. Many of those are explored and articulated in this volume, which hopefully makes a contribution to the quest for new understandings and conceptualizations of this field.

Background

In the early 1990s (1991–1993) the Carnegie Foundation sponsored an international study of the academic profession. Fourteen countries were surveyed, and the detailed responses were captured in a special report edited by Altbach (1996) and an earlier volume by Boyer et al. (1994). The contributing countries were Australia, Brazil, Chile, England, Germany, Hong Kong, Israel, Japan, South Korea, Mexico, the Netherlands, Russia, Sweden, and the United States. The survey instrument contained seventy-two questions ranging from personal details (gender, age, qualifications, length of service, salary, employment status, publication/ conference attendance records, etc.) to sections on working environments, professional activity, service, governance, international dimensions of academic life, and higher education and society.

When it was published, some of the comparative tables attracted attention. For example, only 8 percent of German respondents considered that affiliation with their institution was very important to them. At the other end of the spectrum, 76 percent of Brazilian respondents viewed institutional affiliation as very important (Boyer et al., 1994: 80). By comparison, the spread revealed from answers to a corresponding question on the importance of affiliation to their academic discipline was much narrower (55 percent of respondents in Sweden rated that as very important, as against 95 percent of replies from Brazil). The study produced profiles of the academic profession in the fourteen countries, and enabled broad comparisons to be made about sources of satisfaction and dissatisfaction. For example, only in Japan did a majority of respondents agree with the assertion that top-level administrators were providing competent leadership. Indeed, in the cases of England (49 percent), Germany (49 percent), Hong Kong (48 percent), Chile (42 percent), Israel (41 percent), and the United States (38 percent), sizable minorities disagreed (ibid.: 97).

Broadly, the findings of the survey could be interpreted as providing substantiation for key dimensions of the prevailing paradigm of the academic profession, and its views and values. In the introductory chapter to the Special Report, Altbach and Lewis (1996: 5) noted the importance of context, which the portraits of countries articulated and the comparative data summarized, but concluded that "a community of interest is emerging. The study indicates areas that academics around the world have in common." Among the topics that displayed high levels of consensus were the importance of international scholarly connections, the freedom to choose topics for research, the importance of discipline affiliations, and the belief that faculty in their discipline had a professional obligation to apply their knowledge to problems in society. There was also consensus around the view that academic faculty were not very influential in shaping institutional-level academic policies.

Various responses in the survey conveyed mixed, ambivalent, or partially negative messages about the role and style of institutional managers and administrators. These echo historical tensions, and conflicting beliefs about roles, sources of authority, and allegiances. As the survey demonstrated, and the literature has articulated (Becher, 1989; Becher and Trowler, 2001), academic faculty generally owe their primary allegiance to their discipline, and secondary allegiance to the institution in which they work. By contrast, administrators and other professional staff have tended historically, and in large measure continue today, to attach their primary allegiance to serving the interests of the institution in which they work. That said, the fact that in the United Kingdom the Association of University Administrators operates a code of practice for its members demonstrates a level of collective interpretation of values and behaviors that echoes practice in many statutory professional bodies, but is not a typical feature of the academic guilds or disciplines. In some countries, 'newer' professional groups such as counselors and educational developers have also adopted codes of practice or statements of ethics.

The relationship between academic and administrative structures, academic territories and institutional governance, and the organization of administrative structures have all been, and to a degree continue to be, characterized by inter-system, intersectoral, and temporal variation. At the macro level the scene is set by the relationship to government (national or regional/local) and the degree of autonomy accorded to the institution. As Kogan (2007) enunciates, the history of relationships between administrators and related professionals, and academic faculty, is complex, multistranded and dynamic. One crucial dimension of the relationship is the fact that institutional policies and procedures are at the core of the everyday working lives of senior administrators and related professionals, whereas they tend to be seen as unwanted bureaucratic intrusion by the many faculty who eschew personal involvement in policy formulation and decision making. Moreover, those who do perform that collegial service can devote only a modest proportion of their time and attention to the task.

Structurally, many systems operate bicameral structures, with academic matters being the province of the supreme academic body (senate or academic council), and financial, staffing, and legal issues coming under the scrutiny of the governing body (variously named). Where some of the latter functions were vested not with the institution but with government or some agency of the latter, the scope of governing responsibilities was reduced, as was the need for related managerial capabilities and institutional provision and procedures. Systems where university faculty were, or are, classed as civil servants illustrate this situation, which comes into sharp focus when government decides, as it did in Japan, to cease to class faculty as civil servants. Comparable consequences for institutions follow when government alters existing policy and delegates employment responsibility to institutions. The latter inevitably encounter a whole raft of new human resource-related administrative and professional demands. Additionally, institutions have to work through structural and organizational adjustments, including developing new policies and procedures, and formulating and negotiating ways of addressing the challenges.

Organizational preferences in relation to the structuring of administrative and professional fields tend to fluctuate over time, as well as varying between higher education systems and subsectors. A phase of division into the provinces of the registrar/secretary and bursar in some countries was superseded by arguments for unified leadership of administrative and related fields. More recently, debates have recurred and various formations have been adopted. Writing on entrepreneurial universities, Clark (1998, 2004) emphasized the importance of a "strengthened steering core" in institutions that successfully pursued sustained change. A number of the examples had a unified administration. Even institutions adopting other formations do so with the explicit intention of strengthening steering and enhancing organizational synergies. Some implications for identities and careers of these relationships, issues, and changes are explored later in this chapter.

The Global Context and Interface with Local Contexts

Transformations

Henkel, in Chapter 1, sets out the principal transformations that have affected higher education over the past four or five decades within various theoretical interpretations. She concludes that academics became a less exceptional and less cohesive group. Part of the transformation has also involved a strengthening of the corporate dimension of governance in higher education. Institutional managers have sought, often from legal or quasi-regulatory necessity, to find ways of achieving heightened intra-institutional connectivity. League tables and other comparative measures of institutional performance encouraged actions to monitor performance of units and measures. In many cases there has been a shift in the balance between the various interests within the institution, which researchers have sought to capture (McNay, 1995; Thorne and Cuthbert, 1996).

Widening Participation

Often, several macro factors have interwoven in complex ways. Widening participation or massification inevitably led to a more diverse student population. Reduction in the unit of resource might not be viewed by those working in higher education as an inevitable correlate of massification, but it raises questions about the escalating costs of higher education and how these should be met. Not only did that fuel debates about sources and scale of funding, but it also prompted questions about value for money, and questions about the efficiency and effectiveness of systems and institutions. Many governments (national or regional) used such discussions as an opportunity to influence the shape, structure, workings, and priorities of higher education. In contexts where universities had legal autonomy, governments sought influence through directions to funding sources and/or attaching conditions to specific streams of revenue.

Another dimension of widened participation is the growth of private institutions, be these for-profit bodies or charitably based ones. In substantial measure it offered governments, especially in countries where unmet demand was high, a workable pathway to rapid expansion of provision. A further complication in countries such as the United Kingdom and Australia was the decision to move to a single higher education sector. Thus, polytechnics, higher education colleges, colleges of technology, and other specialist institutes were offered the opportunity to become universities either independently or through institutional mergers. Both systems continue to grapple with some of the implications of those changes. In some senses those systems now more closely resemble the mission and provision span of the system in the United States, save for one vital distinction, namely that the latter is widely accepted as a diversified, although dynamic, system, whereas the systems in the United Kingdom and Australia seek diversity within a unified structure.

Part-time undergraduate study is not a new phenomenon in higher education, but massification and structural changes have resulted in its becoming the dominant mode of study in a substantial cohort of institutions in many systems. It also means that the presumption of an 18–22 full-time residential student population is an inappropriate stereotype, although it continues to be the dominant mode in many research-intensive universities.

Internationalization

In many systems there has been substantial growth in the numbers of international and postgraduate students (taught and research). As Knight (2001, 2003) has noted, the existence of international students studying abroad is only one dimension of the global effects of internationalization. Others include overseas campuses, international mobility of staff, international collaborations on teaching, research, and knowledge transfer, and the internationalization of the curriculum. Onshore and offshore activities also feed back into the trend toward diversification of funding streams, and into an array of human resource issues, strategies, and practices, which in turn have variously affected the operational environment of staff in higher education institutions. Mobility raises issues of support and preparation if institutionally sponsored, and of brain drain or gain if individually sponsored.

Internationalization was one of the key topics explored in a 2004 OECD study *Tertiary Education for the Knowledge Society* (Santiago et al., 2008). Twenty-four developed industrial countries participated. While the study adopted the definition formulated, namely "the process of integrating an international intercultural or global dimension into the purpose, functions or delivery of tertiary education" (Knight, 2003: 2), it did interweave aspects of globalization and respond to the implications of the Bologna process.

Shifts in the Maps of Disciplines

While there have been closures of academic departments in institutions, the overall span of provision has increased as new fields have flourished and as most professions have shifted toward expecting a graduate qualification as the principal, even exclusive, means of entry. That, in turn, has diversified the academic profession and introduced new and diverse perspectives and experiences. Researching the early experience of samples of teacher and nurse educators, Boyd (2007) concluded that the former found important identity continuities between their previous role as classroom teachers and their new role as teacher educators. By contrast, while nurse educators considered their nursing credibility to be a fundamental component of their new role, they suffered a sense of loss of everyday contact with patients, and articulated feelings of searching toward a revised identity that would have to balance new demands of pedagogy, curriculum design, scholarship, and research, while retaining vital practical credibility in their field.

Additionally, professionals in a wide range of fields such as social work or health education often enter academic roles from senior practicing positions. Typically, they have had different life and socialization experience from those of, say, many doctoral students in science or social science. Cumulatively, these trends have contributed to the enrichment and reshaping of the staffing profile of higher education.

Regional Dimensions

Specific trends have affected particular systems or sets of systems. Many could be interpreted as regional manifestations of global phenomena, or responses to global challenges. Thus, the articulation of the concept of a European Research Area, the substantial growth in European Union research and development funding, and the endeavors to foster educational structural commonalities through the Bologna process are explicit attempts to pursue transnational collaboration and cooperation in order to achieve greater collective competitiveness for the participating partners.

Research

At a more localized level the Research Assessment Exercise in the United Kingdom, and equivalent devices elsewhere, have sought greater selectivity in the allocation of research funding, heightened research performance, and enhanced national research competitiveness and status. The procedures and outcomes have attracted comment and criticism (McNay, 1998; Lucas, 2006), but they have also had significant impact upon the freedoms of individual faculty, the nature of individual and collective research strategies, and academic identities. It has led to some interesting collaborative developments as researchers, especially in fields requiring substantial funding, seek ways of securing resources and becoming recognized as part of a center or cluster of excellence. Generally such strategies are institutional or inter-institutional, although external actors such as funding bodies may promote the trend. For example, the Scottish Funding Council has specifically fostered inter-institutional collaboration in research in chemistry and physics, in addition to accommodating inter-institutional merging of provision in various disciplines. Again, new human resource challenges are associated with such developments.

The Knowledge Explosion

The knowledge explosion has been characterized by heightened specialization as well as by exponential growth in publication. The ramifications are extensive, and are covered more fully in several chapters in this volume. Rather than replicate that material, attention here focuses on one dimension, namely implications for the curriculum of conceptions of being up to date in the scholarship of the field. It is increasingly difficult for busy, conscientious faculty to keep abreast of the published output of anything beyond a relatively narrowly defined specialist field or set of fields. They try to address the dilemma by recourse to online searches and reading pre-publication online versions of refereed articles, but even with those strategies it can be difficult to attain a fairly comprehensive picture. At least in part, some publications may not be cited, or their citation may be delayed, simply because they drop below the radar of researchers and come to attention only when cited in a secondary source. Of course, it could be argued that this is not a new phenomenon. In that sense, neither is the challenge of overloaded curricula. However, the sheer volume of output and rapid dating of knowledge in some fields do present testing challenges.

In some senses, academic orientation favors boundarylessness, given that the preferred primary community allegiance is to a discipline rather than the institution. The availability of the World Wide Web could be seen as an enabling extension of the preferred orientation. Increasingly, the Web is having a transformative effect, altering the ways of capturing knowledge production and transfer, and of key dimensions of intellectual inquiry. The trend has also stimulated the need for various support services and facilities, with some demands, such as secretarial support, declining, and others, such as specialized IT support, increasing or being reshaped (e.g. the provision of library services).

E-learning

There has been a marked expansion of blended and virtual learning. Considerable difficulties have had to be overcome to achieve that situation. Reaching agreement over a common institutional virtual learning environment has often been highly contentious. While these environments offer opportunities, they also require the acceptance of protocols and conventions, constraints that can sit uncomfortably with individual academic preferences for considerable personal control over teaching. Differences of opinion over favored virtual learning environments may have contributed to difficulties in establishing viable multi-institutional international provision of e-learning, although that situation could change in time.

Accountability

Expansion of higher education, internationalization and globalization, and changes in relationships between institutions and the state, individually and cumulatively, have all led to growing external expectations of the form and scope of accountability by institutions for academic standards (quality assurance), development (quality enhancement), and performance (various measures of outputs and outcomes). While the multiplicity of these intrusions has been a source of frustration to many within the academy, and remains the subject of ongoing discourses, they have also shaped practices and policies at a variety of levels (sectoral, institutional, intra-institutional). Reference has been made earlier to research selectivity. In the area of teaching and learning, the focus on process dimensions such as the fitness for purpose of quality assurance arrangements, has been succeeded by an emphasis on the impact upon the student learning experience. That recasts or reframes the discourse within the academy, although it also offers the possibility of making more explicit the views of practitioners as educators, as a current project has found (personal communication). Whether such welcomed opportunities for discourse are further facilitated or inhibited by normative generalizations (e.g. Krishnaveni and Anitha, 2007) is a matter of conjecture.

Entrepreneurialism

Various assemblies of the foregoing demands not only have reshaped roles within institutions and generated demands for new roles and services, but have also offered existing staff new opportunities for growth and development, which some at least have grasped enthusiastically. These opportunities include, but are not necessarily restricted to, what Clark (1998, 2004) termed "entrepreneurial" approaches. Clark found that, at least initially, entrepreneurial developments in his illustrative sample happened in what he termed the "developmental periphery". In significant measure that appeared to offer greater freedoms to new ventures than might have occurred within established territories. It was a central part of Clark's thesis that sustained change required the embedding of an entrepreneurial culture, which might be fostered if the "academic heartland" progressively adopted the new ventures. That need not imply a simple maintenance of the established status quo, because the map and territories of the academic heartland can undergo, and in many institutions have undergone, transformations and adaptations in the past two decades as institutions and academic tribes sought to position themselves beneficially in relation to changing markets and opportunities, be these in "Mode 1" or "Mode 2" form (Gibbons et al., 1994).

The wider definition of entrepreneurialism embraces social entrepreneurialism (services to local communities) and other aspects of engagement (services to professions). In the United Kingdom, government has frequently urged higher education institutions to seek a much more prominent role in, and share of the moneys spent on, lifelong learning, skills updating, and continuous professional development. Here a key interface lies at perceptions of skills needs and deficiencies, and visions of future scenarios for employment in successful knowledge-based societies. Almost worldwide, governments hoping to move in that direction envisage higher education as providing the vital platform for the creation and maintenance of a highly skilled, flexible workforce.

Employability

Employability initiatives in higher education have a lengthy history. The fact that they remain government priorities stems not only from the changing nature of societal needs and expectations, but also from external encouragement for some refocusing of output priorities and aspects of graduate skill sets. Scotland provides two recent examples of the interweaving of government expectations and institutional responses. The structuring of funding of Scottish higher education institutions is about to change. It is intended that, henceforth, one component will be from a Horizon Fund, which will be shaped by connectivity of institutional activities with government priorities. Graduate attributes and the employability agenda have been identified as one set of priorities. Recent media reporting of proposals implied that some Scottish institutions enthusiastically welcomed this development, while the ancient Scottish universities were believed to have reservations about a possible departure from the wider purposes of higher education articulated in the Dearing Report (1997).

Nonetheless, the institutions, collectively and voluntarily, recently agreed that the next quality enhancement theme in the sector, with Scottish Funding Council support, should consider institutional understandings of, and initiatives aimed at addressing, the attributes of the twenty-first-century graduate. Moreover, findings from the recent Research–Teaching Linkages theme (Land and Gordon, 2008) found that academic faculty in Scottish higher education institutions preferred the language of graduate attributes to the label "employability", although neither term was sacrosanct from questioning and academic debate.

Labor Markets and Conditions

An Association of Commonwealth Universities survey of around 500 member institutions in thirty-five countries concluded that

> [a]s research and teaching demands increase, competition for academic staff continues to grow both within and outside the sector. If universities are to compete in this environment, effective policies and strategies for academic recruitment and retention need to be established and implemented.
> (Kubler and DeLuca, 2006: 14)

The report emphasized the centrality of a robust human resources function, the need for incentives to attract and retain leading scholars, and, more extensively, the need for innovative approaches to recruitment and retention. While the report concentrated upon faculty members, similar points could have been made in relation to the labor market for professional staff. Competition for knowledge workers was highlighted as the principal driving force for change. Improved strategic and managerial responses were identified as the vital dimensions if institutions were to cope with the growing challenges of competitive labor markets.

On average, institutional responses to the survey revealed that most human resources strategies varied in terms of breadth (e.g. recruitment, recruitment and retention, wider workforce planning) and timescales (i.e. short-term versus long-term). When asked to rank likely and desirable developments, respondents highlighted, in order of importance, a growing emphasis on research output and on teaching excellence, and professionalization of managerial and administrative posts. In similar vein, the top-ranked least likely and least desirable outcomes would be, respectively, an increased movement of faculty into managerial and administrative posts, and growth of fixed-term or part-time contracts.

Kubler and DeLuca (2006) noted that competition varied between countries and disciplines. They argued that mobility may be greater in early career stages, although competition for 'research stars' was recognized as a significant trend. Many of the human resources professionals responding to the survey emphasized the importance of succession planning and expressed concern that fixed-term contracts might undermine that strategy.

Changes to the profile of academic positions in the United States have been analyzed by Schuster and Finkelstein (2006). Two critical trends are that many full-time new hires are not on tenure track, and that there has also been a massive increase in part-time positions. They conclude that these trends are reshaping the academic model (Ph.D., tenure-track appointment, confirmation, tenure review of research/publications, teaching and service, promotion to associate or full professorship). Instead, they argue that a multiplicity of models is developing. If fixed-term appointments continue as the modal category, they would become the twenty-first-century prototype. The tenure model would continue in parallel, as would the part-time model. Indeed, the latter might grow, which again might mean that the former would decline. Many reasons contribute to the growth of part-time and alternative full-time positions. While these might be dictated by economic decisions by institutions, Finkelstein (2007) also highlights the importance of lifestyle choices in shaping newer interpretations of academic careers.

In some countries the growth of fixed-term contracts has been associated with specific types of project-defined positions, such as certain research or development posts. In the United Kingdom, for example, the massive growth over the past twenty years of research assistantships and fellowships was almost entirely correlated with the use of fixed-term contracts. Similar employment patterns correlated with growth of teaching and learning enhancement developments in the past decade or so. Recent changes to employment law provided for greater continuity of appointment for most employees holding fixed-term appointments, although it will take time for the full implications to emerge. Moreover, the scale of the human resource challenge varies between institutions, depending upon the numbers of employees holding fixed-term appointments.

As with other organizations, higher education institutions need to address the demands of both internal and external labor markets. Musselin (2007) noted that the influence of internal labor markets had increased with the growth of internal academic appointments. In fact, many systems have had established traditions of internal promotions up to certain levels, with only the more senior posts being advertised externally. In the past twenty years, largely as a result of the implications of research selectivity alongside other pressures to retain and reward exceptional performance, there has been a marked strengthening of the role of internal labor markets. One illustration would be the huge increase in the United Kingdom of personal professorships—that is, promotion on personal merit, not in open competition. The need to retain stars has become the dominant discourse in strategic academic discussions, with heads of department and/or deans of faculties or schools, or the equivalent, being powerful advocates of the strategy. Generally, the trend meshes neatly with the desire of senior human resources professionals to encourage retention, reward excellent performance, foster succession planning, and enable the pursuit of key institutional strategic priorities.

Further changes in employment law in Europe are likely to heighten the role of internal labor markets as institutions seek to offer alternative posts to individuals as a means of maintaining their continuity of employment in a wide variety of changing circumstances, such as completion of projects, termination of an initiative, closure of an activity, and other causes of redistribution of positions. Such considerations also affect administrative and professional posts. In this case, the significant complication is that there can only be one senior position, for example, one director (or equivalent term), for a specific service or activity. Other sources of recognition and reward, such as salary, then assume greater visibility. Of course, financial reward is an inevitable dimension of all retention and reward strategies and packages, although research has recurrently suggested that it is not the prime motivator for many academic faculty and professional staff. Status may be as important as, if not more important than, salary.

Another internal labor market strategy has been the introduction of a range of new titles such as vice-dean (research) or (teaching and learning) or (resources), or director of teaching and learning at the level of departments and schools. Invariably these positions reward the contractual acceptance of specific strategic roles with financial compensation as well as titular status. The existence of such strategies is not new, although the degree of formalization has generally happened within the past five to ten years. Less formal arrangements coexist, but growing corporate attention to information on websites and other strategic pressures are likely to combine to constrain informal solutions.

Cumulatively, these developments have impacted upon institutional policies and procedures. Enhanced ways of recognizing and rewarding performance require robust, regular, and insightful data, as do judgments about competitiveness and the relationship between internal reward structures and external markets. That has strengthened the role of human resources professionals and/or senior administrators in the design of instruments and procedures, and in the articulation of policy options. Often it has heightened the influence that specific internal academic expertise can provide to an institution. Neither trend inevitably leads to any diminution of academic influence and authority, although it does reshape the detailed nature of discussions and deliberations.

Findings for a recent study for the Higher Education Academy (HEA) in the United Kingdom (2008) illustrate the continuing challenge of demonstrating robustness of data in promotion proposals, and of achieving embedded implementation of policies. The study focused upon reward and recognition for excellence in teaching and learning. It reported on the views of an online survey of over 2,700 staff. Generally, as Diamond and Adam (1995, 2000) had found in the United States, the vast majority of respondents believed that teaching should be recognized appropriately in discussions about promotion, but the majority did not feel that in fact it was. By contrast, senior managers considered that effective policies were in place.

The second part of the HEA study aims to demonstrate ways of assessing teaching effectively, drawing upon existing examples of good practice in institutions. Ramsden, who led the survey, has also encouraged government to allocate funding to enable institutions to improve practice in relation to the assessment of teaching in appointment and promotion discussions. The release of the HEA report coincided with that of one for the Higher Education Funding Council for England (HEFCE, 2008), which questioned the sustainability of the distinctive character of learning and teaching in English higher education institutions without an increase in the level of funding.

Nowadays, procedures and policies for recruitment and retention must be fair and transparent, and comply with legal requirements. For promotions on the grounds of merit, fairness and the appropriateness and robustness of procedures are key considerations. However, when the situation involves a vacancy, a wider range of equity discussions are entailed, including the means of advertising the position and the details of job and person specifications. Typically, such requirements apply to virtually all posts, although arguments are sometimes made to waive policies in exceptional circumstances, such as urgent and/or very short-term replacements. Articulating job and personal specifications may require a shift in established traditions and practices, even within systems that have had a tradition of institutional autonomy over appointments. Essentially, the materials made available to potential candidates must give a fairly clear picture of what is expected in relation to qualifications, the experience and aptitudes of the potential appointee, and the specific roles they will be expected to undertake.

The major sources of increased permeability between higher education systems and other labor markets relate to the growth of professional degree programs; the fact that higher education systems cannot provide posts for all doctoral graduates; the need to recruit individuals with particular specialisms to staff new or expanded professional services within higher education; and the functioning of faculty members as external consultants to industry, agencies, and government, or as academic entrepreneurs in spin-off companies. Permeability is not a new phenomenon, but it has grown massively in scale and complexity, with significant potential implications for institutional strategies and policies, and for individual identities and career pathways.

Increasingly, a major challenge for systems, institutions, and departments or units or centers is to project positive images of attractiveness, performance, working conditions, and employment benefits. Much depends on the degree of freedom of approach available to the institution, but there appears to be a trend toward the use of diversified recruitment strategies. Not all potential implications of equity-related policies necessarily meet with universal support from staff. For example, expressions of good practice in workload allocation policies (Barrett and Barrett, 2007) may be viewed by some participants as constraining expected and valued freedoms. Sometimes, institutions may seek to handle incipient tensions by decentralizing workload allocation decisions to departments, thereby implicitly or explicitly recognizing different disciplinary traditions, expectations, and demands.

In their research, Barrett and Barrett (2007) found a variety of practices in their sample drawn from British institutions of higher education. The range embraced highly detailed and comprehensive examples, others with "an acceptable level of working detail" (ibid.: 475), and informal systems. Despite the variety of possible approaches, reluctance to adopt or adapt was found among responses from heads of departments:

Through the discussions it was apparent that introducing a workload allocation (WLA) model was a time-consuming, resource-intensive, often tense process. Further, the introduction of a WLA system could initially create more managerialism and administrative work in a sector already suffering from high loads (Barrett and Barrett, 2007: 475).

A massive challenge surrounds the adjustment of practice and attitudes in higher education in order to deliver appropriate and equitable enhancing and enriching learning experiences to the increasingly diverse needs and experiences of students. It is not necessarily a simple matter to continue to honor individual academic freedoms while embedding coherent, transparent, appropriate, and sensitized responses to the needs and expectations of diverse student bodies, which nowadays typically span two, three, or more generations (e.g. Baby-boomers, Generation X, Generation Y/Millennials), as well as differentiation on a range of demographic and personal dimensions. An apparently simple, but very real, policy dilemma is to decide whether equity means absolutely equal treatment in all circumstances and, if not, what criteria should guide deviation from that norm.

Academic and Professional Development

The various global contexts discussed earlier have led to increased attention to various dimensions of development, of individuals, teams or groups, and organizations. Some obligations stem directly from legislative requirements, such as health and safety training, training of appointment and promotion committee members on various issues of equality and the application of criteria, and training of all staff on issues of equality, cultural awareness, harassment, and bullying.

From the 1960s on, the research doctorate became viewed as the keystone of academic initiation and socialization (Kogan et al., 1994; Clark, 1992). Three trends have complicated that assumption. First, changes have occurred to the nature and scope of doctorates (Powell and Green, 2007; Green and Powell, 2005; Kehm, 2007). In various ways, those changes have produced some convergence in terms of broadened ideas of the scope of initiation, while significant international and interdisciplinary variations remain in relation to specific expectations and traditions (Powell and Green, 2007). Second, recognizing that many doctoral graduates do not enter careers in academia, revisions to doctoral programs have made varying levels of adaptation in order to demonstrate the relevance of the qualifications to other potential employers of research-trained postgraduates. Third, recruitment to academia has diversified, notably through the growth of undergraduate and postgraduate degree programs in higher education institutions. That altered both the age profile of specific cohorts of entrants to academia, and their curriculum vitae of experiences and qualifications. In substantial measure such entrants have already socialized into their profession, and face both initiation into higher education and possible questions of adaptation of an established identity, rather than the presumed modal phase of initial shaping.

Further permeations complicate the scene, such as research postgraduates who spend some time in industry or other professional roles before re-entering the academic world. Moreover, the expansion of postgraduate education has heightened the visibility of interdisciplinary differences. For example, while it may be atypical to encounter students undertaking part-time doctoral research in chemistry, it is the norm in education.

For more than a decade, efforts have been made to improve the career opportunities, working conditions, and developmental experiences of newer researchers. In the United Kingdom a Concordat was formulated in the 1990s. This has recently been revised and updated. A corresponding Charter and Code, applying to over 3 million young researchers, has been implemented by the European Union. These examples are illustrative of the broadly similar initiatives taken by many national bodies and agencies, often shaped by specifics of local traditions and legislation. Generally, governments support the desirability of finding ways of promoting international opportunities for collaborative research experiences and developmental mobility of newer researchers, although it can be difficult to resolve some of the detailed intricacies of differences in fiscal systems and legislation.

Academic disciplines and related professional societies and associations continue to constitute a major source of developmental provision, notably through conferences, publications, and various networking opportunities. Many of these bodies and societies provide dedicated networking opportunities for specific subgroups and/or subspecialisms such as newer researchers, heads of department, urban geographers, or glaciologists. Some professional bodies require evidence of continuing professional practice and/or development as a condition of maintaining registration. Where that is not the case, many bodies encourage and support it. For example, in the United Kingdom the Association of University Administrators holds a major annual conference and regional lectures and meetings; publishes a journal; provides scholarships for members to attend overseas conferences and/or study tours; runs programs that lead to formal additional qualifications; and expects members to honor an agreed code of practice.

Corresponding provision exists for the newer professions that have grown rapidly within the workforce in higher education, such as human resources professionals; those working in finance, marketing, press and public relations, alumni relations and fundraising, estates management, counseling, student support, and learning support; and careers advisers. Often such individuals may hold membership of several associations and networks, possibly reflecting the blurred boundaries of their roles and varying personal spreads of interest.

There has also been substantial growth in institutional provision of developmental opportunities. Commonplace initiatives include events targeted at orientating and inducting new staff, or addressing the needs of those facing a change of role, such as new heads of department. Reference has been made earlier to the provision of both awareness-raising and detailed training to address changes in legislation or other regulatory or quasi-regulatory (both institutionally and externally defined) requirements. Illustrations of the former might be a new ordering procedure, a way of returning student grades online, recording review of staff performance, registering sickness absence, or standardizing entries to the institutional repository of research activities. Examples of the latter might be changes to the external process of financial audit or quality assurance, or return of statistics to state or national databases. Frequently the various expectations interact. For example, as institutions or departments prepare for an external scrutiny of educational provision, there are typically both compliance and enhancement dimensions. These deliberations generate questions such as: Do we do what we claim? Will that satisfy external expectations and scrutiny? What should be enhanced? How? By whom? That interaction then sparks various developmental initiatives and activities. Indeed, institutions are often moving toward a more continuous review and reflection model across a variety of activities. The implications for developmental provision tend to be a shift toward a more strategic and coherent framework, with greater attention paid to the connectivity between the progression of strategic priorities, and the development of individuals or teams or groups to support those ends.

It is perhaps not surprising that institutions might seek to pursue more focused mission-related development. That might involve monitoring and building research capacity (Hazelkorn, 2004, 2008), enhancing excellence in learning and teaching and student support, enhancing research excellence, promoting commercialization and entrepreneurship, or working closely with regional and professional communities, or indeed various combinations of priorities. Mohrman et al. (2008), writing on the Emerging Global Model for the twenty-first-century research university, imply that no institution may be entirely divorced from such strategic pressures. Among the eight characteristics proposed by these authors is: "Faculty members, as producers of knowledge, are assuming new roles, shifting from traditional independent patterns of inquiry to becoming members of team-oriented, cross-disciplinary and international partnerships, with research directed more often than before toward real-world problems" (ibid.: 7). Additions to the increasingly complex landscape for developmental provision also include supporting sector-wide bodies such as, in the United Kingdom, the Leadership Foundation and the Higher Education Academy.

Identities and Career Pathways

D'Andrea and Gosling (2005) visualized three types of identity, namely personal, institutional, and academic/professional. They suggested three possible strands in the third type: discipline or subdiscipline, profession, and what they termed a universal dimension, for example, "researcher", "teacher", "cosmopolitan". Presumably one could add other descriptors such as entrepreneur or leader to that list. Henkel (2000, 2007), drawing upon her sustained research on academic identities, has outlined various concepts and implications. Later chapters in this volume explore nuances, issues, and trends. Here attention is restricted to a brief consideration of three aspects: the implications of increased complexity and diversity within the workforce in higher education, the links between different strands of identity, and the relationship to career pathways and organizational responses.

Whitchurch (2008a) explored shifting identities and blurring boundaries, with particular attention to what she termed "*Third Space* Professionals". Illustrative examples of institutional projects in *Third Space* included student transitions (welfare, widening participation, careers, and employability), professional development (academic practice, leadership, and management development), and economic and social entrepreneurship and community interactions. More extensively, mainstream academic and administrative roles have also diversified, expanded, and been transformed. New roles have been added, and additional or altered priorities have come to the forefront. Some trends are seen as challenging traditional power balances within institutions. Some phenomena may be ephemeral, examples of Birnbaum's (2000) "management fads" or responses. However, as Schuster and Finkelstein (2006) project the potentiality of current employment trends in American higher education, so it may be appropriate to consider whether some of the trends presently seen as minor notes in the higher education symphony may in fact become recognized as the defining theme over the next decade or two. That knotty problem is examined from various perspectives in other chapters of this volume.

An example of exploration of a new trend within the academic heartland is provided by the study into academic entrepreneurialism among a sample of bioscientists (Duberley et al., 2007). Duberley and colleagues identified three subgroups, namely experienced scientists who could capitalize on their research, colleagues who viewed technology transfer as a new career option, and younger scientists unsure about the direction of their future career. The entrepreneurial faculty members wanted to remain as academic faculty with a spin-out link. The technology transfer professionals sought that focus in their career. The younger researchers were described as career capital builders. Duberley et al. concluded by observing, "Permeating our findings is a strong sense that as a result of institutional changes, the nature of what it means to be an academic is being reconfigured" (ibid.: 495). The evidence from their interviews was that there was a shared sense of change among the researchers, but concern as to whether the implications were fully comprehended by institutional managers.

The role of reference groups may be critical. The reality is that, worldwide, most higher education institutions cannot expect to be ranked as world class in terms of research output. Logically, one might expect that to mean that teaching and service should be highly valued at the very least in a very substantial proportion of institutions of higher education. Yet the Higher Education Academy survey in 2008 found that some 80 percent of respondents believed that performance in research dominated promotion decisions. Institutional managers disputed that proposition, and the report accepted that there was evidence that some institutions operated a range of effective strategies to reward and recognize excellence in teaching and learning, and indeed in service and professional engagement. The survey may reflect imperfect understandings of a slowly changing reality, but it may also demonstrate the continuing power of a dominant culture, and the primacy of the value attached to knowledge production over other roles in contributing to knowledge societies and other forms of creativity.

Archer (2008) examined the ways in which younger academic faculty construct professional identities and define "success". Some of her interviewees felt that they had to suppress aspects of their personal identity, such as social class, in order to fit into their working environment. In line with arguments advanced by Bourdieu (2001), Archer argued that "questions of authenticity and legitimacy are central to the formation of social relations within the academy—with individuals and groups competing to ensure that their particular interests, characteristics and identities are accorded recognition and value" (2008: 386). Her interviewees reported stressful and pleasurable experiences, something that Archer suggested might also be true of more established faculty, especially in an age of increased attention to performance, and expectations that most staff can adapt to new roles and challenges.

In Chapter 5, Strike analyzes some institutional attempts to enlarge and refine the map of career pathways. Whitchurch (2008a) suggested a fourfold categorization of professional identities (bounded, cross-boundary, unbounded, and blended), which could map neatly onto flexible systems of career pathways, but might sit somewhat uncomfortably within rigid systems.

Conclusion

Changes have affected and impacted upon higher education systems, institutions, and structures worldwide, albeit with differences in precise details, profiles, timing and reactions, adaptations or accommodation. Does Whitchurch's (2008a) typology of professional identities (bounded, cross-boundary, unbounded, blended) have potential relevance for changes in academic identities, albeit with an adjustment to the descriptive characteristics associated with each category? Dowd and Kaplan (2005) suggest that this may be the case.

There are substantial cohorts of academic faculty who now perform primarily research or teaching roles, in addition to the numerous varieties of weightings between these traditionally core ingredients (Henkel, 2000) of academic identities. Combinations of management and teaching and/or research roles have increased over the past twenty years, as have examples entailing service, commercialization, community, and other third-stream roles and links. The questions may not be so much whether academic identities are changing, but rather how widespread the trend is and what its principal manifestations and implications are.

Unsurprisingly, institutions have endeavored to respond to the various global challenges that affect their operating environments, adjusting policies, practice, and structures, even promulgating new ones. In an age of increasing emphasis on collective evaluation of performance, even when produced by assembling individual data, attention has focused on ways of assuring and enhancing outputs and outcomes through various environmental, structural, motivational, and evaluative initiatives, processes, and procedures. In aggregate, these can fuel complaints of unwelcome intrusion into the territory of academic self-autonomy in the control of their work, even when contracts may signal that such allocation should occur in discussion with, and with agreement by, the relevant head of department.

Can any analogy usefully capture the nature of perceived attacks upon academic identities? Is it akin to global warming and identifiable by comparatively small but crucial changes in key indicators and relationships? Is it comparable to the creation and erosion of sand and pebble beaches, constantly rubbed, sorted, and sifted by the daily ebb and flow of the tide, but more strikingly altered by occasional storms? Or is the appropriate metaphor one of a modifying and adapting living organism that can adjust to alterations to habitat?

As the later chapters in this volume demonstrate, changes to academic and professional identities are complex, varied, and contested. Sometimes that conception may create tensions (Dobson and Conway, 2004). That raises questions about individual mind maps of the contemporary university. Do these represent the university as having distinct rankings of roles, with certain ranks permitted high levels of individualism and special freedoms? Or is the university a place where all talents are respected, with all roles valued for what they add to the achievement of the reputation and success of the institution? This polarization may be grossly over-simplistic, but it may serve to highlight the key issues, the value attached to respect within the workplace, and the degree to which individuals associate themselves with that workplace.

References

Altbach, P. (ed.) (1996) *The International Academic Profession: A Special Report*. Princeton, NJ: Carnegie Foundation for the Advancement of Teaching.

Altbach, P. and Lewis, L. S. (1996) "The Academic Profession in International Perspective." In *The International Academic Profession: A Special Report*, ed. P. Altbach. Princeton, NJ: Carnegie Foundation for the Advancement of Teaching.

Archer, L. (2008) "Younger Academics: Constructions of 'Authenticity', 'Success' and Professional Identities." *Studies in Higher Education* 33 (4): 385–404.

Barrett, L. and Barrett, P. (2007) "Current Practice in the Allocation of Academic Workloads." *Higher Education Quarterly* 61 (4): 461–478.

Becher, T. (1989) *Academic Tribes and Territories*. Buckingham, UK: SRHE/Open University Press.

Becher, T. and Trowler, P. (2001) *Academic Tribes and Territories: Intellectual Enquiry and the Culture of Disciplines*. Buckingham, UK: SRHE/Open University Press.

Bergquist, W. H. (1992) *The Four Cultures of the Academy*. San Francisco: Jossey-Bass.

Birnbaum, R. (2000) *Management Fads in Higher Education*. San Francisco: Jossey-Bass.

Bourdieu, P. (2001) *Homo Academicus*. Cambridge: Polity Press.

Boyd, P. (2007) "Becoming a Professional Educator: The Professional Development of New Lecturers in Nurse and Teacher Education as Boundary-Crossing Activity." Ph.D. thesis, University of Lancaster, UK.

Boyer, E. L. (1990) *Scholarship Reconsidered: Priorities for the Professoriate*. Princeton, NJ: Carnegie Foundation for the Advancement of Teaching.

Boyer, E. L., Altbach, P. G., and Whitelaw, M. J. (1994) *The Academic Profession: An International Perspective*. Princeton, NJ: The Carnegie Foundation for the Advancement of Teaching.

Clark, B. R. (1992) "Graduate Education and Research Training." In *Research and Higher Education: The*

United Kingdom and the United States, ed. T. G. Whiston and R. L. Geiger. Buckingham, UK: SRHE/Open University Press.

Clark, B. R. (1998) *Creating Entrepreneurial Universities: Organizational Pathways of Transformation.* Oxford: IAU Press and Pergamon, Elsevier Science.

Clark, B. R. (2004) *Sustaining Change in Universities.* Maidenhead, UK: SRHE/Open University Press.

D'Andrea, V. and Gosling, D. (2005) *Improving Teaching and Learning in Higher Education.* Maidenhead, UK: SRHE/Open University Press.

Dearing, R. (1997) *Higher Education in the Learning Society* (the Dearing Report). National Committee of Inquiry into Higher Education. London: The Stationery Office.

Diamond, R. M. and Adam, B. E. (1995) *The Disciplines Speak: Rewarding the Scholarly, Professional, and Creative Work of Faculty.* Washington, DC: American Association of Higher Education.

Diamond, R. M. and Adam, B. E. (2000) *The Disciplines Speak II: More Statements on Rewarding the Scholarly, Professional, and Creative Work of Faculty.* Washington, DC: American Association of Higher Education.

Dobson, I. and Conway, M. (2004) "Fear and Loathing in University Staff: The Case of Australian Academic and General Staff." *Higher Education Management and Policy* 15 (3): 123–134.

Dowd, K. O. and Kaplan, D. M. (2005) "The Career Life of Academics: Boundaried or Boundaryless?" *Human Relations* 58 (6): 699–721.

Duberley, J., Cohen, L., and Leeson, E. (2007) "Entrepreneurial Academics: Developing Scientific Careers in Changing University Settings." *Higher Education Quarterly* 61 (4): 479–497.

Finkelstein, M. J. (2007) "The 'New' Look of Academic Careers in the United States." In *Key Challenges to the Academic Profession*, ed. M. Kogan and U. Teichler. Kassel, Germany: UNESCO Forum on Higher Education and International Centre for Higher Education and Research.

Gibbons, M., Limoges, C., Nowotny, H., Schwartzman, S., Scott, P., and Trow, M. (1994) *The New Production of Knowledge: The Dynamics of Science and Research in Contemporary Societies.* London: Sage.

Gordon, G. (2004) "University Roles and Career Paths: Trends, Scenarios and Motivational Challenges." *Higher Education Management and Policy* 15 (3): 80–104.

Gordon, G. and Whitchurch, C. (2007) "Managing Human Resources in Higher Education: The Implications of a Diversifying Workforce." *Higher Education Management and Policy* 19 (2): 135–155.

Green, D. H. and Powell, S. D. (2005) *The Doctorate in Contemporary Higher Education.* Buckingham, UK: SRHE/Open University Press.

Hazelkorn, E. (2004) "Growing Research: Challenges for Late Developers and Newcomers." *Higher Education Management and Policy* 16 (1): 507–542.

Hazelkorn, E. (2008) "Motivating Individuals: Growing Research from a 'Fragile Base.'" *Tertiary Education and Management* 14 (2): 151–171.

Henkel, M. (2000) *Academic Identities and Policy Change in Higher Education.* London: Jessica Kingsley.

Henkel, M. (2007) "Shifting Boundaries and the Academic Profession." In *Key Challenges to the Academic Profession*, ed. M. Kogan and U. Teichler. Kassel, Germany: UNESCO Forum on Higher Education and International Centre for Higher Education and Research.

Higher Education Academy (HEA) (2008) *Reward and Recognition of Teaching in Higher Education.* Online, available at: www.heacademy.ac.uk/ourwork/research/rewardandrecog.

Higher Education Funding Council for England (HEFCE) (2008) *The Sustainability of Learning and Teaching in English Higher Education.* Bristol: HEFCE.

Hughes, M. (2005) "The Mythology of Research and Teaching Relationships in Universities." In *Reshaping the University*, ed. R. Barnett. Maidenhead, UK: SRHE/Open University Press.

Kehm, B.M. (2007) "The Changing Role of Graduate and Doctoral Education as a Challenge to the Academic Profession: Europe and North America Compared." In *Key Challenges to the Academic Profession*, ed. M. Kogan and U. Teichler. Kassel, Germany: UNESCO Forum on Higher Education and International Centre for Higher Education Research.

Knight, J. (2001) "Issues and Trends in Internationalization: A Comparative Perspective." In *A New World of Knowledge: Canadian Universities and Globalization*, ed. S. Bond and J. P. Lemasson. Ottawa: International Development Research Centre.

Knight, J. (2003) "Updating the Definition of Internationalization." *Boston Center International Higher Education Newsletter* 33: 2–3.

Kogan, M. (2007) "The Academic Profession and Its Interface with Management." In *Key Challenges to the Academic Profession*, ed. M. Kogan and U. Teichler. Kassel, Germany: UNESCO Forum on Higher Education and International Centre for Higher Education Research.

Kogan, M., Moses, I., and El-Khawas, E. (1994) *Staffing Higher Education.* London: OECD/Jessica Kingsley.

Krishnaveni R. and Anitha, J. (2007) "Educators' Professional Characteristics." *Quality Assurance in Education* 15 (2): 149–161.

Kubler, J. and DeLuca, C. (2006) *Trends in Academic Recruitment and Retention: A Commonwealth Perspective.* London: Association of Commonwealth Universities.

Land, R. and Gordon, G. (2008) *Research–Teaching Linkages: Enhancing Graduate Attributes: Sector-Wide Discussions*, vol. 1. Gloucester: Quality Assurance Agency for Higher Education.

Lucas, L. (2006) *The Research Game in Academic Life.* Maidenhead, UK: SRHE/Open University Press.

McNay, I. (1995) "From Collegial Academy to Corporate Enterprise: The Changing Cultures of Universities." In *The Changing University?* ed. T. Schuller. Maidenhead, UK: SRHE/Open University Press.

McNay, I. (1998) "The Paradoxes of Research Assessment and Funding." In *Changing Relationships between Higher Education and the State*, ed. M. H. Little and B. Little. London: Jessica Kingsley.

Mohrman, K., Ma, W., and Baker, D. (2008) "The Research University in Transition: The Emerging Global Model." *Higher Education Policy* 21 (1): 5–28.

Musselin, C. (2007) "Transformation of Academic Work: Facts and Analysis." In *Key Challenges to the Academic Profession*, ed. M. Kogan and U. Teichler. Kassel, Germany: UNESCO Forum on Higher Education and International Centre for Higher Education Research.

Powell, S. and Green, H. (eds.) (2007) *The Doctorate Worldwide.* Maidenhead, UK: SRHE/Open University Press.

O'Meara, K. A. and Rice, R. E. (2005) *Faculty Priorities Reconsidered.* San Francisco: Jossey-Bass.

Santiago, P., Tremblay, K., Basri, E., and Arnal, E. (2008) *Tertiary Education for the Knowledge Society*, vol. 2. Paris: Organisation for Economic Co-operation and Development.

Schuster, J. and Finkelstein, M. (2006) *The American Faculty: The Restructuring of Academic Work and Careers.* Baltimore: Johns Hopkins University Press.

Thorne, M. and Cuthbert, R. (1996) "Autonomy, Bureaucracy and Competition: The ABC of Control." In *Working in Higher Education*, ed. R. Cuthbert. Buckingham, UK: SRHE/Open University Press.

Whitchurch, C. (2008a) "Shifting Identities and Blurring Boundaries: The Emergence of *Third Space* Professionals in UK Higher Education." *Higher Education Quarterly* 62 (4): 377–396.

Whitchurch, C. (2008b) "Beyond Administration and Management: Reconstructing the Identities of Professional Staff in UK Higher Education." *Higher Education Policy and Management* 30 (4): 375–386.

3

Envisioning Invisible Workforces
Enhancing Intellectual Capital

GARY RHOADES

Recent decades have witnessed a marked trend in US universities, and one that is becoming increasingly prominent worldwide, of professors being more actively managed by academic executives to address market demands and pursue market possibilities. Many scholars have written about a more entrepreneurial and commercialized academe in various national contexts (Bok, 2003; Chan and Fisher, 2008; Clark, 1998; de Weert and Enders, 2009; Etzkowitz and Leydesdorff, 1997; Marginson and Considine, 2000). This chapter draws on my concepts of academic faculty being increasingly "managed professionals" (Rhoades, 1998a), and of the rise of non-academic "managerial professionals" (Rhoades, 1998b; Rhoades and Sporn, 2002) working in the context of "academic capitalism and the new economy" (Slaughter and Rhoades, 2004). These concepts point to key developments nationally, and at the campus level, by way of an increasingly specialized and differentiated academic workforce. At the same time, they point to major blind spots nationally, and at the campus level, in higher education policy and 'strategic' management. The chapter's conceptual thrust is to facilitate our ability to envision what are often invisible workforces, and to enhance the intellectual capital of our universities and nations.

From one country to another, universities and higher education systems are experiencing increasing pressure to become more competitive and efficient, more responsive and connected to various external markets, and more focused on the needs and learning outcomes of students. In some settings, such as the United States, these developments have been at play for at least a quarter-century, with the rise of "academic capitalism" (Slaughter and Leslie, 1997; Slaughter and Rhoades, 2004). In other settings these developments are of more recent vintage, coming into play within the past decade or two, with the effect that universities are forced to compete for a greater share of their revenues, and in some cases to become more "entrepreneurial" (Clark, 1998). The implications for the higher education workforce have been profound in terms of the structure and role of the academic profession in particular. More pressure on institutions has translated into more pressure on professors to be more productive, more relevant to and engaged in market-related activities, and to connect more effectively and technologically with a wider range of students than have traditionally been taught in higher education. And, as in the case of institutions, the result has been increased differentiation, of form and function.

The patterns I have described have been unfolding for some time. We can expect that in at least some ways they will be heightened by the global financial collapse.

As public budgets become increasingly strained by declining economic revenues and continued political reluctance to increase taxes, particularly in the United States, universities are becoming more likely than ever to search out alternative sources of revenue and support.

The chapter is organized around four topics, and features developments in US higher education. The first topic addresses the emergence of various relatively invisible categories of academic faculty. In a related vein, the second topic addresses the emergence of various types of other professionals who are also relatively invisible on university campuses. In each of these first two sections of the chapter, not only are the empirical developments highlighted, but so too are the conceptual limitations of, the blind spots in, our current understandings of the academic workforce. The subsequent two sections deal with strategic issues at both the system and the campus level. First, how can envisioning invisible members of the higher education workforce enhance the academy as it confronts significant challenges? Second, how can reconceptualizing the higher education workforce as a key source of intellectual capital better enable the academy to confront what is arguably its most pervasive and profound challenge? Finally, some thoughts are offered about the need to shift from our traditional, individualistic, industrial-era framing of human resource issues regarding employees in academe to a more current collective, and knowledge economy-relevant, construction of professionals.

Invisible Academics: Key Developments and Blind Spots

The word 'professor' conjures up many images. But for all the various images, there are also commonalities in characterizations of professors in the popular consciousness, the public discourse of policymakers, and in the private discourse of many academic administrators. The irony of these pervasive perspectives is that they are largely out of touch with empirical developments in the structure of the academic workforce and academic employment. They render invisible the fastest-growing and now largest segments of academic employees. And they tend to blind us to the most pressing human resource challenge confronting higher education institutions and systems.

Professors are seen as full-time employees who have a great deal of flexibility and freedom in terms of their time. It is not just that professors are seen as having the summers 'off'. It is that they are also perceived to be 'off' in the evenings (when they refuse to schedule classes) and at weekends. Even when they are 'on' work time, the perception is that professors are free not to be in their offices (on Friday afternoons), and not even to be on campus (e.g. to be mowing their lawns instead) on mid-week mornings. They do not clock in or out. They come and go largely as they please. And every sixth year they get at least a semester off, on full pay, for sabbatical. In short, they have it really easy, with even the heaviest teaching 'loads' seeming remarkably light to those who work in the 'real world'. To the average person, the full time of professors is considerably less than full.

Moreover, professors are seen as being relatively untouchable. Once they are tenured they basically cannot be fired, for tenure is a job for life. And even before they get tenure it is extremely unusual for assistant professors to be fired. Compared to professionals in other sectors of society, professors are seen as having extraordinarily secure employment even in extraordinarily difficult financial times, as at present. So, the claims of professors that they are underpaid relative to other professionals with comparable levels of education, and relative to academic administrators, are not particularly compelling to the external world.

In part as a result of their job security, professors tend to be characterized as being resistant to change and to employing new technologies. They are content to remain as 'the sage on the stage', lecturing to large bodies of students. It is hard to get these comfortable old dogs to try any new tricks. Finally, professors tend to be characterized as being more loyal and committed to their careers than they are to their employers or to their students. The view is that discipline trumps institutions and that research trumps teaching. Professors have no incentive to focus on students, or on learning outcomes.

Overall, it is a far from flattering view. More importantly, it is a view that is far from reflecting the reality of the academic profession in the United States. That profession has increasingly become part-time and contingent. More academic faculty are utilizing technology in their classrooms and developing and delivering online instruction. And more and more individual faculty members and categories of academics are focused on instruction in institutions that are less and less committed to their employees.

From the 1970s to the 1990s the proportion of faculty members working part-time in the United States doubled (Rhoades, 1998a). It is now nearly half the academic profession. In the community college sector nationally, about two-thirds of academic faculty are part-time. As is also the case in many developing countries, such as Mexico, where a large proportion of faculty members are part-time, a large proportion in the United States have multiple jobs. Some work at multiple campuses. Others have full-time jobs in professional fields, ranging from education and medicine to business. The part-time designation, then, is in considerable part a misnomer; they are part-time at a particular campus, but may work what is essentially a full-time workload or more at several sites.

In the United States the current term of usage for academic faculty who do not have, or are not eligible for, tenure is contingent faculty, or faculty members working in contingent positions. This category includes an increasing number of faculty members who are working full-time, but are not in tenure-track positions. Estimates are that upwards of 20 percent of academic faculty in the United States nationally are full-time, non-tenure-track (Finkelstein et al., 1998; Schuster and Finkelstein, 2006). As with part-time faculty, the pattern is that these full-time contingent positions are proliferating, even as full-time tenure-track positions are stagnating in numbers. For recent cohorts of new hires, about two-thirds are hired off the tenure track (Finkelstein et al., 1998; Schuster and Finkelstein, 2006).

The reality about the academic workforce today, then, is that flexibility lies more in the hands of academic managers than in the lives of academic faculty. The increased employment of part-time and contingent faculty has systematically and profoundly shifted the balance of power between professional autonomy and managerial discretion, making professors increasingly "managed professionals"

(Rhoades, 1998a). Part-time faculty members have very limited rights and professional perquisites. They can be hired, fired, and non-renewed on extremely short notice, or no notice, with little or no involvement of faculty peers. They have little voice in the governance of the institution. And as larger segments of the curriculum have come to be delivered by part-time faculty members, academic managers have gained increased influence over the curriculum, in terms of what is taught, how it is taught (e.g. online, in distance education, or in hybrid on-campus classes that incorporate advanced instructional technologies). The majority of academic faculty are working with quite limited professional autonomy. And the collective body of the faculty have experienced a decline in their professional influence over the direction of the academy.

The change is so profound that each of the major faculty unions nationally (the American Association of University Professors, the American Federation of Teachers, and the National Education Association) has issued policy statements and recommendations regarding the use of part-time faculty, and more recently on the use of contingent faculty. They have decried the exploitation of part-time and contingent faculty, whose numbers they seek to delimit. And these employees themselves have become considerably more active in the academic labor movement (Rhoades, 2008).

From a human resource management perspective this sector of the workforce is largely invisible. And the practices surrounding their employment are for the most part not codified. Data on the terms and conditions of a complex array of part-time faculty positions are very limited. Whether in regard to salaries, evaluation, or any number of conditions of labor, we simply have few reliable data on part-time faculty. Those studies that have gathered data from national samples of institutions have identified 'best practices' but have also found that few universities employ these practices (Baldwin and Chronister, 2001).

Contrary to the prevailing views about faculty in regard to change, technology, and instruction, contingent faculty members include various categories of faculty who are solely devoted to instruction, and are often very much involved in delivering technology-mediated instruction, often at a distance. Even on the tenure track, more faculty members are utilizing instructional technologies, and more institutions are developing special teaching tracks on which faculty members can obtain tenure.

The patterns identified above are part of what has been called "academic capitalism in the new economy" (Slaughter and Rhoades, 2004). As colleges and universities have engaged in more market-like and market behaviors, they have developed new models of producing research and instruction, and new circuits of knowledge creation and dissemination that have involved blurring the boundaries between universities and the private sector marketplace. Managerial capacity has been expanded in regard to core academic activities and functions, evident in increased institutional claims on intellectual property created by faculty (and students), as well as in increased institutional investment in and management of fields of research and areas of instruction that are seen as being close to the market and as having the potential to generate new revenue streams. In this context, students come to be conceptualized as consumers and customers to be more efficiently served. Instruction comes increasingly to be conceptualized as delivery of an educational commodity or service.

A corollary of the above developments in the prevailing knowledge/learning regime in higher education is that even the tenure-track faculty become, in a sense, invisible—or at least they get pushed more to the margins. A decade ago, I suggested (Rhoades, 1998a) that faculty and their unions should work to assert some control over decision making surrounding the use of instructional technology, not because they were in danger of being deprofessionalized but because they were likely to become increasingly marginalized from exercising professional control over key aspects of the curriculum. And that is precisely what has happened.

Public policy discourse on higher education now centers on accountability, measured in terms of students' learning outcomes. Learning has become less part of a phrase, 'teaching and learning', than a distinct process and product, independent of instruction and professors. The focal point in delivering services to student consumers in an academic capitalist higher education economy shifts from professors to independent and technology-mediated learning processes and communities that are seen as being both more efficient and more effective.

Along these lines, institutional associations such as the Association of American Colleges and Universities (AACandU) and the League for Innovation (consisting primarily of community colleges) seek to foster a transformation and modernization of education, a learning revolution. Such changes involve incorporating and featuring new constituencies (such as other professionals and employers) in shaping and evaluating education (Rhoades, forthcoming). No longer are such matters solely or primarily the purview of faculty members.

The extent to which faculty are part of the consciousness of policymakers is captured concisely in the title of a book by Mary Burgan, a former General Secretary of the American Association of University Professors, *Whatever Happened to the Faculty?* (2006). Burgan notes (ibid.: xvi) not only that there is an absence of faculty representation in national decision making surrounding higher education, but that "I began to observe that the faculty themselves were hardly ever present in the imaginations of the policy makers."

Most recently, that relative invisibility is evident in a 'stimulus package' that was submitted by the Higher Education Secretariat (a group of national higher education associations, with a major force being institutional associations) to the US Congress. The proposal makes the case that higher education is central to the economic recovery of the nation. As might be expected, the package proposed various measures to increase financial aid and facilitate students' access to a college education. It also proposed infrastructure projects to renovate and build new classroom and research facilities. Remarkably, for all the public discourse about our knowledge-based economy in which expertise and innovation are the keys to global competitiveness, no mention is made in the stimulus package about the faculty, about the need to strengthen and expand the professionals who are the key knowledge profession, creating new knowledge and preparing the vast majority of knowledge workers. They are invisible.

The academic workforce has become substantially diversified in recent decades. New categories and strata of academic faculty have emerged and expanded, even as most observers continue to perceive faculty in traditional terms, overlooking defining features of the current academic workforce. As a result, there is a failure to develop the sorts of processes and mechanisms by which to address various aspects of human resource management. There is a remarkable absence of defined, codified practices regarding basic dimensions of employment. Similarly, little attention has been paid to questions of how best to motivate, develop, and reward individuals in these new categories of employment.

Perhaps most remarkably, there is a significant blind spot at national and university levels regarding what is arguably the greatest human resource challenge the United States confronts: the graying of the academic profession. In the United States, roughly half of the full-time faculty are now over 50, compared to less than a third in 1975 (Ashenfelter and Card, 2002; De Francesco and Rhoades, 1987). Whereas in the mid-1970s over 40 percent of full-time faculty in four-year institutions were under 40, by the mid-1990s the figure was less than 20 percent. And it continues to fall. Similar patterns in terms of the overall trend are found in Europe. There is a systematic shifting of the age profile, as the large numbers of faculty members hired in the late 1960s and 1970s move through the system. And that presents key challenges to the academy by way of replenishing the profession, providing professional development, and facilitating professional transitions throughout the career and life course of a professor.

The demographic challenge exists not only nationally, but also within individual colleges and universities. My own campus of the University of Arizona is relatively typical, with over one-quarter of its full-time faculty being aged 60 or older, and nearly half being 50 or older. That sort of demographic profile is a major human resource issue that is receiving minor attention.

The public discourse in higher education points to changing demands on institutions, promotes universities' adaptation to those demands, and calls for increased productivity. Yet there is remarkably limited attention directed to changes in the structure of academic employment; there is much talk about the need to make such employment more flexible and responsive, but little recognition that such flexibility and responsiveness are already built into the large majority of academic positions in the form of various types of contingent categories of academic employment. Similarly, public policy discourse in higher education points to the changing demographics of the student body, and policy discourse more broadly identifies some profound challenges embedded in the graying of the Baby Boom generation (e.g. in the realms of health care and social security). Yet there is remarkably limited understanding of the demographic profile of the academic workforce and the challenges it presents.

Invisible Professionals: Key Developments and Blind Spots

In the eyes of most academic faculty and academic administrators, the only real professionals on campus are professors. It does not matter that professors and presidents walk by, interact with, and depend on a range of other employees on campus with degrees. These people are invisible. It is not that they are seen and yet are unheard. Rather, it is that they are unrecognized and unacknowledged.

The degree of invisibility is such that even when someone points out the existence of other professional staff on campus, academic faculty and academic administrators tend to misunderstand, confusing them with the equivalent of clerical support staff or with low- to mid-level bureaucrats. Much the same can be said of external constituencies. Whether it is policymakers or the general public, the dominant perception is that professors are the principal employees and the only real professionals on campus. The two categories of employees with advanced degrees are assumed to be either faculty or administrators.

Yet a central part of the rise of academic capitalism and the new economy is the emergence and expansion of a wide range of non-academic professionals who, among other responsibilities, mediate between faculty and various constituencies and forces in the external world. They perform such roles within what Slaughter and Rhoades (2004) have called "interstitial units", spaces between existing organizational units that have been developed to manage various new activities in the entrepreneurial university. Neither academic faculty nor senior administrators, they are a category of professional employee with advanced degrees who lack the professional perquisites of professors and the positional power of senior administrators. The human resource practices that apply to these employees follow the model more of administrators (supervisor driven) than of professors (peer driven) in the ways in which they are hired, evaluated, and fired. Yet their identities in many ways take on the trappings of professors in that many such professions have worked to develop technical bodies of knowledge, presented in professional conferences and published in academic journals. Increasingly, in the United States, these professionals have even begun to directly model their program and service delivery on that of professors—for instance, offering for-credit classes to students as part of the undergraduate curriculum.

In the European context, other scholars have identified the emergence of new categories of employee. For example, Clark (1998) has referred to them as part of the "developmental periphery" that constitute one of the organizational pathways for the European universities he studied to become entrepreneurial universities. Scandinavian scholars have also noted and detailed new developments in professional management in European universities (Gornitzka et al., 1998; Gornitzka and Larsen, 2004). And Whitchurch (2004, 2006, 2008a, b) is building a considerable body of work on new spaces and the identities of the people working in these realms.

Why, then, draw on the concept of managerial professionals, and link it specifically to the rise of academic capitalism? In part because other scholarship does not feature these employees as part of a distinctive profession, as being connected to the prevailing managerial project in the academy, and as representing a core feature of a distinctive mode of production. Celia Whitchurch's work on the "Third Space" that has emerged between what she calls professional and academic domains moves in this direction. But Rhoades' work characterizes this space as politically and professionally contested, revealing a growing shift in the balance between managerial discretion and professorial autonomy.

As Rhoades and Sporn (2002) demonstrated, managerial professionals are far from being as prevalent in continental European universities as they are in US universities. But their numbers are increasing. And the sorts of functions that public policymakers are increasingly urging that universities perform, in regard to massification, quality assurance, and intersections with industry, are likely to give rise to some form of specialized professionals (or of seconded professors). Even a cursory review of the jobs advertised in the *Times Higher Education* reveals a range of positions that fall between professors and senior administrators. So it would appear that, at least in some places, new occupations and career tracks are emerging.

In the national datasets of the United States, these managerial professionals are characterized as "support professionals" or "other professionals". Both modifiers underscore the presumed ancillary, subordinate, and residual aspects of these members of the academy. They work in a 'supporting', not a leading, role. They are the unnamed 'other'. Yet in terms of their numerical growth, managerial professionals have greatly outpaced the growth of academic faculty. From 1976 to 1996 these 'non-faculty professionals' went from constituting about 20 percent of the professional workforce in higher education to being nearly 30 percent of that workforce. And that growth continues in recent years, even during relatively tight financial times for colleges and universities, to the point that they constitute about one-third of the professional workforce.

Moreover, the increasing centrality of these employees to some of the most basic production processes of the academy has been highlighted (Rhoades, 2007, 2008). For example, in the area of instruction, various categories of such managerial professionals have utilized instructional and learning technologies as a wedge to establish their professional claims over a domain of work—education—previously dominated by professors. The first step in this process has been for professionals to establish claims of expertise in regard to the use of technology, which is subsequently expanded to, and conflated with, general pedagogical expertise of engagement and student-centered learning. Teaching and learning specialists within and outside the academy in the United States have thereby challenged the claims of professors to know best how to teach their students and, even more importantly, to know about how students learn. Indeed, such professionals have successfully been part of establishing and expanding interstitial units that provide professional development experiences to professors. It is not such a long step from the focus on how to teach to the question of what to teach—for example, what sorts of materials to utilize.

The nature of these interstitial units contrasts with Gibbons et al.'s (1994) conception of a Mode 2 form of knowledge production. Underlying that model is the idea that organizational units are formed around areas of problems that are larger than any particular discipline, and then are reconfigured as the problems being addressed change. Not so in Slaughter and Rhoades' (2004) conception of interstitial units, for such units are part of a systematic restructuring of power within the academy. They are permanent units. A larger proportion of this professional workforce is full-time than is the case for the professoriate. And although managerial professionals do not enjoy the professional privileges of academic freedom and tenure, they are not contingent, flex workers. Moreover, they are not oriented to solving external social problems as much as they are to serving internal organizational interests.

Consider the two other types of managerial professionals identified by Rhoades and Sporn (2002). Those professionals who work in entrepreneurial areas are oriented to generating revenues for the organization that employs them. Over time, some professionals in these realms may develop and adopt orientations that have more to do with directly serving the public good. For example, the Association of University Technology Managers (AUTM) in the United States has very definitely moved in this direction in recent years, including in the reports it does and the metrics it seeks to establish. Nevertheless, the *raison d'être* of these professionals from the standpoint of university managers is to benefit the organization (which in turn is believed to benefit the broader society).

A similar point holds with respect to those managerial professionals who work with students. A central part of their job is to attract and deliver services to captive student markets (Slaughter and Rhoades, 2004: chap. 11). Certainly the professionals in these positions are committed to serving and benefiting students. But just as certainly, from the standpoint of the college or university in question, their role is connected to the interests of the employing institution. Yet for all their centrality in terms of academic capitalist activities, there is a managerial blind spot with regard to managerial professionals. As is explored in a subsequent section of this chapter, they are not conceptualized as intellectual capital. It is as if managers see them as essential providers of valuable services but not as creators of value in their work.

Such a blind spot is unfortunate for at least two reasons. The first is that managerial professionals actually have considerable potential for generating revenue. Some of that potential derives from their independent work. For example, it is not uncommon for some units in student affairs to generate considerable grant revenues for their work with students, either students already in college or students in school who are preparing for college. A second reason that the blind spot is unfortunate is that by virtue of their professional networks in the community, region, and state, as well as in national funding agencies and sources generally relatively untapped by academic faculty, some (units of) managerial professionals could augment the revenue-generating capacity of faculty and their units. But they tend not to be considered in this way. Academic managers and faculty alike are basically blind to these resources and sides of managerial professionals.

Strategically Envisioning Invisible Workforces

It is hard to be strategically effective in preparing, developing, and deploying human resources in the academy if one neither sees nor addresses the major segments of the professional workforce. But that is precisely what is happening in higher education. Therein lies a major source of managerial myopia in strategic planning in colleges and universities. Overwhelmingly, the focus of such efforts is on the academic side of the house, on academic programs, and on professors, traditionally conceived, who are either tenured or on the tenure track.

Equally important strategically is the recognition of the connections among and between various segments of academe and of managerial professionals. It is important not simply to see the entire professional workforce in all its diversity, but also to attend to the intersections, interactive effects, and joint production activities of faculty and other professionals. Otherwise, a variety of strategic and human resource issues are addressed in relative isolation from one another. Again, that is precisely what is happening now in higher education, a pattern that is fostered by the managerial fragmentation of existing managerial structures in the academy. Organizationally, there are various silos in central administration, each with responsibility for segments of the professional workforce, and each developing distinctive and sometimes competing and even conflicting incentives for different patterns and priorities in the behaviors of professionals. Overwhelmingly, this contributes to a lack of focus.

For decades, academic managers have sought to manage colleges and universities more strategically. Part of that strategic management has involved trying to set priorities and provide a vision for the institution. Ironically, however, these efforts have been largely characterized by a managerial myopia evident in plans that primarily involve restructuring/re-engineering/reorganizing (take your pick) academic programs (Rhoades, 2001). Generally led by a provost, such efforts are driven by thinking about various aspects of the academic programs that constitute the provost's basic portfolio. Such organizationally focused efforts concentrate on the configuration of degree programs, not of faculty demography. Their aim generally is to manage traditional faculty so as to make them more productive, responsive, and entrepreneurial; they manage to offer little by way of thinking about the dimensions and productivity of contingent categories of academic faculty. As for non-academic managerial professionals, the strategic schemes largely ignore them, and/or relegate them to a residual concern, to be subject to the processes, norms, and measures designed for (and to some extent by) academic faculty. What is overlooked is the role of these professionals directly involved in producing various educational, research, and service outcomes, or as co-workers indirectly involved in such production activities by virtue of their work with faculty.

Another drawback of prevailing strategic approaches, which seek to focus the institution to get everyone on the same strategic page, is the balkanized structure of senior administration, and the complex and sometimes competing array of incentives they provide to professionals on campus (Rhoades, 2001). Presidents and policymakers outside the university often comment on the diverse, fragmented, and self-interested academic units that inhibit strategic direction. They often aim to get these units and their faculty similarly oriented, moving in the same direction, again with the focus being largely, if not solely, on the academic side of the house. Yet the organizational structure of senior management in the academy runs counter to such efforts. Departmental diversity is complemented by managerial fragmentation among various vice-presidents, who have different backgrounds and distinct and competing portfolios, and who send different messages to academic and other professionals on campus. Even on the academic side of the organization there is not only the provost but also the vice-president for research, each in control of a portion of budgets that offer different incentives for academic units and faculty. Similarly, on the support side of the organization there is generally a student affairs administrator, whose orientation to students and student success is generally somewhat different from that of the provost and vice-provost of undergraduate instruction. In addition, there is often a vice-president of external or public relations, who may provide a different set of messages and incentives to professionals.

Academic capitalism and the new economy tend to augment these managerial shortcomings. The orientation is short-term, which can constitute its own form of myopia. And with the mindset of each unit, and indeed each administrator, being encouraged to generate more activity and revenue, there is a tendency for competition and fragmentation among these units and managers to be heightened. A further strategic shortcoming lies in the failure not only of strategic plans, but also of academic managers and policymakers more broadly to consider the configuration of the workforce in terms of its demographic profile, and key points of transition throughout the lives of professionals. Even on the academic side of the house, in regard only to that segment of the profession that is on the tenure track, as a general rule policymakers and practitioners attend far too little to key points of transition in an academic career. As a result, we are not sufficiently addressing how we deal with academe's demographic profile at this point in time, let alone how we ensure over time that we are establishing policies and engaging in practices to attract future generations of academic faculty, and to ensure that we optimize and facilitate the professional strengths and opportunities of current faculty over the course of their lifetime in the academy.

The situation is even more problematic when it comes to various managerial professionals. We have virtually no data on, understanding of, or attention devoted to matters of careers in various support professions in the academy. There is much by way of national, state, and institutional policy changes to establish a public policy regime that enables, encourages, and incentivizes university connections with the private sector marketplace and activities that generate revenues for universities. Yet we have virtually no strategies, as nations or as universities, with regard to preparing and cultivating professionals working to foster entrepreneurial activity, and thereby to increase new revenue streams in higher education. Similarly, there is much emphasis in public policy discourse on accountability and assessment, as well as on increasing the quality and changing the nature of instruction and learning in higher education through the expanded use of instructional technologies.

Yet we have virtually no systematic discussion of the professionals, inside and outside the academy, on and off campus, who are developing, implementing, and monitoring various metrics and mechanisms of accountability, or of professionals who are similarly purchasing and developing new technologies, as well as providing training in and maintenance of the hardware and software systems involved. Finally, for all the public discourse about college access and success, and the changing needs and learning styles of students, we have virtually no consideration of the professionals who are structuring and providing all sorts of services to increasing numbers of students, of their recruitment, working conditions, or career paths, let alone of their effectiveness and efficiency as professionals.

As noted in the previous section, with some important exceptions there is not even much scholarship in the realm of other professionals, who remain invisible to higher education researchers, including those studying college and university management. In the case of academic faculty there is some scholarship, particularly in the field of higher education, addressing key transition point issues, just as some national policy, mostly in funding agencies such as the National Science Foundation and the National Institutes of Health, seeks to recruit a new generation of students into faculty careers in science and engineering. For example, Ann Austin has done valuable work on preparing the next generation of faculty (Austin, 2002; Wulff and Austin, 2004). Scholarship on recruitment into academic careers in science and engineering maps onto a national policy agenda, although this agenda does not play out in practices and policies at the level of universities. Such work addresses issues of permanent postdoctoral positions and blocked access to such careers for increasing proportions of doctoral recipients, as well as the United States' dependence on international students, a resource pool that is gradually threatened by the growing scientific strength of higher education systems and universities in China, India, and South Korea (Stephan and Ehrenberg, 2007).

A few scholars have examined new faculty generally, in the context of promotion and tenure and the changing demographics, demands, and roles of academe (Austin, 2003; Tierney and Bensimon, 1996). One new book focuses on newly tenured faculty, constructing them as learners and providing valuable insight that connects the human and intellectual dimensions of this stage of the academic career (Neumann, 2009). A recent article addresses the issue of how to re-engage senior faculty who are disengaged but productive (Huston et al., 2008). And a recent book examines the changing academic workplace and identifies key elements that are essential to optimizing the experience and development of faculty (Gappa et al., 2007).

Overwhelmingly, though, with a few important exceptions, research on academic faculty concentrates on tenure-track professors. Even scholars who have tracked the rise of various contingent categories of faculty have not sufficiently considered or examined connections between these segments of academe and the traditional tenure-track workforce. And even they tend to view professional work in academe in terms of a linear career, rather than considering the ways and extent to which professionals move in and out of employment in academe.

The latter perspective of more fluid patterns over time in professional careers is all the more important given the changing nature of professional employment in the larger economy. It is also important in the light of the increased intersection of colleges and universities with the outside world. Such movement across institutional boundaries is central to the organizational idea of academic capitalism and the new economy, in the cases both of faculty and of managerial professionals. That points to the value of envisioning not only thus far largely invisible professional workforces in their segmented settings, but also the intersection and joint activities of professionals across various boundaries within and outside colleges and universities. What is required is a rethinking of professional workplaces and workforces beyond the relatively narrow and, ironically, industrial-era models of professions that currently hold sway.

Strategically Enhancing Intellectual Capital

The current fiscal context promises to heighten national and state governments' tendency in recent decades to seek to maximize short-term efficiency and productivity. Similarly, the heightened fiscal pressures on universities, connected to increasingly stringent governmental budgets and their commitment to academic capitalism, promise to intensify institutional efforts to maximize revenue generation. Particularly in this fiscal context, faculty are seen as a labor cost to be minimized and/or as potential revenue generators whose activities and productivity should be maximized. Managerial professionals are seen almost exclusively in terms of their labor costs. They are not viewed as potential revenue generators because to the extent that they are even considered, they are considered to be low-level support staff or bureaucrats, not professionals with valuable expertise that could be capitalized on. In the case neither of faculty nor of managerial professionals are they regarded as critically important intellectual capital, as a resource that is the key to the United States' future.

Three measures help clarify the extent to which academic managers view faculty as a labor cost to be minimized. The first is a comparison of increases over recent years in the salaries of faculty relative to those of senior central administrators. The American Association of University Professors' 2007 salary survey tracks such salary increases from 1995–1996 to 2005–2006, finding that the increases for presidents were more than six times those for faculty members (AAUP, 2007). And the increases for faculty have in recent years underperformed cost-of-living increases.

A second measure that speaks to a managerial view of academic labor costs is of the increases in tuition versus those in faculty salaries in recent years. Again there is a substantial difference, with tuition increases dramatically outpacing increases in faculty salaries. As Slaughter and Leslie (1997) noted in elaborating the first study of academic capitalism, institutions are de-investing in instructional activities; the pattern of limited salary increases reflects that de-investment.

A third measure that is telling about the managerial perspective on labor costs is the numbers and percentages of full-time tenure-track faculty. As noted in the first section of the chapter, there have been dramatic increases in the numbers and proportion of part-time faculty, and in the numbers and proportion of contingent faculty. Such a pattern of choice at the institutional level, to essentially replace full-time with part-time academic labor, does not suggest a managerial perspective that prioritizes faculty members' labor value as professionals.

Ironically, the same point does not apply to managerial professionals. At the institutional level, across various types of higher education institutions there has been a far greater investment in the past three decades in managerial professionals than in academic faculty. As noted in an earlier section of this chapter, managerial professionals are by far the fastest-growing category of professional employee in the academy. And they are largely full-time employees. That suggests a considerable investment in these professionals at a time when colleges and universities were disinvesting in faculty.

How can the above pattern be explained, particularly if managerial professionals are invisible as professionals? The answer lies in the organizational structure of academic capitalism and the new economy. Part of the pattern of academic capitalism is the proliferation of various 'interstitial' units between academic faculty and administrators. These units emerge as part of the expanded managerial capacity that comes with this mode of production. They afford greater involvement in and monitoring of academic activities by engaging in a range of quality control 'support' functions and services. They also work to address the increased demands from the external world for various types of information and reports. In addition, these units emerge as part of an investment in entrepreneurial efforts to generate and enhance new and existing revenue streams. Finally, these interstitial units and their employees recruit and provide a range of services to students, who in a time of high and rising tuition costs, and growing endowments, are seen as key sources of revenue, as customers to be served and pleased, on campuses marked by dramatic investment (an arms race) in non-academic facilities, and that in many regards have come to resemble resorts, shopping, and fitness centers more than simply educational settings. In short, then, managerial professionals are key players in the academic capitalist enterprise; however, they are seen not as professionals but as employees who staff a range of new non-academic units that are central to the projects of academic executives.

On the other hand, academic faculty are seen as potential revenue generators in their instructional and research activities and intellectual products. The emphasis here is on short-term productivity, prioritizing products that are seen as having potential to generate revenues for the institution in the private sector market. The managerial orientation here is to invest in what are regarded as close to the market fields, and professors in pursuit of revenue-generating possibilities. What is sometimes missing from the prevalent managerial perspective is a sense of and commitment to local, regional, and state (even national) communities. The interests of the enterprise are prioritized. Sometimes those interests can be at odds with the interests of the surrounding society.

One of the key societal interests is the vitality of the academic profession, which provides and prepares the intellectual capital of the nation. Focusing on the short-term economic interests of academic enterprises has not served the longer-term national interest of building, enhancing, and optimizing that capital. Just as in the 1980s, an era of fiscal stress and retrenchment in higher education, much attention is being devoted to the management and finances of universities. Very little has been devoted to the health and quality of academe, including to the generational profile of the profession, and yet the health and quality of the academy are connected to the health and quality of the academic profession.

The systemic dimensions of the profession are perhaps even more important in the European context, where members of the European community are seeking to foster a European higher education community, in some sense to compete with the United States for international students. At the same time, some European countries are investing in developing more world-class universities as a way of competing with the United States not only educationally but also economically. In the case of the former, the principal focus is on student mobility. In the case of the latter, the principal focus is on universities. Both overlook the fundamental importance in the history of American higher education of having a dynamic, mobile academic profession, made possible by a system that facilitated academic innovation.

The strategic oversight in Europe is that in building a European educational space, a marketplace with exchangeable degrees and credits that facilitates the mobility of students across national boundaries, there is virtually no attention devoted to the mobility of professors. And historically, the dynamism of American higher education can be traced in considerable part to the movement and opportunity for innovations in different universities that have been available to professors, particularly to young professors. That movement was intentionally fostered in the United States, for example, by the Carnegie Foundation for the Advancement of Teaching, which helped establish a portable retirement system, later to become the Teachers Insurance and Annuity Association, College Retirement Equities Fund (TIAA-CREF), such that professors could carry their retirement benefits with them when they changed institutions. The explicit aim was to help construct a national profession to the end of enhancing the quality of the profession and thereby of the higher education system. The lack of a pan-European facility in this respect is an inhibitor, although in other respects the European Higher Education Area is a model for collaboration.

Such a systemic strategy required a national perspective and national initiative with regard to professors. It also required a recognition that academic faculty represented key intellectual capital for a country that was rapidly expanding its global presence, economically, politically, and culturally. For the most part, public policy discourse regarding higher education today lacks such foresight and perspective, and remains grounded at the institutional level. The Spellings Commission, for example, sought to leverage institutional accountability and improvement by making more information available to student consumers. The condition and configuration of the professoriate are not taken into account.

At the national level there is something of an important exception to the pattern of national policymakers overlooking the value of academic faculty as intellectual capital. A recent "Issue Brief" of the American Council on Education (ACE) by Jacqueline King (2008) speaks to the problem presented by the small number of young, permanent (i.e. tenure-track) faculty. The paper reports that

[o]nly 3 percent of faculty at four-year institutions are individuals aged 34 or younger working in tenure-line positions. Adding tenured or tenure-track faculty aged 34 to 44 only raises this proportion to 15 percent. Similarly only 3 percent of community college faculty are full-time employees aged 34 or younger. When those aged 35 to 44 are added, this proportion increases to 11 percent.

(King, 2008: 1)

Yet the reason for concern lies less in the intellectual capital that these young academic faculty represent in their professorial roles than in their potential leadership capital, as a pool of future leaders who can eventually move into formal academic administrative positions. In short, professors are framed as a key part of the 'leadership pipeline'.

These data paint a clear picture of an emerging problem: Permanent junior faculty make up a diminishing share of the professoriate, and most of these individuals will not have time to earn tenure (at four-year institutions and some community colleges) and then rise up the traditional administrative ladder from department chair, to dean, to chief academic officer, amassing the kind and amount of experience typical of current leaders (King, 2008: 2).

It makes sense to be concerned about the dearth of young faculty because they are the source of the next generation of academic administrators. It also makes sense, however, to be concerned about the demographic profile of the academic workforce because of what it means for the nation's principal source of intellectual capital, both directly by way of what academic faculty create, and indirectly by way of the knowledge workers they educate. Nevertheless, the ACE's attention to the condition of the academic workforce is welcome, and at least acknowledges the issue as important.

Conclusion

Our current categories and conceptualizations of academic faculty and managerial professionals are insufficient for the task of effectively and strategically managing these increasingly diverse workforces and sets of employees for the future. This is particularly true in the difficult fiscal times of the present. Even as the public policy discourse repeatedly invokes unprecedented changes in higher education that demand corresponding changes in (and responses from) colleges and universities, managers and policymakers continue to operate according to outmoded models of professions and professional employment in the academy. Even as they look to the future, they are stuck in the past.

About one hundred years ago the Carnegie Foundation commissioned a study of teaching and research (of physics) at eight higher education institutions. The analytical focus and origins of the report are evident in the title *Academic and Industrial Efficiency* (Cooke, 1910). The report applied to higher education the principles of scientific management offered by Frederick Taylor (1947), widely utilized in the rising industrial economy. The aim was to estimate and enhance efficiency in colleges and universities, not only on the business side of matters, but also on the academic side, in the organization of teaching and research. The path to that efficiency was by way of organizing work to maximize the productivity of individual workers.

A century later, we have not advanced much in higher education policy when it comes to our conceptions of how to increase academic productivity. Much of public policy discourse is focused on the time allocation of individual faculty members between research and teaching, and on the publication and grants productivity of individual professors, as ways of understanding productivity in higher education. Policymakers and managers seek to provide incentives (including merit pay, bonuses, and shares of royalties) to encourage various types of behavior by individual professors, whether in the conduct of more research, the connection of research to industry, the teaching of more students or classes, or the use of more instructional technologies in delivering instruction.

Such approaches may seem to fit with the idea of academic capitalism. But they are at odds with the idea of a postindustrial, knowledge-based economy and society, and with the character of academic capitalism and the new economy. For a variety of reasons the nature of professional employment in higher education, as in the broader society, has changed dramatically. To conceive of academic work, or the work of managerial professionals on campus, as the result of an individual employee discretely producing a measurable piece of output is to fundamentally misconstrue not only current categories of professional employment in the academy, but also current and future patterns of employment and work.

If we are to construct and implement appropriate and effective policies and practices for organizing and optimizing the work of professionals in the academy, we must be sensitive to new categories of employment and new types and patterns of work that go beyond the individual employee. We must tap into the reality of professional careers in the academy today, careers that cut across various increasingly blurred boundaries within and between higher education, markets, and the state. And we must tap into the reality of professional work today, which is interdependent as much as or more than it is individualistic. Such realities call for a distinctive set of human resource practices within colleges and universities, as well as for a broader set of workforce considerations at a national level. They call for us to envision invisible workforces, and to focus on enhancing the intellectual capital that is so central to our societies.

References

American Association of University Professors (AAUP) (2007) "Annual Report on the Economic Status of the Profession, 2006–2007." *Academe* 93 (2): 21–34.

Ashenfelter, O. and Card, D. (2002) "Did the Elimination of Mandatory Retirement Affect Faculty Retirement?" *American Economic Review* 92 (4): 957–980.

Austin, A. E. (2002) "Preparing the Next Generation of Faculty: Graduate Education as Socialization to the Academic Career." *Journal of Higher Education* 73 (2): 94–122.

Austin, A. E. (2003) "Creating a Bridge to the Future: Preparing New Faculty to Face Changing Expectations in a Shifting Context." *Review of Higher Education* 26 (2): 119–144.

Baldwin, R. and Chronister, J. (2001) *Teaching without Tenure*. Baltimore: Johns Hopkins University Press.

Bok, D. (2003) *Universities in the Marketplace: The Commercialization of Higher Education*. Princeton, NJ: Oxford University Press.

Burgan, M. (2006) *Whatever Happened to the Faculty? Drift and Decision in Higher Education*. Baltimore: Johns Hopkins University Press.

Chan, A. S. and Fisher, D. (eds.) (2008) *The Exchange University: Corporatization of Academic Culture*. Vancouver: University of British Columbia Press.

Clark, B. R. (1998) *Creating Entrepreneurial Universities: Organizational Pathways of Transformation*. Guildford, UK: Pergamon.

Cooke, M. L. (1910) *Academic and Industrial Efficiency*. Bulletin 5. New York: Carnegie Foundation for the Advancement of Teaching.

De Francesco, C. and Rhoades, G. (1987) "Academe in an Era of Retrenchment." *Educational Policy* 1 (4): 461–480.

De Weert, E. and Enders, J. (2009) *The Changing Face of Academic Life: Analytical and Comparative Perspectives*. Basingstoke, UK: Palgrave Macmillan.

Etzkowitz, H. and Leydesdorff, L. A. (1997) *Universities and the Global Knowledge Economy: A Triple Helix of University–Industry–Government Relations*. London: Pinter.

Finkelstein, M. J., Seal, R. K., and Schuster, J. H. (1998) *The New Academic Generation: A Profession in Transformation*. Baltimore: Johns Hopkins University Press.

Gappa, J. M., Austin, A. E., and Trice, A. G. (2007) *Rethinking Faculty Work: Higher Education's Strategic Imperative*. Hoboken, NJ: John Wiley.

Gibbons, M., Limoges, C., Nowotny, H., Schwartzman, S., Scott, P., and Trow, M. (1994) *The New Production of Knowledge: The Dynamics of Science and Research in Contemporary Societies*. Thousand Oaks, CA: Sage.

Gornitzka, Å. and Larsen, I. M. (2004) "Towards Professionalisation? Restructuring of Administrative Work Force in Universities." *Higher Education* 47 (4): 455–471.

Gornitzka, Å., Kyvik, S., and Larsen, I. M. (1998) "The Bureaucratization of Universities." *Minerva* 36: 21–47.

Huston, T. A., Norman, M., and Ambrose, S. A. (2008) "Expanding the Discussion of Faculty Vitality to Include Productive but Disengaged Senior Faculty." *Journal of Higher Education* 78 (5): 493–522.

King, J. (2008) *Too Many Rungs on the Ladder? Faculty Demographics and the Future Leadership of Higher Education*. Washington, DC: American Council on Education.

Marginson, S. and Considine, M. (2000) *The Enterprise University: Power, Governance, and Reinvention in Australia*. New York: Cambridge University Press.

Neumann, A. (2009) *Professing to Learn: Creating Tenured Lives and Careers in the American Research University*. Baltimore: Johns Hopkins University Press.

Rhoades, G. (1998a) *Managed Professionals: Unionized Faculty and Restructuring Academic Labor*. Albany: State University of New York Press.

Rhoades, G. (1998b) "Reviewing and Rethinking Administrative Costs." In *Higher Education: Handbook of Theory and Research*, vol. 13, ed. J. C. Smart. New York: Agathon Press.

Rhoades, G. (2001) "Who's Doing It Right? Strategic Activity in Public Research Universities." *Review of Higher Education* 24 (1): 41–66.

Rhoades, G. (2007) "Technology-Enhanced Courses and a Mode III Organization of Instructional Work." *Tertiary Education and Management* 13 (1): 1–17.

Rhoades, G. (2008) "The Centrality of Contingent Faculty to Academe's Future." *Academe* 94 (6): 12–15.

Rhoades, G. (forthcoming) "Whose Educational Space Is It? Negotiating Professional Jurisdiction in the High Tech Academy." In *Whither the Academic Profession? Its Changing Forms and Functions*, ed. J. C. Hermanowicz. Baltimore: Johns Hopkins University Press.

Rhoades, G. and Sporn, B. (2002) "New Modes of Management and Shifting Modes and Costs of Production: Europe and the United States." *Tertiary Education and Management* 8: 3–28.

Schuster, J. H. and Finkelstein, M. J. (2006) *The American Faculty: The Restructuring of Academic Work and Careers*. Baltimore: Johns Hopkins University Press.

Slaughter, S. and Leslie, L. (1997) *Academic Capitalism: Politics, Policies, and the Entrepreneurial University*. Baltimore: Johns Hopkins University Press.

Slaughter, S. and Rhoades, G. (2004) *Academic Capitalism and the New Economy: Markets, State, and Higher Education*. Baltimore: Johns Hopkins University Press.

Stephan, P. E. and Ehrenberg, R. G. (eds.) (2007) *Science and the University*. Madison: University of Wisconsin Press.

Taylor, F. W. (1947) *Scientific Management*. New York: Harper.

Tierney, W. G. and Bensimon, E. (1996) *Promotion and Tenure: Community and Socialization in Academe*. Albany: State University of New York Press.

Whitchurch, C. (2004) "Administrative Managers: A Critical Link." *Higher Education Quarterly* 58 (4): 280–298.

Whitchurch, C. (2006) "Who Do They Think They Are? Changing Identities of Professional Administrators and Managers in UK Higher Education." *Journal of Higher Education Policy and Management* 28 (2): 159–171.

Whitchurch, C. (2008a) "Beyond Administration and Management: Changing Professional Identities in UK Higher Education." In *Changing Identities in Higher Education: Voicing Perspectives*, ed. R. Barnett and R. Di Napoli. Abingdon, UK: Routledge.

Whitchurch, C. (2008b). "Shifting Identities and Blurring Boundaries: The Emergence of *Third Space* Professionals in UK Higher Education." *Higher Education Quarterly* 62 (4): 377–396.

Wulff, D. H. and Austin, A. E. (2004) *Paths to the Professoriate: Strategies for Enriching the Preparation of Future Faculty.* San Francisco: Jossey-Bass.

4

Innovative University Management

JANE USHERWOOD

Introduction

Universities are places where knowledge is created and disseminated, and where ideas, even tenets of belief, are challenged, refined, or even rejected and replaced. It is surprising, therefore, that more attention has not been paid to the way that universities manage their staff. Whether an institution is progressive in practicing 'human resource management' or traditional in labeling the activity 'personnel' (or even 'staffing') is immaterial. Those involved in management will be aware of the challenges that these practices present, as well as the fact that techniques that work in one set of circumstances may have a different outcome in another situation.

It goes without saying that people are higher education's major asset, whether they be mainstream faculty who teach and research, people in professional functions, or the manual and technical staff who contribute to the environment in which everyone works. Staff costs represent as much as two-thirds of recurrent institutional expenditure, varying only at the margins according to the profile of the individual institution. Universities are not only creators of intellectual capital, but also consumers of it. It is therefore in the university's own interest to ensure that its 'assets' (the staff) are motivated and productive.

In this context, it has been argued that staff perform better if they are 'happy' at work. The philosophy that "happy workers = productive workers" lies behind schemes such as The Great Place to Work Institute, and work such as that by Lundin et al. (2002), which describes how a fish business where there had been low morale and "unhappy" staff changed its fortunes by encouraging more innovative and engaged attitudes. 'Happy' here means at a level beyond merely enjoying the social interaction that is part of the many collective workspaces within universities. The premise is that 'fun' places to work are successful, and therefore 'great', places to work. But does that apply in an environment as diverse as a university? The "Great Place to Work" concept, in both the United States and the United Kingdom, functions on the assumption that a good place to work is a place where employees "trust the people they work for, have pride in what they do, and enjoy the people they work with" (extract from www.greatplacetowork.co.uk). So how can university managers make sure that work is 'fun' and 'enjoyable', and what, if any, replicable measures are there that suit a disparate workforce? If there are such measures, how can a university identify and apply them?

This chapter discusses ways in which employment practices in universities might be different from those of other organizations and sectors, and in what ways experiences from other contexts can translate into the academic workplace. Universities have tended to subscribe to the 'not invented here' syndrome and to distance themselves from changes in management or employment practices elsewhere. Within that context, their 'difference' is examined and challenged, while at the same time recognizing that there are elements that make universities 'different' as places of work, so that not all practices from other workplaces can be transplanted easily. The chapter concludes by considering issues relating to motivation and management, which have been thought of traditionally as 'softer' than metrics or contractual matters, but have come to the fore more recently. It is perhaps ironic that universities are being urged to be more business-like at precisely the same time as other employers are being urged to develop softer management skills and 'emotional intelligence'.

University Contexts

On the one hand, universities are often considered to be different from other workplace environments, even unique, because of their strong tradition as communities of scholars, with associated academic freedoms. They are also major contributors to economic development and the knowledge society, and are therefore centers of innovation and creativity. This can lead to a 'twin dynamic' in which there is potential for the generation of new ideas, as well as a criticality that requires new ideas to be tried and tested before being adopted. This tension may lead to the rejection of examples of good practice from other organizations as being 'not invented here', and needs to be borne in mind when considering how new ways of working might be adopted in individual institutions.

Changing expectations of work by different generations of people labeled respectively Baby Boomers (the post-World War II generation), Generation X (born roughly between 1964 and 1977), and Generation Y or 'Millennials' (born after 1982 and just beginning to enter the workforce) have been highlighted by authors such as Lancaster and Stillman (2002), Shelton and Shelton (2005), and Florida (2002). However, institutional structures have not necessarily adapted to the approaches to work of either current or future generations. Employers who wish to recruit, retain, and motivate younger people may, for instance, need to adopt new forms of reward and incentive. Shelton and Shelton's work suggests that, in common with the Baby Boomer generation, Generations X and Y want interesting work and positive relations with their colleagues, but are less motivated by status or power. Many universities are now using imaginative titles and other non-financial alternatives to promotion as a way of recognizing achievement, particularly as few of them are able to compete with private sector salaries. However, it may be that such initiatives are less attractive to younger generations than creative and challenging opportunities, even if these bring with them an element of risk.

If we accept that the expectations of those in employment are different from what they once were, this suggests that higher education managers need to be innovative in their thinking, to challenge assumptions, and to be creative in their solutions. In these days of the 'globalized university', are the structures and practices of the past still fit for purpose? Furthermore, is a single model applicable to all universities? Although rankings and league tables may have encouraged convergence in a sector that is essentially heterogeneous, uniformity in the management of people is likely to suppress innovation and creativity.

Musselin (2007) has questioned how "success" and "productivity" in higher education might be defined, by examining the experiences of appointment committees in research universities in France. Although each committee agreed that they wanted to appoint the "best candidate" at interview, there was no shared view on what constituted "the best". This research suggests that in the absence of clear guidelines that can be commonly applied, there is the temptation to be influenced by quantitative, rather than qualitative, indicators because they are easier to measure. Furthermore, the increasing heterogeneity of the higher education sector, despite such external drivers as the Research Assessment Exercise in the United Kingdom or national or international league tables, means that it is no longer possible to provide a universally applicable definition of an academic career (as shown by Strike in Chapter 5). Nor is it possible to build 'a great place to work' by having a single set of standards.

The work of Harvard's Collaborative on Academic Careers in Higher Education (COACHE) suggests that attention to the psychological contract, that is to say the unwritten expectations of employment, is as important as attention to the formal contract. The annual COACHE survey identifies satisfaction levels of junior faculty with a variety of elements of their working lives. In 2007 it emphasized the importance of clarity about tenure and performance expectations, and stressed that non-monetary factors were as important as monetary factors in increasing the satisfaction and success of junior faculty. Given that most universities are not able to compete with the private sector in relation to salaries, non-financial elements to the employment package are likely to assume greater significance. Thus, the attractiveness of the work environment is possibly even more important to staff in higher education than to staff in other sectors, where rewards such as higher pay rates or social status are more likely to be available.

Transferring Knowledge and Skills

It could be argued that given a variety of institutions, with differing missions and cultures, differing external and internal drivers, and a workforce that is stratified not only by task but also by generational expectations, practices from one institution or sector are unlikely to transfer seamlessly to others. However, Guest and Clinton (2007: 5) suggest that

> [t]here appears to be no compelling reason why the findings reported in the private sector should not generalise to other parts of the public sector, including higher education. Nevertheless, public sector organisations may possess distinctive features that make it more difficult to introduce strategic Human Resource Management (HRM) and more difficult to achieve an impact on performance.

This suggests that the contemporary university manager needs to practice a kind of *bricolage*, taking the most appropriate ideas from one place and deploying them creatively, adaptively, and resourcefully to meet specific challenges, and having the confidence to reject ideas that do not fit the immediate purpose.

Historically, universities have been places engaged in critical inquiry. Their structures, whatever their origins, have involved management by academic managers that reflects social values and intellectual debate (Hudson and Skaines, 2007). This collegial approach is one in which faculty have confidence, even if it gives rise to, indeed encourages, a multiplicity of views. However, external factors such as increased student choice, more market-oriented funding regimes, competition between institutions, the 'commercialization' of many aspects of university life, and changing expectations of staff and students mean that this model has been subject to modification, for instance, via the recruitment of professional managers with specialist skills. Denman (2005) notes that universities are modifying their internal structures and functions to enhance their competitive edge, and are becoming increasingly business and customer oriented, leading to a form of corporate management. As this is not a culture that academic (and other) staff necessarily choose, it is not surprising that dissonance sometimes arises.

Gappa et al. (2007) note a variety of ways in which the world of higher education is changing, from the exogenous pressures of increased accountability or differing societal expectations, to changes brought about by new ways of delivering learning through increased use of technology. The effect of this is to blur some of the old and accepted boundaries between disciplines. For staff who have been used to greater clarity and certainty, and whose own education probably took place in what they believe to have been more certain times, this provides a challenge, a challenge that Gappa et al. point out not everyone is equally equipped to take on. Also, universities have changed the model of employment from one that assumed tenured posts with guaranteed academic freedom to one that incorporates a mix of staff, some with tenure or in tenure-track posts, but with an increasing number who do not enjoy the same benefits, real or perceived. The increasing number of staff who are on renewable or temporary contracts is a source of disquiet in many parts of academe, for instance, in University and College Union (UCU) campaigns against 'casualization' in the United Kingdom, as it is felt that this brings inefficiency, uncertainty, inequality, and stress.

It could be argued that this dissonance is made more evident by the speed of change and ways in which some universities have embraced corporate models, sometimes confusing the need to be business-*like* with the need to act *as* a business. Acting as a business can have the effect of alienating staff, especially when "[a]cademics increasingly feel that their institutions' overriding concern is narrowly financial" (Fearn, 2008a). Such perceptions are likely to be fostered by language that is not considered to be in tune with academic traditions of collegiality and academic freedom. Adopting the language of 'resource' may mean that there is a danger of losing the 'human' in a globalized world. What university managers at all levels need is to find a way of engaging staff with change while at the same time appreciating that levers which are effective in other contexts may not work if they are simply transplanted without thought and preparation. The culture and context of the organization need to be borne in mind. As an example, it is interesting to note that in the University of Western Sydney's transformation from a federal university facing severe financial constraints in 1999 to a unified institution in 2007, the university sought to follow a process that was "ethical, transparent, fair and fully considerate of our people" (Hudson and Skaines, 2007). That the strategic plan emphasized this, and that managers felt that taking an ethical position was a significant element of the plan, implies that they took into account the environment in which they were operating.

In many Western universities there has been much debate about the importance of branding, for instance, to market their distinctiveness as 'research-intensive', 'ancient', or 'world-class'. Peck and Jackson-Peck (2005) suggest that branding can "help the campus community . . . differentiate service offerings from those of other providers, and underscore the historical mission and educational objectives." However, one consultant described taking part in a "branding workshop" in a university as "not dissimilar to the experience of having to defuse an unexploded bomb", and a member of academic faculty described marketing as a case of "the tail wagging the dog" (Fearn, 2008b). Although many universities have adopted a narrative of themselves for the purposes of internal or external marketing, for many academic faculty this can imply "managerialism", as described, for instance, by Deem et al. (2007). This disconnect between the individual and 'the center' is possibly more pronounced in universities than in other organizations because of their tradition as self-governing communities of scholars. This disconnect, sometimes expressed as allegiance elsewhere, poses particular problems for managers, particularly where loyalties and allegiances to colleagues in other institutions, or to 'the discipline', might seem at variance with institutional priorities.

Differing Loyalties

It is not only the context that is different about universities, but the identification of academic faculty with something separate from, and possibly at odds with, the employer, namely the discipline. To simplify the analogy, in most organizations staff have some loyalty to 'the employer'. The strength of that loyalty will obviously differ from employee to employee, and as a consequence of actions or inactions on the part of the employer or of individual managers. However, by and large it is true to say that the employee wishes the employer to succeed, and vice versa. There is recognition that the success of each is linked, no matter that success may not be commonly measured, and that there is a relationship one with the other. In an academic setting, however, this may not be the case. This is not to suggest that the average academic employee of University X wishes the institution ill, but rather that there is an attachment to something separate from the employer, and in many cases it is seen as more important than the employer.

The way in which an individual academic faculty member achieves a reputation is likely to be more as a result of their disciplinary standing than their institutional standing. Such external influences make the management of the institutional 'whole' more complex. Meyer and Evans (2003) suggest a complex mix of incentives, including interactions with colleagues and students, the development of an academic reputation, and the desire to undertake intellectual activity for its own sake because of the satisfaction it provides. This mix makes academic life attractive even when greater material rewards can be secured in the corporate or other sectors. Therefore, as Meyer and Evans (2005) put it, "[i[f academics already value their disciplines and the potential to benefit society, management incentives to reinforce behaviour can actually have a detrimental impact on such intrinsic motivators."

The most obvious difference between employment in higher education and elsewhere relates to the concept of 'academic freedom'. Although the concept is understood differentially around the world, the idea that academic faculty should be free to question and test received wisdom, and to put forward controversial and unpopular opinions, is enshrined in the UNESCO *Recommendation Concerning the Status of Higher-Education Teaching Personnel* (UNESCO, 1997). This, combined with the criticality of university staff, means that care must be taken in importing techniques from other areas. The point is illustrated by the University of Cambridge's attempts to introduce a new accounting software system known as CAPSA, which did not prove fit for purpose and was not a success for a number of reasons, including the absence of management processes and oversight (Shattock, 2001). Thus, although universities need to guard against the 'not invented here' syndrome, account must also be taken of the culture of universities as places of employment.

Loyalty to the discipline, or the subject, is an important influence on academic thinking, and one that does not have many parallels in other places of employment. As a contributor to the letters page in the *Times Higher Education* remarked,

There is an implication ... that loyalty to a subject is somehow narrower or less worthy than loyalty to an institution. In reality, for most academics, subject loyalty is part of a wider, universalist, ethical commitment to values such as intellectual inquiry and academic standards that transcend institutions.

(Kirkwood, 2007)

Although I have argued that universities are unique places of work that attract people with loyalty beyond their employer, it should not be forgotten that academic faculty are highly motivated and critical groups of people. The Network of Concerned Anthropologists in the United States, for instance, expressed concern that the recently announced money for research from the Department of Defense would shift researchers' agendas to those of the government, and asked scholars to pledge not to accept it. This fund, to support research in the social sciences and the humanities, was welcomed by many university presidents and was to support unclassified (i.e. open) research, but the Network was concerned that "subtle but powerful biases" were at work with any funder of research (Jaschik, 2008).

What motivates staff? And in what way does this differ for academic faculty? It is not possible to come up with clear and simple answers as all individuals, whether academic or not, vary. However, universities must be careful not to use their 'difference' as a cloak under which to hide from lessons being learned elsewhere. Research carried out by the Corporate Leadership Council based in the United States indicated that the most important components of the employment value proposition (EVP) in a global context were compensation, career opportunities, and work–life balance. This is the set of attributes that both the labor market and employees perceive as the value they gain through employment in the organization, and is a useful comparative measure between organizations, sectors, and indeed countries. The attributes vary, but include a mixture of 'hard' and 'soft' measures such as opportunity for growth, reward, the nature of work undertaken, people with whom one works, and work–life balance.

Given that most universities, however they derive their funds, would argue that resources are more limited than the demands upon them, higher education is not able to compete on salary alone with many other employers, particularly those in the corporate or private sector. By concentrating on the total employment package, and emphasizing the 'softer' elements of the EVP, universities may have a unique selling point. However, 'big business' is catching up. Increasingly, large companies are offering increased flexibility of employment as they reach out to Generation X and beyond. They have discovered that these elements of the EVP are relatively low cost and may provide the tipping point in the war for talent. As the COACHE survey (2007) indicated, non-monetary issues are important to junior faculty, the very group who are likely to be drawn from Generation X or Generation Y/Millennials. Although the creative use of rewards such as title and recognition is doubtless relevant for some staff, the importance of culture and other 'softer' issues, such as work–life balance, should not be neglected.

Nevertheless, a lack of money can demotivate. Money has been referred to as a "hygiene factor" (Herzberg et al., 1959), in that it has to be at an acceptable level to make it worth engaging in something, but the presence of more of it does not motivate someone to invest more effort than is strictly required. So, ignoring salary levels, whether absolute or relative, can have a demotivating effect. Most people, if asked, will say they are worth more pay, but many of them will say this in jest if they feel their salary is 'fair' for the effort they put in, or relative to their peers. They are, however, likely to be dissatisfied if they feel that their remuneration is unfair in this respect. Staff, whether in universities or elsewhere, generally want a balance, as the EVP suggests, with no elements of the package having a negative impact on the individual. Maslow (1943) identified a hierarchy of needs, the pinnacle of which he defined as "self-actualization"—that is, the intrinsic desire, when all other needs are satisfied, to strive to fulfill one's ultimate potential. Employment in universities usually provides some degree of self-actualization, not necessarily because of anything universities as employers do, but more as a result of the intrinsic motivation of academic faculty. Some motivational elements, therefore, may be outside institutional control. This does not mean universities should forget the need to satisfy and meet adequately the other levels of need, and to ensure there are no demotivators, which would work against the positive action that they might take.

Supporting the Individual

Concern for the individual and the contribution they can make to the collective is not just an issue being addressed in new, start-up organizations. More traditional, research-intensive universities are also looking at 'the whole person', recognizing that support to stay engaged, productive, 'happy' even, has benefits beyond the individual. Many universities, particularly from countries with well-developed cultures of compensation, offer forms of support such as employee assistance programs. There is no national, let alone international, standard regulating such schemes, many of which are provided by external corporate providers. There has been little research on the effectiveness, or even the validity, of such interventions, and it may well be that the importation of a corporate model has little effect on the 'wellness' of the workforce if it amounts to little more than a general helpline without knowledge of the particular workplace. However, the following example from the United Kingdom gives an indication of innovative whole-university solutions that can be offered at both the individual and the group level, customized to the individual university.

At the University of Birmingham, innovative approaches to workplace well-being have been adopted since 2001 as part of a commitment to becoming an employer of choice in a city that is economically, culturally, and socially diverse. The program is designed to be self-enabling, with multiple entry points available to all staff. The first port of call is the Confidential Assessment Service, which provides an early opportunity for staff to resolve outstanding issues, but also, and more importantly, to signpost various options to help them to work through the matter that is of concern to them. This is based on the principle that only about one-third of all clients who access workplace-based counseling services are likely to benefit (Suvajac Lees, 2007). Others may need mediation, long-term therapy, medical help, or legal or other advice. Counseling, if freely available on demand, tends to deal with the symptoms of concern or distress, rather than the causes. The University of Birmingham's approach is one of 'triage', to assist staff in accessing the most appropriate source of advice to resolve difficulties or disputes. Employee Support Services, of which the Confidential Assessment Service is part, were developed as part of the university's commitment to excellence at all levels in its dealings with staff. The university also wanted to be innovative in its approach and rejected the idea of an externally provided counseling service or employee assistance program, on the basis that these provided non-specific or generic solutions that might not be appropriate (ibid.).

Apart from the Confidential Assessment Service, which is the primary, though not the only, entry point to services on offer, the university has for over ten years also had a team of harassment advisers. These are drawn from volunteers from the university community who provide informal support to staff who feel they are being harassed, or who have been told they are harassing or bullying others. The volunteers are recruited against an identified skill profile and are provided with training prior to appointment to this unpaid role. They also receive two full days' training each year, which means that line managers of harassment advisers are making a commitment to support their staff in this community role.

In addition to harassment advisers, an in-house mediation service was developed on the same voluntary basis. Accredited training in mediation techniques is provided for all volunteers before they are assigned to a mediation 'case', and any mediation is undertaken under the supervision of the employee support manager, who has a background in dispute resolution and is a professional mediator. The employee support manager conducts a preliminary conference for all parties to the mediation to set ground rules for the activity, and ensures that both parties 'buy into' this voluntary process. Then the volunteer mediators, of whom by 2007 there were ten from various departments and all levels of seniority, become involved and aim to help the parties reach a solution that is workable for them. Although external mediators could be retained to do this, there was a feeling that they might not understand the context in which university staff operate, and might introduce a quasi-legalistic element to an approach that was oriented toward problem solving. Whereas an internal service is no doubt cheaper to run, strict rules on confidentiality need to be developed so that staff have confidence in the value and efficacy of the service. Without that confidence, there is always the danger that the situation might not be improved as a result of the intervention.

Also on campus in Birmingham is a branch of the Citizens' Advice Bureau (CAB), an external, not-for-profit organization that offers free information and advice on a range of issues. A dedicated case worker is supplied through a service-level agreement with the local CAB, the first time that this had been made available with any employer. The CAB has a high reputation for independence and the quality of its service, but the demands made on it for advice meant there was often a long waiting list in the offices close to the university. In addition, its opening hours were not conducive to the normal working day. For this reason, in 2003 the university funded the opening of a CAB office for staff on its site so that staff could freely and anonymously access this advice service under the CAB's normal rules of strict confidentiality.

The university evaluates the success of this range of interventions by collecting anonymous statistical data and reporting through appropriate forums within the university. In addition, a client feedback form is used for ongoing quality analysis and control, based on Clinical Outcomes and Routine Evaluation (CORE), the first standardized approach to audit, evaluation, and outcome measurement in the United Kingdom for psychological therapy and counseling services. This allows for progress to be clinically monitored and assessed. Although many employers, including universities, offer employee assistance programs or counseling for staff, the University of Birmingham was one of the first to offer the variety and type of access provided by the Confidential Assessment Service. This ensures that staff access the most appropriate support for them, rather than the only service that is available. The degree of customization allows the effectiveness of interventions to be measured, and aims to prevent the over-medicalization of needs, sometimes associated with over-accessed counseling.

Strategic Human Resource Management

Strategic human resource management is defined by the Chartered Institute of Personnel and Development (CIPD) in the United Kingdom as being a general approach to the strategic management of human resources that is concerned with longer-term people issues and macro-concerns about structure, quality, culture, values, and matching resources to future needs. The example from the University of Birmingham given in the previous section shows how a strategic approach can be taken towards its staff. The following example shows how a macro-strategic approach might be taken at institutional level.

At the University of Melbourne there is recognition that human resource strategies should be integrated within the business and development plan of the university, and that reward systems should be aligned with the university's goals and financial performance (James and Baré, 2007). These aspirations are well understood around the world of human resource professionals. The trick is making it happen in organizations that are as atypical as universities. In order to achieve this, there are four main strands being pursued at Melbourne: the alignment of reward systems with the university's goals and performance, an emphasis on leadership, an emphasis on equity, and the generation and use of comparative data.

Within the context of Australian higher education, where the human resources landscape is heavily shaped by the industrial relations environment, Melbourne has focused effort on actions that have strategic organizational benefit, in the belief that the standard of management influences organizational sustainability and capability. The majority of decisions and actions affecting staff are taken locally, rather than centrally by the human resources department. The 2006 Enterprise Agreement tied rewards to staff with the three agreed strategic goals of the university. For example, staff bonuses or increases are linked to the position of the university in national rankings of teaching and research, as well as institutional revenue growth. Additional financial rewards are also available via 'loadings' (additions) to salary. Thus, faculty are eligible for General Faculty Loadings (GFL) for retention, merit, or additional work.

The university also has an annual performance review and development system known as the Performance Development Framework (PDF), which has an 82 percent take-up among eligible staff. A review had uncovered a belief among some staff that the university had "no effective and efficient means of managing low-performance staff and appeared to be reluctant to use PDF for that purpose." In order to increase take-up and counter the belief that PDF is more of a 'ritual' than a management tool, changes were made to the promotion system for faculty, so that promotion is now conditional on an applicant's performance being assessed as at least 'good' in his or her most recent review under PDF.

The university has around ninety academic leaders at dean and head of department level, together with over a hundred middle- to senior-level administrative managers. Underlining its belief that effective management and leadership is the best way to stave off unproductive disputes and industrial action, it has developed "an outstanding suite of in-house leadership and management programs for both academic and professional staff", which "have greatly assisted in building the management and leadership capacity of the university" (both assessments are according to an internal review of the Human Resources Department, quoted in James and Baré, 2007). These include programs for academic managers (ranging from those aspiring to the role, called Head Start, to a program called Headwork that gives professional and personal support to heads, department managers, and department executive teams), professional and administrative staff, and programs targeted at addressing the university's equity goals.

Melbourne benchmarks itself against similar organizations (the Group of Eight (Go8) research-intensive universities in Australia) as well as against the wider higher education sector nationally. Although the university had higher female participation rates than the Go8 average in 2005 (52.5 percent at Melbourne and 50.4 percent in the Go8), there was still some disparity at senior levels, where 24 percent of senior staff at Melbourne were women, against a Go8 mean of 30.1 percent. Given the relatively smaller number of posts in this group, a change of one or two posts can result in a large swing in percentage points. Melbourne has a number of initiatives to increase the number of women in senior positions at the university. One of the most established is bespoke development activities under the Academic Women in Leadership program, which has been run every eighteen months since 1997. More recently, Melbourne has been targeting promotion support for women, for example, by providing an annual Professorial Promotion and Recruitment Seminar for academic women, and appointing trained equal opportunities observers to academic promotion committees. A network of Equal Opportunity for Women in the Workplace coordinators also develop strategies, and report on progress in gender equity for academic and professional women.

The university uses comparative data from within the Australian higher education sector, as well as from its nearest equivalent institutions, to highlight its performance as an employer of choice. It measures and reports on a number of indices to highlight where it is doing well and where it is doing less well, so that strategic and other interventions can be targeted for both need and impact. A particular issue highlighted for the future is labor shortages. Universities are facing problems in recruiting faculty in some disciplines and are losing, or risk losing, professional staff. This situation of having difficulty in recruiting staff of appropriate caliber, and issues linked with concerns about retention, particularly because of the aging population of academic faculty in many places, is one seen in many countries. It reinforces the importance of a long-term strategy and the exploration of innovative ways of retaining and developing staff, as universities across the globe find themselves recruiting from the same pool of staff.

Conclusion

"HR [human resources] is just another level of management and unfortunately management in universities do not enhance the working lives of academics" (Rogers, 2008). So wrote a member of academic faculty in response to an article in the *Times Higher Education* about bargaining structures in the United Kingdom. That there is tension between trade unionists and human resource professionals during a dispute is not surprising. That a member of staff should feel so strongly about 'management' generally when there is no formal dispute is more significant. Yet, as Lord Franks said in the Report of the Commission of Inquiry into the University of Oxford (1966), "A refusal in the universities to give rational discussion of their administration a high priority must result either in tyranny mitigated by muddle or in time-wasting reduplication of effort." Lord Franks was looking at a specific university and its possible responses to a particular set of circumstances (the expansion of universities in the United Kingdom following the Robbins Report), but his comments resonate today. University managers have to walk the tightrope of engaging groups of staff, many of whom think 'management' is designed to make their lives more difficult, while avoiding falling into the trap of either "tyranny" or "time-wasting". A tough challenge, particularly when, for many, 'management' is just one of the activities they carry out while still undertaking research, teaching, and other academic activities. It is ironic that at a time when many in higher education are stressing the importance of managing as effectively as they perceive to be the case in the industrial or commercial world, many in the private sector are seeking to improve their softer management skills and embracing 'emotional intelligence', or even 'social intelligence' tools, which managers in universities have been obliged to use for some time in the absence of financial levers for rewarding and incentivizing staff.

References

Collaborative in Academic Careers in Higher Education (COACHE) (2007) *2007 Review*. Online, available at: http://gseacademic.harvard.edu/~coache/reports/20070917.html.

Corporate Leadership Council. *Employment Value Proposition Survey*. HR Executive Forum. Online, available at: www.hrexecutiveforum.com/HrForum/index.aspx (accessed April 2, 2009).

Deem, R., Hillyard, S., and Reed, M. (2007) *Knowledge, Higher Education, and the New Managerialism: The Changing Management of UK Universities*. Oxford: Oxford University Press.

Denman, D. B. (2005) "What Is a University in the 21st Century?" *Journal of Higher Education Management and Policy* 17 (2): 9–28.

Fearn, H. (2008a) "Business Divisions." *Times Higher Education*, February 21. Online, available at: www.timeshighereducation.co.uk/story.asp?sectioncode=26&storycode=400672 (accessed March 3, 2009).

Fearn, H. (2008b) "Makeover Mania." *Times Higher Education*, March 6. Online, available at: www.timeshighereducation.co.uk/story.asp?sectioncode=26&storycode=400939 (accessed March 3, 2009).

Florida, R. (2002) *The Rise of the Creative Class*. New York: Basic Books.

Lord Franks (1966) *University of Oxford: Report of Commission of Inquiry*, vol. 1. Oxford: Clarendon Press.

Gappa, J. M., Austin, A. E., and Trice, A. G. (2007) *Rethinking Faculty Work: Higher Education's Strategic Imperative*. San Francisco: Jossey-Bass.

Guest, D. and Clinton, M. (2007) *Human Resource Management and University Performance*. Final Report. London: Leadership Foundation for Higher Education.

Herzberg, F., Mausner, B., and Snyderman, B. (1959) *The Motivation to Work*. New York: John Wiley.

Hudson, S. and Skaines, I. (2007) "Developing and Managing Staffing Strategy in a Large Australian University: A Case Study from the University of Western Sydney." Paper delivered at "Supporting

Success and Productivity: Practical Tools for Making Your University a Great Place to Work." OECD IMHE: September 3–4.

James, R. and Baré, E. (2007) "Implementing Integrated Strategies for Enhancing Staff Motivation and Satisfaction: The University of Melbourne's Approach." Paper delivered at "Supporting Success and Productivity: Practical Tools for Making Your University a Great Place to Work." OECD IMHE: September 3–4.

Jaschik, S. (2008) "Anthropologists Question Minerva Project." *Inside Higher Ed*, May 1. Online, available at: www.insidehighered.com/news/2008/01/01/qt (accessed March 3, 2009).

Kirkwood, R. (2007) "Loyalty, but Not Blind Allegiance." *Times Higher Education*, December 7. Online, available at: www.timeshighereducation.co.uk/story.asp?sectioncode=26&storycode=311385 (accessed March 3, 2009).

Lancaster, L. and Stillman, D. (2002) *When Generations Collide*. New York: HarperCollins.

Lundin, P., Paul, H., and Christensen, J. (2002) *Fish! A Remarkable Way to Boost Morale and Improve Results*. New York: Hyperion.

Maslow, A. H. (1943) "A Theory of Human Motivation." *Psychological Review* 50: 370–396.

Meyer, L. H. and Evans, I. M. (2003) "Motivating the Professoriate: Why Sticks and Carrots Are Only for Donkeys." *Higher Education Management and Policy* 15 (3): 151–167.

Meyer, L. H. and Evans, I. M. (2005) "Supporting Academic Staff: Meeting New Expectations in Higher Education without Compromising Traditional Academic Values." *Higher Education Policy* 18 (3): 243–255.

Musselin, C. (2007) "What Do We Mean by Success and Productivity in Higher Education?" Paper delivered at "Supporting Success and Productivity: Practical Tools for Making Your University a Great Place to Work." OECD IMHE: September 3–4.

Peck, A. and Jackson-Peck, M. (2005) "Look for the Union Label: Brand Marketing for Union Programs and Services." Association of College Unions (ACUI), *The Bulletin* 73: 4. Online, available at: www.acui.org/publications/bulletin/article.aspx?issue=414&id=1050 (accessed April 20, 2009).

Rogers, N. (2008) "Whose Interests Do Unions Really Serve?" *Times Higher Education*, February 14. Online, available at: www.timeshighereducation.co.uk/story.asp?sectioncode=26&storycode=40061 (accessed March 3, 2009).

Shattock, M. (2001) "Review of University Management and Governance Issues Arising out of the CAPSA Project." *Cambridge Reporter*, November 2. Online, available at: http://admin.cam.ac.uk/reporter/2001-02/weekly/5861/5.html (accessed March 3, 2009).

Shelton, C. and Shelton, L. S. (2005) *The NeXt Revolution: What Gen X Women Want at Work and How Their Boomer Bosses Can Help Them Get It*. Mountain View, CA: Davies-Black.

Suvajac Lees, T. (2007) "An Enabling Approach to Supporting Employees." Paper delivered at "Supporting Success and Productivity: Practical Tools for Making Your University a Great Place to Work." OECD IMHE: September 3–4.

UNESCO (1997) *Recommendation Concerning the Status of Higher-Education Teaching Personnel*, November 11. Online, available at: http://portal.unesco.org/en/ev.php-URL_ID=13144&URL_DO=DO_TOPIC&URL_SECTION=201.html (accessed April 20, 2009).

Part II
Implications for Institutions

Introduction

GEORGE GORDON

In Barnett's (2000) age of "supercomplexity", a major challenge for institutional leaders is that of sense making, of understanding trends, identifying patterns, detecting nuances, protecting traditions that should endure, and finding ways of adjusting others to fit more sensibly with the developing needs and expectations that confront the institution.

The four chapters in this part of the book demonstrate different dimensions and facets of these challenges. Musselin (Chapter 8) and Oba (Chapter 6) discuss how traditions in relation to academic and professional appointments are slowly changing in France and Japan respectively. The fact that they both report relatively slow change illustrates the power of traditional structures and the way these permeate identities, which in turn reinforce attitudes and influence the expectations of academic faculty and professional staff, both individually and collectively, through formal and informal groupings and channels of debate and negotiation.

Many institutional leaders may still believe deeply in Johnston's (1996) proposition, from the advantaged position of experience as an institutional leader, that their primary duty is to secure environments that will enable academic faculty, whether in traditional tribes and territories (Becher and Trowler, 2001), "Mode 2" settings (Gibbons et al., 1994) or "Third Space" (Whitchurch, 2008), to perform effectively and then give them as much freedom and operational space as possible to realize their talents and achieve excellence. That idea retains relevance, but now it has to be reconciled with the increased and diverse demands and pressures that institutions face.

Institutions adopting a strategy of working with local industries may discover that their staff lack some vital skills that the new partners value and expect. More generally, there is the significant human resource challenge of ensuring that sufficient staff are willing to practice such activities and have the appropriate skills and experiences to function credibly in such roles. These demands involve issues of motivation, recognition, reward, and performance review, as well as the crucial dimension of career development and the provision of developmental support. They are framed and influenced by traditions, the values of the academy generally and individuals specifically, the procedures and policies of institutions, the degrees of freedom that they have in relation to these matters, and how they choose to exercise them.

Invariably, compromises may need to be made as institutions endeavor to balance conflicting pressures and find ways of achieving acceptance of changes to existing structures, procedures, policies, and criteria. Articulating the challenges that universities face in an age of increasing complexity, Barnett (2000) visualized institutions as complex mosaics, an amalgamation of interconnecting parts, with each part touching some other parts, but the whole structure, and picture, only produced from the totality of the parts. That may appear to be a different conception from one of distinct territories closely guarded by each tribe and policed both by the tribe and institutional managers. Of course, the parts of Barnett's mosaic could still be tribal territories, but they can also be interdisciplinary or multidisciplinary areas, administrative units or professional "Third Space" activities. A crucial challenge in such conceptions may be shifting managerial attention from control and policing to enabling, motivating, and facilitating the effective performance of each part to meet developing demands, and integrating them, providing the necessary organizational glue to achieve a coherent, ideally fluid, mosaic.

Barnett (2000) stressed three conditions that institutions must confront to meet the challenges of increasing complexity, namely knowledge, interaction, and communication. Academic faculty and professional staff need to understand the challenges. Attention should be paid to maximizing contact and connection between the parts, which could be aided by widening traditional circles and networks of communication. In any institution, that demanding set of interconnecting agendas, even after thorough analysis of trends and widespread consultation over options and their implications, may be disrupted by unforeseen events, in addition to being surrounded by uncertainties over the timing of trends and their localized, regional, and national ramifications.

An important task of institutional leaders in such circumstances is that of sense making, discerning key signals from complex, often conflicting, messages and incomplete data and communicating those interpretations in a way that promotes strategic analyses, discussions, and actions. As the Association of Commonwealth University survey (Kubler and DeLuca, 2006) demonstrated, key institutional human resource management implications entail decisions about the recruitment, retention, and development of all categories of staff. However, these must be set alongside, and harmonized with, decisions and practice in relation to staffing profiles and skill sets, and the appropriateness of supporting and enabling structures and procedures.

Institutions, and systems, differ in the degrees of freedom they have over such matters, although the trend, as Oba (Chapter 6) and Musselin (Chapter 8) illustrate, is toward greater localized freedom over recruitment, retention, and development, to enable institutions to address shifting agendas, pursue new opportunities, meet emerging demands, acquire new skill sets, and provide more flexible career pathways and enhanced developmental support. Middlehurst explores various developmental scenarios in Chapter 13.

Structurally, much depends upon the position of the institution and the relevant higher education system. For example, is it a system that incorporates a substantial measure of competition, or one that is largely allocative and less fluid? What is the extent of devolution of powers to institutions? What is the influence of overarching structures, such as national staffing agreements over pay and conditions, or macro-level frameworks to guide decisions on appointment or promotion to senior positions? While every institution wants to recruit 'talented staff', that phrase is interpreted in an increasingly distinctive way by institutions as they seek to position themselves strategically, locally, nationally, and internationally.

At any point in time, political or economic conditions can affect the recruitment attractiveness of institutions in a specific system. Intersystem differences in rates of remuneration and cost of living can be longer-term phenomena. Such disadvantages are not easily overcome without long-term economic shifts and/or shorter-term aid such as donor-country support for specific appointments or secondments.

Conversely, institutions in countries that offer attractive lifestyle choices and/or positive economic options are comparatively advantageously placed as recruitment destinations. Similar differentials can operate at the regional level within countries. Here the key challenge to institutions is to define and promote an attractive and credible prospectus of working in that institution, the "great place to work" philosophy that is explored by Usherwood (Chapter 4) and Gappa (Chapter 12). Such a philosophy also permeates endeavors directed toward retention and motivation.

Staff hold expectations of opportunities which might transpire in changing systems and situations. Smit and Nyamapfene (Chapter 7) discuss that dilemma in the context of recent developments in South Africa. More generally, institutions face the challenge of finding appropriate and meaningful ways of rewarding loyalty and good citizenship within their institutional community. The dilemma is often twofold: first, deciding whether such rewards are to be located within the mainstream structures or handled separately; and second, avoiding accusations of favoritism, or misuses of power and authority, by using transparent criteria and processes. The latter situation can be complicated, even compromised, when institutions understandably seek to retain some discretionary powers.

Removing decisions from local to national control does not obviate such perceived dangers. Nonetheless, some systems have traditionally used centralized vehicles to assure standards for senior appointments. Where that does not happen, a significant degree of independence is sought through the use of external assessors. Periods of instability within a system may lead to calls for a national body, as Smit and Nyamapfene argue (Chapter 7), but the prevalent trend is toward either the accommodation of central and local views (Musselin, Chapter 8), or devolution of decision taking.

The numerous changes that are affecting the map and working of higher education institutions, explored in detail in this volume, can produce a range of institutional responses and adaptations to structures, procedures, and policies. At one end of the spectrum, new frameworks can be formulated, as Strike analyzes in the context of English institutions of higher education (Chapter 5). From interviews with academic faculty, he concludes that many of them retain fairly traditional interpretations of career pathways and of criteria for promotion and reward. Of course, it would be unlikely that such recently articulated new frameworks would have become established and embedded phenomena that had modified perceptions of identity and led to adjustments to value sets or other, even tactical, forms of accommodation. Whether that occurs over time is likely to depend upon three key features: whether perceived benefits are judged to outweigh any limitations; the degree of acceptance that the structure receives from staff, individually and collectively; and the continued suitability of the framework to meet new circumstances and needs.

Institutions can choose a different strategy. Indeed, even where new frameworks such as those analyzed by Strike (Chapter 5) are in place, they may, over time, elect to do so on occasion. Here the options could be described either as exceptionalism or as special initiatives and actions. There is a close correlation to activities in what Clark (1998) termed the "developmental periphery". The fact that some of the staff involved may transfer from the academic or administrative heartland influences some details, since they would typically receive protection of key features of their existing terms of employment.

As the scale of these activities increases, so does the need for greater formality of criteria, procedures, and policies. That can be brought about either by modifying existing frameworks and procedures, as Strike articulates (Chapter 5), or by operating less formalized parallel systems in which the nascent version is treated as separate and, by implication, subordinate. Incrementalist approaches can allow institutions to see how trends develop and avoid premature proposals to change structures and policies. Equally, excessive caution and an absence of attention to the articulation and communication of even rudimentary career pathways may demotivate individual members of staff in newer professional roles, or areas of blended provision.

Yet a degree of caution is understandable, even appropriate. Many of the changes affecting higher education institutions are both complex and contested. From an institutional standpoint they can present important opportunities but also pose significant management challenges. For example, what is the best way for an institution to promote knowledge transfer and links with industry? In the modern era the institution wants to secure an attractive financial return for all participating parties, and take adequate steps to safeguard against any legal actions that might occur. Here the challenge is doing so without the industrial partner or the academic innovator becoming frustrated by the policies and procedures.

In similar vein, the multiple roles that, for example, many academic faculty now perform have led to the use of matrix management structures—that is, where individuals may be responsible to different post-holders for different roles and activities (teaching, research, commercialization, etc.). Here the key challenge is to keep such matrices streamlined, transparent, aligned, and clearly articulated in order to avoid confusion, conflict, disorganization, and demotivation. Ultimately, the priority for any institution is to keep structures, procedures, and policies constantly under review, in order to assure their continuing fitness-for-purpose and effectiveness.

References

Barnett, R. (2000) *Realizing the University in an Age of Supercomplexity*. Buckingham, UK: SRHE/Open University Press.

Becher, T. and Trowler, P. (2001) *Academic Tribes and Territories: Intellectual Enquiry and the Culture of Disciplines*. Buckingham, UK: SRHE/Open University Press.

Clark, B. R. (1998) *Creating Entrepreneurial Universities: Organizational Pathways of Transformation Issues in Higher Education*. Oxford: IAU/Pergamon.

Gibbons, M., Limoges, C., Nowotny, H., Schwartzman, S., Scott, P., and Trow, M. (1994) *The New Production of Knowledge: The Dynamics of Science and Research in Contemporary Societies*. London: Sage.

Johnston, R. J. (1996) "Managing How Academics Manage." In *Working in Higher Education*, ed. R. Cuthbert. Buckingham, UK: SRHE/Open University Press.

Kubler, J. and DeLuca, C. (2006) *Trends in Academic Recruitment and Retention: A Commonwealth Perspective*. London: Association of Commonwealth Universities.

Whitchurch, C. (2008) "Shifting Identities and Blurring Boundaries: The Emergence of *Third Space* Professionals in UK Higher Education." *Higher Education Quarterly* 62 (4): 377–396.

5

Evolving Academic Career Pathways in England

TONY STRIKE

Introduction

Academic careers have changed; at least, they have done so in England, and new models for academic careers have emerged. It has been possible, through my empirical research, to describe what has been happening at institutional level by examining the interplay between higher education institutions' promotion procedures and the social reality as experienced by faculty. English academic career models have evolved, in response to the strategic, competitive, or organizational needs of institutions, to a new diversified form that is less exclusive and recognizes different contributions and career routes. These changes seem to provide educationalists, entrepreneurs, and academic administrators with an opportunity to participate on more equal terms with those following more traditional or balanced academic careers.

This finding might seem attractive, as it recognizes the changes observed and views them as institutionally strategic and academically benign. However, the trend toward a management-led, detailed division of academic labor, basing jobs on the individual task elements of a work process, had tended to fractionalize the academic role. This process of specialization may represent the systematic deconstruction, or demystification, of the craft of academia by managers. If what was observed, in the study described here, was a broad and varied occupation being broken down into describable elements by managers, then it was the start of the destruction, rather than the natural evolution, of the craft profession that was academia. It is not clear from a correlation of career models with the time-contiguous rank order data on research (from the Research Assessment Exercise (RAE), 2001) and education (from the National Student Survey (NSS), 2007) that the localization and fractionalization of academic roles, which tends to break apart the research–teaching nexus and any national homogeneity, has been performance related or of benefit to the academic profession.

The Context for Change

The impact of institutional strategies on academic roles has been noted already (Gordon, 2003), but it has also been suggested that this has been adaptive and evolutionary (Henkel, 2002: 144) in that "the stabilities and continuities in academic identities remained strong." Universities have witnessed the early stages of a change toward greater diversification and fractionalization of academic functions. This change has been the product of a booster effect created by a combination of national policy and local employee relations agreements. The research described here demonstrates how academic careers have changed, and seeks to explain these changes through new career models.

Data were collected from a deliberately varied sample of six English pre-1992 universities. Their promotion procedures were accessed and faculty and human resources directors interviewed. This definition and choice are explained later in the chapter. This was followed by a questionnaire distributed to all forty-two pre-1992 universities in England, which had a 60 percent response rate. Through this research it was possible to achieve new understandings about emerging academic career paths that may replace the concept of a traditional, linear career ladder.

The research started from Henkel's premise that "the concept of identity has been of central symbolic and instrumental significance, both in the lives of individual academics and in the workings of the academic profession" (2002: 137). The view of who was a member of academic faculty and who was not, and a shared sense of level, status, and recognized titles, allowed, for example, peer review for assessing promotion applications internationally. This shared, and relatively stable, view of what an academic career was, which was fixed at least in the collective understanding of the participants, came under pressure as institutions sought to adapt the profession to the requirements of their mission. If institutional policies were causal, then adaptation by a single institution was unlikely to succeed as it would not be universally recognized, and the traditional career structures and their associated behavior patterns could not be outcompeted by any localized alternative. The context in England was, therefore, interesting, as all higher education institutions were required to introduce locally agreed pay structures, including for faculty, by August 2006 (Universities and Colleges Employers Association (UCEA), 2003). This produced many variants, not all of which would persist. The academic profession in England was at the beginning of a period of change without uniformity. The traditional academic career may not have become extinct but it may, if the conjecture here is right, have to live alongside variations of its own species that faculty themselves may not immediately recognize, and may not welcome.

English National Policy Drivers for Dynamism in Human Resources Management

Universities in England are relatively autonomous, self-governing institutions with their own charter and governing council. However, they receive public funding to varying degrees for both teaching and research, and so are subject to public policy made by the research councils or by the Higher Education Funding Council for England (HEFCE). These bodies have various conditions associated with their funding. From a policy perspective the national Committee of Inquiry into Higher Education (in the United Kingdom) chaired by Dearing (1997) and the Independent Review of Higher Education Pay and Conditions chaired by Sir Michael Bett (1999) both stated that improvement in human resource management (HRM) in universities was a necessary condition of future funding.

Recommendation 50 of the Report of the National Committee of Inquiry into Higher Education (Dearing, 1997) recommended that "the higher education employers appoint, after consultation with staff representatives, an independent review committee to report by April 1998 on the framework for determining pay and conditions of service." Dearing, in particular, was concerned that the then current arrangements for determining pay and conditions were hindering the development of the sector. Most universities in England belong voluntarily, by subscription, to the Universities and Colleges Employers Association (UCEA). UCEA has traditionally, through national collective bargaining, set the pay, grading, and conditions rules for universities in the United Kingdom, with the latter's consent. UCEA, which represents the great majority of higher education employers, took forward Dearing Recommendation 50 and, after consultation across the sector, constituted the Independent Review of Higher Education Pay and Conditions, chaired by Sir Michael Bett, with terms of reference as recommended by Dearing.

One outcome of the Bett Report (1999) was the establishment of a national Joint Negotiating Committee for Higher Education Staff (JNCHES). As well as recommending this national committee to replace multi-table bargaining, Bett sought two closely linked pay spines, a national grading framework, job evaluation, and institutional flexibility to reflect markets and performance. The new negotiating body established a National Framework Agreement (Bett, 1999; UCEA, 2003) allowing each institution in the United Kingdom to design its own pay and grading arrangements, provided that they used a single, national fifty-one-point pay spine and adhered to certain common principles. This reform arguably came about as a result of pressure from some larger universities, which threatened to leave UCEA if they were not given latitude to reflect their priorities in their human resource policies. Those institutions that faced the challenge of attracting and retaining quality academic faculty in a competitive international marketplace increasingly strained against national pay scales.

In the grant letter to HEFCE in 2000, the Secretary of State for Education for England made £330 million available to universities for the three-year period 2001–2002 to 2003–2004. Each was required to submit for assessment a human resource strategy in order for funds to be released for the "Rewarding and Developing Staff" (R&DS) initiative (Higher Education Funding Council for England (HEFCE), 2001). An evaluation of this initiative, conducted for HEFCE by management consultants KPMG (HEFCE, 2005), reported a systematic "booster" effect occurring in human resource management practices in universities in England, not seen in the other countries of the United Kingdom.

R&DS funding was paid directly to universities, not through UCEA or JNCHES as national intermediaries. HEFCE's criteria demanded that English universities achieve equal pay for equal work using institution-wide systems of job evaluation (JE). This particular objective, with funding, combined with the National Framework Agreement from JNCHES described earlier, created a particular and nationally localized dynamic for the variant design of institution-specific pay and grading structures. Universities were given a national mandate, the freedom, and the financial resources to localize pay structures, and had the competitive motivation to do so. It was this joining of policy and circumstances that created the important booster effect for structural change to academic careers in England, and made it worthy of study. Significantly, the policy issues of human resource management at national and institutional level, such as pay and conditions of service, bargaining structures, tenure, and competitiveness, are not the same as those issues that individual members of academic faculty raise (Strike and Taylor, 2009).

Competitive Differentiation in Academic Careers

With effect from 2006–2007, universities in England charge variable tuition fees, with most charging the maximum permitted fee of £3,000 but offering differential bursaries or scholarships to attract students. As each competed for students in this new market, the need to offer an integrated, high-quality student experience was highlighted. In addition, universities were, to different degrees, and depending on their mission, pursuing research, enterprise, and innovation agendas, including developing spin-out companies, licensing, and patenting, and offering consultancy services to commercial clients. Pre-1992 universities in England continued to value and to be rewarded for research success. As Henkel stated (2002: 140), these variable institutional missions were a product of strategic choice, "largely in the name of income generation".

This increasing heterogeneity of mission, it was assumed, required the emergence, recognition, and reward of contingent academic career pathways that had descriptive criteria equal in standard and status to those of traditional academic roles, but appropriate to new and varying demands. While traditional academic career structures may have remained strong, they now differed between types of institution and between countries. The simple vertical ladder of lecturer A and B, senior lecturer, reader (within the United Kingdom), and professor, which was well recognized and understood, was defunct as a universal structure. Despite some continued use of uniform nomenclature, differences in academic roles between universities in England quickly emerged to fit divergent missions as the national structures disappeared.

Kogan et al. (1994) reported that a new academic mandate was needed, explicitly linking traditional scholarly values with changing demands on higher education. They noted, however, that academic staffing structures were diversifying without that mandate, creating tensions of status, reward, motivation, and opportunity. By contrast, Henkel (2000) reported that faculty had responded to widespread and powerful policy change in an evolutionary way, retaining core components of their professional identity. This evolutionary metaphor was supported by Høstaker (2000), who suggested that, while he found important differences in the relative influence of institutional policies, the general and continuing trend was toward greater diversification of academic functions, which posed challenges for career paths.

When individual faculty were allowed, or even encouraged, to reshape or reduce what was previously a composite bundle of roles, some differentiation or adaptation was likely to arise. For example, if an outstanding academic researcher sought to buy him- or herself out of teaching activity, this rarely seemed to present problems in the future career path of such successful researchers. However, researchers funded on short-term contracts also did not teach, but did not seem to have the same opportunities, causing tensions of status and reward, as highlighted by Kogan et al. (1994). Likewise, in England, research-intensive universities, in wishing to optimize their academic faculty profile for the Research Assessment Exercise (RAE), sought to exclude those who did not have a high research profile from their submission of 'research-active' staff. Given that such staff would not then attract research funding, they tended to take on teaching or academic administrative activities, perhaps for negative reasons, in that they were escaping an area of weakness rather than exercising a strength. Academic faculty who had positively chosen a career path based on teaching excellence may have felt their choice devalued as a result.

Tuition fees created a different pressure to meet the needs of a diverse set of learners, to prepare academic faculty for teaching roles, and to select, positively and proactively, good educators or educational innovators for these roles. The emergence of the Quality Assurance Agency in the 1990s, and increasing emphasis on quality assurance and assessment of teaching, also began to force universities to recognize and encourage high-quality teaching practice. However, Gordon (2003) suggested that excellence in teaching was still, in most pre-1992 universities, perceived as attracting less prestige and reward than excellence in research, notwithstanding attempts by many institutions to revise their promotion criteria.

Making New Representational Career Models

The representational models described in what follows resulted from qualitative, interpretivist fieldwork in six selected case-study institutions in 2007. The research data underlying the models came from document analysis of promotion procedures, followed by semi-structured face-to-face interviews with the institutional human resources directors on what motivated the documentary changes. To look only at promotions procedures and criteria would be to accept that the reality of academic careers was institutionally defined through ordered procedures, which the participants understood, accepted, and operated within. While this might be a sound ontological perspective, it was possible that the sense of what 'an academic' was, and what made for seniority, was so embedded in the minds of individual faculty that the written procedures of particular institutions had little or no influence. Faculty members would, from this perspective, and through collective influence, impose or create a reality that overcame the particular bureaucratic rules of any one institution.

Interviews were conducted with twenty-one academic faculty in the case institutions who had been promoted or appointed recently, and so were assumed to be knowledgable about the formal or implicit rules. This provided the cultural, subjective career perspective from the participant's viewpoint. By synthesizing the documentary analysis of changed promotion procedures and the intent of the human resources directors with the academic interviews, it was intended to achieve an "interplay between the institutional script and the personal story"

(Arthur et al., 1999: 42). From this interplay it was proposed to offer a career model (or models) that described what the literature reported, and so help understanding. The model(s) would be presented not as ideal types, but as representations of the found reality. After this empirical work the model(s) would be tested, using a questionnaire, to see whether they could be reliably generalized to, or presented as a typification of, academic career design.

The decision was made to restrict the scope to English pre-1992 universities. This exclusion of other English institutions, and pre-1992 universities in other parts of the United Kingdom, requires a short explanation. Before 1992, English universities were private institutions established by royal charter and received funding from the University Grants Committee (UGC), created in 1919. Expansion in higher education through the 1960s and later was largely achieved through the creation of a binary system, forming a new public sector comprising the former polytechnics. Polytechnics were initially, until 1988, run by local government authorities and established with a civic role to provide advanced technical and vocational education, receiving no funding for research. The different legal status, mission, and funding of these institution types meant that their academic faculty originated from very different contracts and grading structures. England, as I have explained, had the benefit of R&DS monies from HEFCE, which were not available in the other parts of the United Kingdom, and the consultancy company KMPG had already reported for HEFCE on the booster effect that this had had on English institutions' human resource management practices (HEFCE, 2005). It was this, therefore, that justified restricting the study to England.

The Making of Formal Promotions Procedures

The first empirical outcome of note from the case studies was that human resource professionals appeared to have one of two means by which they generated their institutions' formal academic career structures. For the sake of simplicity these were termed 'strategic' and 'collegial'. This was overly simplistic, as in both cases one direction was determinative and the other consultative. The choice of which driver had primacy in holding the determinative authority—that is, the management strategy makers or the collegial academic body—was hypothesized as defining the choice of career model, and this was tested by questionnaire.

Strategic Design of Academic Career Structures

Where university management operated as a top-down authority structure, this involved taking policy decisions and implementing executive actions with the aim of maximizing resources and achieving organizational goals. To illustrate, one participant human resources director said of strategy driving change:

> We had a new vice-chancellor start and he introduced a new *strategy* to the university. And if the previous strategy for the university was research, research, research, that being everything, the population who were edu-cationally strong in the university were feeling they didn't count, or they were

disenfranchised, or that they were in the wrong university or not on mission. What he was saying is that the university has three mission domains: Research, we are a research-led university but we also have education, we need to be strong in education and also in enterprise. And following a career in any one of those three business streams was legitimate and that people ought to be able to see a clear career pathway through to demonstrate distinctiveness or success or competence in any one of those streams. And it was really that *strategic intent* of his that *drove* the changes to the academic promotion criteria.

In this strategic model it was the organizational strategy, whether written or advanced by the vice-chancellor or president, that directly influenced the human resources strategy as developed by the human resources director, and caused the production of a new academic career structure. This product was then subject to consultation with, and applied to, the academic population. In short, policymakers adopted a policy, processed with assistance from the human resources department, and introduced it. This model is represented as shown in Figure 5.1.

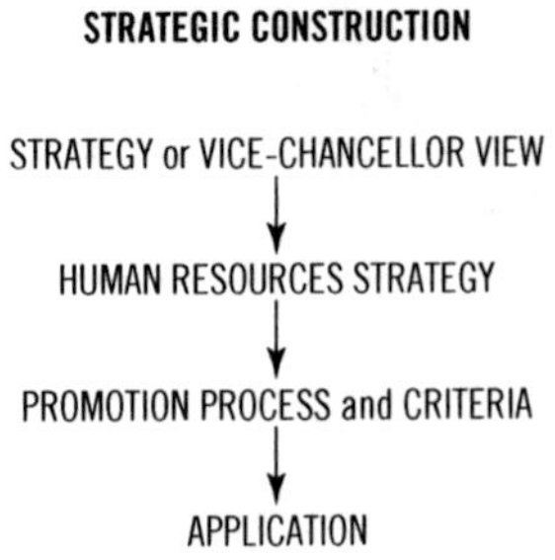

STRATEGIC CONSTRUCTION

STRATEGY or VICE-CHANCELLOR VIEW

↓

HUMAN RESOURCES STRATEGY

↓

PROMOTION PROCESS and CRITERIA

↓

APPLICATION

Figure 5.1 Strategic Construction of an Academic Career

Collegial Design of Academic Career Structures

Farnham (1999: 18) suggested that

[t]he model of university management that best represents the interests of academic staff is the 'collegial' University, which combines high levels of professional autonomy with high levels of staff participation in management. It is a bottom-up 'person'-based organisation in which the focal point of the institution is the collegium of scholars focussed around their academic disciplines.

Illustrating this, and by contrast to the model above, another human resources director talked about the collegial debate driving change:

Every year, the promotion process culminates in a meeting, what's called the main committee on academic promotions. And it is that body which has as part of its agenda having to consider the cases coming through for the year. They also spend a bit of time, and typically perhaps, talking about how the process works, how it is going in the current year and what changes might be beneficial. So it tends to be continuous improvement, if you will, but a learning from the process, rather than anything that is particularly dramatic. The academic division still runs professorial appointments. I think that . . . you know, the way it's been done over the last few years, there is a fair degree of *consensus* now, and indeed I mean, particularly the externals are quite complimentary about both the procedure as written, but also the way it is actually managed in practice. We do get lively debates in the main committee, sometimes about particular issues and, you know, it is not unusual to hear somebody say after about ten minutes, when you just think the plans have been put to rest, you know someone suddenly says, "Well, I don't agree with that". But that's in the nature of *academic debate.*

In this second model, change followed academic debate and a formed consensus. The role of human resources departments was to capture the consensus and then to administer the process that had come from the collegial body. In short, academic faculty proposed a self-definition and the human resources department officially recorded and administered that self-proposition. This model is represented in Figure 5.2.

Figure 5.2 Collegial Construction of an Academic Career

Emergent Career Models

The inductive case study research identified four possible representative academic career models that operated within English universities. These four representational models were termed:

- the slippery pole (unitary, exclusive, and linear);
- the ladder (fragmented and exclusive);
- parallel ladders (inclusive and segregated);
- the climbing frame ((re)integrated).

In summary, the characteristics of each found model were as follows:

The Slippery Pole: Unitary, Exclusive, and Linear

The slippery pole model is the traditional, instantly recognizable, academic career structure in an English research-intensive university, with titles running from lecturer to professor. There is only one career route, so it is unitary. It focuses on research excellence to the exclusion of other academic attributes, and so is exclusive. As one human resources director explained:

> We must recognize what makes this university what it is, and at the end of the day it is the research. So that's what inevitably tends to win out, the research. I mean yes, some do want to teach, but usually that is not at the expense of their research. So to keep it to a fairest minimum we do not have very, at the moment anyway, draconian requirements for teaching, and in fact, as you go up the ladder, the amount of teaching you are expected to do decreases all the time . . . they may, in career terms, if their university teaching dominates . . . in all probability not get above senior lecturer.

Research-only and teaching-only posts might exist, but were not considered to be academic, sat outside the formal career structures, were absent from the formal definitional and promotions procedures, and were referred to as 'academic-related' or something similar. This can be represented pictorially as in Figure 5.3.

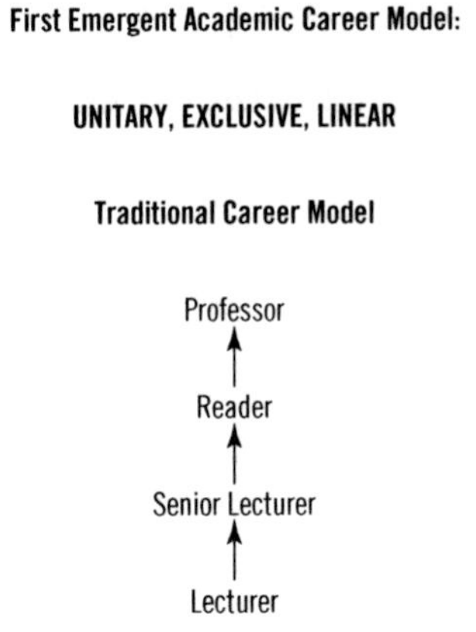

First Emergent Academic Career Model:

UNITARY, EXCLUSIVE, LINEAR

Traditional Career Model

Professor
↑
Reader
↑
Senior Lecturer
↑
Lecturer

Figure 5.3 The Slippery Pole

The Ladder: Fragmented and Exclusive

This second, 'ladder' model (Figure 5.4) recognizes, but has not yet fully assimilated, other forms of academic work in procedural and titling conventions. They were included usually by way of an annex or parallel set of arrangements to the mainstream procedure or convention. Exclusivity remained as the dominant mode, but the required recognition of different types of academic faculty or legitimate contribution caused a (sometimes confusing) fragmentation.

A human resources director struggled to explain this fragmentation of his procedure into research and teaching criteria, while arguing for the continued primacy of research as the 'real' career, as follows:

> There is quite a paradox here. It's ... on the one hand ... the primacy of research. This is a research institution. There are also different research criteria for research in a career strand for researchers and for the mainstream academic. The paradox comes in the fact that in the mainstream academic strand we have teaching elements. And this is the superior stream. Despite the fact [that] there is some teaching element. The fact that there is both some teaching and research is important. Which is a kind of inconsistency. It's peculiar. ... But such is the case. So, research is the fuel for the 'real' kind ... what the culture defines as the mainstream academic career limits. You can't leave behind research in the mainstream academic career.

Research-only or research-dominated roles, and teaching-only or teaching-dominated roles, were considered to be academic, but enjoyed less status or respect from academic faculty in the so-called mainstream. Definitional criteria or promotions procedures may have contained separate annexes or sections referring to or conditionally acknowledging these staff.

Second Emergent Academic Career Model:

FRAGMENTED AND EXCLUSIVE

Traditional Career Model

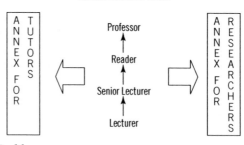

Figure 5.4 The Ladder

Parallel Ladders: Inclusive and Segregated

The third career model accepts and assimilates different types of faculty in a coherent framework of what are sometimes called career pathways or job families. Each different career path is presented as being equally legitimate as a contribution to the success of the enterprise. Each has different criteria but is equal or equivalent in the standards required. However, a clear public distinction or separation is maintained by title, pay scale or promotion process between the different, although parallel, tracks (see Figure 5.5).

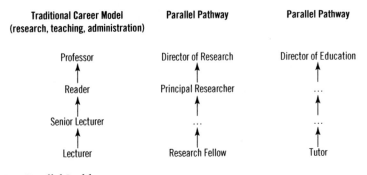

Figure 5.5 Parallel Ladders

For example, a human resources director said:

Those people who were following education career paths were in the main happy with these changes. But they were concerned that the process they go through, and the standards they have to achieve in the education pathway, are seen as being equally rigorous to those that you would have to achieve in the research pathway in order to get the same level of seniority. In other words, what the people in the education career pathway are doing . . . are two things; they say, "Yes, it is good, we like this pathway", but secondly, it is not going to be seen to be as a sort of second-class, second-status, not so good pathway; it has to be seen as demanding, rigorous, you know equally, equally difficult, to carry that equal status.

The Climbing Frame: Integrated

The fourth model joins research or teaching or consultancy or leadership roles as part of an (re)integrated career path. Any visible status labels are removed, so titles, scales, and processes are held in common for roles with differentiated content (see Figure 5.6).

A human resources director explained it as follows:

The last vice-chancellor's view was that we ought to provide an outlet for rewarding people who had made major contributions to teaching and administration, but whose research portfolio was not good enough to be a professor. And, therefore, we dreamed up this title of University Director of Education. People didn't like the title but they liked the money. We looked for national and international contributions to teaching and all sorts of things. We dressed it up. But whatever happened they all still felt that they were not called professors. Professorial research fellows were probably a bit

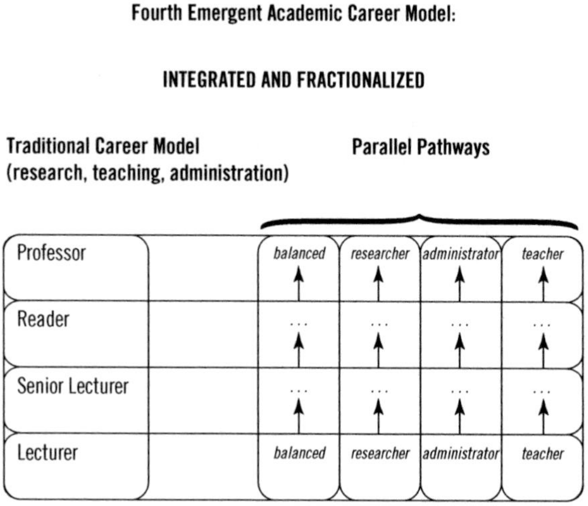

Fourth Emergent Academic Career Model:

INTEGRATED AND FRACTIONALIZED

Traditional Career Model   **Parallel Pathways**
(research, teaching, administration)

Professor		balanced	researcher	administrator	teacher
Reader		...	...	...	...
Senior Lecturer		...	...	...	...
Lecturer		balanced	researcher	administrator	teacher

Figure 5.6 The Climbing Frame

of an anachronism at one level in the sense that it is another research line and didn't do any teaching. Although actually, arguably, a few of them teach. Let's just rationalize this. Let's be brave enough to call people professors who are good at research and teaching and good at administration and good corporate citizens. Let's accept that. So you come to the conclusion that you've got to bite the bullet and you've got to make them professors.

The study's questionnaire design drew on the characteristics of these inductive models and permitted four category responses, independently in the case of both teachers and researchers, as follows:

- cannot be promoted under the general criteria (or will only occasionally be promoted) as they do not meet the necessary criteria;
- have particular/special criteria set out alongside the standard criteria, but with more limited opportunities;
- have their own separately identifiable career track with criteria equal or equivalent in standard to other faculty, allowing them to progress to similar grades but with separate titles;
- have their own career track with appropriate criteria, and can progress to higher grades and be similarly titled to others at the same grade.

Analysis of the questionnaire responses, based on the characteristics of the inductive models above, suggested that nine, not four, models were in operation. Differential treatment of teachers and researchers within the same institution created the additional combinations. This showed the inductive models to be naïve, as they assumed similar treatment of teachers and researchers within each model, but the results affirmed the localization and fractionalization illustrated by the models.

Academia: A Collection of Separate Activities or a Body of Work Belonging to a Single Craft?

Role fractionalization is not necessarily to be perceived as being positive or negative. Kogan et al. (1994: 70) said that the "core functions of academic staff are teaching and research complemented by service to the institution, to the professions, and to society." This does not suggest that they are all performed by each member of academic faculty. Blaxter et al. (1998: 285) gave an extended list of five roles that faculty had to fulfill in executing their work. The roles were teaching, researching, managing, writing, and networking. Houston et al. (2006: 19) went on to describe universities "as concerned with advanced learning, where research and teaching are closely interdependent, and where most teaching is done by people active in advancing knowledge", so suggesting a beneficial link between the tasks. These rather clinical descriptions were given a little more cultural bite by Coaldrake (2000: 15), who described a different ideal that extolled

> individual independence and autonomy underpinned by secure full-time employment, authority derived from academic standing, local control over academic matters, linkage of research and teaching at the individual level, high status for original research, and widespread disdain for what are seen as the lesser tasks of administration and management.

This definition suggests that research and teaching are linked, and that those who performed both require independence.

Dill and Sporn (1995: 16) observed that universities were developing "more creative, adaptable and efficient means of organising academic work." Kogan et al. (1994: 2) described the nature of this impact: "There are changing balances and tensions between different tasks: teaching, scholarship, research, consultancy, community service and administration. Priorities have to be made, by academics and institutions. Differentiation of task is taking place between institutions and within them." The distinction or separation between research and teaching had led to the idea that to gain credibility as an academic, an individual needed to be a respected researcher (Asmar, 2004: 56). Teaching was viewed as an activity that could be outsourced or delegated to part-time or junior lecturers or tutors and held lower status value and significance (Serow et al., 2002). Time spent on teaching was blamed for a lack of research output, since in most universities teaching and research were said to be conducted by the same individuals (Ebong, 2001; Vidal and Quintanilla, 2000). This literature suggested that, far from being integrated, teaching had a negative impact on research if combined in one role.

Whatever the right answer, universities were accountable for both activities, irrespective of how highly ranked they were in research. Teaching formed part of the core functions of universities, although they tended, in the traditional model, to hire and promote academic faculty "on the basis of scholarly distinction" (Serow et al., 2002: 25). This policy was said to tend to increase the institution's ability to produce greater research outputs, but had unintended consequences for education.

Research and teaching were said to be rewarded differently. Coate et al. (2001: 159) said that universities repeatedly set themselves up to fail in education by linking promotion to research productivity, partly because it is easier to measure the outputs. As Kerr noted,

> Society *hopes* that [university] teachers will not neglect their teaching responsibilities but *rewards* them almost entirely for research and publications. . . . Consequently it is rational for University teachers to concentrate on research, even to the detriment of teaching and at the expense of their students.
>
> (1975: 773; emphasis in original)

This literature suggested that research had a negative impact on teaching, and would have made the found models higher-performing and so more attractive.

An Examination of New Managerialism

A new political and ideological intent was set out by the UK government in 1985 with the publication of a Green Paper (Department for Education and Science (DES), 1985). This report, according to Thorne and Cuthbert (1996: 173), "emphasized narrower utilitarian purposes for HE as a servant of the economy". The Jarratt Report (Committee of Vice-Chancellors and Principals (CVCP), 1985) said that institutional leaders should assert their responsibilities as chief executives, and adopt new approaches to strategic institutional leadership. It was important, therefore, to examine the role of new forms of management practice, or new public management, as it affected university structures. Were changed academic career structures the inevitable outcome of a management emphasis on targets, accountability, and performance?

The Taylorist philosophy (Taylor, 1947) promoted, according to Thorne and Cuthbert (1996: 174), the maximization of throughput while retaining quality by "breaking down tasks and limiting their complexity, so that the organization can develop well rehearsed routines and predictable processes to cope with high volume." This description suggested a clear link to observed fractionalization in academic job design. Braverman (1974) argued that an inevitable tendency existed toward the degradation and deskilling of work, as capitalists searched for profits in increasingly competitive environments. Scientific management, or Taylorism (Taylor, 1947), sought to systematize work, designing jobs in their most basic and simple manner. Handy (1993: 165) described the "micro-division" of labor:

- jobs were fractionalized into their smallest elements so that unskilled people could undertake them with little training;
- workers were dispensable;
- individuals could not dictate to management;
- training times were lower;
- standardization of jobs meant better control.

As Hales (1993: 62) said, "Detailed division of labour entails basing jobs on individual task elements of a work process. Employees are, therefore, allocated specific tasks for which they are selected, recruited and trained."

The academic career models represented in Figures 5.3–5.6 show an increased fractionalization, as predicted, but it was unclear to what degree the managerial philosophy described above had led directly to the role designs seen in the study. When one compares the method of making the promotion procedure and criteria, whether strategic or collegial, with the resulting career model, the results from the case studies suggest that a strategic, 'top-down' managerial initiative was more likely to generate an innovative change in the institutional formalization of what an academic career looked like and how roles were described. A managerial approach was assumed to be more likely to produce role fractionalization. This hypothesis was, however, not proven by the questionnaire results.

It was further hypothesized that managerial initiatives to fractionalize academic roles may have been more likely to be pursued where the university found itself subject to, or less able to resist, competitive pressure; or where the university was further down the RAE or NSS rank order. In a high-ranking university the result should be an ability to sustain or defend existing definitions of the academic profession as a single, coherent craft, so avoiding the gradual 'proletarianization' of the academic profession. Or conversely, that the fractionalized models would be more likely to be placed higher in the league tables as they drove performance. These hypotheses were also not proven.

The New Model(s) Explored

In light of the contextual pressures it was not clear initially whether institutions would all adapt in their own way, producing localized role variants and titles of their own, or whether at least some sharing, if not some new uniformity, should be sought. The higher education trade unions in the United Kingdom were one force acting for national uniformity, but in a way that was perceived as a defense of the status quo. The other force was competitive pressure, whereby each institution must not be seen to be disadvantaged for staff recruitment against its peer institutions. Universities seemed to observe or allow an increasing array of academic roles and titles alongside the traditional pathways: teaching and research assistants and fellows, research- or teaching-only faculty, academic administrators, learning and teaching coordinators, academic consultants, enterprise fellows, directors of research, and directors of education alongside the more traditional professor. As was observed, some of these role holders were perceived to be 'academic' and others not, depending on the university's liberal or conservative conception of the profession. In some places a simple, unitary 'ladder' image was, it was assumed, no longer enough to describe the plethora of academic roles and titles required in practice. However, pre-maturity meant that no previous attempt had been made to develop a new model of academic careers.

Torrington, Hall, and Taylor (2002: 453) defined career pathways thus:

A career path is a sequence of job roles or positions, related via work content or abilities required, through which an individual can move. Publicised pathways can help people to identify a realistic career goal within the organisation. Traditional pathways were normally presented as a vertical career ladder, emphasising upwards promotion within a function.

Following this model, the traditional academic career pathway in a research-led English university might have looked like a simple vertical ladder on which not everyone could get purchase, defined here as the 'slippery pole'. Other academic roles may have existed, but they would not be recognized as being within the formal career system as their holders were not perceived as being academic faculty, or they were seen as intending to follow an academic career rather than as actually doing so. Kimber (2003: 41), for example, talked about a two-tiered academic workforce, "the tenured core with security and good conditions and the tenuous periphery with insecurity and poor conditions." Torrington et al. (2002: 454) went on to state, "There is now increasing use of alternative approaches, often designed in the form of a grid, with options at each point, so that upward, lateral, diagonal and even downwards moves can be made."

Any grid showing what academic career paths it was assumed might be emerging is more complicated and choice-ridden. Some of the conceptual models illustrated in this chapter to describe emerging academic career models might be more helpfully seen as climbing frames than as ladders, allowing lateral movements during a career. However, it is appreciated that care is required in using these metaphorical devices, as they may suggest male manual work, and this implication is not intended.

A Perspective on Career Theory

Career models, while perhaps formally documented in organizational procedures, are social constructs that do not exist as tangible objects. Social groups spontaneously develop hierarchical structure (Argyle, 1983). Hierarchy is a relational, social construct and in a work-based organization it is founded on given authority, service, or personal competence. Career progression or promotion through that hierarchy is a social activity conducted between people where some achieve higher rank, earnings, or status (Argyle, 1983; Warr, 1980). In formal, bureaucratic organizations, this process of career management takes the form of grades, titles, pay scales, definitions, and a promotional process for determining progression. Handy (1993: 250) commented that "[c]areer development becomes a human hurdle race, the hurdles being different appointments or different levels of authority. Those who clear a hurdle can progress to the next, until there are no more." In this model, seniority is the reward for success, and pay follows seniority. Kaulisch and Enders stated (2005: 130) that "[l]ike all working people academics go through a sequence of jobs, work roles and experiences; they go through a career." This literature makes career management seem both formal and explicit. However, Schein (1986: 317) suggested:

> We need to build concepts and models around what I call the 'realities' of how things really work in organizations. We need more and better descriptive studies of how things work so that concepts and models mirror what really goes on. Being normative is very comfortable until one starts to take the concept of culture seriously. Then one discovers that the career field is shot through with cultural biases.

Academia is a relational, social world with its own sense of rank or status. For example, the rank or title of reader may be perceived as more prestigious than that of senior lecturer, even if the pay and terms are similar. Researchers may view their social position as different from that of teachers. Those in traditional academic disciplines may have opinions about new or emerging disciplines and their place in universities. Rank exists in ordered societies, such as work-based organizations, in which particular grades or titles are attributed status. It was clear that this changing social dynamic, influenced by those with social capital in each university, was to some extent driving the choice of model.

Sonnenfeld's career systems typology was recognized as a prominent model in career theory (Baruch and Peiperl, 2003). This typology of career systems separated supply—that is, whether a career system was open to new recruits (boundaryless) or closed (bounded) to the external labor market, other than at the entry level. On a second dimension, the assignment flow, the criterion by which promotion decisions were made, was divided into individual and team contributions (Sonnenfeld and Peiperl, 1988). Interestingly, Sonnenfeld and Peiperl attributed the label 'academy' (ibid.: 591) to career systems in organizations that might be characterized as having an internal supply flow (that is, they were bounded) and that focused on individual contributions for their promotion criteria, where professional growth was seen as a personal goal and a community obligation. One characteristic of academies was the existence of "elaborate career paths and job ladders" (Baruch and Peiperl, 2003: 1269).

While academic faculty in English pre-1992 universities may have been in a bounded or closed career, with entry for most through a Ph.D., this was often not an organizational career where work was undertaken for only one institution for the duration of a career. Interorganizational career orientations were said to affect employees' career strategies as they built seniority by moving from one organization to another (Yamamoto, 2006). An interorganizational career was "self-directed by the employees themselves" and required "more self-control on the part of the employee than to develop an organizational career" (ibid.: 244). Defillippi and Arthur (1994) observed that careers characterized by interfirm mobility caused behaviors characterized by a boundaryless career, challenging Sonnenfeld and Peiperl's (1988) typology. In future, English academic faculty would have to pay much more attention to the particular construct given to an academic career by each institution, so that when making interorganizational moves they would appreciate what was valued and promoted in the place they were intending to join.

Conclusion

This chapter was intended to develop the theory around academic careers and how those careers might be structurally represented or described in a changing field. The models derive from empirical research and demonstrate the multiplicity and complexity faced by institutions in designing, and by individuals in following, academic careers. Furthermore, given the local autonomy of institutions, the changes that are occurring tend to be hidden within each institution's internal promotions procedure. By shedding light on the perceptions of academic faculty 'on the ground', it may have been possible to give those with the requisite social capital the opportunity to understand more clearly, and have an influence on, what is occurring.

The first issue to deal with by way of conclusion was the fractionalization of academic roles into constituent, independently performed parts or subunits of what was once an (arguably) integrated whole. As is stated in the Introduction, one possible conclusion from the study was that academia is evolving, in response to the strategic, competitive, or organizational needs of institutions, to a new, diversified form that is less exclusive and recognizes different contributions and career routes. In particular, these changes seemed to provide educationalists, entrepreneurs, and academic administrators, at least in some places, with an opportunity to participate on (increasingly) equal terms with those following traditional balanced careers, thus diversifying and enriching academia. This conclusion was attractive as it recognized the changes observed, and viewed them as both institutionally strategic and academically benign.

Literature on job design offered a different perspective on the empirical findings illustrated in this chapter, one that was not so obviously attractive to those academic participants following the traditional career. Once work was divided and allocated, for instance, into teaching, research, academic administration, and consultancy, it could then be better described, coordinated, and controlled. One finding is that new forms of academic career which came from managerialist initiatives and tended to fractionalize the academic role were less attractive. Hales (1993: 71) suggested that this process of

> rationalisation in general, and scientific management in particular, are the practical and ideological instruments for the systematic destruction of craft organisation, through firstly, deskilling—the separation of conception from execution and the fragmentation of tasks—and secondly, concentration of control in the hands of managers.

If what was observed was a broad and varied occupation being broken down into describable elements by managers, then what this study observes was the start of the destruction, rather than the natural evolution, of the craft profession that is academia.

The second issue to address was the heterogeneity that was found in human resources systems and processes. Little or no commonality existed between pre-1992 English universities' formal written academic promotion procedures, titling conventions, or criteria. What one university meant by, for example, a senior lecturer compared to what another meant by the title lacked any shared meaning in the procedure, definition, and criteria used to achieve or award that rank. Each institution asserted its own meaning, which individual faculty could not avoid, and from which they appeared to have no immunity. Enders identified these trends toward greater heterogenization and decentralization of academia, describing it as a "withdrawal from the former idea or philosophy of legal homogeneity between higher education institutions" (Enders 2000: 13). The academic profession had diversified "into even smaller and more differentiated worlds than was previously the case" (Becher and Trowler, 2001: 17).

Third, it is important to point out that the emerging models appeared to have no obvious correlation to rank orders of universities using the RAE 2001 and NSS 2007 as research and education measures. Academic performance was important. The incentives and possibilities provided by grading criteria for promotion influenced faculty as they sought recognition and seniority. Human resources directors in England were changing the academic titles, pay scales, grade definitions, and career structures for academic faculty, and in so doing were changing what it was to be 'an academic'. The methodology chosen, whether 'strategic' or 'collegial', seemed not to impact on the outcomes. While it is seemingly attractive to assume that the collegial body might sustain a unitary, exclusive career structure and resist fragmentation, this was not supported by the study. On the other hand, the strategic drivers impacting on higher education were generating new alternatives that were either more inclusive or more fractionalized, or both.

Vice-chancellors and others may be concerned that the specific institutional choice of academic career model does not seem to relate to institutional rank in the RAE, or to student experience in the NSS. It is possible that these were the wrong measures, that the institutionally chosen models were not aligned to the organizational strategy, or that the human resource management choices did not impact on institutional performance. Whatever the explanation, the apparent lack of a correlation is troubling, and warrants further attention.

References

Argyle, M. (1983) *The Social Psychology of Work.* Harmondsworth, UK: Pelican Books.

Arthur, M. C., Inkson, K., and Pringle, J. K. (1999) *The New Careers: Individual Action and Economic Change.* London: Sage.

Asmar, C. (2004) "Innovations in Scholarship at a Student-Centered Research University: An Australian Example." *Innovative Higher Education* 29 (1): 49–66.

Baruch, Y. and Peiperl, M. (2003) "An Empirical Assessment of Sonnenfeld's Career Systems Typology." *International Journal of Human Resource Management* 14 (7): 1267–1283.

Becher, T. and Trowler, P. R. (2001) *Academic Tribes and Territories*, 2nd ed. Buckingham, UK: SRHE/Open University Press.

Bett, Sir Michael (1999) *Independent Review of Higher Education Pay and Conditions*. London: The Stationery Office.

Blaxter, L., Hughes, C., and Tight, M. (1998) "Writing on Academic Careers." *Studies in Higher Education* 23 (3): 281–296.

Braverman, H. (1974) *Labor and Monopoly Capital*. New York: Monthly Review.

Coaldrake, P. (2000) "Rethinking Academic and University Work." *Higher Education Management* 12 (3): 7–30.

Coate, K., Barnett, R., and Williams, G. (2001) "Relationships between Teaching and Research in Higher Education in England." *Higher Education Quarterly* 55 (2): 158–174.

Committee of Vice-Chancellors and Principals (CVCP) (1985) *Report of the Steering Committee for Efficiency Studies in Higher Education* (the Jarratt Report). London: Committee of Vice Chancellors and Principals.

Dearing, R. (1997) National Committee of Inquiry into Higher Education. Department for Education. Online, available at: www.leeds.ac.uk/educol/ncihe/ (accessed April 16, 2009).

Defillippi, R. J. and Arthur, M. B. (1994) "The Boundaryless Career: A Competency-Based Perspective." *Journal of Organizational Behavior* 15 (3): 307–324.

Department for Education and Science (DES) (1985) *The Development of Higher Education into the 1990s*. Cmnd. 9524. London: HMSO.

Dill, D. and Sporn, B. (1995) *Emerging Patterns of Social Demand and University Reform: Through the Glass Darkly*. Oxford: IAU Press/Elsevier.

Ebong, I. D. (2001) "Faculty Time and Effort: Analysis for Research Development." *Journal of Research Administration* 2 (1): 11–22.

Enders, J. (2000) "Academic Staff in Europe: Changing Employment and Working Conditions." In *Academic Work and Life: What It Is to Be an Academic, and How This Is Changing*, vol. 1, ed. M. Tight. Oxford: Elsevier Science.

Farnham, D. (1999) "Managing Universities and Regulating Academic Labour Markets." In *Managing Academic Staff in Changing University Systems*, ed. D. Farnham. Buckingham, UK: SRHE/Open University Press.

Gordon, G. (2003) "University Roles and Career Paths: Trends, Scenarios and Motivational Challenges." *Higher Education Management and Policy* 15 (3): 89–103.

Hales, C. (1993) *Managing through Organisation*. London: Routledge.

Handy, C. (1993) *Understanding Organizations*, 4th ed. London: Penguin Books.

Henkel, M. (2000) *Academic Identities and Policy Change in Higher Education*. London: Jessica Kingsley.

Henkel, M. (2002) "Academic Identity in Transformation? The Case Study of the United Kingdom." *Higher Education Management and Policy* 14 (3): 137–145.

Higher Education Funding Council for England (HEFCE) (2001) *Rewarding and Developing Staff in Higher Education*. Online, available at: www.hefce.ac.uk/pubs/hefce/2001/01_16.htm (accessed April 16, 2009).

Higher Education Funding Council for England (HEFCE) (2005) *Evaluation of Rewarding and Developing Staff in HE Initiative 2001/2 to 2003/4*. Online, available at: www.hefce.ac.uk/pubs/rd reports/2005/rd14_05/rd14_05.doc (accessed April 21, 2009).

Høstaker, R. (2000) "Policy Change and the Academic Profession." In *Transforming Higher Education: A Comparative Study*, ed. M. Kogan, M. Bauer, I. Bleiklie, and M. Henkel. London: Jessica Kingsley.

Houston, D., Meyer, L. H., and Paewai, S. (2006) "Academic Staff Workloads and Job Satisfaction: Expectations and Values in Academe." *Journal of Higher Education Policy and Management* 28 (1): 17–30.

Kaulisch, M. and Enders, J. (2005) "Careers in Overlapping Institutional Contexts: The Case Study of Academe." *Career Development International* 10 (2): 130–144.

Kerr, S. (1975) "On the Folly of Rewarding A, while Hoping for B." *Academy of Management Journal* 18: 769–782.

Kimber, M. (2003) "The Tenured 'Core' and the Tenuous 'Periphery': The Casualisation of Academic Work in Australian Universities." *Journal of Higher Education Policy and Management* 25 (1): 41–50.

Kogan, M., Moses, I., and El-Khawas, E. (1994) *Staffing Higher Education: Meeting New Challenges.* London: Jessica Kingsley.

Schein, E. H. (1986) "A Critical Look at Current Career Development Theory and Research." In *Career Development in Organizations*, ed. D. T. Hall. San Francisco: Jossey-Bass.

Serow, R. C., Van Dyk, P. B., McComb, E. M., and Harrold, A. T. (2002) "Cultures of Undergraduate Teaching at Research Universities." *Innovative Higher Education* 27 (1): 25–36.

Sonnenfeld, J. A. and Peiperl, M. A. (1988) "Staffing Policy as a Strategic Response: A Typology of Career Systems." *Academy of Management Review* 13 (4): 588–600.

Strike, T. and Taylor, J. (2009) "The Career Perceptions of Academic Staff and Human Resources Discourses in English Higher Education." *Higher Education Quarterly* 63 (2): 177–195.

Taylor, F. W. (1947) *Scientific Management.* New York: Harper.

Thorne, M. and Cuthbert, R. (1996) "Autonomy, Bureaucracy and Competition: The ABC of Control in Higher Education." In *Working in Higher Education*, ed. R. Cuthbert. Buckingham, UK: SHRE/Open University Press.

Torrington, D., Hall, L., and Taylor, S. (2002) *Human Resource Management*, 5th ed. Harlow, UK: FT Prentice Hall.

Universities and Colleges Employers Association (UCEA) (2003) *Framework Agreement for the Modernisation of Pay Structures.* Online, available at: www.ucea.ac.uk/ucea/filemanager/root/site_assets/framework_agreement/JNCHES_Framework_Agreement.pdf (accessed April 18, 2009).

Vidal, J. and Quintanilla, M. A. (2000) "The Teaching and Research Relationship within an Institutional Evaluation." *Higher Education* 40 (2): 217–229.

Warr, P. (1980) *Psychology at Work.* Harmondsworth, UK: Penguin Books.

Yamamoto, H. (2006) "The Relationship between Employees' Inter-Organizational Career Orientation and Their Career Strategies." *Career Development International* 11 (3): 243–264.

6
Managing Academic and Professional Careers in Japan

JUN OBA

As a result of societal change, university reform has been undertaken continuously in Japan over the past twenty years. The government has revised the regulatory framework relating to organizational and staffing structures so that universities may recruit diverse groups of professionals in different types of units. As the mission and activities of universities have expanded, academic faculty have been expected to fulfill demands that move beyond narrow definitions of teaching and research. As a result, support services have been developed, alongside a process of professionalization for staff. This has resulted in a blurring of the boundaries between academic faculty and non-academic staff. In Japan, academic faculty include professors, associate professors, lecturers, and assistant (professors). Other staff are categorized as non-academic. However, as is mentioned later, the distinction between academic faculty and non-academic staff has become less clear. The first section of this chapter discusses changing academic and professional structures, and the development of support services.

Context

To meet the challenges of a changing environment, including massification, globalization, the increased use of information technology, and the advent of the knowledge society, the Japanese government has continued to reform the regulatory framework of universities. This process was accelerated in the 1990s: In 1991, by amending the Standards for the Establishment of Universities (SEU), the Monbusho (Ministry of Education, now MEXT; hereinafter referred to as 'MEXT') deregulated university education and permitted each institution to develop programs on its own initiative, thus diversifying higher education provision. In the same year the University Council (UC), an advisory body to the Minister of Education, recommended that graduate education expand in response to a growing need for knowledge workers, both inside and outside academia. Other measures taken to enhance the responsiveness of universities included industry–academy collaboration, self- and external evaluations, information disclosure, development of academic faculty, and governance reforms.

Reforms implemented since the 1990s have focused primarily on deregulation in the context of marketization, the development of a quality assurance system, increased competition among institutions, and a reinforcement of universities' managerial capability. Universities have become more autonomous, have seen their roles and responsibilities expand significantly, and have become increasingly complex in the face both of a major shift from teaching to learning, and of increasing demands from industry. Such reforms have required different types of organization and staff—both academic and non-academic—in universities.

Changing Academic Organizations and Profession

Reform of Academic Structures

Historically, Japanese higher education has been characterized by a closed structure supported by a chair (*koza*) system and research-oriented academic faculty (Arimoto, 1996). The Japanese chair system, established in the nineteenth century and consolidated in research universities before World War II, has been criticized for its rigidity and lack of responsiveness to society (Amano, 2001). Clark (1983) pointed to the problem associated with the chair system—reduced adaptability to change in the expanded higher education system—and this was especially true in Japan (Ogawa, 2002). In other postwar universities[JO1], as a rule a 'department subject' (*gakkamoku*) system has been adopted, in which academic faculty are allocated according to programs instead of disciplines (chairs) and not necessarily expected to undertake research (Amano, 2001).

Contrary to these general principles, some new structures were established. The University of Tsukuba, founded in 1973, was an initiative to overcome such problems by developing clusters of schools that did not consist of chairs. The 1976 amendment to the School Education Law made it possible to define as a university an institution offering graduate courses only (thus as an independent graduate school). Four national universities of this type have been established. In the meantime, interuniversity research institutes were also founded, crossing individual university boundaries to undertake nationwide research activities.

In other universities, particularly in national universities, organizational structures developed outside academic units and faculties, such as research centers, interdisciplinary graduate schools crossing multiple faculties, and independent graduate departments (sometimes entire schools). By 2003, eighty independent schools had been founded in thirty-five national universities, and seventy-eight independent departments in thirty-eight national universities. In addition, new collaborative schemes, such as a united graduate school (*rengo-daigakuin*: a graduate school at the doctoral level created by multiple universities, whose degrees are awarded by the leading institution) and a cooperative graduate school (*renkei-daigakuin*: a program in collaboration with external research institutes) were created. In 2003 a professional graduate school (*senmonshoku-daigakuin*) system was added to university structures.

Traditional academic units have also been restructured. Along with the expansion of graduate education, chairs were amalgamated into large chairs (*daikoza*) to break down disciplinary boundaries. By 1996, chairs had been amalgamated in 277 faculties in ninety national universities out of ninety-eight. For example, at the Graduate School of Education and Human Development at

Nagoya University, twenty-four small chairs were reorganized in 2000 into eight large chairs (Ogawa, 2002). In 2001, universities were no longer required to adopt one of the systems (*koza* or *gakkamoku*) but could design a new form of academic unit. In 2007, finally, both systems were withdrawn from national regulation and each university is now free to organize its own structure, even though it is still under the control of MEXT via program approval procedures.

Changes in the Professoriate

Alongside the structural reforms, MEXT has continuously revised the qualifications required for academic faculty, so that institutions may recruit different types of professional and promote mobility. In 1985, by virtue of an amendment to the SEU, universities were enabled to employ people with specialized knowledge and experience in fields of study from outside academia. The 1988 UC report recommended recruiting people from a wider cross-section of society to contribute to graduate education. Other measures to promote mobility and exchange included opening professorships in public (national and local public) universities to overseas candidates, the development of endowed chairs and research units, and the abolition of the regulation controlling the ratio of full-time to part-time academic faculty. Before the reform, the number of part-time teachers was not permitted to exceed half the number of full-time teachers. Academic faculty employed from outside universities rose from 1,152 in 1982 to 1,837[JO2] in 1991, while in the same period the total number increased from 107,422 to 126,445, and the number of non-academic staff from 150,259 to 162,299.

This policy was revised in the 1990s, and the 1994 UC report recommended the following measures:

- employment of people with diverse backgrounds and experience, including graduates from, or with experience of, other universities, non-academics, women, and overseas recruits;
- greater use of open recruitment;
- greater attention to the philosophies and objectives of individual universities and faculties when determining selection criteria, and openness of selection methods;
- organized efforts for teaching improvement.

In 1997 a law relating to fixed-term employment of university teaching staff was introduced, which enabled universities, in particular public universities, to employ academic faculty on a fixed-term contract basis. The number of academic faculty to whom this regime was applied, or who were employed on the basis of this law, rose from seven in 1998 to 3,546 in 2002 in national universities, while the total population remained relatively static, rising slightly from 60,205 in 1998 to 60,930 in 2002.

Implications of the Reforms

Questions remain, however, about the extent to which the measures implemented up to the 1990s were effective. In reality, even toward the end of the 1990s universities continued to be closed and unresponsive to society, and more openness and flexibility was called for. Amano (1999) admitted that university education had been little improved by the preceding reforms. The most recent reforms, including the 2004 incorporation of national universities (Oba, 2007), and the certified evaluation system, are expected to improve the responsiveness of institutions significantly. According to the latter reform, all universities should be institutionally evaluated once every seven years by one of the evaluation agencies recognized by MEXT.

Along with the reforms of the academic profession and structures, support services and their staff have become more professionalized. This change is discussed in the following section.

Development of Support Services and Professionalization of Staff

Policy Recommendations for Promoting Professionalization

One of the earliest proposals in the postwar period for professionalization of functional areas in universities was made by a group of American student services experts commissioned by the US–Japan bilateral agreement. In 1952 the group recommended to the Japanese government various measures to promote student services, including provision of professionally trained staff with status in keeping with their responsibilities, which were classified as educational rather than as clerical. Furthermore, the group recognized that these staff should carry some limited teaching responsibilities (Lloyd, 1953).

The recommendations were subsequently studied by the Student Welfare Council of MEXT, including establishment of an employment system allowing universities to recruit professional staff. The Council's 1958 report defined an employment system for professional staff and suggested creating a new employment category in addition to that of teaching staff. However, recognizing the incompatibility of a US-type system with the traditional Japanese system, and the under-professionalization of student services, the Council proposed providing professional staff in student services with an academic rank, so that the idea of a separate category of non-academic professional staff was not adopted.

In the 1980s the National Council on Educational Reform, an advisory body to the prime minister, called for deregulation of universities in its recommendations for reforming the entire education system. In the 1990s, MEXT, in consultation with the UC, proceeded with diverse reforms and, in 1991, with deregulatory measures such as the simplification of the SEU, as mentioned earlier. As a result, university autonomy was significantly enhanced, demanding development of a stronger managerial capability. In 1995 a UC report called for the improvement of administrative organization and enhancement of partnership between academic faculty and non-academic staff, in addition to stronger leadership by university presidents.

Furthermore, in its 1998 report the Council recommended the development of support functions and encouraged professionalization of certain areas, including international affairs and admissions.

Elsewhere, numerous recommendations were made in relation to the professionalization of non-academic functions. The 1999 report of the Central Council for Education, an advisory body to the Minister of Education, called for the development of admissions offices staffed by professionals. The 2000 report of a ministerial expert panel on student support exhorted universities to switch their emphasis from "teacher-centeredness" to "student-centeredness" and recommended numerous measures, including collaboration between academic faculty and non-academic staff, professionalization of non-academic staff, and recruitment of specialists such as counselors and careers advisers from outside universities. Other recommendations for professionalization were to be found in areas such as university–industry cooperation, information technology, and financial management.

Nevertheless, most of the proposals were not fully implemented, partly because of inflexible employment structures and traditional university cultures. One of the objectives of the incorporation of national universities was to introduce flexibility into the governance of universities, eliminating constraints on human resource management (Oba, 2005). The 2002 ministerial report on this incorporation urged that the duties of non-academic staff should not be limited to the support of education and research. It suggested that they should participate actively in university management in collaboration with academic faculty, and in the light of the expansion of functional areas requiring a high degree of specialization, it recommended creating employment systems to accommodate this. After incorporation, neither academic faculty nor non-academic staff had civil servant status, and national universities were able to recruit non-academic staff without holding a national civil service examination. Some universities have recruited professionals for managerial posts requiring specialized knowledge and skills from outside higher education, but the number of non-academic positions that are advertised remains limited. It should be noted, however, that centers specializing in certain services, such as admissions and placement, have developed significantly in universities. In the next section, the establishment of centers specializing in academic support—academic support centers—is addressed.

Academic Support Centers and Their Staff

DEVELOPMENT OF ACADEMIC SUPPORT CENTERS

A survey on university governance was conducted in 2006 (Research Institute for Higher Education (RIHE), 2007) in which a questionnaire was sent to all universities at three levels of academic administrators (presidents, faculty deans, and department heads). The responses were classified by legal status (national, local public, and private) as well as by category (see the Annex to this chapter). According to the survey, academic support centers (ASCs) have been or are being established in nearly two-thirds of universities. They are more frequently developed

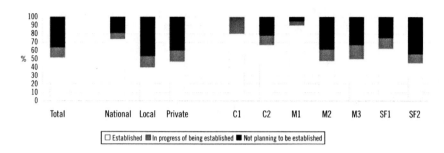

Figure 6.1 Establishment of Academic Support Centers (ASCs) by Legal Status and by Category

Source: Research Institute for Higher Education (RIHE) (2007). Reproduced with permission.
Note: N = 270 responding institutions. See Annex for definition of categories.

in national universities than in local public and private universities, and are particularly well developed in universities of categories C1, C2, and M1, which are large, comprehensive, multidisciplinary institutions having their origins in the prewar period (Figure 6.1). Thus, professionalization of academic support functions is being developed principally in larger universities that are more likely to have additional resources.

These centers have different missions (Figure 6.2), ranging from development of academic faculty to general education (general education is not necessarily a function of ASCs in the strict sense of the word, but centers in charge of general education are often responsible for campus-wide academic support activities; in this section, the general education function is not addressed, apart from the survey results). In local public universities, centers have fewer functions than those in national and private universities (centers in a university are addressed as a whole; the functions referred to here are those carried out by all relevant centers in a university). Staff development (intended mainly for academic faculty) and general education functions are most developed in national universities, and careers services in private universities, which have been more attentive to graduate employment than have public universities. However, many local public universities plan to develop centers, as do national and private universities in relation to less developed functions. As a whole, centers at all three types of universities are likely to develop in order to fulfill all the functions addressed in the survey, as shown in Figure 6.2.

STAFF IN CENTERS

Most centers in national universities have their own professional staff; in the local public and private institutions they tend to rely on other academic units for staff (Figure 6.3). If one analyzes the staffing by category (Figure 6.4), centers in the larger comprehensive or multidisciplinary universities are seen to have their own staff or staff allocated by central offices. Many other universities seem to

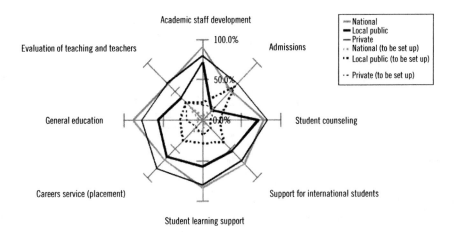

Figure 6.2 Functions Assigned to Academic Support Centers

Source: Research Institute for Higher Education (RIHE) (2007). Reproduced with permission.
Note: N = 261 responding institutions.

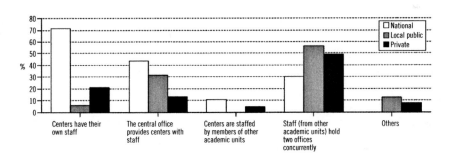

Figure 6.3 Professional Staffing of Academic Support Centers by Legal Status of the University

Source: Research Institute for Higher Education (RIHE) (2007). Reproduced with permission.
Note: N = 270 responding institutions (multiple answers allowed).

have difficulty in staffing their centers owing to scarcity of resources. Even though centers are set up in smaller universities, they are poorly staffed and most often funded at the expense of academic units, which may in turn be a source of tension.

Table 6.1 shows the situation in relation to professional staff in student services. Apart from counseling and career support, over half of the universities have no professional staff, and recruitment from outside—either as academic faculty or as non-academic staff—is not common. Professionals coming from outside universities are most often found in counseling, which is the only functional area in the survey where externally appointed professionals outnumber those from

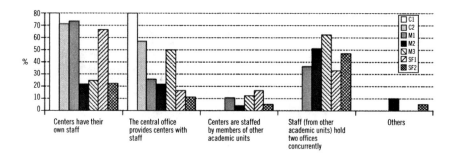

Figure 6.4 Professional Staffing of Academic Support Centers by Category of the University

Source: Research Institute for Higher Education (RIHE) (2007). Reproduced with permission.
Note: N = 270 responding institutions (multiple answers allowed). See Annex for definition of categories.

TABLE 6.1 Number of Universities Having Professional Staff in Student Services by Functional Area (Current State)

	Instructional support	Learning support	Student life support	Counseling	Career support
Employ professionals from outside as non-academics	9	6	10	128	60
Employ professionals from outside as academics	7	10	1	43	17
Develop professionals inside the university	90	89	106	80	96
No professionals in the university	141	143	128	36	94
Total	239	234	240	240	237

Source: Onuki (2009).
Note: N = 243 responding institutions (multiple answers allowed).

inside the system. Table 6.2 shows that very few universities intend in future to reduce recruitment of professionals from outside, but well over half the universities have no intention of changing their current practice. With a limited number of universities intending to develop professionals internally, professionalization seems to be a gradual process.

In national universities, many of the professionals recruited externally and located in ASCs have academic rank (Table 6.3). This is partly (but importantly) because, before incorporation, except for part-time employment, national universities could employ as non-academic staff—professional or otherwise—only

TABLE 6.2 Number of Universities Having Professional Staff in Student Services by Functional Area (Future Directions)

	Instructional support	Learning support	Student life support	Counseling	Career support
Employment from outside	8	12	2	56	51
Employment from outside will decrease	0	1	1	2	3
Develop professionals inside the university	52	44	41	28	45
No change is expected	157	163	171	146	137
Total	215	216	215	216	216

Source: Onuki (2009).
Note: N = 243 responding institutions (multiple answers allowed).

TABLE 6.3 Number of Universities Having Professional Staff in Student Services by Type of University, with Percentage of Academic Faculty Included in Professional Staff

	National universities	Local public universities	Private universities
Employ professionals from outside as non-academics	27	34	152
Employ professionals from outside as academics	31	4	43
Develop professionals inside the university	37	33	374
No professionals in the university	111	101	327
Percentage of academics among professional staff	33	6	8

Source: Onuki (2009).
Note: N = 243 responding institutions (multiple answers allowed).

those who were qualified in the national public service examination. Moreover, for certain kinds of functions, academic rank was regarded as indispensable for working with academic faculty, and as providing a preferable status for recruitment of professionals externally.

Issues and Challenges

Centers discussed in the previous section are not always highly regarded and are often viewed with skepticism by academic units. Attitudes to the centers can diverge among different groups of decision makers. Less satisfaction is shown by department heads than by presidents, with the views of deans being somewhere between the two (Figure 6.5). The gap between the views of presidents and those of department heads is the greatest in relation to development of academic faculty (65 percent against 40 percent). There seems to be little consensus on the effectiveness (and probably on even the *raison d'être*) of centers on each campus.

Such undervaluation by department heads may derive from the perceived administrative nature of centers' activities, many of which are characterized by normative approaches. It seems that although their professional staff may be classified as 'academic', the mode of their activities generally differs from that of the academic units; the values developed by the centers do not seem to converge with those of the latter. The centers, rather, develop their own set of values, as Becher and Kogan (1992) argue in relation to non-academic administrators.

Values shared by the centers seem much closer to those of the central administration than do those shared by the academic units. Institutions have now largely been released from national regulations, but academic faculty are more exposed to various pressures as part of institutional management, driven largely by the quality assurance system. Centers are often looked upon as management advocates, or at least as channels through which these pressures are exerted. Furthermore, centers compete for resources not only with academic units but also with administrative units. In the future, competition is likely to be harsher in an environment where enrollments of 18-year-olds and block grant allocations by government are declining.

The future position of ASCs, because they are seen as being neither academic nor administrative, and because of the different cultures associated with the two forms of professional activity, would appear to be insecure.

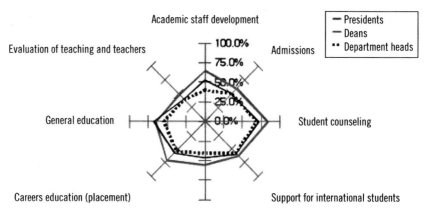

Figure 6.5 Effectiveness of Academic Support Centers, as Evaluated as Satisfactory by Academic Administrators

Source: Research Institute for Higher Education (RIHE) (2007). Reproduced with permission.
Note: N = 141–152 (presidents); 378-402 (deans); 1,332–1,363 (department heads).

Conclusion

Regardless of the differences that exist among national systems, higher education institutions are facing similar challenges in an increasingly knowledge-based society. To meet these challenges, the government in Japan has revised regulatory frameworks on an ongoing basis and encouraged diversification of higher education institutions' structures and workforce, changing the nature of the academic profession and careers. Extended discussion of professionalization has resulted in numerous recommendations in relation to non-academic staff. Nevertheless, most of these have not been fully implemented, principally because of the persistence of a binary division of staff—academic and non-academic—supported by the traditional university culture and rigid employment systems.

Since the 1990s the government has proceeded with deregulation and has developed a quality assurance system. These changes have enhanced the autonomy and responsibility of higher education institutions and significantly diversified their activities, involving complication of tasks and calling for a more diverse range of expertise not only in teaching and research, but also in management and support services. Up until now, the professionalization of non-academic tasks has been promoted largely by staffing centers with professionals, particularly in national universities.

At the same time, these changes have blurred the traditional academic and non-academic boundary. Although professionalization of non-academics is limited, many professional staff positions have been created in academic support areas, and they are now filled most often by people holding academic rank. Despite value differences, possession of an academic rank may be helpful for these professionals when working with academic faculty. Their main function remains that of support or advice, but, as shown by Henkel (2000), they are also regarded as change agents in what has been accepted as uncontested academic territory. The traditional divisions between academic faculty and non-academic staff and tasks now seem oversimplified, as shown in multiple previous studies (Gordon and Whitchurch, 2007; Henkel, 2007; McInnis, 1998; Whitchurch, 2008). Askling (2001) also reports that special support units in Swedish universities are often staffed with highly specialized academic faculty. In an environment of declining government resources and a scarcity of new positions, components such as ASCs seem vulnerable to tensions arising over differences of values and resource allocation, not only with traditional academic units, but also with secretariats.

Finally, in a shift from teaching to learning, where the focus has increasingly been on learning outcomes, collaboration between all categories of staff—academic and non-academic—is critical (Barr and Tagg, 1995). It is important to recognize the complementarity of the two cultures, regardless of the possibility of the convergence of staff categories, and, by promoting professional careers and creating shared commitments, to assure their collaboration in enhancing the student experience.

References

Amano, I. (1999) *Challenges to Japanese Universities*. Tokyo: University of Tokyo Press [in Japanese].

Amano, I. (2001) *The Future of University Reform: From Imitation to Creation*. Tokyo: Tamagawa University Press [in Japanese].

Arimoto, A. (1996) "The Academic Profession in Japan." In *The International Academic Profession*, ed. P. G. Altbach. Princeton, NJ: Carnegie Foundation for the Advancement of Teaching.

Askling, B. (2001) "Higher Education and Academic Staff in a Period of Policy and System Change." *Higher Education* 41 (1/2): 157–181.

Barr, R B. and Tagg, J. (1995) "From Teaching to Learning: A New Paradigm for Undergraduate Education." *Change* 27: 12–25.

Becher, T. and Kogan, M. (1992) *Process and Structure in Higher Education*, 2nd ed. London: Routledge.

Clark, B. R. (1983) *The Higher Education System: Academic Organization in Cross-National Perspective*. Berkeley: University of California Press.

Gordon, G. and Whitchurch. C. (2007) "Managing Human Resources in Higher Education: The Implications of a Diversifying Workforce." *Higher Education Management and Policy* 19 (2): 135–155.

Henkel, M. (2000) *Academic Identities and Policy Change in Higher Education*. London: Jessica Kingsley.

Henkel, M. (2007) "Academic Boundaries: Are They Still Needed?" *Higher Education Forum* 4: 33–45.

Lloyd, W. P. (1953) *Student Counseling in Japan: A Two-Nation Project in Higher Education*. Minneapolis: University of Minnesota Press.

McInnis, C. (1998) "Academics and Professional Administrators in Australian Universities: Dissolving Boundaries and New Tensions." *Journal of Higher Education Policy and Management* 20 (2): 161–173.

Oba, J. (2005) "The Incorporation of National Universities in Japan: Initial Reactions of the New National University Corporations." *Higher Education Management and Policy* 17 (2): 105–125.

Oba, J. (2007) "Incorporation of National Universities in Japan." *Asia Pacific Journal of Education* 27: 291–303.

Ogawa, Y. (2002) "Challenging the Traditional Organization of Japanese Universities." *Higher Education* 43 (1): 85–108.

Onuki, Y. (2009) "A Study on Organizations and Division of Roles of Student Affairs." In *Developing Staff in Universities: Identity and Professionalism*, ed. J. Oba. Reviews in Higher Education no. 105. Hiroshima: Research Institute for Higher Education (RIHE) [in Japanese].

Research Institute for Higher Education (RIHE) (2007) *Transforming Universities in Modern Japan*. COE Publication Series no. 27. Hiroshima: RIHE [in Japanese].

Whitchurch, C. (2008) "Shifting Identities and Blurring Boundaries: The Emergence of *Third Space* Professionals in UK Higher Education." *Higher Education Quarterly* 62 (4): 377–396.

ANNEX 6.1 University Categorization Used in the Research Institute for Higher Education (RIHE) Survey

Category	Description	Number of institutions	Number of responses		
			President	*Deans*	*Department heads*
Comprehensive university 1 (C1)	Former imperial university	7	5	44	68
Comprehensive university 2 (C2)	Comprehensive university, founded on the core of a university under the old system	14	9	69	144
Multidisciplinary university 1 (M1)	Multidisciplinary university with a faculty of medicine, not having its origin in a university under the old system	34	23	91	228
Multidisciplinary university 2 (M2)	University with at least two faculties without a faculty of medicine, not having its origin in a university under the old system	309	116	309	666
Multidisciplinary university 3 (M3)	Multidisciplinary university founded on the core of a university under the old system, without a faculty of medicine	22	13	42	110
Single-faculty institution 1 (SF1)	Single-faculty institution (medicine)	25	9	9	8
Single-faculty institution 2 (SF2)	Single-faculty institution (apart from medicine)	289	99	60	205

Source: RIHE (2007). Reprinted with permission.

Being an Academic in Contemporary South Africa

PATRICIA SMIT AND KINGSTON NYAMAPFENE

Introduction

Many countries now recognize the importance of education as an agent for social change and as an instrument through which policy changes may be propagated and executed. South Africa has perhaps reflected this more clearly than countries where relationships between the state and higher education have been based on a broader consensus and where a mandate for policy was achieved via democratic processes. For many years this was not the case in South Africa and the relationship between state and higher education was, at best, tenuous. The advent of a democratically elected government in 1994 represented a watershed for higher education in both its relationship with the state, and the role higher education was expected to play in shaping a new nation. In some ways, higher education institutions had anticipated this change by adopting measures to undertake activities that would be consonant with the new policies and roles. A keyword for this process was 'transformation'. Several institutions had 'transformation forum(s)', which, in turn, linked into a network known as the National Transformation Forum. What was sought by these initiatives was a change in roles and relationships among stakeholder groups within the institutions, and between the institutions and other agencies. This change in relationships could not take place without a change in expectations, and a redefining of the roles and identities of the players.

Possibly the most significant change was the call to create a more diverse workforce, not only to reflect the demographics of the nation, but also to put in place a leadership that would be sympathetic to the new policy framework at the national level and would champion it within their institutions. Many of the 'new' academic faculty entering the system during this phase had some attributes in common. They were either relatively young and had completed postgraduate programs recently, or were academic faculty who, until then, had worked at historically disadvantaged institutions. The latter group tended to be from racial groups other than the 'Whites', who had hitherto dominated or been the exclusive players in the system. The groups also comprised those who had opposed the policies of the Apartheid era and remained the custodians of the transformation process and, almost by default, found themselves playing a role that was much broader than that associated with academic faculty of the previous era (Ramphele, 2008). Thus, the "transformation" that institutions underwent resulted not only in structural reorganization but also in changes in the roles and identities of academic faculty. A rapid and ongoing process of workforce diversification continues to present challenges to the system as tensions arise around, for instance, achieving appropriate levels of diversity and maintaining standards; and providing support for students from less advantaged backgrounds and resources for research and staff development.

Such changes have challenged institutions to review their missions, their service delivery approaches, and the recruitment and progression processes they have adopted in relation to their staff. The study suggests that institutions have been slow to recognize and act upon these challenges, and a sense of policy ambiguity can lead to the kinds of problems that form the focus of the study, namely a changing view among academic faculty of their own identity in an environment in which the institutional policy framework does not seem to take into account the dichotomy between the perceptions of staff when they enter the institution, and the reality of their day-to-day experiences.

Because of its political history and the effects of former policies on higher education, another factor to take into account when looking at the challenges currently facing the system is that of 'culture conflict'. This arises from the fact that, in order to address the issues of racial and gender inequity in the workforce, South Africa found itself with a somewhat limited pool on which to draw in the initial stages of transformation. Some institutions sought to address the problem quickly by bringing in as many South Africans as possible from the diaspora. Some brought in non-South Africans whose profile fitted whatever 'equity' gap the institution sought to bridge (Ramphele, 2008). This alone created a clash of cultures. Those who had been in the system when it was less open felt that they were being disadvantaged in relation to career progression by people who had not been subjected to educational and other forms of discrimination under the previous regime. Even when those entering the sector from outside came in with higher qualifications and more experience, they were seen on occasion as having been unfairly fast-tracked. Many of the 'outsiders' also came in with different views about how to conduct research and achieve a publication record, and a different understanding of the expectations of being 'an academic'.

Later in the chapter there is more detailed discussion about what it means to be 'an academic' in the South African context, using data from respondents in the study. We examine the perceptions and lived experiences of South African academic faculty against institutional definitions of the concept of 'an academic', with the objective of understanding institutional notions of 'an academic' as compared to the perceptions of respondents when they were asked, "What does it mean to be 'an academic' in South Africa today?"

The Nature of Higher Education

Higher education institutions can be considered as complex organizations (Barnett, 2000). That complexity is increased by the effects of 'globalization', as more higher education systems find themselves linked internationally in a variety of ways. Furthermore, higher education has become marketized, with economic rationalism and corporate interests becoming prominent features. Managerialism is seen to have introduced into higher education a number of new elements, such as entrepreneurial activity to counter a decrease in public funding, and a requirement for public accountability, as well as demands for efficiency, effectiveness, and increased productivity (Ozga and Deem, 2000). Other values associated with managerialism include an emphasis on individualism as opposed to collaboration and collegial enterprise, and on the customer rather than the producer (Trowler, 2001). These conditions have implications for those who work in higher education. Budget constraints, for example, put pressure on institutions to achieve more from a pool of employees that is not expanding in relation to increased workload (Currie et al., 2000). The South African higher education system has much in common with other systems, including conflicting expectations between state and institutional aspirations, increasing diversity of the workforce, the increasing complexity of work, and the impact of globalization. In addition, like other public services in the country, the system has had to respond to sociopolitical changes and the ensuing policy developments.

Against this background the study sought to understand what it means to be 'an academic' in South Africa. This question arose from an earlier investigation into the meaning of leadership in South African higher education (Smit, 2006). During this earlier study, different views about the concept of academic identity became apparent, suggesting that a review was timely. Possible questions were: How do people view the concept? Why do they view it that way? Is it time to develop a different set of definitions? The following section is based on a review of the literature, a study of a selection of job advertisements, and a small-scale qualitative study conducted with twelve academic members of faculty drawn from eight institutions and representing a range of disciplines in the humanities, social sciences, and natural and applied sciences.

Method

In order to understand the context in which the investigation was carried out, key policy documents that have shaped higher education in South Africa were examined. These included the report of the National Commission on Higher Education (1996), the *Higher Education Act* (Department of Education, 1997), and the *National Plan on Higher Education* (Department of Education, 2001). Formal sources, such as internal guidelines for grading and promotion of academic faculty, and informal ones such as newspaper advertisements for vacant academic posts, were reviewed to obtain a sense of the views of institutions on the subject, and what their expectations were of the people they appointed to academic positions. The content of twelve academic job advertisements placed by seven South African higher education institutions in the national press in late 2007 and early 2008 was analyzed.

With an understanding of what could be considered the 'formal position' on higher education, together with the authors' own experience, a questionnaire was designed to solicit the opinions both of newly recruited academic faculty and of those who had been in the system longer. While it would have been beneficial to interview at least one representative from each of the country's twenty-three universities, this was not possible within the time frame of the study. There was also an additional challenge in trying to find subjects who were willing to invest the time required to answer the questions. Therefore, the time was used to undertake a more thorough survey of fewer respondents, whose views were thought to represent 'typical' clusters within the system. Semi-structured interviews were conducted, with the goal of exploring the activities and experiences perceived as being central to the concept of being an academic member of faculty. Questions around the following issues formed the basis of the interviews:

* the conversations that do or do not take place about the concept;
* institutional expectations of academic faculty;
* career paths and related issues.

Findings

Academic Faculty Members' Perceptions of Their Roles

There was general agreement among respondents that being 'an academic' meant playing certain well-defined roles and participating in specific activities, as well as having certain attitudes. These roles, activities, and attitudes included being a teacher, researcher, administrator, mentor, and consultant (involving possession of very specialized knowledge in a given area). Extended professional activities included community outreach or service, development of teaching materials, student supervision, knowledge sharing, and participation in the activities of professional bodies. The attitudes identified included taking risks, having a questioning mind, and representing the conscience of society.

While there was some agreement on the general meaning of the concept 'academic' among academic faculty, there was no common understanding of the expectations associated with the concept. It was evident that the perception of what the term meant was dependent on such factors as the different contexts in which teaching occurred, for instance:

* the discipline being taught;
* the level at which teaching was taking place;
* institutional factors, including the historical background of an institution;
* the institution's teaching and learning culture;
* facilities to support teaching and research, its location, and its ethos.

Respondents gave various reasons for differences in the understanding of the concept of 'an academic', including the following:

* there has never been a general debate on the concept;
* individual preferences of members of academic faculty toward research or teaching, or a combination of the two, influence how they view themselves;
* the academic background of individual faculty, especially their postgraduate experiences, influences their understanding of academic activity;

- external influences, such as interaction with peers in different environments, for instance, overseas higher education institutions and institutions external to the sector, may play a part.

The respondents concurred that their understanding of what it meant to be 'an academic' had changed over time. Although most of them had encountered the concept for the first time when they were undergraduate students, they acknowledged that at that stage they had had a somewhat rigid and monolithic view of 'an academic' as a person who was very knowledgable. Some of them suggested that, as students, they had seen members of academic faculty as somewhat eccentric and out of touch with the real world, engaging more with their own ideas than with matters that might interest other people, leading to the perception that it was difficult for some academic faculty to communicate with students—the stereotype of an 'absent-minded professor'.

At that stage, therefore, respondents' understanding was based almost exclusively on their perception of an academic member of faculty as a 'teacher' who was the ultimate source of information and knowledge in their discipline. It was also a reflection of the type of pedagogy that dominated academic culture at that time. All the respondents had been educated in a teaching and learning environment that was not highly interactive and did not seek to encourage the exploration of ideas, but rather took the approach of delivering information to students who were not expected to challenge or interrogate it. When some of the respondents were undergraduates, they had not been aware that an important part of university work was the conduct of research. Therefore, they did not see teachers also as scholars who were seeking more knowledge about their discipline. However, once they had become academic faculty themselves, their understanding of academic activity changed. As one of the interviewees observed, they no longer saw academic faculty as all-knowing, but rather as people who were "on a constant road of discovery of knowledge and . . . who should know how to teach and share the message effectively . . . who are more in touch with reality". They therefore perceived academic faculty as being able to define and think through problems, to develop options to solve these, and as knowing how to develop ideas. In their new understanding they saw 'an academic' as someone who should be prepared to acknowledge to their students a lack of comprehensive knowledge, while at the same time showing them how to find out the answers to questions. Some respondents pointed out that this approach made them more accessible and connected to their students.

Institutional Expectations

Although it was clear that institutions had broadly similar expectations of academic faculty, there was also evidence that there was no common understanding by different institutions of the term 'academic'. This, respondents suggested, was due to the fact that institutions did not, in general, create a platform where discussion and debate of the concept could take place. One respondent suggested that "the notion of the entrepreneurial university and 'managerialism' collide horrifically with the purpose of higher education". However, there was also a counterview which argued that the fact that institutions seemed to have similar expectations for academic faculty suggested that there was a common understanding at the institutional level. However, in our view, this may be a case of dissonance between what institutions assume is a given, and how individuals interpret it. So, the problem may lie in a communication gap between what institutions expect and how individuals respond to those expectations, influenced in their interpretation by factors affecting their own perceptions of their roles. This affirms the statement about the absence of a platform for discussion of concepts and roles in academe. Such concepts are themselves dynamic and subject to change, influenced by contexts, geography, politics, and historical pathways. What is also clear from the apparent disconnect between the perceptions of the institutions and those of their staff is that the staff seem to understand that there is something unclear about their perceived roles, whereas institutions tend not to take account of the contexts and circumstances in which procedures and regulations were established. Thus, in a sense, the communication gap also reflects a gap in analysis of the situation by institutions, and a failure on their part to modify their perceptions over time. In that regard the staff appear to be ahead of policymakers.

The view that institutions seem to have a common understanding was examined against the requirements that institutions declare when they advertise vacant academic positions. Twelve such advertisements were examined. All required potential recruits to be able to:

- teach;
- undertake research;
- undertake community outreach and engage in some administrative activities.

This represents the traditional 'trinity' of the principles on which contemporary higher education institutions operate.

In broad terms there was little ambiguity about the expectations of institutions. However, analysis of the advertisements revealed that institutions were also asking for more than these basic requirements, that they were being broken down in more detail, or that they were being expanded to include elements demanded by the state and the market.

Thus, institutions were also looking for people with a range of non-academic skills, such as leadership, management, and facilitation, and the ability to work as team members with communication skills and adaptability. 'Adaptability' suggests a continual renewal of professional identity, reflecting the idea of identity as a "project" (Giddens, 1991; Henkel, 2000). Institutions also now appear to be looking for people with entrepreneurial skills. Some advertisements required candidates to be able to attract postgraduate students and external funding, as well as being able to identify opportunities for the development of short courses. Some of the respondents cited this as an example of work that they considered to be outside the realm of academic work, yet throughout history academic faculty have always been expected to attract 'apprentices', the difference being that in contemporary institutions they are more likely to 'advertise' who they are and what they have to offer, whereas in the past the reputation of scholars was more self-propagating, based mainly on other people's esteem of their work or the impact it had on society.

Respondents also identified roles and activities that they did not expect to be part of the work of academic faculty, such as detailed administrative duties. They cited activities such as recruiting contract staff to support teaching, budgeting, the cross-checking of marks, and attending meetings. One respondent described meetings as "endless", while a second regarded the meetings as of little value because "very little real discussion of critical issues or constructive action takes place". There was a view that some of this work could be viewed as 'student services', such as tracking information on students, library orientation, induction in the use of online resources, and student welfare and support, especially in relation to Black students. This is one area in which the views of respondents may be justified, because in many well-resourced institutions it would be the expectation that such activities would be assigned to professional support services. However, as a result of becoming involved in such activities, some respondents became skilled in areas in which they had never anticipated becoming involved. For instance, one became the webmaster of the department as a result of experience gained through networks that they had formed outside his primary discipline. Another became an e-learning coordinator, while another is now an expert on the requirements of the South African Qualifications Authority (SAQA) after being part of the team that prepared courses for approval by the Authority.

While some of these additional responsibilities could be considered as falling outside the central concept of academic activity, they can also be seen as career development opportunities, since the academy tends to create its own middle managers. It is not uncommon in South Africa for people to move from purely academic roles to roles that involve some, or only, administration. Academic administration might be said to benefit from being staffed by people who have been in close contact with the student body and faculty, making them better able to understand issues relating to academic policy or student matters. This kind of career progression has been the route that enabled some vice-chancellors and their deputies eventually to reach their current positions.

In one sense the activities that are identifiable as central to the definition of 'an academic' in the South African context are, by and large, no different from those found among institutions elsewhere, namely teaching, research, community outreach, administration, and academic citizenship in the form of membership of various institutional or academic bodies. What is different is the depth of understanding of academic contexts and cultures. This is not only a young and rapidly evolving academic culture, but also one that has a history characterized by various tensions in the fight for and in defense of academic freedom. Some of those tensions seem to be ever-present, with continuing contestations around new agendas that have been defined by government policies and priorities, in particular in shaping the continuing agenda for 'transformation'. Therefore, the development of the sector continues to be intertwined with the political environment, so that, for instance, the structure, role, and composition of something so central to the life of an institution as the Senate have been shaped more by legislation (the National Plan on Higher Education) than by academic debate.

The Missing Elements

Some respondents noted an absence of features that would be regarded by academic faculty in other systems as integral to their work. These included a lack of opportunity and resources to visit other institutions or to be visited by colleagues from other institutions; a lack of joint projects with colleagues at other institutions; limited access to journals and conferences; and difficulty with resourcing online teaching, because the majority of students did not have access to personal computers. Such problems tend to be more pronounced in some institutions than others and, in some cases, in particular departments or disciplinary areas. On the other hand, some South African higher education institutions compare favorably with prestigious institutions elsewhere (see, for example, Ramphele, 2008: 218–219). In these cases there are active international linkages and a free flow of academic faculty between institutions participating in joint and collaborative research projects. This is an area in which national policymakers might need to be encouraged to take steps to even out an uneven landscape and to create greater equity between institutions in a supposedly unitary national system of higher education.

Respondents also mentioned that they wished to be more involved in activities such as:

- community work with students;
- engaging in academic debate;
- releasing time for keeping up with reading relevant to their disciplines.

There was also a desire to be able to undertake these activities during normal working hours. However, some of this may be achieved by better time management and being more creative in utilizing the available resources, including an appreciation of the potential of postgraduate students in supporting research.

Career Paths

It can be argued that a better understanding of the concept and role of 'an academic' might arise from the adoption of more clearly defined career paths or options. Respondents were therefore asked whether they were aware of the existence of such career paths in their own institutions. Their views were also sought on what they perceived or understood to be their career prospects and levels of job satisfaction, and what support they received from their institutions to foster their development along the identified career path. The respondents who believed they recognized the existence of an academic career path identified a traditional one whereby the member of staff starts as a lecturer and then moves on to a senior lectureship, then to an associate professorship, and finally to a full professorship. They suggested that this path was well documented and therefore clear. There were, however, difficulties in the implementation of such a career pathway. Respondents indicated a need for a mentoring process as well as for a more liberal interpretation of the criteria for promotion.

Respondents were asked whether institutions had policies that guided career development. Fifty percent replied in the affirmative. When asked whether they were familiar with the details of the policies, only 33 percent replied in the affirmative. Sixty percent of the respondents who were familiar with institutional policies had also utilized these at some stage in their careers. Their familiarity with the policies was largely in the area of staff development, which they took advantage of mainly to fund their studies with a view to bettering their qualifications, particularly in those cases where respondents did not hold a doctorate or appropriate terminal degree in their field. As one of the respondents observed, "If you do not get a higher qualification, you won't have a job". This statement reflects the fact that a significant percentage of South African academic faculty do not have doctoral degrees.

Respondents were also asked what means institutions were using to promote career development policies, and what support they provided for implementation of the policies. One institution used regular messages on the intranet and faculty meetings. However, the majority of respondents asserted that there was very little support and, in some cases, no funding earmarked for the implementation of the policies. One of the respondents was of the opinion that "managerialism does not support career development", suggesting that it was regarded as a personal goal rather than as an institutional imperative.

The results of this study suggest that an important link exists between clarity of institutional policies and the level of satisfaction with career development opportunities among individuals. On the other hand, there appears to be so much vagueness in several of the institutions examined that the defining of a career path is left to individual departments or the individuals themselves. One respondent pointed out that in many cases "there is a lot of talk and no action". Another suggested that at the policy level there was a conflict of expectations in that one was expected to fulfill the criteria for advancing one's career, largely based on research output, while also carrying a full teaching load—a concern also noted in another study (Wolhuter et al., 2006).

Respondents were also clear that where institutions do not create supportive environments in which career development can take place, the concept of career development may be clear but will remain nothing more than an idea. They pointed out that their environments were characterized by understaffing; no or limited sabbaticals; no resources set aside for research and administrative support, a factor also reported by Mapesela and Hay (2006); and insufficient mentoring to guide academic faculty about career development. There was also a feeling that conditions not only change all the time, but are continually moving in a direction that erodes those elements that would favor career development, so much so that one respondent said that they no longer "know where [they] stand".

The majority of the respondents were in favor of having clearly defined institutional policies for career development and the active promotion thereof. One of the respondents expressed this quite clearly by saying:

It is important to outline what the university values in terms of learning and teaching and knowing, in order to ground policies covering, *inter alia*, leave, intellectual property, curriculum, what staff activities are valued, student life, and the institution's approach to social responsibility.

The respondents suggested that issues related to career development could be addressed at both the institutional and the sector levels. At institutional level they suggested that academic faculty needed to have access to appropriate development programs that would build capacity in research and writing for publication. Academic development centers could actively guide academic faculty, and the need for mentorship in this process was, again, emphasized.

At the 'system level', respondents felt there was a need for a nationally coordinated effort in relation to the formulation and implementation of career development policies, as well as a standardization of procedures and regular monitoring and evaluation of career progression. National training could also include academic development and incorporate such programs as effective teaching; how to conduct research; creating networks with the community, especially the business sector; and academic management. The latter could include such matters as time management, tutoring students, and assessment processes and techniques.

When asked about job satisfaction, respondents highlighted two main sources of satisfaction: first, engagement with students (one of the foremost reasons why people choose to work in higher education, as reported by Astin and Astin, 2007); and second, reaching personal milestones, particularly where this involved overcoming difficulties that led to institutional reform. Factors contributing to respondents not experiencing job satisfaction included:

- a lack of focus by the system on the job satisfaction of rank-and-file academic faculty (as opposed to an apparent focus on senior managers);
- a lack of recognition for tasks such as the nurturing or motivation of students, which are an integral part of academic work, especially in these environments, but not necessarily recognized as such;
- the tendency for some institutions to adopt a 'managerial' rather than a collegial approach to adoption and implementation of policies;
- more demands on individuals, combined with lack of prospects for promotion or recognition of effort.

Respondents were clear that job satisfaction could not be measured by salary or titles, but was likely to come, in the words of one respondent, "with a sense of having made a difference to the way the people of the world, especially South Africans, live".

Conclusion

As in other countries, higher education in South Africa has been affected by competing demands, not only by globalization but also by local factors. These include issues such as 'massification' and its implications for teachers; pressures to undertake applied research rather than 'blue skies' research; the diversification of the workforce without appropriate resources to support this; internal and international competition for talented staff; and competition with the private sector for managers who also have an academic background. South Africa, therefore, finds itself in the same position as many other countries in the types of challenges facing the sector.

More specifically, the study suggests that being 'an academic' in South Africa involves a combination of roles, activities, and attitudes affected by institutional factors such as the ethos, history, and practices of the institution. The lived experiences of academic faculty as evidenced by the responses of our interviewees clearly demonstrate a sense of uncertainty about what their identity *is*, or should be. Part of the 'conflict' in how these players view their role arises from perceptions they held prior to attaining these positions, but that has been exacerbated by the fact that, in reality, there *has* been a change from what that role may have been in the past. The old view of a 'linear' career path has less currency today, and the boundaries between academic work and supporting activities have become blurred. The demands of institutional and public accountability are such that the record keeping and information management necessary to protect the individual and the institution, as well as to provide a customer-focused service to students, have added to the number and complexity of tasks associated with the management of academic work.

However, it would appear that institutions are not always aware of a shift in the roles and expectations of their staff, and that an open and formal debate would assist in understanding these, and to make clear institutional expectations. This has to be a negotiated process, to maximize understanding. It also needs to be a national process, to minimize uneven conditions.

References

Astin, A. W. and Astin, H. S. (2007) "The Leadership Role of Faculty." *Project Kaleidoscope*. Online, available at: www.pkal.org/documents/LeadershipRoleOfFaculty.cfm (accessed January 5, 2008).

Barnett, R. (2000) *Realizing the University in an Age of Supercomplexity*. Buckingham, UK: SRHE/Open University Press.

Currie, J., Harris, P., and Thiele, B. (2000) "Sacrifices in Greedy Universities: Are They Gendered?" *Gender and Education* 12: 269–291.

Department of Education (1997) *The Higher Education Act (101 of 1997)*. Pretoria: Government Printers.

Department of Education (2001) *National Plan for Higher Education in South Africa*. Pretoria: Government Printers.

Giddens, A. (1991) *Modernity and Self-Identity: Self and Society in the Late Modern Age*. Cambridge: Polity Press.

Henkel, M. (2000) *Academic Identities and Policy Change in Higher Education*. London: Jessica Kingsley.

Mapesela, M. and Hay, D. H. R (2006) "The Effect of Change and Transformation on Academic Staff and Job Satisfaction: A Case of a South African University." *Higher Education* 52 (4): 711–747.

National Commission on Higher Education (NCHE) (1996) *A Framework for Transformation*. Pretoria: Department of Education.

Ozga, J. T. and Deem, R. (2000) "Carrying the Burden of Transformation: The Experiences of Women Managers in UK Higher and Further Education." *Discourse: Studies in the Cultural Politics of Education* 21: 141–153.

Ramphele, M. (2008) *Laying Ghosts to Rest: Dilemmas of the Transformation in South Africa.* Cape Town: Tafelberg.

Smit, P. (2006) "Leadership in South African Higher Education: A Multifaceted Conceptualisation." Unpublished Ph.D. thesis, University of London.

Trowler, P. R. (2001) "Captured by the Discourse? The Socially Constitutive Power of the New Higher Education Discourse in the UK." *Organization* 8: 183–201.

Wolhuter, C. C., Higgs, L. G., and Higgs, P. J. (2006) "The South African Academic Profession and Transformation of Higher Education." *Higher Education Review* 38 (2): 3–20.

The Impact of Changing Recruitment Practices on Academic Profiles

CHRISTINE MUSSELIN

At a time when competition among institutions is rising and higher education, research, and innovation are seen by national governments as strategic goals for the economic development of knowledge economies, two main issues are at stake. The first relates to the structure of higher education systems and the kind of institutional design that might be adopted in order to improve their efficiency. In many countries, similar, but sometimes conflicting, answers are found in relation to, for instance, the transformation of relationships between the state and organized higher education interests on the one hand, and autonomous higher education institutions on the other (see, for instance, Brunsson and Sahlin-Andersson, 2000; Amaral et al., 2002; Musselin, 2006; Krücken and Meier, 2006).

The second issue is at the heart of this book. It deals with human resources and includes two interrelated questions: First, should the academic profession be managed in a different way? Second, should the profiles of academic faculty be subject to adaptation? In both cases the self-regulatory practices traditionally adopted by the profession are being modified. Many authors (e.g. Slaughter and Leslie, 1997; Henkel, 2000; Enders and Musselin, 2008) describe the increasing influence of institutional leaders (be they 'academic' or not) in decision-making processes that affect the individual careers of faculty members, including those in research posts. In recruitment processes the search for new academic profiles has induced a shift in appointments criteria and in recruitment procedures and practices. These two questions are linked in that the recruitment of individuals with new types of profile fulfills expectations related to the diversification of institutional missions (what some authors, such as Enders and de Boer (2009) term "mission stretch"). This accompanies the introduction of new practices in the management of academic faculty.

While acknowledging the interdependence of these two questions, this chapter focuses on the transformation of recruitment procedures and practices. The following developments will be based for the most part on the results of three different studies in France and Germany undertaken over ten years, one aimed at understanding how academic faculty recruit their future colleagues (Musselin, 2005), one on the influence of gender on academic careers in France (Carrère et al., 2006), and one on the impact of recent changes that have been introduced in Germany.

Two different models will be analyzed: First, a distinction is made between recruitment decisions relying on (national) competition, with a central pool of candidates and where all positions are considered as equivalent; and 'recruitment', defined as a matching process between the specific needs of a recruiting department (and/or institution) and the specific characteristics of a candidate. It will be argued that, partly because higher education institutions are increasingly differentiated, the 'recruitment' model tends to become the norm even in countries where a process of national competition previously existed. Second, it will be shown that, at the same time, recruitment practices are changing to become more formalized, to include more steps in the process, and to rely on new types of criteria.

Specific Recruitment versus 'National' Competition for Homogeneous Candidate Profiles

Recruitment procedures are still very different between countries (Altbach, 2000; Enders, 2001; Enders and de Weert, 2004). They reflect the national characteristics of different higher education systems and the way they are configured—that is, the frame within which the type of governance developed by universities, the steering style of the overseeing ministry, and the internal regulation modes of the disciplines are inscribed, make sense, and relate to each other (Musselin, [2001] 2004: 112). Thus, appointment procedures reflect the differences in system configurations in different countries and point to two main models, which I shall now describe.

Differing Conceptions of Recruitment

On the one hand, in countries that developed strong and autonomous higher education institutions (mostly the English and North American systems), recruitment has always been the responsibility of the institutions, which are the employers of their staff. As a result, each institution recruits its candidate of choice and finds a fit between the profile of the selected candidate and its own institutional profile. The notion of "organizational saga", developed by Clark in a seminal paper published in 1972, helps in understanding this fit between a higher education institution and its personnel. For Clark, the notion of organizational saga refers to "the story of special performance [which] emerges not in a few months but over a decade or two", and which is "embodied in many components of the organization, affecting the definition and performance of the organization and finding protection in the webbing of the institutional parts" (1972: 179). The saga that characterizes a specific institution is known externally and therefore encourages applications from candidates who share its values and norms, while appointing committees will prefer candidates who offer these values and norms. In such countries the match between the institution and the candidate is a feature of recruitment decisions and practices.

This form of matching is very different from the principle prevailing in some other countries, and in particular in Germany and France until a few years ago, and still persisting in some cases. The belief (whether or not this is based on reality) was that academic appointments in each institution were made on an equivalent basis. Little differentiation was recognized or expected among universities. As a result, all were expected to recruit homogeneous types of candidates. In France this principle of equality was pushed further, as little differentiation was recognized among French academic faculty, for instance, in terms of salaries or careers. In Germany, by contrast, while institutions are considered broadly equivalent, differentiation between candidates has been accepted for a long time (Enders and Teichler, 1997).

Nevertheless, beyond these nuances, in neither of these countries did recruiting a professor involve matching the specific characteristics of a candidate with the specific needs of an individual institution, because of the supposed equivalence between institutions. All universities were supposed to offer equivalent positions, or to look for a similar profile of a professor within his or her discipline. Universal criteria were supposed to exist for the purpose of deciding who would be part of the professoriate and who would not.

In the case of France this explains why recruitment procedures depended on nationwide competition, and why strong weight was accorded to discipline-based national committees of peers. In the mid-1980s, in order to recruit an assistant professor (who in France holds a tenured position termed a *maître de conférences*), local appointment committees were agreed partly by election and partly by appointment for each discipline at the university level, and ranked up to five candidates in order of preference. A national body, the Conseil National des Universités (CNU), made up of nationally partly elected and partly nominated discipline-based committees, examined the rankings established by each recruiting institution for each discipline and could decide either to change the order of the ranking, to reject the decision, or to confirm it. Its role was thus to ensure that the decisions made at the institutional level were in conformity with the criteria of the discipline concerned. In particular, it checked that the choices neither reflected local, as opposed to universal, preferences, nor resulted from local bias.

In some disciplines (economics, political science, law, and management) there still exists in France a specific competition or *'concours'* (called *agrégation du supérieur*) for those *maîtres de conférences* who want to become professors. Every second year a national panel of professors is established for each of this group of disciplines. A president of the panel is designated by the French ministry from among the professors who have the highest level of seniority. The president then designates the other members of the panel and generally has to respect some balance among them in terms of location (Paris versus province), academic specialties, and, more recently, gender. The candidates have to undergo a series of assessments before this panel within a period of about six months. After each step of this national process a number of candidates are rejected. At the end, the national panel ranks the remaining candidates. This number is often equal to the number of professorial positions made available by the national ministry, but it can also be less than this number if the panel decides that there are fewer excellent candidates than positions available. The candidate ranked first on the list can then choose the institution where he or she wishes to go from the available slots. The next candidate does likewise until the last one on the list takes the position that remains. Thus, higher education institutions do not select their professors, but are in fact 'chosen' by the successful candidates. This type of allocation of personnel to positions is clearly different from what was previously defined as 'recruitment'—that is, a process of mutual matching between a candidate and an institution.

The Expansion of the 'Recruitment' Concept over the Competition or 'Concours' Concept

The idea that academic positions are homogeneous—that for any position within a specialty, for instance, medieval history, all recruiting universities require the same profile, and that the best way to allocate manpower between identical positions and heterogeneous candidates is a national competition—is still current in France. It has, nevertheless, been challenged in two ways: First, the supposed impartiality of such national procedures (often opposed to the presumed bias of local decisions made at the institutional level) has often been criticized, either by arguing that national bodies reproduce the mainstream views of each discipline and block potential innovations, or by showing that national procedures do not escape the influence of the disciplinary networks that characterize more decentralized processes. A recent publication shows that there is a significant impact on a candidate's success in the *agrégation du supérieur* if his or her doctoral supervisor is a member of the panel (Combes et al., 2008). The same phenomenon was observed in relation to the *agrégation du supérieur* in management in a recent study (Sabatier and Pigeyre, forthcoming). Second, and more importantly than the recurring debates between the supporters of national procedures and the supporters of a more decentralized process, the increased autonomy of higher education institutions has cast doubt on the credibility of purely national processes.

This evolution has been progressive in France as the path to autonomy has been incremental. But it can be shown that each time institutional autonomy has increased, some of the national processes that frame career development in France have been modified. The introduction of contractual policy (Musselin, [2001] 2004) is a good example. By the end of the 1980s the ministry had transformed the allocation of recurrent budgets among French universities. While the larger share was allocated according to fixed criteria (e.g. number of students, space), the remaining share depended on the quality of the four-year strategic plan each university was asked to prepare, and was fixed through a four-year contract between each university and the ministry. With this process, the emergence of stronger higher education institutions became possible, all the more so as this evolution has been reinforced by a revision of the role of the CNU in the same period.

Since 1992 the CNU has no longer been expected to control (and modify) the decisions made by institutions. Apart from during a short interruption between 1995 and 1997, the discipline-based commissions of the CNU receive the portfolios of the candidates who wish to apply for a position of *maître de conférences* (or professor) before these positions are made available by universities. These commissions check whether the candidates are sufficiently qualified to apply for such a position. Those who are declared 'qualified' by the CNU are then allowed to apply for any position available in any institution within the next four years. Each institution can therefore decide whom to recruit from among the group of qualified individuals. It should nevertheless be added that some disciplines in the CNU resist this reduction of their power by being very selective in the approval of candidates. For instance, in law it is not unusual for the number of approved candidates to be very close to the number of positions available. Thus, the approval rates may differ significantly from discipline to discipline. In 2007 the ratio of approved candidates to the total number of candidates applying for approval, or 'qualification', reached about 60 percent on average, but only 22 percent in public law and 86 percent in optics. Despite such discrepancies, the role and the influence of the CNU have tended to decrease since 1992.

The Act of August 2007 is reinforcing this evolutionary process. It did not revoke the national 'qualification process', the CNU, or the *agrégation du supérieur*, but it increased the weight given to individual higher education institutions in the recruitment process taken as a whole. First, it gave each university president the power to appoint the local recruitment committees. Second, the president now has the possibility of rejecting the choice made by these committees if he or she does not agree with the ranking. The president can therefore exercise a veto.

Because the CNU and the *agrégation* have been maintained, it is too soon to speak of a shift from the principle of '*concours*' to the principle of recruitment in France. But a further phenomenon, which is common to France and Germany, is also encouraging moves in this direction. As a result of the contractual policy in France (see above) and of the Acts of 1998 and 2005 in Germany (which both provided each *Land* with more margin of maneuver vis-à-vis federal legislation), the differentiation among higher education institutions increased, and they are expected to become further distinguished from each other. This supports a shift toward the idea that each vacant position is specific (i.e. different from others) and that this specificity derives from the particular needs and orientations of the local institution where the recruitment takes place. A good indicator of the increasing influence of the local institutional setting in academic recruitment procedures can be detected in the advertisements for vacant positions. If one looks at the positions available in sociology in some well-known sociology departments in large French universities on the one hand, and in less prestigious sociology departments in medium-sized French universities on the other hand, the differences between the advertisements posted on the websites of the two types of institution are clear.

To illustrate this point, two examples are drawn from the recruitment process in France in spring 2008 (Boxes 8.1 and 8.2). The advertisements have been downloaded from the websites of two French universities, one in Paris (called Socio-Paris) and one in the provinces (called Socio-Province). Both relate to a position for a *maître de conférences* in sociology, but each has been slightly modified in order to maintain the anonymity of the universities concerned. It is clear that the institutions are looking for very different profiles, even if both are in the same discipline. The vocational orientation of the advertisement of Socio-Province strongly contrasts with the theoretical expectations of Socio-Paris, while the somewhat detailed expectations expressed for the first differ from the very short description provided by the second. Of course, these advertisements may be

---

BOX 8.1 Advertisement Posted on the Website of Socio-Province

Through his/her fundamental and applied research on urban issues, the candidate is expected to consolidate the fit between the vocational training programs of the university in this field and the needs of vocational training in the urban sector.

S/he will teach on a Master's program on the urban sector, a Master's program on "Analysis and Urban Intervention", a Bachelor's program on "Cities and Regulations", and a vocational Bachelor's program.

S/he will have teaching responsibility for these training programs and for relationships with professional schools of urban studies, and with urban professionals in the region. A good knowledge of teaching practices specific to vocational training will be required.

Teaching expectations

To lecture in urban sociology (identities and professional practices within the urban sector, social exchanges and exclusion processes, methodology and epistemology in social and human sciences applied to the urban sector).

In collaboration with the vocational training center, to provide legitimacy to the professional bachelor's and Master's programs; to review the adaptation of training programs to vocational training, and to promote them within the department of sociology.

Research

The candidate will be required to adapt his/her research agenda to the four-yearly strategic plan of the university, and to the section on "urban dynamics" of the XXXX research institute. S/he will focus on the impact of local public intervention, and also lead international or European research programs. S/he is, furthermore, expected to develop interdisciplinary research projects on urban public policies by answering calls for proposals.

---

strategic: the precision of the first may be explained by the fact that this university already has someone in view and, therefore, the recruiters may have adapted the profile of the position to the profile of this candidate. Thus, it would be dangerous to over-interpret the advertisements without having more empirical data. Nevertheless, it seems reasonable to suggest that Socio-Province has a precise need to fulfill, and is therefore looking for a specialist, while Socio-Paris does not have such clear specifications in relation to specific areas, and is looking for a theoretical profile regardless of the field the candidate works in.

While the Ministry of Education still publishes very formal and succinct advertisements in official journals, these examples clearly show that French institutions expand these legal advertisements via versions published on their

---

BOX 8.2 Advertisement Posted on the Website of Socio-Paris

Position in sociological theory; epistemology of social sciences

Teaching

Bachelor's degree in sociology; Master's degree in sociology.

Objectives: The candidate will be familiar with, and be able to teach, the main theoretical paradigms in the sociological tradition, as well as contemporary sociology.

Using empirical studies, s/he will be able to raise issues on the nature of the sociological paradigm and on its relationship with other social sciences. S/he will lecture to audiences of sociologists as well as psychologists.

Research

The candidate will be a member of the XXXX research center.

---

websites and no longer publish a 'call for applications' that refers only to the field covered by the position (as they did before). They now give more detailed information on their websites, including details about teaching expectations, the research agenda, and the future affiliations of the candidate. They therefore tend to develop advertisements in the same way as commercial organizations. They are no longer simply looking for a theoretical sociologist or an urban sociologist, but rather define (more so in the case of Socio-Province than in the case of Socio-Paris) a specific profile adapted to their specific needs. It is therefore clear from the case examples that the two universities are not searching for people with similar profiles. Socio-Province is not looking for just *any* urban sociologist; he or she must be interested and experienced in vocational training. Although Socio-Paris might be interested in a theoretical sociologist specializing in urban issues, this would not be attractive for Socio-Province, even though the candidate appointed might work on urban issues. Both cases show the importance of the local situation and local needs in the search for an appropriate appointee. As a result, posts are no longer necessarily homogeneous and substitutable. The pool of posts is heterogeneous, and seems likely to become more so.

In the following section it is argued that this diversity of role profiles also has an impact on the criteria used to define the 'best' candidate, and to select him or her.

Changing Recruitment Practices

While recruitment procedures remain different between countries, there appears to be some convergence in that individual positions are likely to be defined according to the specific needs and situation of the recruiting institution. This change affects countries where the competitive '*concours*' tradition prevailed, and it is accompanied by a general evolution in the requirements that candidates have to fulfill in order to have a chance of being recruited. From this perspective, three main developments are noticeable: a formalization of procedures, a more complex mix of dimensions, and new forms of competency.

The Formalization of Recruitment Procedures

There would appear to be an overall trend toward more formalized procedures and requirements. In many countries the advertising of a position has hitherto been very succinct, often being limited to a very short description such as "Sociology of organization. Skills in quantitative methods required". Such concise descriptions are less common today, and each recruiting department or institution is expected to provide some detail of the specific programs on which the appointee would be expected to teach, their research interests, and also service activities. In countries such as the United Kingdom (Bessy et al., 2001), where this is common for all types of post, advertisements about academic positions are likely, also, to mention the level of salary.

Parallel with these developments is the growth of candidates' portfolios. These tend to be increasingly specific. It has long been the custom to require a curriculum vitae and a list of publications, but many institutions now also ask candidates to provide, for instance, details of the classes they have already taught, and a teaching portfolio. A number of publications may be included in the portfolio, although these may not always be required for the first round of interviews: Musselin (2005) found that in German mathematics departments, publications were required only from the candidates who survived the first round of assessments. The appointment panel would be likely to send them for assessment to external experts rather than reading them themselves. Referees' reports are mandatory in many countries, while in France the '*rapport de soutenance*' (i.e. the document written by the members of the panel who attended the defense of a Ph.D. candidate) is always required. This assists the appointment panel to understand the composition of the doctoral panel (who was on it and what their background and reputation are), and the quality of the dissertation or thesis (whether the panel's report is fair and accurate).

Beyond these changes affecting advertisements and the provision of portfolios, recruitment procedures themselves have tended to become more complex and to last longer. They are no longer informed solely by subjective criteria, as was the case until very recently in France. But even in France, with the implementation of the 2007 Act the rapid interview (lasting twenty to thirty minutes) of the candidates by a single local appointment committee is likely to be replaced by a process that is both more open and prescribed. Some French universities are already considering how appointment processes might be improved, and thinking about introducing more assessment tools. In many other countries the examination of the portfolio is complemented by an extensive assessment of a shortlist of candidates who are invited onto campus. It is no longer unusual to ask candidates to give a lecture and/or a research seminar, then to undertake interviews with different groups of people: the appointments committee, the department chair, the dean, sometimes even the president of the institution. In a Belgian university a psychological test and an interview with a human resources manager have been introduced recently.

This expansion and formalization of appointment procedures does not apply only to tenured or tenure-track positions. In many countries, recruitment processes for support posts and short-term contracts now follow more formal procedures. A shortlist for an appointment involving a five-year contract in Norway, for instance, required each candidate to produce a portfolio including topics such as training, professional experiences, and teaching, as well as the submission of all published work. Such an in-depth process remains unusual, and informal networks often continue to be used. This is particularly the case in Germany for non-professorial staff. But there is a trend across many countries, including Germany, toward the introduction of more formal selection processes for doctoral and postdoctoral candidates (Sadowski et al., 2008).

A More Complex Mix of Dimensions

While it is possible to demonstrate that contemporary procedures are more complex, in that, for instance, favored candidates are likely to combine a mix of qualities, it is less easy to track changes over time, as no studies exist of how appointment decisions have been made in the past. Moreover, the literature about recruitment processes in the past came to somewhat varying conclusions. On the one hand, authors such as Hagstrom (1965) and Cole and Cole (1973) concluded that processes relied on universalist, objective criteria. On the other hand, authors such as Crane (1970) and Long and Fox (1995) contested these assumptions and revealed that less objective criteria were playing a role. While this second group of authors showed that universalist criteria were not the only, or crucial, factors, and that recruitment was in some respects already multidimensional, they saw this as being a problem, rather than as representing good practice.

Drawing on a comparative study of appointments committees in France, Germany, and the United States (Musselin, 2005), the discussion here will focus on the multidimensional character of appointment decisions, rather than engaging in a debate about the pros and cons of different approaches. Despite differences between the twenty-two history or mathematics departments, located in research universities in the three countries, all of them paid attention to three main features of candidate profiles: The first was their academic activities. There were variations in the precise factors and indicators that each discipline and/or each country used, but all valued academic productivity. Second, teaching ability was also taken into account, even if all interviewing panels recognized that the assessment of this might be problematic. Third, the 'social fit' of candidates was invariably a crucial aspect. Almost all respondents in the twenty-two departments reported asking questions such as 'Will this candidate fit in with our students?', 'Do I want this person to be my colleague in the coming years?', and 'Will this candidate participate in the collective duties of the department?'

Although these three dimensions were always present in the departments studied, the balance among them varied from one department to another. The profile of the department or the profile of the advertised position, which were related to each other, affected the relative weight given to each dimension. In summary, departments with a strong academic orientation and reputation are likely to attach more importance to the academic dimension, while departments that have a heavy student load or are more teaching oriented will lay more emphasis on the pedagogical and collegial dimensions. Thus, a multidimensional assessment of candidates is common in contemporary research universities, even if the balance between dimensions may vary.

New Forms of Competency

The final change to note relates to the evolution of the criteria applied to successful candidates. Most criteria continue to be very 'academic', in the sense that they are clearly related to the norms and standards of a given discipline. For French historians, for instance, the way that the archives are used in research constitutes a crucial aspect of whether a candidate is a worthy and capable historian. This factor is, of course, specific to this discipline and to the evaluation of the academic quality of the portfolios in (French) history. Such academic and research-oriented criteria have not disappeared, but they are increasingly accompanied by new forms of requirement and criteria.

One of these is the increasing attention given to teaching skills. Even in research-oriented institutions, teaching abilities are assessed and taken into account. But again, criteria vary according to the discipline, and thus reflect discipline-based requirements. Musselin (2005) found that many mathematicians, for instance, pointed to the importance they attached to the way that candidates used the blackboard, while this factor was not mentioned by historians.

In addition to these 'classical' and discipline-based criteria, the emergence of less 'purely' academic criteria can be observed. In a mathematics department in Germany it was, for instance, common in the recruitment of professors to review their success in obtaining grants (*Drittmittel*). Of course, it can be argued that obtaining grants demonstrates academic quality. As in all countries, the failure rates in obtaining funding from national research councils are increasing. As a result, obtaining grants becomes an indicator of the academic worth of individual members of faculty. But other outcomes attach to this criterion. For instance, it suggests that the department is likely to attract more resources if the candidate is recruited. A grant-holder's track record, such as number of publications and research grants, also testifies to his or her managerial abilities as a project leader in motivating a team. In some cases, such skills are now explicitly required in order to obtain promotion. In the French national research organization, the Institut National de la Recherche Agronomique (INRA), those applying for a position of director of research (*directeur de recherche*), which is the highest status one can reach in this institution and is equivalent to a chair, it is expected that the candidates will have demonstrated managerial skills (Carrère et al., 2006). Thus, only those who have exercised responsibility as team leaders in their laboratories have an opportunity to achieve such positions. A high level of publications is also required in their portfolio, but this is no longer sufficient for someone to be promoted to director of research.

There may also be more overtly commercial expectations. The advertisement published by Socio-Province and the emphasis put on vocational training mean that the candidate must be interested in activities providing revenue to the department, and in developing training programs meeting a social demand, rather than solely in relation to his or her academic interests. A recent interview with a German university president pointed in the same direction. Among the objectives negotiated with the newly recruited professors was their commitment to vocational training, and their ability to bring resources to the university was increasingly required as an indicator of performance.

There is, therefore, a shift toward a diversification of the requirements for either recruitment or promotion, and the addition of new skills that hitherto have not been regarded as 'academic'. Simplistic conclusions should not, however, be drawn from these observations. The inclusion of new and supplementary criteria does not mean that academic values are being ignored. They remain central, but are contextualized by broader considerations. The reverse may also apply in some disciplines. In a study on management departments in France there was a clear fracture among the faculty members (Musselin and Becquet, 2008). On the one hand, some believed in the recruitment of professionals—that is, candidates with academic credentials but also with professional experience in commerce or industry. On the other, some faculty members strongly (and successfully) argued for an 'academicization' of their discipline, and the use of 'pure' academic criteria; they thought that publications in top-rated journals should be the key factor. While the former were defending the profiles that dominated when this discipline developed within French universities in the 1970s, the latter were defending what they considered to be the future of their discipline, and won the debate.

Similar movements are observable within many French business schools, which have long been elite teaching institutions but were not research institutions. In the mid-1990s these schools discovered that they needed to engage in high-level academic activity if they wanted to be recognized internationally. Like management departments within universities, business schools increased the importance attached to academic criteria in their recruitment processes. For instance, they recruited holders of doctorates trained in international business schools, whereas in the past their staff had consisted primarily of former students. Similar developments are also observable in professional fields that have been integrated into universities in recent years, such as nursing and architecture. The introduction of 'less' academic criteria in recruitment is therefore not generalizable, and it more directly affects the traditional, core disciplines. For these, there is clearly increasing attention, even by peer faculty, given to criteria that might be said to relate as much to the institution as to the academic discipline.

Conclusion

This chapter has argued that appointment procedures, and their requirements and practices, are evolving. In countries where the prevailing view was that individual academic positions were homogeneous, and therefore interchangeable, general, universal criteria have been used to select candidates. This view is increasingly being challenged, and the specific characteristics of institutional contexts are taken into account. This has led to greater heterogeneity in relation to the types of post available.

Transformations are also affecting appointment processes, which are becoming not only increasingly complex but also more formalized and multidimensional. They therefore combine different aspects and tend to incorporate criteria that are less 'purely' academic, in particular in the more traditional disciplines.

Although these transformations are not radical, they are progressively affecting academic recruitment and the profiles of the newly recruited staff. Thus, younger staff who have been through a series of assessments are likely to be less reluctant than their senior colleagues to participate in ongoing appraisal and review processes that are more management oriented, such as were introduced in Germany for newly recruited professors. This might be said to be a natural progression from more complex initial entry procedures into an academic career. In other words, new forms of recruitment become part of the socialization process for incoming academic faculty.

References

Altbach, P. (ed.) (2000) *The Changing Academic Workplace: Comparative Perspectives.* Boston: Boston College Center for International Higher Education.

Amaral, A., Jones, G., and Karseth, B. (eds.) (2002) *Governing Higher Education: National Perspectives on Institutional Governance.* Dordrecht, the Netherlands: Kluwer Academic Publishers.

Bessy, C., Eymard-Duvernay, F., de Larquier, G., and Marchal, E. (eds.) (2001) *Des marchés du travail équitables, approche comparative France/Royaume-Uni.* Brussels: PIE-Peter Lang.

Brunsson, N. and Sahlin-Andersson, K. (2000) "Constructing Organizations: The Example of Public Reform Sector." *Organization Studies* 21 (4): 721–746.

Carrère, M., Louvel, S., Mangematin, V., Musselin, C., Pigeyre, F., Sabatier, M., and Vallette, A. (2006) *Entre discrimination et auto-censure: les carrières des femmes dans l'enseignement supérieur et la recherche. Une analyse comparée sur trois disciplines: biologie, histoire et gestion.* Final Report, Convention 02R4680, Paris.

Clark, Burton R. (1972) "The Organizational Saga in Higher Education." *Administrative Science Quarterly* 17 (2): 178–184.

Cole, J. R. and Cole, S. (1973) *Social Stratification in Science.* Chicago: University of Chicago Press.

Combes, P.-P., Linnemer, L., and Visser, M. (2008) "Publish or Peer-Rich? The Role of Skills and Networks in Hiring Economics Professors." *Labour Economics* 15 (3): 423–441.

Crane, D. (1970) "The Academic Marketplace Revisited." *American Journal of Sociology* 75 (6): 953–964.

Enders, J. (Ed.) (2001) *Academic Staff in Europe: Changing Contexts and Conditions.* Westport, CT: Greenwood Press.

Enders, J. and de Boer, H. (2009) "The European Higher Education Area. Various Perspectives on the Complexities of a Multi-Level Governance System." In *European Integration and the Governance of Higher Education and Research: The Challenges and Complexities of an Emerging Multi-level Governance System,* ed. A. Amaral, P. Maassen, C. Musselin, and G. Neave. Dordrecht, the Netherlands: Springer.

Enders, J. and de Weert E. (eds.) (2004) *The International Attractiveness of the Academic Workplace in Europe*. Frankfurt am Main: Materialen und Dokumente, Hochschule und Forschung.

Enders, J. and Musselin, C. (2008) "Back to the Future? The Academic Professions in the 21st Century." OECD *Higher Education 2030*, vol. 1: *Demography*. Paris: OECD Editions. (*L'Enseignement supérieur en 2030*, vol. 1: *Démographie*. Paris: Éditions OCDE.)

Enders, J. and Teichler, U. (1997) "A Victim of Their Own Success? Employment and Working Conditions of Academic Staff in Comparative Perspective." *Higher Education* 34 (3): 347–372.

Hagstrom, W. (1965) *The Scientific Community*. Carbondale and Edwardsville: Southern Illinois University Press; London and Amsterdam: Feffer & Simons.

Henkel, M. (2000) *Academic Identities and Policy Change in Higher Education*. London: Jessica Kingsley.

Krücken, G. and Meier, F. (2006) "Turning the University into an Organizational Actor." In *Globalization and Organization*, ed. G. Drori, J. Meyer, and H. Hwang. Oxford: Oxford University Press.

Long, J. S. and Fox. M. F. (1995) "Scientific Careers: Universalism and Particularism." *Annual Review of Sociology* 21 (1): 45–71.

Musselin, C. ([2001] 2004) *The Long March of French Universities*. New York: Routledge. (First published in French: *La Longue Marche des universités*. Paris: PUF, 2001.)

Musselin, C. (2005) *Le Marché des universitaires. France, Allemagne, États-Unis*. Paris: Presses de Sciences Po.

Musselin, C. (2006) "Are Universities Specific Organisations?" In *Towards a Multiversity? Universities between Global Trends and National Traditions*, ed. G. Krücken, A. Kosmützky, and M. Torka. Bielefeld, Germany: Transcript Verlag.

Musselin, C. and Becquet, V. (2008) "Academic Work and Academic Identities: A Comparison between Four Disciplines." In *Cultural Perspectives on Higher Education*, ed. J. Välimaa and O.-H. Ylijoki. Dordrecht, the Netherlands: Springer.

Sabatier, M. and Pigeyre, F. (forthcoming) "Les Déterminants de l'agrégation du supérieur en gestion." Working paper submitted for publication.

Sadowski, D., Schneider, P., and Thaller, N. (2008) "Do We Need Incentives for PhD Supervisors?" *European Journal of Education* 43 (3): 315–329.

Slaughter, S. and Leslie, L. L. (1997) *Academic Capitalism: Politics, Policies, and the Entrepreneurial University*. Baltimore: Johns Hopkins University Press.

Part III
Implications for Individuals

Introduction

GEORGE GORDON

The three chapters in Part III examine how the changing landscape of higher education has impacted upon different sets of individuals, namely academic faculty, administrators and providers of professional expertise, and librarians respectively. In each case the professional dimension features prominently in the detailed analyses. Understandably, individual nuances are more muted, although all of the authors in this volume fully recognize that they can become paramount, especially at critical moments such as in relation to decisions about tenure or promotion or adjustment to role; location within an institution; and adjustments to measurement of performance or other changes to (or threats to) terms of employment that an individual considers likely to be significant or to have potentially negative, destabilizing, or disruptive consequences.

That is not, of course, surprising. The concept of the psychological contract is founded upon what are often unwritten mutual expectations of how two parties, the employer and the employee, will behave—what might be encapsulated in the phase 'the unwritten deal'. For example, the employee usually expects to receive appropriate recognition for his or her endeavors, including for displays of loyalty or good citizenship, in addition to reward for appropriate levels of performance. Broadly, employees hold a notion of what they believe constitutes the institution acting as a good employer, even though that notion may crystallize only under certain, normally adverse, circumstances. A second complication is the influence of competition between individuals, especially in situations where individual performance is an important criterion in promotion and reward. Such is increasingly the case in many institutions in countries that have devolved such decisions to institutions, or in which that degree of autonomy is an integral component of the statutory authority of the institution. Even where younger professionals may express distaste for elitism and prevailing hierarchies, as Whitchurch in Chapter 10 reports, it should not be presumed that that can be interpreted as signaling a lack of interest in their endeavors being justly recognized and rewarded.

McInnis, in Chapter 9, introduces his analysis of academic identities by exploring claims that academic faculty have made to be treated not only as autonomous professionals, but as ones with special rights. That caveat is vital, if contentious, because many professions accord a considerable degree of autonomy to their members. Here the position of the academic as a member of an academic profession is a fascinating one. Kogan et al. (1994: 28) argued that reference to the term started to feature more prominently in the relevant literature in the United Kingdom, the United States, and Australia in the 1980s and 1990s. They argued that disciplinary grouping was the primary point of professional allegiance for academic faculty, with the broader conception of an academic profession resting upon features such as conditions, status, functions, and values. Growth and diversification of higher education led them to conclude that a multiple profession was emerging, something that is amply illustrated by McInnis in Chapter 9, Whitchurch in Chapter 10, and Law in Chapter 11.

Some might question the use of 'profession' in relation to the broader concept of an academic profession. While the doctorate might be advanced as evidence of necessary credentials, it is not a universal requirement. Moreover, the nature of the doctorate is diversifying (Kehm, 2007). Regulation is another common characteristic of a profession. As McInnis demonstrates in Chapter 9, academic faculty firmly believe in the primacy of self-regulation. Arguably, the communities of the disciplines, through the use of external assessors, can exercise a quasi-regulatory role in relation to appointments and promotions, although that is not a universal function. As the chapters in this volume report, consensus over characteristic functions is being eroded, although it remains a topic of considerable debate. Certainly the range of functions has been extended, and there have been related adjustments to expectations about desirable and acceptable combinations of roles and balances of tasks. Eraut (1994) added a client orientation to his characteristics of a profession. That term may be slightly less contentious within the academic community than the concept, for example, of students as customers, although it would, nevertheless, probably meet with a fair degree of suspicion, even outright opposition. Yet some universities are now describing their services as student facing, staff facing, or industry facing. In other words, they are apparently explicitly thinking in the language of the relationships between their professional and academic services and specific sets of clients.

Notwithstanding these challenges to the concept of an academic profession, other trends may provide some support. Staff unions and professional groupings, seeking to address the changing needs of their members and the challenges that they report, conduct and publish surveys, produce position papers, and commission and publish research which collectively and separately are intended to contribute to and shape debates about roles, rewards, conditions, values, and purposes. Provision for initial and continuing professional development for faculty and professionals has mushroomed and is becoming more coherent and formalized. It may progress in very interesting directions, as Middlehurst (Chapter 13) suggests in a fascinating set of scenarios.

Rice (2005) advanced an "ideal" for the future of scholarly work, based around the elaboration of Boyer's (1990) four forms of scholarship. This built upon Rice's (1996) ideas for the new American Scholar. In essence, could the proposition demonstrate at least one, and more probably two or more, of the four forms of scholarship that provide the intellectual foundations for a modern conceptualization of the academic profession? Furthermore, the tendency for academic faculty to describe the impact of some changes as creating a sense of deprofessionalization

(McInnis, Chapter 9; Rhoades, Chapter 3) conveys the implication that they may hold stronger perceptions of what constitutes professionalism than one might have suspected. Torstendahl (1990) associated professionalism with the use of knowledge as social capital. That theoretical position differs in subtle but significant ways from what might be described as more practice-based conceptualizations of professions and professionalism.

Kolsaker explored the impact of managerialism on academic professionalism in a small-scale study at six English universities. She concluded that "much of the literature is overly negative in claiming proletarianisation and demoralisation" (2008: 523). Harman (2003) qualified prevailing negative views of the impact of change on the basis of his Australian study of how faculty and prospective faculty reacted to a changing commercial environment. He acknowledged that "the transition to the new higher education environment has been painful and damaging for the profession, with many academics feeling deeply frustrated, disillusioned and angry" (ibid.: 121). He proceeded to comment that "[m]any have made successful transitions to productive involvement in research links with industry and in other entrepreneurial activities without jeopardizing their academic integrity" (ibid.: 121).

Two important points flow from these and other research studies: First, many views exist, and possibly even coexist. For example, it surely must be possible to be pleased as an individual about how a new opportunity has affected oneself, while nevertheless holding broad concerns about trends and implications. Second, the overwhelming balance in the recent research has been on either detailed small-scale studies or broader interpretations and arguments. There is a paucity of large-scale data, especially continuing datasets that explore the experiences and aspirations of academic faculty and professional staff. A potential exception to that generalization would be the Staff Survey covering participating American universities (the equivalent to the large and more established National Student Survey). Broadly, those data seem to show a range of responses of perceptions of opportunities and challenges. What is needed is a wider survey of practices, expectations, experiences, and identities.

Librarianship might seem to present a simpler professional category for analysis since it tends to have clear professional requirements in terms of entry credentials and, at least historically, as Law (Chapter 11) outlines, a clear sense of internal structures, roles, and relationships to other parts of the university. However, over the past twenty-five years it has been transformed. Academic programs in librarianship have become degrees in information science. Practicing librarians within university libraries have developed, often willingly, "blended" professional roles, as described by Whitchurch (2009), through, for example, providing instruction to students on information searching or some other dimension of information literacy.

As Law observes, the trend toward bringing together library and institutional information technology provision has been more problematic than some advocates might have imagined. Perhaps the intellectual convergence was insufficient, or has still to mature sufficiently to spark the desired synergy. Certainly traditions tended to differ greatly, as did profiles of skills and aptitudes. Given such experiences, it is understandable that institutions may have sought to address managerial capacities as a possible solution, perhaps unintentionally leading to perceptions among practitioners that managerial skills rated much more highly than professional expertise and credibility.

Of course, Law (Chapter 11) does not propose any 'winding back of the clock'—some return to a previous set of professional territories. Equally, he is questioning whether a meaningful new professional tribe has, as yet, emerged. Drawing upon his experience of leading this merged area of activity for more than a decade, he is concerned about how effective synergy can be developed and progressed, what that would entail, how it should be staffed, and where it should sit within the organizational map. Here Whitchurch's (2008a, b) conceptualization of roles and spaces may offer helpful insights. These activities could certainly be viewed as "Third Space" functions. They may need permeable and fluid structures to work effectively, with multiple partnerships and lines of communication rather than singular reporting routes and chains of command.

In 2001 the American Association for Higher Education undertook a web-based survey of chief academic officers to explore views on Boyers' four forms of scholarship (O'Meara, 2005). Using the catch-all term 'chief academic officer' (CAO) was doubtless primarily a device to avoid clumsy lists of equivalent roles. Yet it also captured, perhaps subconsciously, an important dimension of developments in management in higher education. Currently a small number of universities have adopted, or are considering adopting, the titles chief operating officer and chief financial officer in place of historic titles such as registrar, university secretary, or bursar. The activities reporting to these post-holders are categorized as 'professional services', and, indeed, staff working in those areas are described as members of a specific professional service (e.g. strategic planning, finance, estates, human resources, careers, student services).

Titles such as chief operating officer or chief financial officer may seem redolent of the world of industry and commerce rather than academia. Presumably proponents would claim they are necessary to support the transformation and modernization of the management of universities. They might possibly argue, perhaps privately, that older titles have too much baggage associated with them. Indeed, the responses of some of those interviewed by Whitchurch (Chapter 10) might add support to the view that there is a need to shift the established balance of professional power. Of course, these innovations may be very limited in time and uptake, manifestations of Birnbaum's (2000) "management fads". However, if any of the experiments appear to enhance the standing of their institution successfully, that would be likely to attract interest from other potential adopters. Nor is the experiment without attractions, even at this early stage.

In Chapter 2 we referred to the large numbers of staff in universities, Rhoades' "invisible workforce" (Chapter 3), who are hugely under-represented in the research, for example, on identities in higher education, and who are often depicted in analyses, as Whitchurch explains in Chapter 10, as secondary and subservient players rather than crucial contributors to the collective endeavor. Thus, identifying such staff as part of professional services might be a helpful step toward enhancing understandings of their roles and contributions, and perhaps also toward opening improved career pathways. Whitchurch (2008a, b; and Chapter 10) has articulated frameworks that could be used to develop 'climbing frames' akin to those that Strike reported in Chapter 5 for academic faculty and research staff. Such structures should be enabling and readily capable of adjustments as circumstances change. Middlehurst (Chapter 13), Whitchurch (Chapters 10 and 14), and Gappa (Chapter 12) implicitly argue that 'one size fits all' solutions may not satisfy the expectations of individuals, or the evolving needs of institutions.

Stromquist et al. (2007) used six national vignettes to explore whether the contemporary professoriate was becoming diversified or segmented. They concluded that diversification should be welcomed, provided that safeguards were put in place over academic standards of programs and the working conditions of staff. Without such assurance, perhaps the full potential of creativity cannot be achieved, or staff be motivated and feel valued and rewarded, yet there seems to be a significant, although not necessarily incompatible, difference between these two agendas. Perhaps both agendas must be pursued. However, it would be singularly unfortunate to exhaust too much of the available energies and resources on the pursuit of standards and working conditions at the expense of fostering and nurturing the creativity of *all* staff, of effectively motivating them and of implementing ways of responding to their expectations, aspirations, and changing needs.

References

Birnbaum, R. (2000) *Management Fads in Higher Education.* San Francisco: Jossey-Bass.

Boyer, E. L. (1990) *Scholarship Reconsidered: Priorities for the Professoriate.* Princeton, NJ: Carnegie Foundation for the Advancement of Teaching.

Eraut, M. (1994) *Developing Professional Knowledge and Competence.* Oxford: Pergamon.

Harman, G. (2003) "Australian Academics and Prospective Academics: Adjustment to a More Commercial Environment." *Higher Education Management and Policy* 15 (3): 105–122.

Kehm, B. M. (2007) "The Changing Role of Graduate and Doctoral Education as a Challenge to the Academic Profession: Europe and North America Compared." In *Key Challenges to the Academic Profession,* ed. M. Kogan and U. Teichler. UNESCO Forum on Higher Education and International Centre for Higher Education Research. Kassel, Germany: INCHER-Kassel.

Kogan, M., Moses, I., and El-Khawas, E. (1994) *Staffing Higher Education.* London: Jessica Kingsley.

Kolsaker, A. (2008) "Academic Professionalism in the Managerialist Era: A Study of English Universities." *Studies in Higher Education* 33 (5): 513–526.

O'Meara, K. (2005) "Effects of Encouraging Multiple Forms of Scholarship Nationwide and across Institutional Types." In *Faculty Priorities Reconsidered,* ed. K. O'Meara and R. E. Rice. San Francisco: Jossey-Bass.

Rice, R. E. (1996) *Making a Place for the New American Scholar.* Washington, DC: American Association for Higher Education.

Rice, R. E. (2005) "The Future of the Scholarly Work of Faculty." In *Faculty Priorities Recommended,* ed. K. O'Meara and R. E. Rice. San Francisco: Jossey-Bass.

Stromquist, N. P., Gil-Anton, M., Colatrella, C., Mabokela, R. O., Smolentseva, A., and Balbachevsky, E. (2007) "The Contemporary Professoriate: Towards a Diversified or Segmented Profession?" *Higher Education Quarterly* 61 (2): 114–135.

Torstendahl, R. (1990) "Introduction: Promotion and Strategies of Knowledge-Based Groups." *Academic Work: The Changing Labour Processes in Higher Education,* ed. R. Torstendahl and M. Burrage. London: Sage.

9

Traditions of Academic Professionalism and Shifting Academic Identities

CRAIG McINNIS

Introduction

Academic faculty have long claimed special privileges and status as autonomous professionals within their institutions and society in general: "As if it were a birthright, they struggle for self-government, invoking powerful doctrines— academic freedom, community of scholars, freedom of research—which serve both as guild ideologies and as the justification for unusual personal liberties" (Clark, 1987a: 372). The core values underpinning a tradition of autonomy and self-regulation in the workplace are still invoked by academic faculty in response to ongoing government intervention and institutional reform. Individual autonomy in the workplace is vigorously defended even, in extreme cases, where it runs counter to the strategic goals of institutions or threatens the survival of academic departments. In particular, the loss of academic identity is cited as a self-evident consequence of a higher education managerial environment driven by market competition and the pressure to generate income.

In this dramatically changed landscape the operation of the contemporary university relies on a burgeoning cadre of strategic and support specialists (Finkelstein, 2007; Whitchurch, 2006, 2008). As a consequence, new dynamics in the workplace are testing the core elements that traditionally define and sustain academic identities, including their sense of authority, autonomy, and capacity for self-regulation. Understanding the sources of academic identity, and appreciating its significance in the fabric of university operations, is critical to institutional success. Indeed, Clark argues that the identities that evolve from the academic socialization process "may be more powerful than those of mate, lover, and family protector, or those that come from community, political party, church, and fraternal orders" (1987b: 80). Likewise, Henkel points to the special nature of academic identity: "as of central symbolic and instrumental significance both in the lives of individual academics and in the workings of the academic profession" (2000: 13).

This chapter is concerned with the impact of the changing composition of the workforce in universities, alongside the increasingly systematic efforts to manage academic work roles, and on what it means to be 'an academic'. The chapter provides examples of issues affecting the roles and status of academic faculty as professionals, particularly with respect to the centrality of academic freedom and self-regulation in the workplace. The significance of these values for academic productivity, and as sources of work satisfaction, is considered in relation to the institutional management of work and professional development, and their impact on the roles and status of academic faculty.

Academic Identity under Pressure

Henkel explores three major sources of academic identity—the discipline, the institution, and the profession—to assess "the extent to which major change in the politics and structures of higher education has also meant major change in what it means to be an academic in the UK" (2000: 13). The underlying assumption is that academic identity drives the commitment and productivity of individuals and, importantly, the workings of academic systems characterized as "loose coupling mechanisms, horizontal distribution of authority, and collegial governance likely to depend heavily on exchange relationships" (ibid.: 20). The problematic nature of the academic profession and the notion of professional identity are discussed in the following section, with particular emphasis on the challenges to academic authority, freedom, and self-regulation.

A Fragmented Profession

Perkin (1969) argued that academic faculty are the "key profession" in that they are the primary educators for the professions. However, the very notion of an academic profession is contested and generally regarded at best as a weak source of academic identity (Henkel, 2000: 21), and, as Clark observes,

> [i]t is not astonishing that the academic profession as a whole is primarily fragmented rather than integrated by professionalism, because professional attachment forms first around the discipline. The academic profession is qualitatively different from all other professions in the extent of this fragmentation. It is inherently a secondary organization of persons located in numerous diverse fields that operate as primary centers of membership, identity, and loyalty.
>
> (1987a: 381)

Nevertheless, there are signs that a new era of professional identity is emerging for academic faculty, partly as a product of adaptation to the managerial environment and partly as a response to the presence of the new generation of specialist staff in the contemporary university who increasingly expect parity of status as professionals in their own right, and who also compete with academics for status and authority. With that in mind, it is useful at this point to consider what it means to be a professional across a range of occupations and, in turn, what this means for academic identity.

Sullivan (2000) suggests three perspectives of professionalization. The first focuses on the control over the market for services gained by superior knowledge combined with claims of special moral integrity. The second emphasizes the cultural and social authority to define and control a specific area of expertise, particularly scientific knowledge, and therefore to assert autonomy in the workplace and prestige in society. Finally, there is the perspective of professionalization as an ideology of social reform, with social responsibility as the primary characteristic.

The notion of professionalism underpins the formation of professional identity in all fields of endeavor involving advanced knowledge, particularly in those fields traditionally associated with a sense of vocation or calling, where moral values and work values are closely interrelated to the point where they become relatively indistinguishable (Sullivan, 2000). When professionals are threatened by external regulation, or their knowledge and expertise are challenged in the workplace, they invariably raise the loss of professional identity and the undermining of their professionalism as an issue.

Professionalism is generally characterized in terms of the level of self-regulation and personal autonomy professionals have over their decisions about how their expertise will be applied. The professions are also collegial in their defense of the collective good, their control over the education and induction of members, and their adherence to a code of ethical practice. These observations are made with reference to the medical profession and the threats to its collective professional identity from a curtailment of the "privileges of self-regulation and self-policing" (Sullivan, 2000: 673). This is due, in part, to the rise of new professions and "para-professions" that has accompanied the need across all professions for higher skill levels to manage more complex technologies, to respond to intensified external scrutiny and regulation, and to deal with the myriad challenges associated with working in globalized knowledge economies. The deference shown to these professions in workplace hierarchies that once confirmed and reinforced their sense of professional identity is no longer assured. The general principles, and threats, apply to professionals more generally as well as to academic faculty.

The work of the learned professions has long been understood to require a significant domain of discretion in individual practice. It has therefore been thought to require a stronger sense of moral dedication than most occupations (Sullivan, 2000: 673). Professionals in this sense, and particularly academic professionals, believe they have a moral obligation to assert their freedom. Professionals operating at this level are also assumed to be focusing on higher values associated with responsibility to clients and the public good. Service is valued more highly than personal profit. Indeed, the public support for their long and intensive training, and the infrastructure in which they work, is considered to be part of the social contract between the professional and the public.

Identity can be interpreted as a sense of sameness and of being recognized with others of the same kind. It suggests the possession of a distinctive set of characteristics including roles, values, and behaviors developed in both formal and informal processes of socialization. These qualities are relatively stable over time and readily recognized as distinctive attributes of both the role and the person. Identity is therefore more than a persona adapted to suit particular circumstances. Academic faculty share key characteristics of identity with other professionals: their moral and work values are closely tied, perhaps more intensely than most; their core values are exceptionally stable, sometimes to the point of intransigence and self-defeat in the face of new realities; and their commitment to an ideology of reform and the public good remains undiminished. Most striking is their continued preference for service over personal profit, with salary taking second place to the pursuit of knowledge. They hold collegiality high on their list of defining values.

The professionalization of fields such as medicine and law has resulted in collective mobility in terms of social status and economic security, although some fields, such as teaching and nursing, have been less successful in achieving these outcomes (Sullivan, 2000: 673). In contrast, there are generally negative observations on the status and security outcomes for academic faculty, particularly with respect to their sometimes "bizarre" career paths (Altbach and Musselin, 2008: 2), and the impact of casualization, which appears to be a common element across national systems in otherwise idiosyncratic academic employment and working conditions (Enders, 2000: 31).

Discipline and Institutional Allegiances

It is commonly observed that academic faculty are divided in their loyalties between their disciplines and their institutions, with the latter generally taking second place. However, Ruscio (1987) argues that the discipline and the institution do not compete with one another. Nor does he see the competition resolved by individuals falling into identities fixed around being either a "cosmopolitan", active in the wider international research community, or a "local", bounded by the institution and concentrating efforts on teaching and administration. Instead, Ruscio describes a "subtle, intricate interaction with many nuances . . . as we move through the various disciplines and across the many institutions, each with its own culture." In systems with highly diverse institutional settings, such as the United States, the academic profession is more obviously "a creature of its organizational setting" (Ruscio, 1987: 331). In contrast, in national systems that are almost entirely public, such as those of Australia and the United Kingdom, the level of diversity tends to be limited to variations around a relatively standard model of comprehensive universities meeting local and regional needs. Institutional differences in mission and in the profile of faculty are not as pronounced.

Becher's (1989) investigation of academic "tribes and territories" provides a comprehensive picture of the myths, unifying symbols, and contested borders that reflect and reinforce the complex and overlapping disciplinary cultures in which academic identities are forged. Accommodating the subtle and sometimes arcane differences between the many disciplinary cultures can confound the best-laid plans for institutional workplace reform:

> In the world of scholarship, the activities . . . centre on each discipline. Thus, theoretically at least, we have the academic profession, one for each discipline. Each discipline has its own history, its own intellectual style, a distinct sense of timing, different preferences for articles and books, and different career lines.

> (Light, 1974, cited in Becher, 1987)

Ruscio's analysis (1987: 332) works from the premise that "[i]nstitutional differences ... remain in the shadows. Institutional affiliation comes after the training, after the socialization." However, this should not diminish the significant role of the institution in the development of academic faculty as professionals. As Parsons (1951) observed, the status of the faculty of a university gave individuals a clearly institutionalized role with a source of remuneration and a "market" for their products—that is, students and professional colleagues, and the provision of facilities for their research.

Change and Diversity in Professional Socialization

Two key points of difference between academic faculty and other professional groups concern those identified earlier as control over entry to the market, and the authority to define the specific area of expertise. In the absence of an overarching professional registration body that might manage entry or set boundaries, academic faculty have only limited and indirect control over the membership of the academy. Once qualified and appointed to a position, they were, traditionally, not directly accountable to their colleagues. The expectation of self-regulation is derived partly from a sense of egalitarianism, sometimes to the point of benign neglect: "Once admitted to the academic profession, individuals, who might be quite young, were assumed to be functioning, independent practitioners, within the dominant norm of self-regulation" (Henkel, 2000: 169).

In contrast to the education and development of the traditional professions, Becher (1989: 110) observed that for academic faculty "there is no such thing as a standard career pattern which spans the range of intellectual activity." With this cautionary note in mind, it is generally the case that the professional socialization process for faculty begins during postgraduate studies and the acquisition of a doctorate, although the development of an interest in a field of study emerges earlier, in the undergraduate years, when students are drawn to particular subjects as well as to people of like skills, passions, and outlooks. As part of a longitudinal study of graduate education, Austin and colleagues examined the graduate experience as preparation for the academic career:

> Aspiring faculty members begin their graduate education with enthusiasm and idealism about engaging in meaningful work. Some used the term "passion" to describe their excitement about the questions in their disciplines or fields they wanted to pursue. For others, sharing their enthusiasm for the discipline or field with students is a primary motivation. . . . They want to engage in work that has a positive impact on the students with whom they come in contact or on the broader society and work that has personal significance for them.
>
> (Austin, 2002: 106–107)

There are considerable discipline-based variations in the socialization process and the ways identities are shaped. Graduate students in hard-pure subjects such as physics are expected to behave like employees "in an enterprise that requires their collaboration and their conformity", whereas those in soft-pure disciplines such as history "are treated like self-employed persons or individuals of independent means" (Becher, 1987: 282). Nevertheless, while academic faculty may research and teach in collaboration with others, for the most part their training as research students involves a significant amount of work conducted in isolation, they are examined as soloists for their dissertations, and if there is company behind them it is muted, thus establishing or perhaps reinforcing a lifelong preference for individual achievement.

The range of alternative pathways into the academic profession is increasing. One of the most salient features of the new workplace realities is the growth in the range and complexity of enterprises and external partnerships in which universities are now involved. Individuals now work in diverse local and global settings that require engagement with multiple organizations, some of which overlap while others operate in parallel. As universities strive to work more closely with employers, academic appointments in vocational areas demand experience in the relevant industry. In an effort to maintain their credibility, some individuals insist on extending their multiple identities to embrace their vocational origins as lawyers, accountants, psychologists, and so on, even when their work as practitioners in the field has become negligible.

In the case of vocationally oriented fields, where experience in the workplace is a prerequisite, the doctorate may follow appointment to an academic position, and may even be a condition for ongoing employment and promotion. These alternative pathways are increasingly common with the casualization of the academic workforce and the increase in adjunct positions as institutions grapple with the competition for talent and skills shortages in many fields.

Challenges to Academic Authority, Autonomy, and Freedom

The elements of professional identity common to academic faculty, regardless of the considerable diversity in disciplinary and institutional contexts, center on their authority in the field of study, personal autonomy, and academic freedom in the workplace. This is, for many, the major attraction of an academic career over more favorable salaries and conditions in other walks of life. The dominant academic values in a classic autonomous university and department are typically considered to be concerned with "the disinterested search for knowledge, the critical approach to received knowledge and forms of social arrangements, and respect for logic and evidence" (Kogan, 1996: 244). In the research-intensive universities these values assume that academic faculty are, first and foremost, people engaged in scholarly pursuits as specialists in specific branches of study. Being regarded by peers as an authority on a specific subject area is a significant element in academic identity, with 'expert of international standing' as the highest accolade. In these contexts, peer-assessed research drives performance and reinforces identities; the same cannot be said for faculty with more generalist teaching roles and little or no research profile.

Chief among the distinctive characteristics of academic identity associated with autonomy is the universal expectation on the part of individuals that they have the freedom to pursue their own intellectual interests. That is, they believe they should be able to decide what they will research and teach, usually, although not always, within the limits of their disciplinary expertise. Henkel's empirical work confirms that "[b]elief in the importance of academic freedom as a source of motivation and as a necessary condition of the advancement of knowledge remains a powerful force in academic cultures" (2005: 151).

Universities have generally protected the freedom of academic faculty to carry out their functions "in the face of forces of society which tend to interfere with it" (Parsons, 1951: 343). While high-profile cases of universities curtailing academic freedom might suggest that this is no longer the case, academic freedom remains a contested and complex area of debate, as evidenced by the submissions to a recent inquiry into academic freedom (Australian Senate, 2008). There is little systematic evidence to support the view that institutions are less likely to protect academic freedoms now than they were fifty years ago. Nevertheless, significant threats are raised by a number of recent developments influencing the behavior of institutions, including the commercialization of research, the difficulty in obtaining research funding, and the impact of counterterrorism legislation (MacDonald and Williams, 2007).

Most academic faculty have little cause in their careers to exercise the academic freedoms that might bring them into public conflict with their institutions and governing bodies, but they reserve the right to do so. However, they are increasingly likely to encounter mission-driven initiatives that threaten their right and capacity to make choices about what they research and teach, and, to some extent, how they work. The in-principle freedom to research and teach as they choose means in effect that academic faculty have traditionally defined and owned their work. Their value-rational orientation pushes them to explore issues that may or may not be in the interests of government agendas, the institution that employs them, or external stakeholders that fund their research or employ their graduates. Indeed, the issues that absorb faculty may have little immediate consequence outside a small circle of colleagues with similar interests. To translate this ownership into everyday terms, when they are asked about their working week it is not unusual for them to respond that they have been very busy but have not had any time for their 'own work'. This is almost incomprehensible for those who define work as something that occurs in a time and place managed and supervised by an organization.

In contrast to most workers, academic faculty have also been able to declare their preferences for the type of work that best suits their interests and the subjects about which they are enthusiastic at a particular point in time. They are generally able to build their careers accordingly, and may even choose to change direction and the emphasis they give to teaching and research to align with their career stage or to maximize their chances of ongoing employment or promotion. The respondents in the Henkel sample focus mostly on their own work, and their perspectives are concerned with exploring the issues, questions, and problems that they as individuals choose to pursue (Henkel, 2000: 189). The primary motive is to maintain continuity in the themes of research and teaching. This provides them with a sense of personal satisfaction and credibility among the particular community of scholars, satisfies the desire to make an original and ongoing contribution to knowledge, and creates opportunities to open up new areas of discovery. It is not surprising to find that there is a high level of migration among academic faculty across disciplinary subfields and specialisms as they follow their interests (Becher, 1989: 118).

However, making choices about teaching and research is increasingly less likely for large numbers of individuals. Most prefer to do both, although the trend has been toward a preference for research. The casualization of the academic workforce—mostly in teaching positions—is the obvious example of change in this respect. That does not necessarily mean that all academic faculty on casual or fractional appointments are unhappy about their lack of choice; many have chosen to take casual appointments for a range of lifestyle reasons, and are on the whole more satisfied with their jobs than those with full-time tenure (McInnis, 2000: 137). The issue is that as the critical mass of those without these choices grows, there are fewer left to argue the case for autonomy and freedom to pursue their personal intellectual interests, and of course the norms that reinforce academic identities shift. Moreover, the nature of freedom and autonomy among tenured faculty over what is researched and taught can no longer be taken for granted. The pressure to generate income from teaching and research means that increasing numbers are teaching in subjects for which they do not feel qualified, and are involved in research and commercial activities that are not necessarily of great personal interest. These are pragmatic responses to current institutional and personal realities.

Decline of Self-Regulation and Work Satisfaction

The workplace challenges facing universities that directly impact on academic identity over the past decade or so have been widely discussed (Coaldrake and Stedman, 1999; Henkel, 2005; Whitchurch, 2008). In emphasizing the impact of the discipline and the institution in the formation and maintenance of academic identity, Henkel (2000) acknowledges the risk that this ignores the significance of the everyday reality of academic working lives. Self-regulation in the management of work and its implications for academic identity are easily underestimated as a defining element in academic identities. Academic faculty place a premium on the freedom they have to manage their work in ways that suit their personal priorities and approaches to research and teaching.

Autonomy over what individuals will teach and research extends to setting their own priorities and organizing daily work patterns within the relatively permeable constraints of institutional structures and processes. While their idiosyncratic approach to the management of time and task is often a source of tension between them and others in the workplace, it is justified on the grounds that self-regulation is a prerequisite for discovery, and correlates with productivity. This creates a key point of tension with the increasingly professionalized cadre of specialists in the workplace who have less autonomy over their work, time, and location, and who are entirely focused on the achievement of institutional strategic goals. The way in which these tensions are being resolved is of considerable significance for the future of academic identity and productivity, which is in turn critical to the performance of institutions.

The growing complexity of university operations and the pressure of external demands have also led to the fragmentation of academic work and challenged the extent to which academic faculty can continue to maintain traditional levels of self-regulation and control. The fragmentation has led to excessive workloads, fueled largely by administrative work, particularly that associated with compliance and performance management. This accounts for most of the increase in work-loads over the past decade (McInnis, 2000: 125) and has major implications for individuals and their sense of autonomy with respect to the self-regulation of work.

Reconceptualization of what it means to be 'an academic' is occurring incre-mentally as the form and management of their work change by default. The integrity of academic identity is tested by the extent to which individuals are able to choose to give priority to a plethora of initiatives in the contemporary university. Their capacity for choice is also being reshaped by the changing context of everyday work practices, accountabilities, and compliance demands, which gives them little or no room to opt out of institutional mission-driven goals. This presents major challenges to the sources of work satisfaction that sustain the distinctive nature of academic identities.

Coaldrake and Stedman examined the impact of changing roles and policies on academic work. Their analysis points to the gap in policies that recognize the need for change in work roles at an institutional level, but fail to address the realities of academic culture that underpin the organization of universities and thus limit capacity for change:

> In the main, academic work has stretched rather than adapted to meet the challenges posed by transformations of the higher education sector. The preference of many universities and individual academics is to allow accumulations and accretion rather than to undertake the more difficult and threatening task of making strategic choices and reconceptualising what it means to be an academic.
>
> (1999: 9)

This requires close consideration of the relationship between academic work motives and sources of satisfaction. A review of theoretical perspectives on academic work satisfaction by Lacy and Sheehan (1997: 306) identified Herzberg et al.'s (1959) two-factor theory of satisfaction as an explanatory model for the academic profession. The intrinsic factors are those related to the actual content of the tasks. Extrinsic factors include salary, security, and benefits. The important point here is that each factor can be high or low with respect to satisfaction—that is, while the extrinsic context factors can be significant sources of dissatisfaction, the intrinsic factors can remain as sources of satisfaction. These factors are directly tied to the central elements that maintain a sense of academic identity. Changes in the workplace that impact on these factors threaten the strength and stability of academic identity, and that in turn undermines academic productivity.

The main predictor of work satisfaction for academic faculty, clearly ahead of salary and job security, is the opportunity to pursue their own academic interests (McInnis and Anderson, 2005: 143). The second most important set of predictors concern factors that hinder academic work, such as the negative impact on teaching too many students, or the difficulty of obtaining adequate funding for research activity. A particularly strong negative predictor is "having to teach outside your area of academic expertise", which is obviously at odds with the need for a sense of authority in the subject area. However, it appears that otherwise bad conditions are somewhat mitigated by individuals' commitment to particular tasks, pre-eminently their love of research. This commitment is most likely to be sustained if it reinforces the sense of academic identity that attracts academic faculty to their careers in the first place. In contrast, where the opportunity to pursue individual interests in teaching and research is limited, commitment declines.

Identity and Organizational Cultures

The presence of contrasting and competing discipline-based organizational cultures within universities amplifies the idiosyncratic nature of academic identities. It provides an additional layer of protection for academic freedom and autonomy, and challenges institutional preference for uniform policy implementation. Strategic and operational plans of universities are invariably written with caveats that their successful outcomes are conditional in that they allow for faculty and school differences in interpretation and application.

In Clark's study of academic life in the United States he refers to the "enclosures of culture" (1987b: 105). Academic identity and the disciplinary cultures in schools and departments are tightly bonded and create distinct local organizational cultures. The perspectives and values that characterize the local permutations of academic identity are cultural biases, "worldviews or ideologies entailing deeply held values and beliefs defending different patterns of social relations" (Dake and Wildavsky, 1990: 42). The disciplinary cultures generate significantly different organizational cultures within institutions at the level of the school or department that sharpen differences in academic identities (McInnis, 1996).

Each culture sets the boundaries for membership and the norms for interaction and work roles. For example, there are major differences in the ways in which doctoral research is supervised. Whereas some disciplines assume that supervisors are actively engaged in the research of their graduate students, others are comfortable with supervisors having little or no detailed knowledge of the student's topic. These relationships are reflected in the preferred organizational forms of disciplinary cultures that shape and reinforce the identities of their members.

In disciplines that lean toward hierarchical organizational arrangements, the forms of knowledge and traditions of scholarship tend to create relatively sharp social divisions that prescribe the ways in which the members interact. The values central to the academic identity of the members in these cases are focused on continuity and stability rather than on change. This contrasts strongly with egalitarian academic cultures, where, in keeping with the social ideology of the disciplines, formal lines of authority and hierarchy are likely to be opposed. Without clearly articulated roles and regulations, the relationships between individuals are ambiguous, and departments prone to factional splits. In these cases, academic identity is closely tied to the value of unity within the group in terms of ways of thinking about the subject or field and the socialization of new members, including students.

A third example of an academic culture shaping academic identities is one that puts the individual academic at the center, where identity is achieved rather than ascribed. The culture is one of performance defined by a high level of competitive individualism. Academic faculty in these organizational cultures prefer the mutual convenience of loose social arrangements between individuals. They maximize their choice and freedom to resist regulation. Entrepreneurialism and market competition lead, for example, to course structures that provide students with a wide array of subject choices that reflect the idiosyncratic interests of the academic faculty.

A fourth academic culture is of the type characterized by Douglas (1978) as an insulative culture, in that it is strongly prescriptive in its control over the behavior of individual faculty members, but somewhat weak in the social bonds that hold the group together. This is the kind of environment in which doctoral research students are loosely linked to highly specialized subgroups. At this point in the socialization process, those outside the institution play an especially strong role in the formation of academic identities.

The Impact of Institutional Management on the Roles and Status of Academic Faculty

As universities strive to meet the demands of their key stakeholders, compete in local and global markets, and advance their reputations, it is hardly surprising that they have taken a more systematic and whole-of-institution approach to managing the performance of academic faculty. This is evident in the rise of formal induction processes and workload management plans, and the development of leadership capabilities at all levels of operation. Institutions are also motivated by strategic goals that require, for example, a uniformly high level of quality in the student experience, and the integration of information technologies across the whole institution. These and other areas of mission-driven changes are having a direct impact on the roles and status of academic faculty, and indirectly reshaping their identities.

There is of course debate as to the extent to which the management reforms of recent years such as these have actually reduced the powerful role of collegiality, or shifted power relations between managers and academic faculty, to the point where the latter no longer consider themselves as "self-directing beings acting autonomously within a relatively liberal environment" (Kolsaker, 2008: 517). The management of individuals is likely to become more obviously shaped by institutional goals. It is also likely that academic faculty, particularly the new generation, are not necessarily as uncomfortable with these developments as their predecessors (ibid.).

Institutional Management of Academic Productivity

Universities are working at improving academic productivity on a number of fronts, with almost seamless programs that incorporate professional development, appraisal, and reward systems. The academic profession has not been formally responsible or accountable for the training of juniors, and there are no rewards and sanctions involving the profession as a collective entity. As noted earlier, in the past many junior faculty experienced benign neglect in their formative years. Some disciplines do have ways of influencing, but not controlling, the behavior of their members. Ultimately, the primary source of control over the workplace behavior of academic faculty is the institution in which they are employed, with varying levels of collegial input.

Driven largely by external accountability demands, institutions almost universally now take responsibility for inducting academic faculty and training them for their core roles. Academic identities are being shaped for teaching by a range of in-house specialists based in academic development units. Specialists from human resources departments, experts in organizational leadership, and professional development staff at institution and school level are assuming more prominence in structuring and delivering systematic programs to ensure that individuals are guided and supported in their endeavors.

Systematic preparation of early-career faculty members is now the norm at both national and institutional levels in the United Kingdom, the United States, and Australia. Almost all universities now have comprehensive professional development programs for both research and teaching, although their reach and impact vary considerably. These mandatory programs frequently provide formal qualifications in university teaching, which, despite early resistance, appear to be gaining acceptance as a part of the natural order. These activities are supported with formal mentoring arrangements, supervisor training, annual performance appraisals, and career planning. The disciplines exert a stronger influence in the case of large faculties and schools where local development units establish their own systemic induction and support programs. The comprehensiveness of the programs, the level of compliance, and the accountability of supervising academic faculty and leaders clearly challenge notions of academic status and authority.

Concerns about institutional productivity and performance have also led to more systematic institution-wide arrangements for the management of academic workloads. This is partly in response to the reality of more demanding and complex workloads, and partly in response to government and market pressure on universities to improve productivity levels. Full Economic Costing requirements in the United Kingdom have generated an array of strategies to manage workloads

(Barrett and Barrett, 2008), and their effectiveness varies accordingly. It is important to recognize that increasing numbers of academic faculty no longer work within the framework of a single campus, many work in more than one department, and most now teach and manage large classes of students from diverse backgrounds. The logistics of managing work time across multiple locations and learning settings present a further and formidable set of challenges. Notwithstanding well-intentioned efforts to address issues of overwork and work-related stress, institutional codification of work time and activity strikes at the core value of self-regulation.

Workload management plans are closely tied to institutional strategic plans and operational targets. They provide an opportunity for institutions to articulate the preferred emphasis in the balance of work activities as they relate to the institutional mission. While diverse disciplinary interests are generally acknowledged, research activities that contribute most to institutional performance are given priority status. Similarly, the institutional priorities given to teaching activities might give emphasis to particular modes of course delivery, types of students, or the amount of time and energy spent on managing the student experience.

Occasionally, motivated by concerns about both the welfare of academic faculty and perceptions of institutional performance, some universities have decreed that individuals should keep prescribed office hours. However, these proposals are generally short-lived, and more collegial and creative solutions to workload issues have emerged. These appear to have some success where collegiality and transparency are evident. The pattern in Australia and the United Kingdom is for workload management plans to be devised in general terms at the institution level, and then interpreted to accommodate local and disciplinary conditions in schools and departments. Nevertheless, establishing common principles for the allocation of workloads, even where allowances are made for the diversity of disciplines, promotes normative models of how faculty ought to work. There is little evidence to date that the plans necessarily improve productivity, performance, or work satisfaction. The implementation of institutional norms for academic workload is also problematic, since it may well work against advice from successful scholars on ways of improving personal productivity (Wildavsky, 1989).

The Impact of Learning Technologies

The proliferation of new information technologies provides perhaps the most striking example of contemporary pressures on academic identities, specifically their authority and autonomy in the workplace. It presents a volatile mix of forces with the potential to transform academic identities. The outcomes of this transformation have direct implications for the creation, preservation, synthesis, and transmission of knowledge at the heart of academic endeavor. New technologies have also opened up opportunities for specialists in flexible delivery to claim a central role in managing the teaching and learning process, as well as the broader experience of students. The online delivery of subjects and resources has given specialists in learning management systems a central role in the process of developing curriculum content, the pattern of learning sequences, and forms of assessment: "It is not uncommon for academics to find their professional judgement and preferences overridden by institutional solutions to technical incompatibilities with learning management systems or enrolment and results processes" (McInnis, 2005: 86).

The impact of technology is not confined to knowledge production or new approaches to curriculum design and delivery. The nature of the work is being reconceptualized, with new expectations about the management of academic performance and productivity made possible by course delivery technology. Coaldrake and Stedman (1999) identify possibilities created by information technologies for the "unbundling" of academic work and its redistribution within institutions. They suggest a number of areas involved in the transformation of teaching that can be managed almost exclusively by specialist professional staff, including, for example, the assessment of students' credentials and giving credit for entry; advising students through choices of study options; designing and developing resources used in learning, including textbooks, videos, and computer packages; delivering instruction, for example, by lecturing or demonstrating practical work in laboratories; and assessing, evaluating, and providing feedback on student progress. These technology-based teaching and advisory activities, and the associated administrative tasks, "shift the focus of academic time from designated face-to-face contact hours to more distributed patterns of activities" (ibid.: 7).

While some of these tasks are not necessarily technology dependent, in the complex world of mass higher education the search for efficiencies has given priority to technologies. In the process, the sharing of control over what were formerly academic domains has created significant role ambiguity for academic faculty. New technologies require individuals to share their work with others, partly because of the need for technical expertise and partly because the scale of the teaching enterprise requires the kind of systematic planning and sophisticated delivery that are beyond the capacity of a single person. Since technologies are being used to accommodate large numbers of students and to capture bigger markets, major changes to the way in which work is organized are involved (McInnis, 2002: 59).

The technologies also enable the collection of information about the time, location, and nature of student activity to be readily accessed and analyzed. Although academic faculty find it to their advantage to cite such measures as student usage rates and the reach of their electronic delivery modes in support of their performance reports, the same data sources are being used by supervisors, senior executives, institutional planners, and quality auditors with a strategic interest in student progress and learning outcomes. The potential impact on the academic identity of individuals is significant, and the measures that are most readily available set the standards for individual performance. Instead of a "broad repertoire of assessment methods ... needed to capture the work of the faculty" (Braskamp and Ory, 1994: 22), a fragmented picture of academic work, and therefore identity, is likely to be the outcome of greater technical specificity in the measures made possible by institutional databases.

Institutional Management of the Student Experience

The student learning experience in universities is in a process of continuous and significant transformation. In response to national priorities for productivity and skill development in the workforce, the focus of policymakers has shifted to more formal approaches to the governance and management of the student experience in order to ensure successful learning outcomes. For individuals, this means, among other things, more evidence-based performance management, participation in systematic professional development programs, and close working relationships with support specialists. The activities of the specialists who share responsibility for the quality of the student experience include involvement in a wide range of activities: managing, for example, student transition and retention, work-integrated learning, study abroad programs, study skill development for international students, and graduate employment opportunities.

The strategic interest in the management of the student experience has also generated closer partnerships between academic faculty and external stakeholders. In a market-oriented environment—where graduate employability is a pre-eminent measure of institutional performance—members of faculty need to work closely with professional registration bodies in defining and managing the student experience. In some professional areas, particularly those with a diffused disciplinary base such as nursing and teacher education, registration boards exert considerable influence over the content and form of the curriculum, as well as approaches to teaching. The threat of courses not being accredited, and of graduates being rendered unemployable, leaves academic faculty in vocationally driven schools and departments with little option but to comply with the demands of registration and accreditation bodies.

Professionalizing Leadership

Unlike professionals in other fields who move into management roles, academic leaders often maintain some research and teaching activity to sustain a fundamental passion for knowledge in their field. Department heads go to considerable lengths to downplay their leadership roles and characterize them as temporary positions; indeed, fewer than 10 percent of academic faculty indicate a career interest in administration (McInnis, 2000: 123). Even those who change career paths into senior executive leadership positions find it difficult to let go of their primary source of identity. The connection with the discipline may also serve a number of other purposes. It allows the leader to assert credibility as a 'card-carrying' member of academic faculty in the collegial decision-making process. It also keeps them up to date with changes in teaching and research that might inform and legitimize decision making, and maintains a presence in the field for re-entry into full-time teaching and research, or for post-retirement continuity in adjunct appointments. But these are perhaps trivial against the primary motive of satisfying the deep personal need to be respected as a member of a scholarly community engaged in the life of the mind—that is, to maintain an academic identity.

New academic leadership roles have emerged in recent times to manage strategic goals of institutions, to address accountability requirements, and to position institutions for grants and rewards flowing from a range of new national bodies such as the Higher Education Academy in the United Kingdom. The proliferation of academic leadership roles reporting to deans and heads of department include associate dean positions with specialist designations such as teaching, research, international development, industry, or community relations. These are often mirrored at the school or department level with, for example, associate head positions. The creation of leadership opportunities, and the professional development provided, has become a significant attraction for academic faculty since it provides a reward for demonstrated commitment and competence, increases opportunities for promotion, and provides alternative career paths.

This does not mean that individuals in these positions are any closer to central decision making; these leadership positions are essentially line-management roles. The everyday realities of the academic workplace are pushing collegial governance opportunities to one side, as individuals are increasingly faced with the prospect of choosing between being involved in governance or being mainstream academic faculty. Mid-career tenured faculty, who were once most likely to be involved in governance and decision making, are declining in numbers relative to the total academic workforce. Casualization not only reduces the critical mass of individuals involved in administration and governance, but also makes great demands on the reduced core of tenured faculty with respect to supervision and coordination responsibilities (McInnis, 2006: 124).

Conclusion

The impact of the changing dynamics in the workplace has significant implications for individual academic faculty and their sense of identity. Failure to acknowledge the importance of academic identity by institutions and policymakers puts the primary sources of motivation, commitment, and productivity at risk. The importance of self-regulation in the workplace, as a central element of academic identity, cannot be overstated. It is clearly possible for institutions to undermine academic productivity and to lose faculty by failing to address the values and work preferences of individuals that attract them to the profession and their positions in the first place. This has ramifications for institutional performance in the core business of teaching and research. The harsh reality for universities in the global competition for academic talent is that they face significant challenges in attracting, rewarding, and retaining outstanding faculty.

There is evidence that external forces are impinging on the values and work patterns of individuals that, if poorly understood and managed, can have a negative impact on morale, work satisfaction, and productivity (Finkelstein, 2007; McInnis and Anderson, 2005). Contrary to Ruscio's (1987) view that the discipline and the institution do not compete, there are signs of new tensions emerging. The competition from within the institution comes increasingly from the impera-tive to create seamless strategic plans that enhance national and international positioning. Moreover, the mission-driven agendas of the new cadre of professionals depend heavily on their capacity to engage academic faculty in collaborative initiatives. If there is an exchange relationship, it is an uneasy one for faculty, since the demands of new initiatives add to the already fragmented nature of their work and draw them away from their discipline-centric sources of rewards and satisfaction. It also means that individuals lose the sense of ownership that drives many of them to subordinate most aspects of their lives to their work (McInnis, 2000).

However, some caution is needed against overstating the trends assumed to be undermining traditional forms of academic identity. Recent evidence indicates that the traditional work roles and preferences of individuals have considerable resilience. For example, although the intensified competition for research funding in many national systems has pushed academic faculty into collaborative arrangements, they continue to conduct most of their research alone (Coates et al., 2008: 5). Likewise, the influence of the disciplines remains significant for individuals (McInnis, 2000; Henkel, 2005; Coates et al., 2008).

There is also a view that the literature has been overly negative, and that a process of adaptation is currently under way, with emerging evidence that academic faculty "appear to be crafting and re-crafting their identities as conditions change, possibly as elements of professionalism are appropriated by managerialist practices" (Kolsaker, 2008: 522). This is perhaps illustrated by the increasingly positive responses to professional development requirements, and to new leadership opportunities that are likely to be accepted as a sign of professionalism in the next generation of faculty. There also appears to be growing acknowledgment of the benefits of national and institutional accountability processes, despite the onerous nature of compliance requirements.

How successful universities are in responding to these challenges will depend on a shared understanding of the importance of academic identity to individual productivity and satisfaction. It will also require considerable adaptation and adjustment on the part of individual faculty if they are to learn how to share space with their specialist professional colleagues (Whitchurch, 2008). The diversity of organizational cultures within institutions complicates matters. The permutations of academic identities shaped by local settings include contrasting shades of individualism, and social arrangements that quickly become obvious when whole-of-university policy on such issues as academic workload management is introduced.

The question remains about how the presence of an increasingly large and diverse body of professional specialists, with considerable claim to status and power (and not merely 'parity of esteem') on campus, is likely to influence the values and behavior of individual faculty in the workplace. As the operational roles in universities become blurred and the lines of reporting more permeable, individuals have been forced incrementally to redefine their identity and work relationships, and to loosen their hold on traditional sources of authority.

The impact of the transformed higher education workplace on the values, motivation, and commitment of individual members of faculty has potentially negative consequences on their work satisfaction and productivity. However, the changing workplace also has the potential to enhance their standing and expertise, to their collective and individual advantage. The key to turning potential negatives into positives in the new academic workplace is to recognize and cultivate the core elements that sustain academic identities—that is, being an authority in a field of study, and being able to conduct work with an exceptionally high level of personal control.

References

Altbach, P. and Musselin, C. (2008) "Academic Career Structures: Bad Ideas." *International Higher Education* 53 (Fall): 2–3.

Austin, A. (2002) "Preparing the Next Generation of Faculty: Graduate School as Socialization to the Academic Career." *Journal of Higher Education* 73 (1): 94–122.

Australian Senate Standing Committee (2008) *Allegations of Academic Bias in Universities and Schools.*

Barrett, L. and Barrett, P. (2008) *The Management of Academic Workloads: Full Report on Findings.* Research and Development Series. London: Leadership Foundation for Higher Education.

Becher, T. (1987) "The Disciplinary Shaping of the Profession." In *The Academic Profession,* ed. B. Clark. Berkeley: University of California Press.

Becher, T. (1989) *Academic Tribes and Territories: Intellectual Enquiry and the Cultures of Disciplines.* Buckingham, UK: SRHE/Open University Press.

Braskamp, L. and Ory, J. (1994) *Assessing Faculty Work.* San Francisco: Jossey-Bass.

Clark, B. (1987a) *The Academic Profession.* Berkeley: University of California Press.

Clark, B. (1987b) *The Academic Life: Small Worlds, Different Worlds.* Princeton, NJ: Carnegie Foundation.

Coaldrake, P. and Stedman, L. (1999) "Academic Work in the Twenty-first Century: Changing Roles and Policies." Occasional Paper Series, September. Canberra: Department of Education, Training and Youth Affairs.

Coates, H., Goedegebuure, L., Van der Lee, J., and Meek, L. (2008) *The Australian Academic Profession in 2007: A First Analysis of the Survey Results.* Melbourne: ACER/CHEMP.

Dake, K. and Wildavsky, A. (1990) "Theories of Risk Perception: Who Fears What and Why." *Daedalus* 119 (4): 41–60.

Douglas, M. (1978) "Cultural Bias." Occasional Paper no. 35. London: Royal Anthropological Institute. In *In the Active Voice,* ed. M. Douglas. London: Routledge & Kegan Paul.

Enders, J. (2000) "Academic Staff in Europe: Changing Employment and Working Conditions." In *International Perspectives on Higher Education Research,* vol. 1: *Academic Work and Life: What It Is to Be an Academic and How This Is Changing,* ed. M. Tight. New York: JAI Elsevier.

Finkelstein, M. (2007) "Negotiating the New Academy." *Academic Matters: The Journal of Higher Education* (April): 14–18.

Henkel, M. (2000) *Academic Identities and Policy Change in Higher Education.* London: Jessica Kingsley.

Henkel, M. (2005) "Academic Identity and Autonomy Revisited." In *Governing Knowledge: A Study of Continuity and Change in Higher Education—A Festschrift in Honour of Maurice Kogan,* ed. I. Bleiklie and M. Henkel. Dordrecht, the Netherlands: Springer.

Herzberg, F., Mauser, B., and Snyderman, B. (1959) *The Motivation to Work.* New York: John Wiley.

Kogan, M. (1996) "The Institutional Aspects." In *Higher Education and Work,* ed. J. Brennan, M. Kogan, and U. Teichler. London: Jessica Kingsley.

Kolsaker, A. (2008) "Academic Professionalism in the Managerialist Era: A Study of English Universities." *Studies in Higher Education* 33 (5): 513–525.

Lacy, F. and Sheehan, B. (1997) "Job Satisfaction among Academic Staff: An International Perspective." *Higher Education* 34: 305–322.

Light, D. (1974) "The Structure of the Academic Profession." *Sociology of Education* 47 (1): 2–29.

MacDonald, E. and Williams, G. (2007) "Banned Books and Seditious Speech: Anti-terrorism Laws and Other Threats to Academic Freedom." *Australian and New Zealand Journal of Law and Education* 12 (1): 29–46.

McInnis, C. (1996) "Academic Cultures and Their Role in the Implementation of Government Policy in Higher Education." In *Higher Education and Work*, ed. J. Brennan, M. Kogan, and U. Teichler. London: Jessica Kingsley.

McInnis, C. (2000) "Changing Perspectives and Work Practices of Academics in Australian Universities." In *International Perspectives on Higher Education Research*, vol. 1: *Academic Work and Life: What It Is to Be an Academic and How This Is Changing*, ed. M. Tight. New York: JAI Elsevier.

McInnis, C. (2005) "The Governance and Management of Student Learning in Universities." In *Governing Knowledge: A Study of Continuity and Change in Higher Education*, ed. I. Bleiklie and M. Henkel. Dordrecht, the Netherlands: Kluwer.

McInnis, C. (2006) "Renewing the Place of Academic Expertise and Authority in the Reform of University Governance." In *Governance and the Public Good*, ed. W. Tierney. Albany: SUNY Press.

McInnis, C. and Anderson, M. (2005) "Academic Work Satisfaction in the Wake of Institutional Reforms in Australia." In *The Professoriate: Profile of a Profession*, ed. A. Welch. Dordrecht, the Netherlands: Springer.

Parsons, T. (1951) *The Social System*. London: Routledge & Kegan Paul.

Perkin, H. (1969) *Key Profession: The History of the Association of University Teachers*. London: Routledge.

Ruscio, K. (1987) "Many Sectors: Many Professions." In *The Academic Profession*, ed. B. Clark. Berkeley: University of California Press.

Sullivan, W. M. (2000) "Medicine under Threat: Professionalism and Professional Identity." *Canadian Medical Association Journal* 162 (5): 673–675.

Whitchurch, C. (2006) "Who Do They Think They Are? The Changing Identities of Professional Administrators and Managers in UK Higher Education." *Journal of Higher Education Policy and Management* 28 (2): 159–171.

Whitchurch, C. (2008) "Shifting Identities and Blurring Boundaries: The Emergence of *Third Space* Professionals in UK Higher Education." *Higher Education Quarterly* 62 (4): 377–396.

Wildavsky, A. (1989) *Craftways: On the Organization of Scholarly Work*. New Brunswick, NJ: Transaction.

10
Convergence and Divergence in Professional Identities

CELIA WHITCHURCH

Introduction

This chapter considers issues arising for staff who are loosely termed 'professional', who are likely to have both management responsibilities and specialist knowledge but who are also increasingly mobile with respect to their career paths, spheres of interest, and portfolios of activity. At the same time as universities have employed increasing numbers of specialist staff with expertise to deal with functions such as business development, marketing, and public relations, roles and identities have also become more fluid. Diversification, therefore, has been accompanied by a convergence not only between functions such as student recruitment and the promotion of the institution to new student markets, but also between professional and academic spheres of activity.

The chapter suggests that amid (and perhaps in spite of) pervasive discourses of "managerialism", joint working between professional and academic colleagues, which may include overlaps and crossovers of activity, is increasingly common, facilitating opportunities and outcomes for both groups of staff. However, such joint working tends to remain hidden from view because it is not easily articulated via formal organizational structures and processes. It is, therefore, likely to depend on individual initiatives, the skillful use of networks, and tacit understandings. In this context the concepts of "managerial" and "borderless professionals" offered by Rhoades and Middlehurst respectively in Chapters 3 and 13 are reviewed, alongside that of the "blended professional" (Whitchurch, 2009). While faculty are not excluded from these considerations, for the purposes of this chapter the focus is on people employed on professional contracts (albeit some of these may have shifted from academic contracts earlier in their careers).

These developments have been recognized in the United Kingdom, to some extent at least, in the introduction of a national Framework Agreement (Universities and Colleges Employers Association (UCEA), 2003), one aim of which was to give greater flexibility to institutions in rewarding and developing the different contributions that might be made by a range of staff. Such changes raise issues for both individuals and institutions about what it means to be a 'professional', and also 'a manager', in contemporary higher education. These are considered, alongside the implications of a loosening of boundaries, which may, as suggested by Strike in Chapter 5, lead to accommodations in formal structures, such as the creation of "career climbing frames" alongside step-by-step career ladders.

A Melting Pot?

While Becher's classic account (1989) of academic identity gives primacy to knowledge groupings ("territories") and disciplinary cultures ("tribes"), its second edition acknowledges that it is difficult to maintain firm parameters for these "tribes" and "territories" in more fluid, contemporary environments: "these properties are not only relative rather than absolute ... their attributions may change over time and space" (Becher and Trowler, 2001: 184). Furthermore, Becher and Trowler (2001: 194, 197) acknowledge that more identity work is needed to take account of the increasing diversity of institutional functions and locations, and the implications of these for institutions. Since 2001, evidence has accumulated that rigid boundaries are becoming less sustainable, not only between academic disciplines, but also between academic and other forms of professional activity. Increasingly, staff without academic contracts contribute to teaching and learning (Rhoades, 2007), research spin-out (Allen-Collinson, 2007; Hockey and Allen-Collinson, 2009), and a range of institutional projects in quasi-academic areas such as widening participation, outreach, and regional partnership (Whitchurch, 2008a, b). Likewise, Law in Chapter 11 demonstrates how those occupying converged library and information roles undertake teaching and research in relation to information literacy and digital resources. In common with staff in academic practice or educational development (Land, 2004, 2008), and institutional research (Harrington and Chen, 1995; Whitchurch, 2008b), these groups have their own professional associations, bodies of knowledge, and literatures.

These movements arise partly from the development of broadly based, extended projects across the university, which are no longer containable within clear boundaries and create new functional portfolios (Whitchurch, 2008b). These projects, such as student transitions, community partnership, and professional development, require staff who are capable of moving across boundaries and understanding ways in which different elements impact on the project as a whole. For instance, the student transitions project now encompasses contiguous activities such as marketing and recruitment, widening participation, student funding, welfare and disability, careers advice, and alumni relations. The human resources function, as well as encompassing all the legislative requirements associated with employing staff, incorporates staff development, equality and diversity, and work–life balance. These extended projects split and re-form to create new fields of activity. Professional staff in these types of areas are, therefore, increasingly mobile, and become involved in activities that in the past might have been regarded as the sole preserve of academic faculty, such as:

- authoring documentation associated with, for instance, major funding bids and learning support;
- speaking at outreach, induction, and study skills events;
- conducting recruitment visits at home and overseas;
- conducting negotiations with community and business partners;
- representing their institutions on national and international agencies.

Thus, increased functional specialization to meet legislative and market requirements is accompanied by less boundaried forms of working.

Both groups of staff are also likely to work and study side by side on senior management and leadership programs run by, for instance, the Harvard Graduate School of Education (in the United States), the Leadership Foundation for Higher Education (in the United Kingdom), and the L. H. Martin Institute for Higher Education Leadership and Management (in Australia). Furthermore, a growing number of professional staff have, or are acquiring, academic credentials, including doctoral qualifications, and/or teaching or management experience in post-compulsory education. Some of these people see themselves as moving into senior management roles that have traditionally been occupied by academic faculty, for instance, a pro-vice-chancellorship or provostship.

At the same time as changes are occurring for professional staff, academic faculty with traditional portfolios including teaching, research, and third-leg activity, work alongside other academic colleagues who may focus primarily on teaching or research, as well as with, for instance, contract workers who move from project to project (research or other types of project). Some faculty may move in the direction of 'management', taking on a top team role; others may move in a 'professional' direction, teaching on and researching into professional development or learning support. Such people may be co-located in a department of educational development that also caters for professional staff seeking management development.

No doubt because of the movements described above, it has proved difficult to encapsulate professional groupings within generic employment classifications, which contributes to a lack of clarity in understandings about roles, functions, and identities (Whitchurch, 2006). Kehm (2006) suggests that "new higher education professionals" represent emergent expertise, and Whitchurch (2008a, b) has described the development of a "Third Space" between professional and academic spheres of activity, in which "blended" roles occur, comprising components of what have been thought of traditionally as purely academic or purely professional activity (Whitchurch, 2009). Middlehurst (Chapter 13) demonstrates how the globalization of higher education has led to greater fluidity, and even instability, between academic disciplines, functional responsibilities, and institutional approaches to role definition, leading to concepts of professionals and professionalism that are "borderless", in that they cannot be fixed in time and space.

The following posts, advertised in a single issue of the UK publication *Times Higher Education* (February 26, 2009), offer a snapshot of the trend toward an increasingly fluid mix of activity within individual roles:

- *Learning and Teaching Manager in an academic department* (p. 57)
- *Head of Employer Led Curriculum Development* (p. 57)
- *Deputy Vice-Chancellor (Operations)* (p. 61)

Between them, these roles demand:

- a facility for developing networks;
- a confidence to operate in different milieus;

- an ability to conduct bridging activity with external partners;
- organizational skills, as well as an appreciation of the specific teaching and learning environment;
- management of multiple functions in complex environments;
- an ability to "deliver a sweeping transformational agenda".

Only one of the advertisements specified an academic qualification, although all required a track record in management. Furthermore, the fact that management roles are increasingly incorporated within academic schools, faculties, and departments, and are therefore embedded in Clark's "academic heartland" (1998), implies an expectation of joint working alongside academic colleagues, in management arrangements that are increasingly distributed (Bolden et al., 2008).

It is also significant that another post, advertised in the same issue of the *Times Higher Education*, which is described as what might be thought of as a traditional Director of Student Services role, places greater emphasis on experience of matrix management and customer relations per se than on experience in higher education, requiring someone "who may currently be leading a customer service function in the public or private sectors . . . [and] have experience of leading multifunctional teams and of developing and improving systems and processes" (p. 62). Another role, entitled Project Manager (Academic Development), which might well in the past have been seen as a 'service' role in relation to quality assurance, curriculum management, and governance, requires project experience in a higher education setting. The latter is written in a way that indicates an expectation of developmental rather than process-oriented activity, and is framed in terms of "work[ing] effectively in complex situations and with changing priorities . . . build[ing] alliances for change among stakeholders . . . liaison with colleagues in similar roles at other HE institutions" (p. 78).

This increasingly diverse mix of activities within and between roles may be parallel, complementary, or even conflicting. It has impacted on both professional identities and working practices, as described in Table 10.1, and contributes to a more complex institutional dynamic. The movements described above might also be seen as having a political dimension, in that they give rise to a broad spectrum of views. At one extreme, professional staff are seen primarily as having a service or support role, in which they "provide services and are therefore subservient. . . . They are not initiators or developers of the institution" (Pro-vice-chancellor, post-1992 UK university, quoted in Prichard, 2000: 190). Such views derive from an "academic civil service" tradition (Sloman, 1964; Lockwood, 1986). In this scenario, professional staff would be expected to provide technical, regulatory, and policy advice as members of a homogeneous cadre, whether they were in generalist or specialist roles. The prime purpose of these functions was to support decision making by academic colleagues, whose management responsibilities were likely to be additional to their academic interests, and to be for fixed terms of office. Such traditions may, in part, be responsible for claims of "invisibility" in an Australian context (Szekeres, 2004: 7) and also in a U.S. context (Rhoades, Chapter 3). They also continue in a number of European countries, where professional (and also

TABLE 10.1 Changes in Identity and Working Practices

Identities	Working practices
Specialization of expertise, e.g. marketing, business development	Mixed teams comprising professional staff and academic faculty making equivalent contributions
Professionalization, e.g. development programs; qualifications; establishment of body of knowledge; professional standards	Lateral leadership on the basis of expertise rather than seniority
'Academicization', e.g. applied research, publications, conferences	Cross-boundary working (between functions, center and periphery, academic and professional domains, internal and external partners)
Internal consultant and interim manager roles	Roles linked to major institutional projects such as widening participation
Portfolio careers (which may involve movement into and out of higher education)	Staff performing internal consultant roles, moving from project to project on a contractual basis
Mixed backgrounds, with experience that includes both academic and professional components	Joint working between academic faculty and professional staff, who cross backwards and forwards into each other's spheres of activity
"Blended" identities comprising elements of both academic and professional activity	Incorporation of staff with "blended" identities in areas such as learning support, academic practice, community partnership, student life, and welfare
Less stable understandings, by professional staff themselves and by their colleagues, about the precise parameters of their roles	Fluidity between roles and nomenclatures, for instance, between pro-vice-chancellors with portfolios that might include human resources or the student experience, and their professional colleagues

academic) staff are employed directly by the government as civil servants, and in Japan, where they are, however, subject to change as the government relaxes the regulatory environment so as to permit recruitment of individuals from a greater diversity of backgrounds, as described by Oba in Chapter 6.

Such arrangements offer a system-wide framework, so that an individual in one institution is assumed to have similar skills and knowledge sets to those of someone occupying a similar post in another institution. In some cases there are national pay structures, reflected in generic job titles and career paths. In this scenario, professional identities are primarily positional, and common understandings about roles, relationships, and legitimacies derive from formal organization charts. One legacy of this overarching framework is that professional staff are seen as a source of continuity, as "guardians of the regulations" (Barnett, 2000: 133) and "keeper[s] of the community memory" (McNay, 2005: 43). However, the increased accessibility of information via the internet, and its rapid outdating, mean that this type of function has reduced in significance in contemporary institutions.

At the other end of the spectrum, professional staff have been linked directly to the rise of "academic capitalism", the generation of institutional income, a transfer of power to "managerial professionals", and a consequent "de-professionalization" of academic faculty (Slaughter and Rhoades, 2004). Thus, information technology specialists who assist with "instructional production" in the United States are referred to as "'unbundl[ing]' traditional faculty instructional practices . . . reducing professors to content [i.e. information rather than knowledge] experts" (Rhoades, 2007: 6). This view parallels the concept of "managerialism" in the United Kingdom, a government approach that obliges public-sector organizations to operate in accordance with market imperatives (Ferlie et al., 1996; Ranson et al., 1998; Deem et al., 2007). This is framed in terms of:

- government policies that require universities to bid competitively for public sources of funding, as well as to compete in external markets;
- the introduction of an ethos of "enterprise", whereby institutions are expected to foster activities the prime aim of which is to generate income (rather than solely on the basis of their academic merit);
- increased accountability to government via, for instance, quality assessment processes;
- government policies that stress the role of universities in serving socio-economic agendas;
- increased regulation of the work of faculty by those with management responsibilities, be they professional or academic managers.

'Managerial' approaches, therefore, reinforce the sense of a separation and even a polarization of academic and management activity, and an 'othering' of management. In this scenario, professional staff are seen as "pivotal for the new self-understanding of higher education institutions as increasingly autonomous actors in the emerging global markets for knowledge and education" (Kehm, 2006: 170).

Competing perceptions about the roles of professional staff, which can and do occur simultaneously, set up tensions that provide an edge to day-to-day working relationships. These tensions arise partly from problems of definition, partly from a lack of understanding about roles and identities, and also from the way that professional staff are perceived in relation to academic faculty. The fact that they are portrayed as providing a service to academic colleagues, and also as agents of "managerialism", with variations in between, illustrates the difficulty of developing clear understandings about such a diverse grouping. Tensions also arise from issues of comparability, and the way that these are managed can be critical to local cultures. For instance, where professional staff and faculty work side by side in a department such as learning partnerships or professional/academic practice, staff without academic contracts may not have the same rights as their academic colleagues in relation to, for instance, intellectual property or study leave. However, it is argued in this chapter that while these dichotomies and tensions continue, substantial numbers of professional staff are operating in partnership with academic colleagues, and that such forms of joint working enhance the opportunities available to both groups, and to their institutions, in achieving their goals.

Joint Working: A Case Example

The following case example illustrates ways in which convergence between the roles of two colleagues, one on a professional and one on an academic contract, achieved an outcome that was of benefit to all parties. The collaboration was voluntary; neither individual was line-managing, or being line-managed, by the other; and both were attuned to what the other might be able to offer in putting together a complex bid for funding.

A Case Example of Joint Working between Dr Celia Whitchurch (CW), Lecturer, Institute of Education, University of London, and Jack Peffers, European Development Officer (EDO), Institute of Education, University of London

Profiles

CW, who is employed on an academic contract, and the European Development Officer (EDO), who is employed on a professional contract, collaborated on the submission of a bid to the European Union (EU) for research funding. Both had mixed academic and professional backgrounds. CW had had a career as a professional higher education manager before becoming a lecturer, and in this capacity had submitted bids on behalf of academic colleagues to agencies such as the UK National Health Service and Regional Development Agencies. She had been involved in the development of professional staff at national level and had published regularly on higher education management. However, she was relatively new to the process of profiling her own academic work in a way that would attract funding, and had no experience of bidding to the EU. The EDO had undertaken research, education, and training in the context of education/ business collaboration and the development of international partnerships. He had spent a significant period of time in senior research roles, had published regularly on education–industry partnerships, had detailed knowledge of European funding opportunities, and had an extensive international network of contacts, facilitated by his knowledge of several European languages. Our combined experience, therefore, maximized the joint contribution that

---

we were able to make to the submission of a major bid to the EU for research funding.

Background

Research funding from the EU for higher education projects is commonly tied to policy initiatives aimed at creating opportunities for people in the European Higher Education Area. To achieve a successful outcome, therefore, academic proposals need to be written in such a way that they contribute to EU policy, for instance, in relation to knowledge transfer, student mobility, or professional development. The bidding process is complicated and time-consuming. Not only do the policies, programs, and criteria change year on year, but deadlines are often relatively short, and bids usually require a minimum of half a dozen or so European partners. Higher education institutions, therefore, often have a dedicated European officer with knowledge of the process, who publicizes calls for proposals and has extended networks through which he or she can bring together partners in areas of common interest to access appropriate sources of funding. Such professionals are able to assist academic faculty in the application of their research in new (and perhaps unthought-of) areas, to enhance their and their institution's research profile, and to generate income.

Process

CW became involved in the bidding process after attending one of a series of seminars run by the EDO about funding streams offered by the European Lifelong Learning Directorate. This led to a series of conversations about an idea that CW had had to extend her research into continental Europe. In all, the process took three months, and involved weekly meetings interspersed with email contact. Activities included:

- *inviting five European partners to join the bid, and gaining their agreement to the allocation of work and anticipated income;*
- *collecting detailed information about each partner and their institutions, and incorporating this appropriately;*
- *completing a 100-page proposal, on an interactive online form, with detailed specifications in relation to alignment with European higher education policy objectives; practical benefits for institutions and individuals; project milestones; the development of work packages that met EU criteria; and the division of each work package into components that were allocated among the partners;*
- *developing a budget that costed each component of each work package, and allocated the associated income among the partners;*
- *inputting the budget on an interactive online spreadsheet in such a way that it was accepted by the online system (if there were inconsistencies between the various costing elements, the spreadsheets were automatically rejected);*

- *submitting the bid electronically, with accompanying legal documents, again in such a way that it was accepted by the system.*

Analysis

On the one hand, the EDO was alert to the potential of CW's work in the context of European policy initiatives (and had her draft a 'pilot' early on in the process to verify this). Having substantial experience of how an academic piece of work was likely to map onto EU priorities, he was able to help her orient the application toward the appropriate EU program. On the other hand, CW was sensitive to advice proffered that the EU would not fund the proposal solely on the basis of its being high-quality or original research, and that the application should be written in such a way as to be aligned to European policy thinking. As part of this process she "learned the language" of the EC Lifelong Learning Framework so as to make the case.

The EDO acted as 'pacemaker' in relation to the agreed critical path and in encouraging regular contact with partners to keep them informed and in agreement. He also acted as 'critical friend' in reviewing the ambitiousness of the proposal in the light of budgetary implications and constraints. CW for her part continuously revised drafts so that judgments could be made about its shape, and so that the various strands (balance of partner contributions/research and professional practice; work packages and costs) could be adjusted on an ongoing basis. The proposal, and the final budget, went through multiple iterations. Both of us were willing to 'go the extra mile' in order to achieve an outcome, which at times involved 24/7 working and availability.

Although we submitted the bid thirty-six hours before the deadline, we received an email the following day to say that in view of the fact that significant numbers of applicants had had difficulty in completing the online form, the Agency was extending the deadline by two weeks and reverting to paper submissions. Although we had not worked together before, we attribute our success in completing the online application on time and according to the due process to the adoption of a critical path, and the building of confidence step by step via our respective contributions. Thus, the EDO made himself available on a regular basis, and as the need arose, to offer mechanisms for solving specific problems, and CW followed up advice given at each stage. Both had an appreciation of the academic, policy, and practical issues arising from the bid, and by crossing over into each other's territory moved forward with an application that played to all three considerations.

The process illustrates elements of "managerial", "borderless", and "blended" working as described earlier in this chapter. In a "managerial" capacity the EDO acted as entrepreneur in spotting the potential of an academic idea for income generation, and helping to translate this into a "Mode 2" form of research that would be eligible for funding. There was also a sense in which the project was then 'sold on' to European partners by CW on the basis of its funding potential. CW was able to self-manage so as to accommodate the bidding requirements, editing her material so that it was oriented toward innovation in professional practice and multilateral institutional cooperation, and writing it in a language that 'spoke to' EU agendas.

"Borderlessness" was demonstrated by the fact that the project involved working with partners (who might or might not be known to each other) across geographic boundaries, in which CW's academic networks and the EDO's European networks were critical. In a different sense the project required both of us to adopt a "borderless" approach to the work required to frame the proposal in accordance with EU requirements. This involved specifying, for instance, "milestones", "deliverables", "work packages", partner contributions, and ways in which it met EU award criteria and policy objectives; putting together a budget that related costs both to partners and to the individual components of the work packages (neither of us had an accounting background); and getting to grips with the technical aspects of the online submission process, which was being used by the EU for the first time.

The EDO's "blended" background enabled him to:

- *act as 'ideas broker' in developing the institution's intellectual capital;*
- *act as mentor and guide in empowering an academic colleague to take advantage of a funding opportunity by offering clear signposts, timely assistance, enthusiasm, and encouragement;*
- *use the 'social capital' conferred by internal and external networks to open doors;*
- *be client focused in bringing together the aspirations of an academic colleague, the institution for which we both worked, and the prospective funding body.*

CW's "blended" background enabled her to:

- *accommodate and adapt to EU requirements and specifications;*
- *respond to advice, especially in relation to pragmatic aspects of the bidding process;*
- *remain sensitive to the needs, aspirations, and academic interests of prospective partners;*
- *write the proposal so that its academic originality was extended to incorporate innovatory professional practice that would optimize the chances of success;*
- *adopt a systematic approach, for instance, assembling all the material before entering it on the online form (a process that itself took several days).*

We do not suggest that we, or the process of collaboration described above, are exceptional, but we use it to illustrate the type of joint working that enabled a complex process, conducted under tight time and workload constraints, to be completed successfully. It was made more manageable by an appreciation of the need to contextualize research in an appropriate policy framework, and a willingness to pool resources. Therefore, a combination of imagination, pragmatism, and political understanding, together with an ability to work systematically in addressing problems as they arose, enabled us to deliver what we considered to be an innovative proposal according to the requirements of a potential funding body. In this type of scenario, therefore, where each might defer to the other in one instance and take the lead in another, traditional notions of who might be managing whom do not apply. Although the immediate aim was to generate research income from which our institution as well as ourselves would benefit, motivations also included 'social' objectives of extending and developing CW's research in a European context, of benefiting professional practice, and of creating development opportunities for fellow professionals. By sharing the tasks involved, whether at the more creative or operational end of the spectrum, we were able to develop a synergy that we could not have achieved single-handedly.

Reconceptualizing the Professional Manager in Higher Education

It is suggested that the case example above offers an alternative to approaches that are seen primarily as 'service and support' or as 'managerial', in which professional staff might be characterized respectively as 'uncritical friends' or 'power brokers'. However, both of these concepts imply a division of labor, whereas in joint working a professional member of staff is more likely to be seen, rather, as a critical friend and dealmaker. This process might be seen as fulfilling a definition of "management" that "multipl[ies] human accomplishment" by "amplify[ing] and then aggregat[ing] human effort" (Hamel, 2007: 250). It might also be seen as addressing the challenge noted by Florida (2002: 22), in which:

the biggest issue at stake in this emerging age is the ongoing tension between creativity and organization. The creative professional is social, not just individual, and thus forms of organization are necessary, but elements of organization can and frequently do stifle creativity.

The case example demonstrates how space might be found for a less divisive approach that brings together "creativity" and "organization".

Joint working also raises questions about what it means to be 'a professional' or 'a manager' in contemporary institutions. As is suggested in Whitchurch's study (2008b), it is possible not to know 'what sort of professional I am any more'. Despite the process of 'professionalization' that is seen to have occurred in countries such as the United Kingdom and Australia, the Whitchurch study (ibid.) suggests that younger staff saw the concept of 'professionalism' as conveying an elitism with which they were not comfortable, and which was felt to militate against a common purpose of colleagueship. Thus, one person suggested that "[p]rofessionalism is 'old school'". This reflects the less hierarchical approaches said to be favored by people belonging to Generations X and Y, described in Chapters 4 and 13, who, it is said, value interest and work–life balance above the organizational status they may have.

The case example also suggests that the concept of "democratic professionalism" (Whitty, 2008) may have currency in higher education as well as in the schools sector, to which it was originally applied. As Whitty (2008: 42) suggests,

> [I]t is not necessarily appropriate to view such developments [inter- and multi-agency working in schools] as an example of de-professionalization, but rather as an attempt at re-professionalization—that is, the construction of a different type of professionalism, perhaps more appropriate to contemporary needs.

Higher education might, therefore, adopt for its own purposes Sachs's (2003) concept of the "activist professional" who "works collectively towards strategic ends, operates on the basis of developing networks and alliances . . . these alliances are not static, but form and are re-formed around different issues and concerns" (Whitty, 2008: 45). The adoption of this type of agency may well be critical to staff working across professional and academic boundaries, to the development of a "community of professionals" (Association of University Teachers (AUT), 2001), and to Rhoades' (2005: 5) call for "non-faculty" to become more integrated in decision-making processes:

> Faculty are not the only professionals on campus; the number of non-faculty managerial professionals is growing rapidly. Increasingly, they participate in institutions' basic academic work, and like faculty, they have important expertise about the academy to contribute in shared governance. In short, we need a more inclusive, democratic academic republic.

A 'networked' approach to professional life is also linked to the potential for greater movement between higher education and other sectors, of which there is already evidence (Whitchurch, 2008b). In the United Kingdom, a traffic of professional staff can be observed between higher education and the National Health Service, regional development agencies, further and adult education (the college sector), non-governmental organizations (NGOs), and the charitable sector. An influx of staff from outside has brought new forms of expertise into higher education. There is also some evidence of senior staff being imported in areas such as human resources and finance because of a perceived lack of qualified applicants for posts (Lauwerys, 2009).

In Australia, and also to some extent in the United Kingdom, the concept of the 'internal consultant' also appears to be gaining currency, in which people move from project to project and are paid on that basis, with or without an institutional retainer. Individuals in this position might have a number of concurrent, part-time contracts with different sections of an institution or institutions, have a 'special projects' portfolio with one employer, or spend part of their time as a private consultant. In addition, it is becoming more common to employ 'interim managers', a practice that is common in other sectors and may become more widespread as the global economic environment impacts on institutional finances. An advertisement by a firm of management consultants in the *Times Higher Education* (March 26, 2009: 11) illustrates that there is a pool of people looking for these types of roles:

> Our team at Veredus has particular expertise in providing Higher Education clients with experienced senior interim management consultants in the following areas:
>
> • Directors of HR
> • Directors of Finance
> • Directors of ICT
> • Heads of Estates/Facilities
> • Heads of School and Faculties
> • Programme/Project Managers in a variety of disciplines (eg HR)
> • Organizational change and policy development specialists.

'Interim managers' may be people who have worked in higher education, or they may come from outside. Their presence is likely to raise boundary issues about their relationships with both professional and academic colleagues. There may be dependencies on both sides as interim managers seek to understand and work in local cultures, and existing staff may have to cope with discontinuity, particularly if interim managers are employed as change agents. Professional staff also work increasingly with colleagues outside the university, for instance, with information system providers, partners in local communities, and colleagues on offshore campuses. Such relationships may involve professional staff working at boundaries to perform a translational function with external colleagues, again with mutual dependencies. All these developments could be said to parallel the casualization observed in relation to academic faculty (Rhoades, Chapter 3). They also raise questions about whether or how the concept of allegiance or belonging to an institution, a function, or the higher education sector itself might pertain. New loyalties may emerge, for instance, to teams and projects, which may be short- or long-term, and there may also be re-entry issues if and when individuals return to the mainstream.

Whereas the twentieth century was dominated by large-scale bureaucracies, it has been suggested that the twenty-first century will increasingly be characterized by working "on the move" (Moynagh and Worsley, 2005), "ethical leadership" (Mendonca and Kanungo, 2007), and innovative organizational practice (Dodgson et al., 2005). Moynagh and Worsley (2005: 3) also suggest that social capital, as opposed to organizational structure, will be paramount in twenty-first-century working: "As human interactions become more central to work, organisations employing individuals who work well together will secure a competitive advantage."

Thus—and if, as Hamel (2007) claims, "the work of managing will be less and less performed by 'managers'"—institutions are likely to become increasingly cognizant of ways in which, as demonstrated by the case example above:

Capability counts for more than credentials or titles . . .
Commitment is voluntary . . .
Authority is fluid and contingent on value-added . . .
Ideas compete on an equal footing . . .
Decisions are peer based . . .

(Hamel, 2007: 253–254)

To this might be added the possibility of sourcing information, or understandings about how to perform a specific task or process, on a need-to-know basis without relying unduly on specialist experts, bureaucratic solutions, or precedents. The internet has, since the turn of the century, made this increasingly possible, and has thereby had a leveling effect in relation to the capabilities of individuals.

In considering the recruitment and development of professional staff, and the conditions under which they work, therefore, institutions may wish to review:

- how organizational structures might inhibit or encourage lateral forms of working;
- how professional staff might be accommodated in a "career climbing frame" (as described by Strike in Chapter 5), and how crossovers between professional and academic spheres of activity might contribute to a career portfolio, whichever type of contract is held;
- critical success factors associated with joint working between professional and academic spheres of activity;
- the aspirations and relationships of people undertaking joint working on projects or in teams;
- issues of 'parity' between people working in mainstream and boundary space;
- appropriate management and leadership styles;
- the use of:
  - internal and external networks;
  - consultancy or interim management roles;
  - job titles, job descriptions, and employment categories.

Conclusion

It would appear that there are forces for both divergence and convergence around the identities of professional staff in higher education. In addition to recognized cadres of staff in generalist, 'academic civil service' roles, which exist to a greater extent in some countries than in others, there are now also specialist staff in a wide range of fields, including, for instance, enterprise, marketing, widening participation, and quality. Alongside a divergence in the composition of and expectations around individual roles, however, there is also evidence of convergence and crossover, particularly between activities traditionally associated with either professional or academic spheres of activity, as exemplified by the case material in this chapter. Such a complex scenario leaves the way open for fissures to open up between 'managers' and 'managed', and for regroupings to occur when, for instance, teams or partnerships form around specific projects, and joint working takes place.

The global economic downturn may foster such divisions, for instance, between those in permanent posts and those in short-term, project-specific roles. If the funding environment becomes increasingly uncertain, as seems likely, with a continued squeezing of units of resource, institutions will wish to have the scope to adjust their salary commitments year on year. Not only will they be less willing to take a chance on loss-leading activity, but restructuring of existing activity may be ongoing. Relationships between a permanent core of staff and those on fixed-term contracts, therefore, are likely to be critical to maintaining teaching and research programs, with associated comparability issues vis-à-vis workloads and career prospects. Notwithstanding what commentators say about the predilections of younger staff for flexible portfolio lifestyles, there could also be a retreat toward a desire for greater clarity and certainty about career paths and futures. Nevertheless, it may be that resource constraints also help to stimulate joint working from the bottom up between colleagues who perceive advantages in pooling their resources to maximize the chances of successful outcomes.

Finally, it is suggested that as well as augmenting the "revenue generating capacity of faculty and their units" (Rhoades, Chapter 3), professional staff are also responsible for generating non-financial rewards, for instance, in the form of social capital, represented by friends of the institution in local communities, as well as wider national and international networks and partnerships. Such connections may lead to new spin-off activity, or extensions of existing activity, such as bespoke programs for local business or international partners. In particular, when involved in joint working with academic colleagues, they may provide a stimulus for innovation and growth, bringing together colleagues so as to add synergy to current portfolios. Thus, joint working could be said to be an example of how the higher education workforce might be "reconceptuali[zed] . . . as a key source of intellectual capital" (Rhoades, Chapter 3). A critical issue for institutions, therefore, is to create the conditions through which tensions might be used creatively. Maintaining this delicate balance might be described as the key challenge for 'professionals' and 'managers' alike.

Acknowledgment

I wish to acknowledge the collaboration of my colleague Jack Peffers, European Development Officer, Institute of Education, University of London, in constructing the case study used in this chapter.

References

Allen-Collinson, J. (2007) "'Get yourself some nice, neat, matching box files!' Research Administrators and Occupational Identity Work." *Studies in Higher Education* 32 (3): 295–309.

Association of University Teachers (AUT) (2001) *Building the Academic Team: A Report on the Contribution of Academic-Related Staff to the Delivery of Higher Education.* London: Association of University Teachers.

Barnett, R. (2000) *Realizing the University in an Age of Supercomplexity.* Buckingham, UK: SRHE/Open University Press.

Becher, T. (1989) *Academic Tribes and Territories: Intellectual Enquiry and the Culture of Disciplines.* Buckingham, UK: SRHE/Open University Press.

Becher, T. and Trowler, P. (2001) *Academic Tribes and Territories: Intellectual Enquiry and the Culture of Disciplines,* 2nd ed. Buckingham, UK: SRHE/Open University Press.

Bolden, R., Petrov, G., and Gosling, J. (2008) *Developing Collective Leadership in Higher Education.* London: Leadership Foundation for Higher Education.

Clark, B. (1998) *Creating Entrepreneurial Universities: Organizational Pathways of Transformation.* Paris: International Association of Universities Press and Elsevier Science.

Deem, R., Hillyard, S., and Reed, M. (2007) *Knowledge, Higher Education, and the New Managerialism: The Changing Management of UK Universities.* Oxford: Oxford University Press.

Dodgson, M., Gann, D., and Salter, A. (2005) *Think, Play, Do: Technology, Innovation, and Organization.* Oxford: Oxford University Press.

Ferlie, E., Ashburner, L., Fitzgerald, L., and Pettigrew, A. (1996) *The New Public Management in Action.* Oxford: Oxford University Press.

Florida, R. (2002) *The Rise of the Creative Class.* New York: Basic Books.

Hamel, G. (2007) *The Future of Management.* Boston: Harvard Business School Press.

Harrington, C. and Chen, H. Y. (1995) "The Characteristics, Roles and Functions of Institutional Research Professionals in the Southern Association for Institutional Research." Paper delivered at the Thirty-fifth Annual AIR Forum, Boston, May 28–31. Online, available at: www.eric.ed.gov/ERICWebPortal/custom/portlets/recordDetails/detailmini.jsp?nfpb=true&_&ERICExtSearch_SearchValue_0=ED386136&ERICExtSearch_SearchType_0=no&accno=ED386136 (accessed April 21, 2009).

Hockey, J. and Allen-Collinson, J. (2009) "Occupational Knowledge and Practice amongst UK University Research Administrators." *Higher Education Quarterly* 63 (2): 141–159.

Kehm, B. (2006) "Strengthening Quality through Qualifying Mid-Level Management." In *Prospects of Change in Higher Education: Towards New Qualities and Relevance—Festschrift for Matthias Wesseler,* ed. M. Fremerey and M. Pletsch-Betancourt. Frankfurt am Main: IKO Verlag für Interkulturelle Kommunikation.

Land, R. (2004) *Educational Development: Discourse, Identity and Practice.* Buckingham, UK: SRHE/Open University Press.

Land, R. (2008) "Academic Development: Identity and Paradox." In *Changing Identities in Higher Education: Voicing Perspectives,* ed. R. Barnett and R. Di Napoli. Abingdon, UK: Routledge.

Lauwerys, J. (2009) *The Development of Professional Careers in UK Higher Education.* London: Leadership Foundation for Higher Education.

Lockwood, G. (1986) "The Rise of the Administrator." *Times Higher Education Supplement* (April 11): 17.

McNay, I. (2005) "Higher Education Communities: Divided They Fail?" *perspectives: policy and practice in higher education* 9 (2): 39–44.

Mendonca, M. and Kanungo, R. N. (2007) *Ethical Leadership.* Maidenhead, UK: Open University Press.

Moynagh, M. and Worsley, R. (2005) *Working in the Twenty-first Century.* Leeds: Economic and Social Research Council and The Tomorrow Project.

Prichard, C. (2000) *Making Managers in Universities and Colleges.* Buckingham, UK: SRHE/Open University Press.

Ranson, S., Martin, J., McKeown, P., and Nixon, J. (1998) "The New Management and Governance of Education." In *The New Management of Local Governance: Hierarchy, Markets and Networks,* ed. G. Stoker. London: Macmillan.

Rhoades, G. (2005) "Capitalism, Academic Style, and Shared Governance." *Academe* 91 (3).

Rhoades, G. (2007) "Technology-Oriented Courses and a Mode III Organization of Instructional Work." *Tertiary Education and Management* 13 (1): 1–17.

Sachs, J. (2003) "Teacher Professional Standards: Controlling or Developing Teaching?" *Teachers and Teaching: Theory and Practice* 9 (2): 175–186.

Slaughter, S. and G. Rhoades (2004) *Academic Capitalism and the New Economy: Markets, State, and Higher Education.* Baltimore: Johns Hopkins University Press.

Sloman, A. (1964) *A University in the Making.* London: British Broadcasting Corporation.

Szekeres, J. (2004) "The Invisible Workers." *Journal of Higher Education Policy and Management* 26 (1): 7–22.

Universities and Colleges Employers Association (UCEA) (2003) *Framework Agreement for the Modernisation of Pay Structures.* Online, available at: www.ucea.ac.uk/en/Pay_and_Conditions/Framework_Agreement (accessed April 21, 2009).

Whitchurch, C. (2006) *Professional Managers in UK Higher Education: Preparing for Complex Futures.* Interim Report. London: Leadership Foundation for Higher Education. Online at: www.lfhe.ac.uk/publications/research.html (accessed April 21, 2009).

Whitchurch, C. (2008a) "Shifting Identities and Blurring Boundaries: The Emergence of *Third Space* Professionals in UK Higher Education." *Higher Education Quarterly* 62 (4): 377–396.

Whitchurch, C. (2008b) *Professional Managers in UK Higher Education: Preparing for Complex Futures.* Final Report. London: Leadership Foundation for Higher Education. Online, available at: www.lfhe.ac.uk/publications/research.html (accessed May 9, 2009).

Whitchurch, C. (2009) "The Rise of the *Blended Professional* in Higher Education: A Comparison between the UK, Australia and the United States." *Higher Education* 58 (3): 407–418.

Whitty, G. (2008) "Changing Modes of Teacher Professionalism: Traditional, Managerial, Collaborative and Democratic." In *Exploring Professionalism*, ed. B. Cunningham. London: Bedford Way Papers.

11

The Changing Roles and Identities of Library and Information Services Staff

DEREK LAW

Reg Carr retired as Bodley's Librarian in 2006 and, as many senior professionals have done, he published a sort of *apologia pro vita sua* (Carr, 2007), reflecting on changes throughout his career. As a young graduate contemplating a career in librarianship in the late 1960s, he had a clear and predictable potential future mapped out: assistant librarians were aged in their early twenties, and this was the normal career grade: one became promotable to sublibrarian (a departmental head) from age 30 onwards, deputy librarian at 40 and, for highfliers, the university librarian aged 50 or so. Retirement age was often still 67, and although the universities had seen some expansion of student numbers in the 1960s, the role was largely unchanged from what it had been a century earlier. Technology did not exist in any meaningful way, with even photocopying being a novel, rather messy, and certainly expensive toy.

Throughout the 1960s the growth in student numbers in the United Kingdom had led to a slow parallel growth in library staff numbers. As a result, and often in the 'new' universities of the 1960s, there was some experimentation with the concept of subject specialists as opposed to the old functional departmental divisions of cataloguing, reference, and reader service. Although first degrees in library science existed, a much more common qualification route was a first degree in almost any discipline—English and history being prevalent—with a one-year diploma course taken at a library science department, and two years of on-the-job training leading to Associateship of the Library Association. Formal training and career development were non-existent, with skills developed by example. Some practical skills were gained through involvement in the committees of the Library Association—often a sandpit for Young Turks—and attendance at conferences was rare, usually national, and only very exceptionally international.

Many librarians pursued a sort of dual career undertaking scholarship in a small way, publishing in decently obscure journals, usually in the humanities. Very rarely a doctorate might be pursued in an academic discipline, but it was certainly not seen as a requirement. The skill set acquired at age 22 could last a professional lifetime. Almost without exception the entire university passed through the doors of the library. No serious researcher, scholar, or undergraduate could work without the collections of the library and the interlibrary loan service. There was as yet no national library service and very little cooperation with other libraries beyond the local. The University Grants Committee Annual Report for 1921 (University Grants Committee, 1921) had famously stated, "The character and efficiency of a university may be gauged by its treatment of its central organ—the library. We regard the fullest provision for library maintenance as the primary and most vital need in the equipment of a university." The Parry Report (University Grants Committee, 1967) cited this statement with apparent approbation, maintaining that it was as true as ever, but noted without comment that little was known about the adequacy or efficiency of libraries.

That state of affairs continued largely unchanged until around 1990. Then, as Carr noted, "those who have worked in academic research libraries since the mid-1990s have been through a time of 'white water' change such as none of their predecessors ever knew." Within the span of a single professional career, this part of the university community had experienced a period of quite unparalleled seismic change, which shows no sign of abating. The very *raison d'être* of libraries is open to question, while the skill set required appears to change almost by the week.

The position in computer centers was to a degree analogous. In 1970, computers were still novel and mainframe based, and researchers had to visit the computer center to use them, usually to run batch processing jobs. Computing center staff typically had science degrees in vaguely related disciplines ranging from physics to biology and were much more likely than librarians to have a Ph.D. The capacity of computers was almost in inverse proportion to their size, the usual wry view being that the university computer of 1969 had the power of a microchip running a household central heating system forty years later. Indeed, computers were sufficiently expensive and rarified that their replacement was managed by the Computer Board, an agency of the University Grants Committee, on a seven-year cycle with visitations by members of the Board, who would solemnly adjudicate on university plans and agree, and at least partially fund, an investment strategy. The computer center was an arcane and exciting place of new research opportunities for new scholars in science, but at the periphery of university life. No real career paths had yet been created or developed, and technical skills were at least as valued as management skills in what were still quite small operations in terms of staff numbers. The skills required were technical and programming skills. The role of computers in management of the institution was non-existent. Again the operation was local. JANET (the Joint Academic Network) was not created until 1983, and even then was limited and partial in its availability.

E-learning, of course, did not exist, but there were always academic faculty who developed an interest in pedagogy, and there was some thread of instructional design using images in particular. They would typically be based in subject departments; the idea of pedagogic centers had yet to take root. The creation of the Open University in 1969 spurred interest, and the 'new' universities of the 1960s were also particularly interested in novel approaches to instruction for the broader student body that the expansion of the system had created. Many universities had what were usually termed audiovisual departments. Equipment was bulky and relatively primitive. Expensive production facilities with studios and recording areas were required for the keenest universities. As for the rest, content creation tended to be of slides and sometimes tape recordings, with video beginning to make a mark. Medical schools often led the way in developing audiovisual materials, but tended to have separate and dedicated facilities. Classroom support revolved around slides, overhead projectors, and acetates, and, above all, the provision of chalk. There were no clear qualifications or requirements throughout the system, with each university recruiting technical staff to meet the individual needs of the institution.

Thirty years on, these groupings have all changed in quite fundamental ways and are now commonly aggregated to form the information services of the university. How this has come about, and the human resource challenges it has posed and continues to pose, offer object lessons for the future. For there is no sign that the information revolution has run its course. Of the three groups, librarians were the only one with the sort of professional knowledge base that is a defining characteristic of a profession. The erosion and supplanting of that knowledge base has blurred the distinction between the groups, so that 'information professional' is a term that can apply in any of them.

1970–1990

The characteristic feature of the period 1970–1990 was the inexorable growth and spread of technology, and a move from purely locally based activity to national and international cooperative systems. In libraries, much of the period was spent in developing the mechanization of existing processes. Librarians by and large spent a generation developing library housekeeping systems with all sorts of glittering features, but these were and are gold-plated dinosaurs. As a general rule, throughout the period, library users still had to visit the library, still go to a catalogue hall and write down the call number on a scrap of paper, still go to the shelf, still find the book they really wanted was not there, and still come to the issue desk to argue about paying fines. Such reskilling as went on was a consequence of purchasing commercial systems and associated training. Conferences and special interest groups grew in number to exchange experience. If there was a change, it was a cultural one that reflected wider cultural sensitivities. Carr (2006) describes this succinctly:

> In fact—in this country [the United Kingdom] at least—it was not generally until the 1980s that the "customer-oriented" ethos of the service industries really made serious inroads into the reader service departments of the older and larger university libraries. Until then, the emphasis in those more "traditional" libraries tended to be placed more overtly on collections (rather than on services to users), on administrative procedures (rather than on ease of use), and on rules and regulations (rather than on what users wanted). Thankfully, the world has now changed for the better in this respect; but "old habits die hard", and even now there are still a few library staff here and there who prefer, mistakenly, to think that their libraries exist primarily to provide them with employment, rather than first and foremost to serve their users.

As the use of IT systems began to spread, the library and the computer center began to have some real contact, developing small products and routines. Similarly, university administrations began to develop an interest in the use of IT to mechanize administrative processes. To a degree, the computer center had begun to provide basic IT skills training to administrators and librarians. Pedagogical concerns remained detached. For the library this still meant little more than trying to acquire reading lists to make sure that the books were in the library, while the computer center might offer some skills training for undergraduates in science disciplines. More generally, the development, in particular, of European Union programs for higher education and for research began to expose staff to new influences and new thinking, which meant that the environment was seen as stimulating and skill-enhancing through learning from others. JANET was, of course, the preserve of the computer center, but librarians were quick to grasp the potential significance of networks as a means of resource sharing, and from the mid-1980s a febrile debate began on the opportunities that were emerging.

In practical terms, libraries began to undertake major projects to convert their catalogues to machine-readable forms. These huge projects represented a major investment, and many staff received formal training in project management, usually from external consultants. As a side benefit, this gave a confidence in management and an appetite for developing technology. And a new range of skills was expected but never provided for. Along with other university staff, information services staff were expected to develop skills in areas as wide-ranging as fund-raising, marketing, human resource management, and resource management. Most universities were now prepared for this, and a range of internal and external courses were made available, as well as a much more formalized process of assessment and goal setting.

Technological Drivers and Organizational Change

Electronic information resources had existed since the mid-1960s, particularly in the sciences. However, access to them had been significantly restricted. The resources were abstracting and indexing tools rather than primary sources, and all searching was mediated and batch processed. In many universities, while online searching operated from the library, it was conducted by externally funded individuals whose principal skill was disciplinary. It was very much at the edge of library life. Technology slowly and inexorably spread, although it was not until the early 1980s that the possession of a personal computer became relatively common in universities. What had begun to change, however, was the thinking about the future of libraries. In a seminal paper in 1978, Lancaster stated, "We are already very close to the day in which a great science Library could exist in a space less than ten feet square."

By 1990 the new technology in libraries was CD-ROM. Most libraries had by now set up IT systems departments, buying in technical skills rather than retraining staff. Libraries still looked back. A raging debate took place in libraries on whether users should be allowed unmediated access to CD-ROMs and, if so, whether they should have to attend mandatory training courses. Pedagogy was slowly developing to take account of computing. The now ubiquitous PowerPoint was launched only in 1987, but by 1990 was not in common use. Teaching remained largely traditional.

Perhaps the largest change came in 1990–1991 when the Computer Board was finally closed down. Until then, much of higher education was required to have an IT strategy, and that was a well-understood process defined and refined by the Computer Board. At about that time, when the Computer Board became the Information Systems Committee, there was a strong push to make institutions produce an information systems strategy. This recognized that the days of the mainframe had largely gone, that much of the purchasing power was at departmental or grant-holder level, but that the university still needed to have a view of what it was trying to achieve, rather than what it intended to buy. Before that concept had been defined, far less refined, the notion of information strategies began to take hold, perhaps precisely because it was an imaginative but ill-defined concept. Computing was now seen as a local responsibility, not a nationally driven issue. The days of the central procurement of a major mainframe every seven years had in effect been swept away by the personal computer.

Finally, and presciently, the Computer Board had appointed a librarian to its board, recognizing the convergence of library and IT interests. It was a period of intense ferment. In 1991 the first-ever national site license was signed with the Institute for Scientific Information, to create the BIDS (Bath Information and Data Services) service. This confirmed the position of the United Kingdom as the leading country in developing both the theory and the practice of electronic information provision. The short-lived Information Systems Committee became the Joint Information Systems Committee (JISC) as the home nations set up their own funding councils. The Joint Funding Council (Joint Funding Council, 1993) promptly commissioned a review of libraries—in part driven by the addition of the polytechnics to the sector. This reported in December 1992 and foresaw a major expansion of electronic library activity. That was picked up by the JISC. It funded electronic resources, it adopted a mission of promoting cultural change, it promoted training groups and activities, and it required all institutions to adopt an information strategy. It consciously set out to involve every institution in projects and activities and training and considering the future. This forced library and computer managements to work together to consider joint futures. Then, in 1993, the World Wide Web was invented and the world changed forever. The first Web browser came in 1994. In the four years after that, it achieved a phenomenal acceptance, in what has been characterized as the largest mass migration in human history. It was adopted by 50 million users in fifty months. Radio took thirty-eight years to gain such an audience, and television some thirteen years (Law and McSean, 1999).

Convergence

The response of many institutions was to bring the library and computer center under common management (Royan, 1990). This model and its variants spread like wildfire through the higher education system in the United Kingdom— although, curiously, almost nowhere else in the world. Perhaps unsurprisingly, and despite the huge cultural differences between librarians and computer center staff, no real effort was made to consider human resource issues. The larger groupings required a broader range of management skills, and there was a general growth in the use of management training courses for senior managers. As for all other staff, the JISC played a seminal role in developing staff. The nationally driven eLib program was crucial, but was aimed very much at library staff. The recent evaluation of the program was clear on its impact:

> There was agreement across the board that theirs is a highly risk-averse profession. Nevertheless, they have taken on board a huge raft of changes in the ways in which they deliver services. Indeed, they have taken almost complete ownership of the changes that have occurred, showing a degree of imagination and breadth of vision that is striking. Such ownership explains the lack of memory of eLib, despite the fact that its aims and objectives have become so widely embedded.
>
> (Duke and Jordan, 2006)

Computer center staff also faced a whirlwind of technological change. Nor was this just technological growth. A common complaint was that while IT had moved from supporting a handful of departments to supporting the whole university, resources had not grown at the same pace. Whole new areas of skill had developed, from networking to personal computing and software support. Computer centers now supported a mass market, and not just a few technically competent areas. Perhaps as a result, computer centers recruited much more from industry, effectively buying in skills rather than simply reskilling those already in the sector. It was quickly discovered that mistakes could be expensive—as the disastrous national MAC (Management and Administrative Computing) initiative, aimed at developing university administrative systems, demonstrated. Many converged services included learning services, which had also been overtaken by this huge personalization of access to information, resources, and learning materials. As well as developments in pedagogy, roles were developed in staff and student training in the use of software.

A Crisis of Identity

But library professionals were perhaps the most affected group. The very title 'librarian' had become very unfashionable. In the United Kingdom even the venerable name of the Library Association was changed to the anonymous and anodyne CILIP (the Chartered Institute of Library and Information Professionals), following merger with the Institute of Information Scientists. This lack of confidence in their name was, in turn, reflected in the professional library schools. Undergraduate courses soon all but disappeared from the United Kingdom, partly because of the impossibility of defining a credible shared corpus of knowledge for the discipline, leaving one-year Master's courses, while departments themselves underwent a Damascene conversion to departments of information science, or merged with departments of computing, or simply disappeared. Even postgraduate courses reduced greatly in number, although courses in topics as varied as electronic publishing and information management appeared to flourish, taught by the same academic faculty. These schools were typically too small to survive in a difficult economic environment, and even the larger ones have had to follow this path of diversification, with many of their graduates taking up employment outside the traditional library sector (Feather, 2003). The same experience is evident in other major countries, from Australia to the United States, and there is a real fear that the next generation of professional managers of library services is simply not being created.

At first, the tendency was to assume that this new type of converged information service would recruit or retrain a generation of Renaissance men and women armed with a copy of Dewey in one hand and a screwdriver in the other, capable of resolving any user need. When these paragons failed to appear, a more realistic approach emerged, which created small teams of experts each with their own set of skills, albeit still with some understanding of how to resolve issues in computing or web searching. New mantras inspired by American business then began to appear, and the wish was to become 'user-centered' and 'customer-focused'. So, while the skills of the librarian were again seen as relevant within converged services, these were to be presented in quite new ways. And so titles changed again.

Oyston (2003) offered case studies of what happened when libraries were replaced by or rebadged as learning resource centers at four quite different universities, and reports what happened at Sheffield Hallam, Aberdeen, Lincoln, and Leeds Metropolitan Universities. In Sheffield Hallam, reorganization followed the creation of the new Adsetts Learning Resource Centre, where "the most significant change was that of assistant librarian to information adviser"; in Leeds Metropolitan University the role of assistant librarian took on some computing support functions and became senior information officer; in the University of Lincoln, learning advisers were developed as multiskilled individuals working to support curriculum design and delivery, and the transmission of generic skills to students; in Aberdeen the faculty subject librarians became faculty information consultants, while assistant librarians became site service managers.

These four cases are fairly typical of what has been happening in many universities. In the same way, a brief analysis of four issues of a CILIP recruitment magazine revealed a whole range of new titles: Information Officer, Taxonomist, Heritage Information Manager, Learning Resource Centre Manager, Database Manager, e-Resources Librarian, Outreach Librarian, Web Services Manager, and the rather more established Systems Librarian all featured, all with elements of more traditional skills and roles (Law, 2004).

Until the late 1980s, librarians had a clear sense of professional identity, and happily fell within Eraut's description (1994) of the characteristics of professionalism. The profession prided itself on having a long tradition, going back four thousand years to Ashurbanipal's great library of tablets of stone. They fondly remembered Thomas Young, the natural philosopher and polymath who, when he died in 1829, was recorded as the last man who knew everything. Since then, society had required intermediaries to manage and organize knowledge in all its published forms. The organization of knowledge, with cataloging and classification as its core, provided the basic, but arcane, competences as the set of skills and knowledge that defined the professional knowledge base.

Eraut's list of the classic professional concepts of moral integrity, confidentiality, and neutrality, as well as a service ethos, permeated the profession. A professional association and the attendant provision of qualifications, pupilage, and a code of ethics were all in place late in the nineteenth century. A major research library might contain a million volumes, and academic faculty had little alternative to finding what they needed in the collections. Apart from visits to other universities or archives in the long vacation and interlibrary loans (again controlled by library staff), there were only vestigial alternatives to using these professional intermediaries to gain access to knowledge. Even abstracts and indexes were in a primitive state until the late 1960s, and non-existent in some disciplines. Although the point was not clearly understood by the profession, much of its professional skill rested in practice on a deep knowledge of the local collection, and significant practical experience, rather than on a set of generic rules or skills. There was a clear sense of partnership in the academic life of the institution—an unequal partnership no doubt, but nonetheless a partnership.

What one can see with hindsight is the paradox of an increase in 'professionalism' but a loss of public need for the core skills of the profession. Librarians now are much less clearly partners in the academic enterprise and much more a provider of services in an increasingly hierarchical relationship characterized by the division of university staff into 'academic' and the very pejorative 'non-academic'. Libraries have arguably never been better run. Professional skills have been blurred as more managerial competences have been eagerly acquired from other areas. Financial management, marketing, strategic planning, technology, and training have all been eagerly adopted and practiced as research libraries have grown in scale and complexity. This has led to a poor differentiation of specialist (information-related) skills from generic ones shared with other professions.

At the same time, the growth of the internet and its associated tools such as search engines has led to a growing public view that the library is only one of multiple sources of information, while there is a growing body of evidence that users would rather interact with search engines than with people. Cataloging and classification, the twin arks of the professional covenant, are increasingly seen as of little value, even by librarians, having in effect been replaced by natural language searching. Google is now seen as displaying the attributes of moral integrity, confidentiality, and neutrality, previously the hallmarks of the profession. We can see that this passing of trust has weak foundations, as Google collects masses of information on individuals, information that has been passed on to government. Interestingly, this is happening at a time when librarians in the United States display huge professional courage and resist the USA PATRIOT Act's requirement to pass on user data to government agencies.

A further interesting blurring of identity has occurred through a convergence of interests around e-delivery, which has led to a blurring of functional and disciplinary boundaries leading to librarians—and others—beginning to encroach on teaching and research, the traditional domains of academic faculty. Partly as a result of the very large funds made available by both the European Union and the JISC, a substantial cadre of young staff has emerged who undertake and publish research on areas related to digital resources and their many uses. A significant amount of this activity has related to teaching. Much of the development of Managed and Virtual Learning Environments (MLEs/VLEs), the exploration of social networking, and a variety of digitally based tools has been led from libraries and converged services. The reluctance of many existing academic faculty to devote time and energy to such areas of teaching has, arguably, left a vacuum, which has been filled by these "blended" or "third space" professionals (Whitchurch, 2008a, b) who straddle academic and professional domains. Even conventional librarians increasingly see training students in information literacy, and in research and discovery skills, as being part of their core competences. The reaction of academic departments and faculties to this varies dramatically, ranging from harmonious partnerships to outright hostility.

International Comparisons

The crisis in librarianship as a profession is found in every country. Converged services proved to be a peculiarly British response to the development of digital services and resources. Although the model was tried at individual institutions in many other countries, it never really found the same degree of dominance as in the United Kingdom. In the United States a partnership approach between libraries and IT remains the dominant model. This was, and is, undoubtedly colored by the way in which US professional library staff enjoy tenured positions and are seen as much more analogous to academic faculty. Nonetheless, American library schools are closing, and the same level of professional angst exists as elsewhere. There is more commonality of experience in northern Europe, in part because the development of IT-based resources and services works with, and is often based on, the UK JISC experience. There are notable comparisons with the Dutch experience, for example. While converged services are not as common as in the United Kingdom, links between library and IT services are strong. The European Union has also proved a very effective mechanism for sharing experience and practice. Much joint work has also gone on with Australia and Hong Kong, which also resonate with UK experience.

The Future

The pace of change shows no signs of abating. The sheer wealth of information now available on the web dwarfs the collections of even the largest library. In particular, Google plans to digitize literally millions of volumes, while most scholarly journals are now available electronically. A recent major *Guardian* supplement (Guardian, 2008) collected a range of generally upbeat views from senior managers. It claimed that the technological developments "have put the library back at the heart of teaching, learning and academic research." This seems wildly optimistic, given the general decline in many of the measures of library usage. A major issue for library managers is that most members of the university no longer need to darken the library's doors. Funding and policy decisions are increasingly made by people who do not use the library. And yet one very common response has been to build new library buildings (often renamed resource centers) without any clear idea of their future purpose or function.

The same optimism can be seen in the professional literature. Some face the future with confidence and certainty:

> Librarians are professionals trained in the acquisition, organization, retrieval, and dissemination of information. In essence, the practice of librarianship in the virtual library environment will not be very different from that in the traditional print-based library. The librarian's role will continue to include selection of suitable resources, providing access to such resources, offering instruction and assistance to patrons in interpreting resources, and preserving both the medium and the information contained therein.
>
> (Burke, 2002)

Pinfield (2001) makes the same point about subject librarians seeing their role as repurposing existing skills, rather than developing entirely new ones. Others are less clear, but still want libraries to remain:

> [I]f these decisions [on the future role of libraries and librarians] are made wisely, the academy may be able to maintain much of the ineffable, inspirational value associated with academic libraries while retaining their practical value through altogether transformed activities and functions built upon a new mission designed for a more digital world.
>
> (Campbell, 2006)

But there is a much darker alternative. Marc Prensky (2001a, b) is perhaps best known for his formulation of the concept of digital natives and digital immigrants. Less well known, but even more chilling, is his proposition that the very nature of knowledge and information is changing:

> It seems to me that after the digital 'singularity' there are now two kinds of content: 'Legacy' content (to borrow the computer term for old systems) and 'Future' content. 'Legacy' content includes reading, writing, arithmetic,

logical thinking, understanding the writings and ideas of the past, etc.—all of our 'traditional' curriculum. It is of course still important, but it is from a different era. Some of it (such as logical thinking) will continue to be important, but some (perhaps like Euclidean geometry) will become less so, as did Latin and Greek. 'Future' content is to a large extent, not surprisingly, digital and technological. But while it includes software, hardware, robotics, nanotechnology, genomics, etc. it also includes the ethics, politics, sociology, languages and other things that go with them.

(Prensky, 2001a: 4)

The underlying trends are fortunately relatively clear. They are toward ubiquity and portability. Wireless technology, the convergence of personal digital assistants (PDAs), mobile phones, and laptops, and government policies aimed at delivering broadband to the home all lead to a situation of great power being put in the hands of individuals. Much of higher education's power base has depended on the concentration of resources. Knowledgable teaching and research staff, laboratories, and libraries have provided a magnet that draws students and research. The technology, at least theoretically, removes that advantage. The growth of simulations, whether for chemists or lawyers, digital libraries, and webcams means that it is entirely possible to create a virtual university. Google (and others) have begun huge programs of digitization. There seems a certain inevitability that once 30 million or so volumes are available on the web, the question will be asked whether a university needs a library at all. Already in institutions as varied as Bangor University and London University's School of Oriental and African Studies (SOAS), plans have been proposed to shed library staff explicitly on the basis that the (so-called) easy availability of material on the web renders the role of subject specialists redundant.

What is less well noticed is the uncontrolled growth of born-digital material in all institutions. A simple list would include:

Forms of e-Content

- research papers
- conference presentations
- theses
- wikis
- blogs
- websites
- podcasts
- reusable learning objects
- research data
- e-laboratory books

- streamed lectures
- images
- audio files
- digitized collections
- e-archives
- email
- human resources records
- student and staff records
- corporate publications
- national heritage artifacts

All of these are growing. No one controls them all; policies for selection, preservation, curation, and access are not in place, or generally even discussed.

There is an obvious role here for information services staff to develop new content systems and to revivify the fundamental skill of the organization of knowledge.

One perceptive commentator has remarked on this:

> Although these emerging, digital-age library services may be important, even critical, in the present era, there is no consensus on their significance to the future academic library—or even on whether they should remain as library functions carried out by librarians. In addition, at this point, the discussion of the future of the academic library has been limited to librarians and has not widened, as it should, to involve the larger academic community. Consequently, neither academic librarians nor others in the academy have a crisp notion of where exactly academic libraries fit in the emerging twenty-first-century information panoply. Because of the fundamental role that academic libraries have played in the past century, it is tremendously difficult to imagine a college or university without a library. Considering the extraordinary pace with which knowledge is moving to the web, it is equally difficult to imagine what an academic library will be and do in another decade. But that is precisely what every college and university should undertake to determine. Given the implications of the outcome, this is not an agenda that librarians can, or should, accomplish alone.
>
> (Campbell, 2006)

And yet there is something of a paradox here. Institutions in general and libraries in particular have in recent years focused on client- and service-oriented approaches. This has led to services aimed particularly at students and in support of teaching. Service to academic faculty has diminished in that many, or most, faculty acquire their information at the desktop. Nor is it often obvious to the individual that the information has been acquired, licensed, and managed by librarians. This focus on commercially available material has moved librarians well away from their roots. There is no debate on, no theory or philosophy of, the curation and preservation of born-digital resources. It is at least possible that some institutions will allow the management of digital resources to be diffused among a number of parts of the university, and that the library will cease to have any real function other than that of museum.

There is a very real need for professional leadership and debate on this future. Some of this debate is emerging from among professional educators rather than practitioners. For example, Corrall (2005) has articulated three key questions:

- Will we see more explicit technical specialization emerging within library and information science (LIS) practice and education?
- How will future information management roles be divided among information professionals, IS/IT professionals, and others with information-oriented backgrounds?
- Can we identify and define different levels of information-related competencies for 'specialist', 'intensive', and other types of information users?

Corrall identifies two diverging paths for professional growth. First, there might be technical "infostructure" specialists charged with designing, developing, managing, and supporting the organization's information infrastructure. Second, there would be functional "biz-focus" specialists whose task would be to align information to business and personal needs, applying information solutions to client problems. Such a structure sits well with perceptions of what is happening in practice. It is then a matter of taste and perception whether one sees this as a rather rapid but natural evolution of the proud four thousand-year-old tradition of librarian, or the replacement of a Neanderthal tradition by a more developed and new species.

Conclusion

Universities create and consume information and knowledge. The development of technology has both globalized and increased that creation and consumption, while quite plausibly creating routes that allow information users to bypass what were previously centrally provided services. Staff involved in the provision of information services have found the skill sets they require on the one hand changing at an impossibly rapid pace, and on the other merging and overlapping. Web managers, content management system managers, repository managers, VLE managers, and so on can be employed by any or all of the units that constitute these information services. Perhaps oddly, while the majority of universities have brought together all their information services in a single management structure, only a very few have attempted to break down the traditional departmental boundaries.

Linked to this is the absence of any emerging view of what type of staff should be employed and what skill sets they should possess. Career paths are no longer clear, but at least there is a general commitment to developing generic management and leadership skills. Personal and softer skills are perhaps more valued by interview panels than are specific professional competences, if only because the life span of such professional competences can be measured in months rather than decades. The organization of knowledge will remain a key requirement for universities, but where and by whom it is organized is a much more open question. It can only be a question of time before a university outsources library provision to a third party as no longer being part of the core business. A more cheerful view is that the information profession, however defined, will move past its mid-life identity crisis and define a set of skills and competences in managing locally produced e-resources, for quality-assuring externally accessed data, and for teaching information literacy. This provides the core of competences that would ensure a settled and satisfying career. How and where those skills will be taught and assured remains a much more problematic question.

References

Burke, L. (2002) "The Future Role of Librarians in the Virtual Library Environment." *Australian Library Journal*. Online, available at: www.alia.org.au/publishing/alj/51.1/full.text/future.role.html (accessed April 21, 2009).

Campbell, J. D. (2006) "Changing a Cultural Icon: The Academic Library as a Virtual Destination." *EDUCAUSE Review* 41 (1) (Jan.–Feb.): 16–18, 20, 22, 24, 26, 28, 30.

Carr, R. (2006) "What Users Want: An Academic 'Hybrid' Library Perspective." *Ariadne* 46. Online, available at: www.ariadne.ac.uk/issue46/carr (accessed April 21, 2009).

Carr, R. (2007) *The Academic Research Library in a Decade of Change*. Oxford: Chandos.

Corrall, S. (2005) "Developing Models of Professional Competence." Paper given at the Sixth World Conference on Continuing Professional Development and Workplace Learning for the Library and Information Professions. Online, available at: www.ifla.org/IV/ifla71/papers/cpdwl-Corrall.pdf.

Duke & Jordan (2006) *Impact Study of the Electronic Libraries Programme*. Bristol: JISC. Online, available at: www.jisc.ac.uk/publications/publications/elibimpactstudyreport.aspx (accessed April 21, 2009).

Eraut, M. (1994) *Developing Professional Knowledge and Competence*. London: Routledge.

Feather, J. (2003) "Whatever Happened to the Library Schools?" *Library and Information Update* 2 (10): 40–42.

Guardian (2008) *Libraries Unleashed*. Supplement published with the newspaper on April 22, 2008. Online, available at: http://education.guardian.co.uk/librariesunleashed.

Joint Funding Council (1993) *Libraries Review Group Report* (the Follett Report). Bristol: Higher Education Funding Council for England.

Lancaster, F. W. (1978) *Toward Paperless Information Systems*. New York: Academic Press.

Law, D. (2004) "Bibliographes spécialisés et bibliothécaires de référence: questions actuelles au Royaume-Uni." In *Bibliothécaire, quel métier?* ed. B. Renoult. Paris: Cercle de la Librairie.

Law, D. and McSean, T. (1999) "Net-Knitting: The Library Paradigm and the New Environment." In *Libraries without Limits: Changing Needs, Changing Roles*, ed. S. Bakker, European Association for Health Information and Libraries. Proceedings of the Sixth European Conference of Medical and Health Libraries, Utrecht, June 22–27, 1998. Dordrecht, the Netherlands: Kluwer.

Oyston, E. (2003) *Centred on Learning*. Aldershot, UK: Ashgate.

Pinfield, S. (2001) "The Changing Role of Subject Librarians in Academic Libraries." *Journal of Librarianship and Information Science* 33: 32–38.

Prensky, M. (2001a) "Digital Natives, Digital Immigrants." *On the Horizon* 9 (5): 1–6.

Prensky, M. (2001b) "Digital Natives, Digital Immigrants Part 2: Do They Really Think Differently?" *On the Horizon* 9 (6): 1–6.

Royan, B. (1990) "Staff Structures for Today's Information Services." *British Journal of Academic Librarianship* 5: 165–169.

University Grants Committee (1921) Report, February 3. Cmd. 1163. London: HMSO.

University Grants Committee (1967) *Report of the Committee on Libraries* (the Parry Report). London: HMSO.

Whitchurch, C. (2008a) *Professional Managers in UK HE: Preparing for Complex Futures*. Final Report. London: Leadership Foundation for Higher Education. Online, available at: www.lfhe.ac.uk/publications/research.html (accessed April 21, 2009).

Whitchurch, C. (2008b) "Shifting Identities and Blurring Boundaries: The Emergence of *Third Space* Professionals in UK Higher Education." *Higher Education Quarterly* 62 (4): 377–396.

Part IV
Challenging Boundaries

Introduction

CELIA WHITCHURCH

The concluding chapters, in Part IV, offer suggestions as to ways in which the challenges arising from a diversifying workforce might be met. It may well be that the implications of the global economic downturn, which began to become apparent in the autumn of 2008 after most of the chapters for this book had been written, will cause some of the phenomena that have been observed, such as the casualization of the workforce, to gather pace. What seems clear is that financial levers for attracting and rewarding staff are likely to be increasingly scarce in the foreseeable future, and that other aspects of the employment 'package' will continue to assume importance—for instance, opportunities for career development, conference attendance, secondments, coaching and mentoring, or responsibility at local level for, say, teaching and learning.

A changing external environment is likely to impact not only on formal contracts of employment, but also on what is known as the psychological contract, which has been defined as "[t]he perceptions of . . . two parties, employee and employer, of what their mutual obligations are towards each other" (Guest and Conway, 2002, quoted in Chartered Institute of Personnel and Development (CIPD), 2009). This more informal contract is based on interpretations and understandings by both employer and employees of formal terms and conditions of employment. Expectations and aspirations are likely to be influenced by staffing policies and working practices, as well as by relationships between colleagues and, in the case of higher education, membership of a disciplinary or professional community, and the status and mission of the employing institution. The significance of the psychological contract is recognized by the increasing use of, for instance, surveys of staff satisfaction and levels of stress in higher education (e.g. Knight and Harvey, 1999). Whether or not such surveys are seen as having a practical effect, they illustrate an awareness that staff well-being can have an impact on the quality of the contribution that they make.

These considerations bring into view the fact that contracts of employment, formal or informal, involve a partnership between employers and employees. Yet, as shown in the chapters of this book, understandings about that partnership are not necessarily fixed or stable. A 'push' from those with responsibilities for shaping institutional activities and aspirations is likely to be balanced by a 'pull' from those whose activities contribute to an institution's particular mission. This is an ongoing and iterative process, the outcome of which accounts for an institution's precise character and shape at any one time. Thus, while institutions are subject to pressures from governments and markets, individuals are subject to a matrix of relationships and crosscutting strands, at the same time interpreting, yet seeking to influence, the demands being made on them. Senior managers interpret external requirements as they shape the internal operating environment, and line managers interpret, and also seek to influence, the cultures and strategies of their institutions.

Therefore, while it is possible for institutional structures to remain static, the situation on the ground, as people go about their day-to-day activities, is likely to be more fluid. Given these dynamics in contemporary institutions, it is not surprising that a number of the contributions to this volume raise the question, implicitly or explicitly, of what it means to be an academic or a professional in higher education. This reflects not only diversifying identities and activities across institutional communities, but also a complex web of relationships at all levels. The traditionally discrete roles of teaching, research, technology transfer, and/or administration are overlaid by, for instance, community and business partnership, widening participation, outreach, and the student experience. As pointed out by Gappa in Chapter 12, e-learning and its implications for learning design and support have added another dimension. However, while for some this may imply an identity crisis, for others it enables new identities to be forged.

As pointed out by Whitchurch in Chapter 14, clear distinctions between 'managers' and 'managed' are increasingly difficult to maintain, reflecting Kolsaker's suggestion that "dichotomous analyses of managerialism and professionalism are now outmoded" (2008: 523). It may be more appropriate to think in terms of the relationship between the institution, its various parts, and the individual, and the variables influencing the way that this is played out. The PricewaterhouseCoopers (2007) model of Blue, Green and Orange Worlds, referred to by Middlehurst in Chapter 13, may help us to understand such relationships in institutions that are increasingly amoeba-like, rather than being represented solely by hierarchical or matrix structures. Furthermore, the three scenarios, as shown in Table IV.1, may well coexist and are not necessarily mutually exclusive.

Like all such models, this one is intended as a conceptual tool to assist with thinking about organizational cultures, what might be occurring, and what might be appropriate in a specific institution or institutional segment. In the context of higher education this model also maps onto existing conceptualizations. Thus, the Blue World might be seen as reflecting 'managerial' approaches, in which individuals are regarded as a resource much as other resources, and there is a focus on performance management. In this scenario, individuals adopt a negotiating position in relation to their roles and careers on the basis of their perceived value. The Green World might be seen as reflecting traditional ideas of collegiality, and also as incorporating concepts of "democratic professionalism" (Whitty, 2008) and "ethical leadership" (Mendonco and Kanungo, 2007). The Orange World reflects ideas about the "casualization" of the workforce (Slaughter and Rhoades, 2004), and the emergence of project and portfolio working in "Third Space" (Whitchurch, 2008).

On the one hand, it would seem that the need for management and leadership capability is unlikely to diminish in a world that is not only less certain but also

TABLE IV.1 Approaches to People Management

	Blue World Corporate Capitalism (cf. "managerialism")	Green World Social Responsibility (cf. "collegiality"; "ethical leadership")	Orange World Collaborative Networks (cf. "Third Space")
Approach to people management function	"People and Performance" ("a hard business discipline")	"People and Society" ("innovative solutions", e.g. secondments in a downturn)	"People Sourcing" ("a flexible workforce")
Organizational challenges	Maximizing human capital Performance management	Risk of non-socially responsible behavior Sustainability	Lack of organizational infrastructure Based on social capital Multiple contracts
People profile	Individuals negotiate their roles on the basis of their value as human capital	Socially engaged Value placed on overall employment package	Fluid roles Portfolio careers Skill and knowledge networks

Source: Adapted from PricewaterhouseCoopers (PWC) (2007).

more risk-laden. On the other hand, whether or not such activities are given the labels of 'management' or 'leadership', the opportunity to take responsibility for, for instance, a program module, or elements of a research project, is likely to be valued as an opportunity for development. Thus, a relatively junior member of a self-managing team might take on responsibility for the health and safety aspects of work in a specific laboratory. As a result, demand for management development programs dedicated to managers from both academic and professional back-grounds is likely to continue. Nor are these likely to be aimed solely at those at the most senior levels. A flyer for a project leadership program (facilitated by an external organization, Humentum UK) at the Institute of Education, University of London, circulated in the spring of 2009, illustrates the 'ripple-down' effect of traditional concepts of management and leadership. The program aimed to enable participants to:

- lead a project team so that it meets its potential for productivity and effectiveness;
- facilitate an effective project work environment;
- influence the project team to work on and support the project;
- look beyond the critical path (Humentum UK, 2009).

A key phrase is "look beyond the critical path", which focuses attention not only on the next step in the process, but also on the need to contextualize local activity in both institutional and wider policy environments. This may mean looking across academic and functional domains of activity, for instance, in the development of an appropriate e-learning environment for learners of different disciplines and levels of experience. Thus, "Effectively leading a team requires influencing skills and conflict management know-how . . . factor in today's virtual team issues, and managing a project takes on a new level of complexity" (Humentum UK, 2009).

Although it is not possible to predict the way that higher education systems will evolve, it could be that one response to increased financial stringency will be a stronger steer from the corporate center in a Blue World, at the same time as further casualization of the workforce fosters ways of working characteristic of the Orange World. Such a scenario would create further institutional dynamics, and could also have the effect of squeezing opportunities to develop more sustainable and ethical forms of activity in a Green World. However, whatever happens, it seems likely that tension between pressure for a more controlled operating environment and pressure for one that is more fluid and networked will be a challenge for the higher education sector and people working in it, particularly if this tension is to be used to positive effect. Nevertheless, those with responsibilities for people are likely to seek the spaces and flexibility to develop approaches that are appropriate to their locale in relation to, for instance, workloads and schemes of recognition and reward. This is likely to involve not only the creative use of existing mechanisms, but also a search for opportunities that assist individuals in extending their reach for the future. The chapters that follow give a glimpse of some of these possible spaces and opportunities.

References

Chartered Institute of Personnel and Development (CIPD) (2009) *The Psychological Contract*. Online, available at: www.cipd.co.uk/subjects/emptreltns/psycntrct/psycontr.htm (accessed April 14, 2009).

Guest, D. and Conway, N. (2002) *Pressure at Work and the Psychological Contract*. London: Chartered Institute of Personnel and Development.

Humentum UK (2009) *Improving Project and Change Management Performance*. Online, available at: www.humentum.co.uk (accessed April 21, 2009).

Knight, P. and Harvey, L. (1999) "The Use of a Staff Satisfaction Survey at the University of Central England in Birmingham." *perspectives: policy and practice in higher education* 3 (2): 56–62.

Kolsaker, A. (2008) "Academic Professionalism in the Managerialist Era: A Study of English Universities." *Studies in Higher Education* 33 (5): 513–525.

Mendonca, M. and Kanungo, R. N. (2007) *Ethical Leadership*. Maidenhead, UK: Open University Press.

PricewaterhouseCoopers (2007) *Managing Tomorrow's People: The Future of Work 2020*. London: PricewaterhouseCoopers. Online, available at: www.pwc.co.uk/pdf/managing_tomorrows.pdf (accessed April 18, 2009).

Slaughter, S. and Rhoades, G. (2004) *Academic Capitalism and the New Economy: Markets, State and Higher Education*. Baltimore: Johns Hopkins University Press.

Whitchurch, C. (2008) "Shifting Identities and Blurring Boundaries: The Emergence of *Third Space* Professionals in UK Higher Education." *Higher Education Quarterly* 62 (4): 377–396.

Whitty, G. (2008) "Changing Modes of Teacher Professionalism: Traditional, Managerial, Collaborative and Democratic." In *Exploring Professionalism*, ed. B. Cunningham. London: Bedford Way Papers.

12
Rethinking Faculty Work and Workplaces

JUDITH M. GAPPA

In baseball, successful managers recognize the importance of each team member, from the star pitcher to the second-string infielder. They motivate their players to perform at their best by helping them to understand and value the unique role of each team member. Likewise, individual players must be able to function autonomously in their roles and work effectively as part of a team. The star pitcher cannot defend the entire playing field; he needs help when a ball is put into play. He must count on the outfielders communicating effectively with each other when a fly ball threatens to drop between them.

This simple sports analogy shares many similarities with the importance of supporting and valuing a college or university's faculty members. Just as managers must rely on their players to win, colleges and universities rely on their faculty members, who, individually and collectively, are the means by which institutions achieve their missions. Faculty members represent each college or university's primary resource: its intellectual capital. As such, they are each institution's major, and only renewable, asset. Colleges and universities invest heavily in the intellectual capital that their faculty represent because these are the means by which institutions achieve their missions (Gappa et al., 2007).

Today, dramatic changes are occurring in higher education and in the environments in which colleges and universities work worldwide. Because each institution's success and well-being are directly related to the quality of work its faculty produces, collectively and individually, faculty productivity is becoming more and more critical. But faculty productivity is closely related to the treatment individual faculty members receive, and to their satisfaction with their career choice and institution. Therefore, to meet current and future challenges, every college and university must pay attention to the recruitment, retention, and well-being of its faculty members.

To do so successfully, they must understand how much faculty members and their working environments have changed. America's decentralized system of public and private higher education has seen enormous expansion and diversification of its institutions, its faculty members, and its students in the seventy-five years since the widespread adoption of the tenure system as the prototype for defining and employing faculty. From 1940, when tenure was formally adopted, to 2003, the population of the United States more than doubled, the number of students increased from 1,494,000 to almost 17,000,000, and the size of the faculty grew from 147,000 to 1,139,000 (Gappa et al., 2007: 60). These faculty members are now employed at highly diverse institutions: research universities, liberal arts colleges, state systems of education, community colleges, and for-profit institutions.

This chapter begins by examining the results of this growth and diversification: in colleges and universities, in faculty members themselves and their varied roles, in different types of academic appointments, in work patterns, and in contributors to job satisfaction generally. A Framework of Essential Elements of faculty work is then proposed as a resource for rethinking faculty work and workplaces in order to maximize faculty satisfaction and productivity in today's changed environment. The Framework and its Essential Elements are more fully developed in Gappa et al. (2007). When this chapter discusses themes and ideas from this text, such as the Framework of Essential Elements, it is not continuously cited. However, all other data sources and references are cited.

A brief word about terminology: in recognition of the complexity and diversity of today's faculty, this chapter uses the term 'faculty' as an inclusive term that covers all those occupying a faculty position. Three types of faculty appointments are now widely used in the United States (Gappa et al., 2007: 67ff.):

- tenure-track or tenured appointments, with their guarantee of continuous employment;
- contract-renewable appointments, which offer potential for long-term employment through renewal of contracts for specified periods;
- fixed-term appointments, which are temporary by nature and occupied largely by part-time workers.

Why Rethink the Academic Profession?

Changes in US colleges and universities, in faculty work, in faculty members themselves, and in employment trends and components of worker satisfaction in general all mandate a reconsideration of who today's faculty members are and of their working conditions, in order to ensure institutional ability to recruit and retain excellent faculty, now and in the future.

Changes in Colleges and Universities

Higher education institutions in the United States have grown in number from approximately 1,700 in 1940 to almost 4,200 today (Gappa et al., 2007: 60). These colleges and universities and their leaders are faced with numerous societal challenges that seem to grow more difficult with each passing year. Examples abound. They must:

- create environments that enhance student diversity and attract potential students who are well matched to the institution's mission;
- find new sources of revenue as traditional sources decline;
- continuously maintain and enhance their technological infrastructures within budgetary constraints;

- respond effectively to additional accountability requirements imposed by a public that wants to see wider access for more students, high-quality research that solves societal problems, engagement with surrounding communities, and contributions to economic development.

Fiscal constraints and shifts in financial support are putting added pressures on American colleges and universities as they face ever-increasing costs of operating expenses, employee compensation packages, and growing enrollments. Financing technology infrastructure, providing additional student services, addressing deferred maintenance, and handling increasing energy costs are only a few examples of rising expenditures. In addition, public institutions are faced with volatile state budgets and stagnant federal support.

At the same time that colleges and universities in the United States are struggling with fiscal constraints and increased competition for scarce resources, they are faced with more calls for accountability, and more government and public oversight. Increased federal regulation regarding student financial aid and research funding also requires additional reporting and review.

Changes in Faculty Work, Appointments, and Demographics

The effects of changes in faculty work, appointments, and demographics in their colleges and universities are being felt by faculty members, who are experiencing declining autonomy in their work, escalating workloads, an increasingly diverse student body, and, for some, a change in the nature of the academic community. Historically, the American faculty has been defined according to membership of the professoriate, which included both employment and organizational roles (Schuster and Finkelstein, 2006). Faculty employment operated in accordance with the structure, definitions, and rules for tenure promulgated by the American Association of University Professors (AAUP) in 1940 and widely endorsed by American colleges and universities (AAUP, 2001). Faculty members were seen as "complete scholars" engaged full-time in teaching, research, professional service, and academic citizenship (Rice, 1996). They occupied tenure-track or tenured appointments, and they had defined roles in and responsibilities for the governance of a college or university.

Over the past seventy-five years, however, the tenure system has eroded as the academic profession has grown, diversified, and changed. Gradually, those concerned about the well-being of the professoriate have realized that a new conceptualization of who faculty members are, and what they do, is now needed. In order to preserve what is best about American higher education in a period of national and global change, this new conceptualization of faculty members and their work is likely to incorporate faculty who occupy alternative appointments to the tenure system, and also to accommodate the professoriate, both as an aggregated workforce that does the necessary work of a particular college in its unique setting, and as a collection of people who, through their individual experience and knowledge, make significant contributions to institutional success. In other words, the academic profession must take into account the work of the faculty as a whole and the aspirations, needs, and contributions of each individual who is a member of the professorial "vocation" (Plater, 2007).

But a new conceptualization of the role and purpose of the faculty must also accept and incorporate the fundamental restructuring that is occurring in many professions. For example, the restructuring of the medical and legal professions led to an increased emphasis on efficiency and revenue generation. Higher education is now experiencing a similar reallocation of revenues, and emphasis upon revenue generation, which has led to changes in faculty working conditions and employment (Rhoades, 1998). In addition, there has been explosive growth over the past decade in for-profit institutions of higher education. Because they operate as businesses, these new institutions differ from the more traditional colleges and universities in important ways. Courses are developed by core staff or experts in the field, and faculty members are hired to teach the courses assisted by various technology experts. For the most part these faculty members work part-time and do not have tenure. Many for-profit institutions rely solely on the internet to teach audiences worldwide (Kinser, 2007).

These new developments have led to significant changes in faculty careers and academic workplaces in American colleges and universities. In the past, the work of the faculty—the creation, presentation, dissemination, and preservation of knowledge—was based on simple and familiar technologies: the book, the classroom, and the face-to-face course. Today, information technology makes it possible to disaggregate the educational process, thereby reconfiguring faculty work. New organizations such as Blackboard and E-College allow colleges to outsource instructional platforms. Or courses can be offered worldwide over the internet, and student remedial and supplemental education services (such as Sylvan Learning Systems or Stanley Kaplan) can be outsourced. This unbundling of course design and development from course delivery and student interaction and assessment allows institutions to reduce their fixed costs (Finkelstein, 2007). New activities such as writing proposals, developing e-learning programs, or working on technology transfer are tasks that now engage faculty members, in addition to the more traditional activities of teaching, research, and service to the community. And these diverse activities are no longer considered peripheral. Instead they are recognized as important aspects of academic work, and essential to success as a faculty member (Musselin, 2007).

The effects of these changes on faculty members are widespread. They include changing patterns of faculty appointments, a decline in faculty autonomy and control of their work, escalating workloads, increasingly entrepreneurial and high-pressure environments that hinder faculty commitment to their institutions and communities, and the need for continuous career-long professional development.

The enormous growth of the higher education enterprise in the United States since the 1940s, when tenure predominated as the employment system, also has led to widespread changes in faculty appointments. By the early twenty-first century only 27 percent of all new faculty appointments and 56 percent of all new full-time appointments were in tenure-track positions (US Department of Education, 2004). Slowly but inexorably, colleges and universities have migrated from tenure-eligible to non-tenure-eligible appointments that do not have the academic freedom or job security associated with tenure. Today the majority of faculty members in American colleges and universities occupy non-tenure-bearing positions, both contract-renewable and fixed-term.

The demographics of faculty members have also changed. Women now represent 44 percent of new faculty members (those in their first six years of employment) and 34 percent of senior faculty (those with more than seven years of full-time employment) (US Department of Education, 2004). And this increase in the number of women faculty members is likely to continue, because they are being awarded an increasing share of doctoral degrees across all disciplines (Hoffer et al., 2005). In 2003, for the first time, women received more that half of all doctorates awarded to American citizens (51 percent).

Similarly, the percentage of people of color, either native born or citizens born outside the United States, receiving doctorates has grown 64 percent in the past ten years. In 2004, 20 percent of US citizens awarded doctoral degrees were members of racial or ethnic minority groups. Increases in the number of international students who have earned doctoral degrees in the United States have also enlarged the pool of potential faculty. Only 67 percent of recent doctoral recipients are US citizens (Gappa et al., 2007: 62ff.). Data about the diversity of doctoral recipients by gender, ethnicity, and citizenship are good news for colleges and universities that want to recruit new faculty. But they also force institutions to consider how to make the faculty career attractive to potential faculty when the academic profession is compared with other possible careers.

Changes in Employment Trends

The employment of the professoriate has always followed societal norms for workers in general. Current tenure policy developed in the early twentieth century, when employment policies in the United States focused on job security obtained through long-term employment with one company. This was possible at that time because it was presumed that the household unit contained both a 'breadwinner' and a stay-at-home housekeeper and carer of children. Thus, household and family responsibilities were divided and differentiated between two people occupying distinctly different roles (Gappa et al., 2007).

These societal norms that defined the employment relationship in the past have changed partly as a result of dramatic changes in households. Women are now full participants in the workforce. Thus, there is no longer a traditional housekeeper at home. The result is that women and men have significant house-hold and caregiving responsibilities beyond their work. Also, many of today's workers, including faculty, view job security differently. While they still value security, they no longer necessarily seek it through long-term employment with one entity. Instead, today's professionals carry job security with them in their portfolios of accomplishments and skills. They enhance their "employability" through on-the-job professional development and career growth (Waterman et al., 1994).

In their research on the attitudes of tenure-track faculty members, Dowd and Kaplan (2005) labeled faculty as either "probationers" with a "boundaried" (limited to one institution) view of their careers, or "mavericks" with a "boundaryless" view (focused on discipline, not institution). "Maverick" tenure-track faculty members with a "boundaryless" view perceive their careers very differently from "boundaried" faculty, as this quotation from a "boundaryless" faculty member suggests: "You have to keep your vita in shape and be ready to move when the time comes, and if you do that, you'll be a happy guy . . . I don't find it [being on the tenure track] particularly stressful here". Their colleagues who view their careers as being limited to one institution, or "boundaried", perceive their careers differently: "I like teaching. I enjoy the research but have little time for it. . . . I give more priority to my professional life because I am on the tenure track and work about eighty hours a week" (ibid.: 710).

The quotation from the "boundaried" faculty member is an example of the feelings of today's faculty who are working longer hours. The proportion of faculty members reporting that they work more than fifty-five hours a week has grown from 13 percent in 1972 to 44 percent in 2003, with no differences between men and women (Schuster and Finkelstein, 2006). Tenure-track faculty, in particular, cite their workloads as a major source of stress and dissatisfaction with the academic career (Gappa et al., 2007: 108–109).

Faculty Satisfaction with the Academic Career

Faculty members choose an academic career because it offers autonomy, intellectual challenges, and freedom to pursue their interests. Overall, they are very satisfied with their career choices (US Department of Education, National Center for Education Statistics, 2004). But they also indicate dissatisfaction and stress with their current employment. Faculty generally express dissatisfaction with their salaries, and cite as sources of stress their workloads, their ability to manage both work and household responsibilities, and tenure and promotion review processes.

With demand for faculty increasing, institutional leaders need to consider how they can attract highly qualified doctoral recipients (who are increasingly women and ethnic minority group members) into faculty careers. Researchers for the "Heeding the New Voices" project showed that the tenure process was a major source of stress and dissatisfaction for probationary faculty (Rice et al., 2000). In interviews, probationary faculty members cited vague, unclear, shifting, and conflicting performance expectations, insufficient feedback on their performance, the tenure review process itself, and the six-year up or out timeline as major sources of dissatisfaction and stress. The authors found that while probationers looked forward to an environment characterized by respect, collegiality, collaboration, community, and connectedness, they actually experienced something quite different: "In short, we learned that the evaluation and tenure system, in its current form at many institutions, is undermining the very creativity, energy and commitment that make new faculty of such value" (ibid.: 12). More recently, Archer (2008) interviewed a group of young academic faculty at a British university. In her interviews with diverse faculty members in different types of academic positions, she found that becoming an academic is not just smooth, straightforward, linear, or automatic. Instead, it involves conflict and instances of inauthenticity, marginalization, and exclusion. Academic success was viewed as constrained by race/ethnicity, social class, gender, and age by the young academic faculty she interviewed.

In sum, five themes run through the research findings about faculty members' job satisfaction and career priorities:

- Faculty members value equity. When they perceive inequitable treatment, their job satisfaction diminishes.
- Collegial relationships, both with their colleagues and with administrators, are important to faculty.
- Faculty members are more satisfied when they believe they are growing professionally, and when they have autonomy, control over their careers, and access to the resources they need to do good work.
- Faculty members place a high value on security in employment, either in the form of tenure or in other forms such as rolling contracts that guarantee sufficient time to find another position.
- Support from department chairs and institutional administrators, and recognition for their work and contributions, also lead to high levels of satisfaction (Gappa et al., 2007: 117).

These five factors are particularly important to consider when recruiting and retaining faculty members who are not in the traditional tenure system. Today's challenge is to provide an environment where, regardless of appointment type or individual demographics, all faculty members are treated fairly and have the opportunity to grow professionally, to have their work respected, and to be members of their academic communities. Optimizing these qualities in faculty work can help colleges and universities improve their faculty recruitment and retention, and increase faculty productivity.

Rethinking Faculty Work and Workplaces

The changes in higher education in the United States outlined in the first part of this chapter have resulted from its tremendous expansion and diversification in the seventy or so years since tenure became the model for American academic employment. Growth in the number of faculty members and institutions of higher education has caused a proliferation of various types of faculty appointments, with differences in compensation and support structures. In turn, this proliferation of faculty appointments has raised important questions about whether or not all faculty members are treated equitably and with respect by their institutions, and whether or not their talents are being fully utilized. When any member of the academic community is not respected or valued, or when his or her talents are not fully utilized, both the faculty member and the college or university lose the full benefits of his or her intellectual capital. Today, to remain competitive and to accomplish its many societal mandates, the higher education community must rethink faculty employment and careers, the organization of faculty work, and how best to utilize and support all faculty members.

How can academic work be organized in ways that more fully achieve institutional and faculty goals and priorities? To paraphrase a well-known quotation from Albert Einstein, "problems cannot be solved by thinking within the framework in which the problems were created." While colleges and universities and their faculty members must retain important academic traditions, they must also ensure that essential elements of faculty work are incorporated into the employment of all faculty members, regardless of the type of appointment they have.

Changing Faculty Employment while Retaining Academic Traditions

The employment of the professoriate has always followed general workforce norms. For example, when tenure became the model for faculty employment in the early twentieth century, faculty members, like other workers, were seeking job security during rough economic times. However, today's faculty members, like their counterparts in other professions, seek more flexibility in their working environments in order to manage dual-career households and other responsibilities. To recruit and retain faculty now, colleges and universities must ensure that their employment policies and practices address the important priorities of current faculty for their work and workplaces (Gappa et al., 2007).

Fortunately, what today's faculty seek is not incompatible with what is sought by their colleges and universities. For example, faculty members now seek flexibility to meet their lifestyle and household demands, while colleges and universities want their priorities met. These are not necessarily incompatible objectives. Why not structure a working environment that enhances the well-being of the faculty while simultaneously producing excellent work? If a valued faculty member can reconfigure her work responsibilities in order to take care of household and child-care responsibilities more effectively, she will likely remain at the institution for many years. But when a new, probationary faculty member carries a heavier advising load and is assigned to more committees than his departmental colleagues, when he is seldom invited to join informal conversations, and when he feels his research interests are not valued, concerns about tenure review, frustration with colleagues, and intellectual isolation may lead him to look for a position at another institution.

Second, important traditions of the American academic profession such as shared governance and academic freedom can be preserved. But these key traditions—academic life within a collegial community, participation in the governance of their college or university, job security and academic freedom—must be redefined so that they include today's diverse professoriate in a variety of academic employment arrangements, while simultaneously meeting institutional needs and mandates.

Third, fundamental academic beliefs about what it means to be a professor, and the values underlying tenure as an employment system, can be retained while changes are made to meet the needs of today's colleges and universities and their faculty members (Gappa et al., 2007). For example, one of the hallmarks of tenure is the shared responsibility between faculty and administrators for the well-being of the faculty and the institution. This shared responsibility must be preserved, but not necessarily through a tenure commitment. Today's reciprocal relationship emphasizes faculty members' commitment to institutions' success, and the use of their intellectual capital for institutions' benefit during their time of employment. In return, colleges and universities commit to enhancing individual faculty members' employability by providing new forms of job security for those outside the tenure system through continuous professional growth and multiyear contracts. For faculty members in contract-renewable appointments, employment security can reside in their portfolios of demonstrated competencies (Waterman et al., 1994). In this reciprocal relationship, faculty members owe their institutions good work and participation in institutional governance during their time of employment, while the institution owes them respectful treatment, fairness, opportunities for professional development, and some measure of job security.

Fourth, the tradition of shared governance in American higher education is as important today as it has ever been. This tradition envisions a partnership between the institution and its faculty members. Everyone has a responsibility to participate in governance of the institution: faculty members individually and collectively in appropriate roles, department heads, deans, provosts, presidents, and governing bodies. Today, faculty members in every academic appointment and administrators must continue to work together to assess current institutional policies and practices governing faculty employment and support for faculty work. Together, they must identify and prioritize specific ways to improve the institution's working environment and each faculty member's contribution to the institution.

Finally, employment policies, practices, and environments that focus on the well-being and productivity of the faculty are likely to be tailored to each institution's profile, and to be sufficiently flexible to meet new needs of faculty members as they arise. The higher education enterprise in the United States has become too large and complex for there to be one vision of the 'ideal' professor and one commonly endorsed policy or practice that defines the profession, such as the adoption of tenure in the 1940s. Instead, today each individual college and university has become the locus of change in employment policies and practices for its faculty members. Each individual institution will adopt faculty appointment and employment policies and practices that enable it to recruit and retain the most talented faculty available to meet the challenges of today's competitive world. This institutionally based competition for talent will drive the recruitment and employment of the twenty-first-century professoriate.

But what will guide this new working environment and its continuous reassessment and improvement within individual colleges and universities? How will important academic traditions be maintained? Matching the traditions of the academy to the present realities of faculty members and their institutions requires an understanding of the critical attributes of the workplaces that faculty members now seek.

The Essential Elements of Faculty Work

Today, all faculty members seek meaningful work, regardless of whether they are in tenured, contract-renewable, or fixed-term appointments. To successfully recruit and retain excellent faculty, colleges and universities must focus on the important priorities of their faculty members for their work and workplaces, while retaining key traditions of the academic profession, such as shared governance and academic freedom.

Gappa et al. (2007) labeled these priorities as the Essential Elements of Faculty Work. These Essential Elements were developed from research findings on faculty satisfaction and career priorities discussed earlier. They are the glue that holds individual faculty members and their college or university together in a mutually rewarding, reciprocal relationship. They must be incorporated into every faculty member's appointment and employment conditions in order for each faculty member to contribute his or her best work to the institution. The five Essential Elements are:

- employment equity;
- academic freedom and autonomy;
- flexibility;
- professional growth;
- collegiality.

These Essential Elements enable colleges and universities to match important academic traditions to the present realities of their faculty members' lives and employment. They also incorporate the findings of worker satisfaction theorists such as Hertzberg (1966), Maslow (1970), McClelland (1975), and Alderfer (1972). Their research indicates that employees in general find their work satisfying if they have meaningful relationships with coworkers, challenging work, respectful treatment, ownership or sense of responsibility for their work, autonomy, recognition and opportunities for advancement, and feedback about their work (Gappa et al., 2007).

In Figure 12.1 the Essential Elements are placed in a circle surrounding a core of respect. Preceding the circle of Essential Elements are two smaller circles. They represent the roles of faculty members and administrators in ensuring the presence of the Essential Elements in a college or university's workplace. The arrows connecting the two small circles delineate the reciprocal relationship or mutual dependence between faculty and administrators, while the arrows connecting the

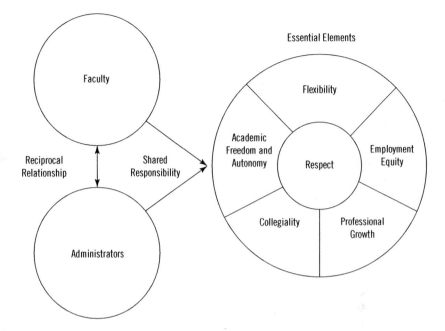

Figure 12.1 Impact of Faculty and Institutional Characteristics on the Essential Elements

Source: J. M. Gappa, A. E. Austin, and A. G. Trice, *Rethinking Faculty Work: Higher Education's Strategic Imperative* (2007: 137). Copyright 2007. This material is reproduced with permission of John Wiley and Sons Inc.

two small circles to the large circle delineate the shared responsibility of faculty and administrators for incorporating the Essential Elements into the working environments of all faculty members.

Respect, defined as the basic human valuing of each faculty member as an individual for who they are and for what they uniquely contribute to their institution, is placed at the center of the circle because it is a prerequisite for, and influences, all the other elements. Respect is a fundamental entitlement of every faculty member and is at the core of any reciprocal relationship between faculty members and their institutions (Gappa et al., 2007). The five Essential Elements of faculty work cannot be effective without the core of respect, because unless and until all faculty members (in fact, all employees) feel they are respected, they are less likely to place much importance on the other elements or to benefit from them (Campbell and Koblenz, 1997).

Sennett (2003: xix) critiques the lack of positive expressions of respect and recognition of others in modern society:

Lack of respect, though less aggressive than an outright insult, can take an equally wounding form. No insult is offered another person, but neither is recognition extended; he or she is not *seen*—as a full human being whose presence matters. When a society treats the mass of people in this way, singling out only a few for recognition, it creates a scarcity of respect, as though there were not enough of this precious substance to go around. Like many famines, this scarcity is man-made; unlike food, respect costs nothing. Why, then, should it be in short supply?

As Sennett suggests, faculty members in and outside the tenure system in many US colleges and universities can find themselves in environments that fail to respect their work and contributions. For example, in one department, faculty mailboxes for part-timers were set up as a separate class, positioned below those for full-time faculty. After the part-time faculty protested, the department integrated all faculty mailboxes in alphabetical order, which made the part-timers feel included and valued. However, in another department all new faculty members were invited to a reception, but the part-timers were not introduced to their department colleagues. They felt like non-persons (Gappa et al., 2007: 147).

Each of the five Essential Elements that surround respect is related to a unique dimension of faculty work. Thus, each element stands as a separate attribute of faculty work that makes its individual contribution to the quality of every faculty member's work experience. But the elements are placed in a circle because they are interdependent and non-hierarchical, and they also interact with each other. Benefits derived from practices developed to enhance one of the elements can, and do, impact on and enhance other elements at the same time. For example, the achievement of equity in faculty employment is not possible without simultaneously providing flexibility to enable all faculty members to work productively and manage their personal lives and responsibilities.

Definitions of the five elements accompanied by examples to illustrate the element in practice are given below.

Employment Equity

Employment equity is the right of every faculty member (regardless of appointment type or time base) to be treated fairly in regard to all aspects of his or her employment by the institution and its departments, to have access to the tools necessary to do his or her job, and to have status as a fully fledged member of the faculty (Gappa et al., 2007: 140, 195ff., 220).

EXAMPLES

- Develop faculty employment policies such as probationary periods, evaluation criteria and processes, and equitable compensation for each type of academic appointment in accordance with institutional guidelines, and provide these policies in writing to each faculty member. Ensure that institutional policies are carried out consistently in every academic department.
- Provide faculty in fixed-term (part-time or temporary) appointments with sufficient office space, equipment, and support services to successfully accomplish their jobs. Include part-time or temporary faculty in the eligibility for

recognition and rewards for exemplary accomplishments, and publicize their noteworthy contributions to the campus.

Academic Freedom and Autonomy

Academic freedom and autonomy refers to the right of all faculty members to express freely their professional views in research and in the publication of results, in the classroom in discussing their subjects, and as academic citizens without institutional censorship when such views are appropriately and responsibly expressed (AAUP, 2001; Gappa et al., 2007: 140; 227–238).

EXAMPLES

- Clearly define what constitutes academic freedom and include the definition in the employment contracts for contract-renewable and fixed-term academic appointments. Publish academic freedom policies and protections through grievance procedures in faculty handbooks.
- Ensure that all faculty members are informed about their academic freedom rights and responsibilities through regular written communications and periodic emphasis at campus convocations and faculty development events.

Flexibility

Flexibility means the ability of faculty members to construct work arrangements that maximize their contributions to their institution while they simultaneously manage household responsibilities and lead meaningful personal lives (Gappa et al., 2007: 141, 197, 246, 270).

EXAMPLES

- Allow variable time bases in tenure-track and tenured appointments, and adjust probationary periods accordingly.
- Redefine the length of the probationary period to a maximum number of years of full-time service or its equivalent, and allow faculty members to work toward tenure at varying time bases and/or with occasional breaks in service over an extended period of calendar time.
- Provide work–life leave policies that support faculty members during specific periods of personal and family-related need.
- Place and regularly update listings of resources on campus websites to support individual faculty in managing their personal responsibilities, such as referrals for services of child or elder care.

Professional Growth

Professional growth involves opportunities that enable faculty members to broaden their knowledge, abilities, and skills, to address challenges, concerns, and needs, and to find deeper satisfaction in their work (Gappa et al., 2007: 141, 285, 298).

EXAMPLES

- Embed faculty development in the daily work of faculty members by assigning faculty members, including, when appropriate, contract-renewable and fixed-term faculty, to institutional committees, task forces, and responsibilities where they can simultaneously foster their professional growth, fulfill their work responsibilities, and participate in governance in a collegial environment.
- Help early-career and new faculty make the transition to successful faculty careers by welcoming them to campus through comprehensive orientation programs designed for each type of faculty appointment.

Collegiality

Collegiality requires opportunities for faculty members to feel that they belong to a mutually respectful community of colleagues who value their contributions, and who are concerned about their overall well-being (Gappa et al., 2007: 142, 305ff.).

EXAMPLES

- Encourage faculty members individually to take personal responsibility for the quality of their academic community and the professional behavior of their colleagues.
- Invite all new faculty members, regardless of appointment type, to participate in departmental meetings, faculty development programs, and campus-wide events, and ensure that they feel welcome and included.
- Provide all faculty members with sufficient office space and staff support services, as well as parking privileges, library cards, and access to campus health and recreational facilities.

When these essential elements are incorporated into faculty work and work-places, benefits accrue to faculty members and to their colleges and universities. Faculty who are treated equitably and with respect, who have access to professional development opportunities and the flexibility to organize their work to accommodate their personal lives, and who participate actively in decision making about their work are more likely to find satisfaction in their work and to have a greater commitment to their institutions. In turn, colleges and universities that have incorporated the Essential Elements should expect greater success in their efforts to recruit and retain excellent and diverse faculty members and increased organizational commitment from them.

Conclusion

No one knows what higher education will be like twenty or thirty years from now, in the United States or anywhere else, but we do know that it will be different from what we see today. We also know that the pace of societal change will be too fast to allow institutions more time than they have now to make decisions or to adjust to new demands. It is unlikely that the financial status of higher education will improve greatly either, at least in the near future. It is certain, however, that faculty members will be increasingly more diverse in terms of who they are, the appointments they fill, and the work they do. We also know that the work that colleges and universities have traditionally undertaken will continue to be critical to the future of society. The world will need educated citizens more than ever as the demands for new knowledge to solve complex world problems increase. But the pace of change is accelerating. Thus, colleges and universities today, more than ever before, must pursue strategically their mandate to recognize and understand the significance of the changes taking place around them, and act appropriately, rather than simply letting the environment control them or operating as if nothing was changing.

To stay ahead of their competition requires institutions to focus continuously on creating supportive working environments that utilize the talents of their faculty, their primary and only renewable asset, as fully as possible. The Essential Elements of faculty work and workplaces build on the traditional values underlying the academic career, including academic freedom, sufficient job security to engage in the thoughtful long-term work necessary for discovery and transmission of knowledge, continuous professional development, and participation and collegiality in a scholarly community. They are a beginning point for rethinking academic work and establishing attractive workplaces for today's diverse faculty.

References

Alderfer, C. P. (1972) *Existence, Relatedness and Growth: Human Needs in Organizational Settings.* New York: The Free Press.

American Association of University Professors (AAUP) (2001) *AAUP Policy Documents and Reports*, 9th ed. Washington, DC: AAUP. Online, available at: www.aaup.org (accessed April 21, 2009).

Archer, L. (2008) "Younger Academics' Constructions of 'Authenticity', 'Success', and Professional Identity." *Studies in Higher Education* 33 (4): 385–403.

Campbell, A. and Koblenz, M. (1997) *The Work and Life Pyramid of Needs.* Deerfield, IL: Baxter Healthcare Corporation and MK Consultants.

Dowd, K. O. and Kaplan, D. M. (2005) "The Career Life of Academics: Boundaried or Boundaryless?" *Human Relations* 58 (6): 699–721.

Finkelstein, M. J. (2007) "Negotiating the New Academy." *Academic Matters: The Journal of Higher Education* (April): 15–18.

Gappa, J. M., Austin, A. E., and Trice, A. G. (2007) *Rethinking Faculty Work: Higher Education's Strategic Imperative.* San Francisco: John Wiley.

Herzberg, F. (1966) *Work and the Nature of Man.* Cleveland, OH: World.

Hoffer, T. B., Welch, V., Williams, K., Hess, M., Webber, K., Lizek, B., Loew, D., and Guzman-Barron, I. (2004) *Doctorate Recipients from United States Universities: Summary Report.* Chicago: National Opinion Research Center.

Kinser, K. (2007) "For-Profit Institutions Need to Be Classified, Too." *Chronicle of Higher Education* 53 (March 30): 30. Online, available at: http://chronicle.com/weekly/v53/i30/30b00901.htm (accessed October 14, 2008).

McClelland, D. C. (1975) *Power: The Inner Experience.* New York: Irvington Press.

Maslow, A. H. (1970) *Motivation and Personality*, 2nd ed. New York: Harper.

Musselin, C. (2007) *The Transformation of Academic Work: Facts and Analysis.* Center for Studies in Higher Education, Research and Occasional Paper Series: CSHE.4.07. Berkeley: University of California at Berkeley.

Plater, W. M. (2007) "Background Paper for Consideration of a Project on the Future of the Professoriate." Seminar Presentation, Carnegie Foundation for the Advancement of Teaching, Palo Alto, CA (March 6).

Rhoades, G. (1998) *Managed Professionals: Unionized Faculty and Restructuring Academic Labor.* Albany, New York: State University of New York Press.

Rice, R. E. (1996) *Making a Place for the New American Scholar.* New Pathways Working Paper Series, no. 1. Washington, DC: American Association for Higher Education.

Rice, R. E., Sorcinelli, M. D., and Austin, A. E. (2000) *Heeding New Voices: Academic Careers for a New Generation.* New Pathways Working Paper Series, no. 7. Washington, DC: American Association for Higher Education.

Schuster, J. H. and Finkelstein, M. J. (2006) *The American Faculty: The Restructuring of Academic Work and Careers.* Baltimore: Johns Hopkins University Press.

Sennett, R. (2003) *Respect in a World of Inequality.* New York: W. W. Norton.

US Department of Education (2004) *Digest of Educational Statistics, 2004.* Washington, DC: NCES Publication 2004–331.

US Department of Education, National Center for Educational Statistics (2004) *National Study of Postsecondary Faculty.* Washington, DC: NSOPF:04.

Waterman, R. H., Waterman, J. A., and Collard, B. A. (1994) "Toward a Career Resilient Workforce." *Harvard Business Review* 72 (4): 87–95.

13
Developing Higher Education Professionals
Challenges and Possibilities

ROBIN MIDDLEHURST

Introduction

The art and practice of 'developing professionals' is a multilayered enterprise involving a variety of contexts, many different actors, and a range of processes over time. When designing developmental opportunities, one must ask some obvious questions such as 'What kind of higher education professional is needed in future?', 'What kind of developmental opportunities lead to the emergence and growth of professional skills and identity?', 'What capabilities and capacities need to be developed to grow as a higher education professional?', and 'In which settings and circumstances will these capabilities and capacities be exercised in future?' These are broad questions that do not have simple or definitive answers. Indeed, there are likely to be many possible answers since higher education is not homogeneous, either within or across countries. The UK sector is likely to become still more diverse in the next decade, as the missions of traditional universities evolve and as new providers emerge onto the scene. Furthermore, there is no single professional group within institutions; instead, many different professionals work in higher education carrying out diverse roles and portfolios, even where formal titles are similar. While there are common challenges arising from external trends and environmental conditions, both subtle and substantive differences also exist, with a range of choices available to institutions and individuals. Finally, a dynamic external environment is already creating—and doubtless will continue to create— uncertainty about the precise nature of future roles and associated capabilities and capacities. For all these reasons, development routes and opportunities are likely to be non-linear and varied in form and scope.

This chapter is deliberately exploratory. It seeks to examine three main themes: the changing context for professional practice, for higher education professionals, and for developmental agendas. While these will be dealt with discretely, there are numerous interconnections between the themes, both conceptually and in practice. A conceptual framework (drawn from research on "borderless education") is offered through which to consider the themes. This framework leads to the notion of "borderless professionals", a concept that offers a way of thinking about professionals, their roles and identities, and their development. The chapter is based on multiple sources of evidence, including my own research, the wider literature, experience of developmental work with professionals in higher education over some twenty years, reflection on working in a range of higher education settings, and analysis of recent studies that explore scenarios for the future of higher education and work.

A Conceptual Framework: from "Borderless Education" to "Borderless Professionals"

The term "borderless education" was originally coined by a team of Australian researchers. They were commissioned in 1997 by the Australian Ministry of Higher Education (the Department of Employment, Education, Training and Youth Affairs (DEETYA)) to elicit and test the available evidence for the interest and involvement of global media in higher education provision, and to draw out the short- to medium-term policy implications arising for Australian higher education (Cunningham et al., 1998). The contextual issues and drivers behind the research questions and research focus included globalization; media and information and communication technology (ICT) convergence; the impact of ICT and media on higher education; the impact of public sector reform on higher education; the context of distance, open, flexible, and lifelong learning in Australia and internationally; and the notion and emergence of the "virtual university" (ibid.: 7).

The research brief included the development of a set of scenarios for Australian higher education, and nine different scenarios were created. The key elements that contributed to the concept of "borderlessness" in education in this first study were the provision of education across boundaries, including national and regional boundaries, and boundaries of time and space through use of ICT. The concept also examined "borderlessness" in terms of convergence across previously discrete sectors. This included convergence of types of higher education provision and modes of operation, across media corporations and universities, public and private sectors, and business and corporate cultures.

A second Australian study (Cunningham et al., 2000) extended the focus of research from media businesses to the leading non-traditional providers of postsecondary education in the United States—the corporate, for-profit, and virtual providers—and the extent to which they presented threats to, and opportunities for, traditional universities in the United States and Australia. The motivation behind this study was more strongly stated than in the first, namely an increasingly competitive postsecondary learning environment, "with the pre-eminence of traditional universities as the major providers of higher education being challenged by non-traditional organizations such as corporate and virtual providers" (ibid.: 1).

The contextual issues and drivers behind the research noted the growth of the information society and the importance of knowledge-based rather than manipulative skills; the scope arising from ICT for "disintermediation", meaning the removal of a human intermediary in the teaching process; the growing demand for continuing professional education as an element of lifelong learning as well as off-campus (home, workplace) provision of courses to a growing population of "time-pressed adults"; employer demand for tailored education and training as well as servicing of the learning needs of employees in globalized businesses; and alliances between universities and private organizations in order to gain leverage through a combination of areas of strength to generate new sources of non-governmental income. The concept of "borderlessness" in this study built on the previous research and identified new elements such as heightened competition, challenges to traditional modes of learning and delivery of teaching, and alliances across organizations (and sectors) to create leverage and generate revenue. These elements were captured in the title of the researchers' final report: "The *Business* of Borderless Education" (italics added).

A third, UK, study, linked to the second Australian study (CVCP, 2000), added further dimensions to the concept of "borderlessness". In common with the parallel Australian research, the UK study focused on corporate universities and for-profit education, media, and publishing businesses, but added professional bodies and associations, educational services, and educational brokers. The study was international, investigating developments in the United Kingdom, the United States, continental Europe, and the Commonwealth. The UK team accepted the Australian reports' existing dimensions of boundary crossing (time, space, national, regional, sectoral, and organizational boundaries) and identified other emerging themes. Trade in education was becoming an important theme, with reference to "import" and "export" opportunities for higher education, accompanied by sometimes fierce debate about new delivery mechanisms for education "as a commodity" that crossed national borders and legal jurisdictions. Identifying transnational education as a traded service brought these forms of higher education into the international negotiating frameworks for liberalizing and deregulating trade established through the World Trade Organization's General Agreement on Trade in Services (GATS). With further developments in ICT, the researchers also noted the potential for "disaggregation or unbundling" of the teaching and learning system into discrete functions that could be delivered by different providers (as in the case of franchising of teaching or the separation of teaching from the provision of examinations). These providers might be private, for-profit, or public educational organizations.

The UK study drew upon analyses of trends in higher education and other sectors (Department of Trade and Industry (DTI), 1999; Chatham House Forum, 1998). Burton Clark captured many of the key developments identified in the United Kingdom's borderless education study when he commented that "knowledge expansion *and* specialization, *and* reconfiguration are self-propelling phenomena" (1998: 130). Clark's assessment resonated with a Chatham House Forum prediction that the intellectual capital base of the world was likely to double by 2020. This Chatham House Forum report provided corroboration for some of the trends highlighted by the Australian research team in their second study, including an increase in competition, convergence across industries, and coupling of economies, cultures, political centers, and many interest groups across national boundaries, creating greater complexity in sociopolitical issues. The UK report brought the various analyses together and, from its investigation of developments and trends, drew out a number of notable elements in borderless education. These were professionalism (a highly professional and customer-focused approach to education and training, particularly in the "earner-learner" markets); technology dependence and a need for technological compatibility for joint operations; the blurring of boundaries between previously discrete territories, alongside difficulties of categorizing new roles and entities; new emerging boundaries, as non-core business was outsourced; emergence of different forms of educational value (such as company certification over traditional qualifications); fluidity of educational level; growth in collaboration; and the rise of corporate branding among institutions, to signify reputation and market position.

These three reports covered a wide conceptual, geographical, and analytical terrain in an effort to map an increasingly competitive and commercial world of borderless education, in which the role of universities and their relationships with each other and with other sectors were increasingly being—or needing to be—redefined and reconfigured. To help make the link to borderless professionals, the key elements of "borderlessness" from these reports are captured in Table 13.1.

How might these reports, and the concept of "borderlessness", be applied to higher education professionals? There are several levels that could be considered:

- the level of context, in that the reports highlight important elements of a changing external and internal institutional context;
- the level of professions and professional roles, in terms of the impact of changes on the waxing, waning, and emergence of professions, and the configuration and reconfiguration of professional roles;
- the level of capabilities, particularly as a core capability will include the ability to work across boundaries;
- the level of development, in that developmental opportunities need to be 'fit for purpose' and designed to match the needs of "borderless professionals".

At this stage of the discussion one could postulate that a "borderless professional" is one who is aware of, and sensitive to, the context of borderless education, and who actively seeks to develop the capabilities to succeed in this context.

External and Internal "Borderless Contexts"

External Environments

Since the publication of the series of reports on "borderless education" there have been many other studies that have sought to apply one or more lenses to the future. Some have taken the form of scenarios such as those produced by the OECD Centre for Educational Research and Innovation (CERI) (Vincent-Lancrin, 2004) or by the Centre for Higher Education Policy Studies (CHEPS) (Enders et al., 2005). These scenarios focus on many similar themes to those of the borderless reports (developments in ICT, growth of competition and emergence of new providers,

TABLE 13.1 Key Elements of "Borderlessness" Drawn from Australian and UK Studies

Key elements	Explanatory note
Crossing (traditional) boundaries	Includes geographical and time and space boundaries as well as definitional boundaries, boundaries of operations, sectors, identity, and culture
Convergence	Covers the merging of activity and operations
Coupling	Includes linking of countries, sectors, and organizations through a variety of forms of collaboration
Disintermediation	Removal of human intermediaries, particularly in teaching and learning, and shift to ICT-mediated forms
Knowledge expansion, specialization, reconfiguration	Dynamic components of the "knowledge economy and society", which are core to the higher education business
Disaggregation or unbundling of functions within a system	Creates the potential to outsource, share, or divest particular functions and roles within and across organizations; also referred to as "commodification"
Deregulation	Liberalization of trade and removal of barriers to the free flow of goods and services
Emerging boundaries	New configurations of roles, operations, and organizations
Technology dependence	ICT is fundamental to most, if not all, operations, and creates new possibilities for interconnectedness; developments in technology are a major driver of change in and across organizations, roles, and working practices
Fluidity of educational level	Levels and types of educational opportunity are becoming more fluid and blurred, based on need and demand
Variety of educational value	What is valued as an educational opportunity or outcome is becoming more diverse, with different market (and non-market) values attached
Competition	Higher levels of competition and extended scope of competition across organizations, sectors, countries
Complexity	Greater levels of complexity through extended scale and scope of operational contexts and activities
Commercialization	Applies to higher education institutions as they seek revenue-generating opportunities and operate as "businesses" with a range of commercial activities within their portfolio. Linked to public sector reforms and to the dynamics of a knowledge-driven economy
Professionalism	Incorporating both traditional and new elements, notably increasing customer focus, and specialized and expanded skills
Branding	Exploiting reputation, signaling position and standing in the marketplace

more flexible learning structures, and variations in demand and supply of higher education in different markets). They also highlight other important factors, such as changes in state–university relationships and issues of governance; funding patterns and the market as a coordinating mechanism for higher education; demographic trends and their impact on types of demand for higher education in different parts of the world; and the quality issues that may arise from a more fragmented teaching and learning system, and less coherent student experience.

Developments in the research landscape are no less significant. One scenario in the CHEPS study, for example, highlights the increasing separation of teaching from research, and the organization of research into interfaculty and interuniversity units comprising flexible and semi-permanent teams in self-organized centers. These teams have a great deal of contact with partners in business, and in other organizations and interest groups. Another scenario points to increases in the volume of "applied research", and the separation of "big science" from applied sciences in funding and organizational terms. The former is now located mainly within cross-national consortia, which draw on researchers from universities as well as researchers from the public and private sectors. These scenarios pick up on the separation of knowledge production into "Mode 1" (knowledge arising from developments within and across disciplines) and "Mode 2" (knowledge created in the context of application), distinctions first made by Gibbons et al. (1994).

In the United Kingdom a number of other future-focused studies are being conducted (2007–2008), including a strategic foresight project and a study on the size and shape of the UK higher education sector. The former draws attention to phenomena that have developed further since the original borderless reports, and discusses their implications for higher education. These include the use of open-source content and software in education, the development of web-based communities and their impact on the dissemination of knowledge, the significance of mega-research collaborations involving "intense knowledge sharing and collaboration", and the continued growth of alternative sources of knowledge production outside universities. This report views UK higher education as part of a "global economy of learning" in which the key features include "a complex, dynamic and continually moving system, based on both economic and inter-personal interactions, in multiple context." This system is "highly interdependent, with its separate functions or strands inextricably interwoven, manifested and experienced on many different levels" (Universities UK (UUK), 2007b: 5). A number of "borderless dimensions", as set out in Table 13.1, are clearly visible.

The second of the UK reports (Universities UK, 2008) is again presented as three scenarios, as in the case of the OECD and CHEPS papers. The focus is more localized, considering elements such as changes in UK government policies toward higher education, changes in pre-18 higher education and training, changes in aspirations toward higher education within different student markets—18-plus, people in work, and the retired—and the degree of divergence of the four UK higher education systems (in England, Scotland, Wales, and Northern Ireland).

The four reports quoted here all focus on the environment for higher education, particularly in terms of the social and economic role of higher education, and the place of institutions in a global and regional higher education system. While the drivers of change identified are similar, the reports typically offer multiple possible futures, from greater homogeneity of the sector (based on slow adaptation to change and consolidation through institutional merger) to greater diversity (based on increased stratification of the sector into different types of institution, operating within different markets, with different missions). Creating choices and taking decisions that lead to successful outcomes will clearly depend on the skills and capabilities of the professionals of the future.

Internal Contexts

The four reports are less clear about the internal structure and overall shape of institutions and the nature of the internal working environment, although one can glean some clues from them. Variously, they highlight:

- increases in the size of institutions through mergers within the higher education sector and intersectorally;
- institutional failure and its consequences (merger and acquisition or bankruptcy);
- specialization of function (e.g. developing teaching materials for use across Europe; a shift in research and development activity outside Europe);
- institutional management as a career path;
- institutional differentiation and stratification involving differences in size, structure, funding, ownership, and modes of employment;
- horizontal and vertical integration of functions via the web;
- intra- and interorganizational networks;
- a holding company combining public and private entities with decentralized structures;
- a combining of university and company laboratories.

Two examples echo the borderless reports, and illustrate different dimensions from complexity of organizational function within a web of interconnections to a diversity of coexisting forms. The first vision involves

> fuzziness ... which encourages ... much finer-grain and [more] flexible differentiation of institutions than those of the age of institutional "types". Nowadays universities bundle and un-bundle their tasks in teaching, research and service, their multi-disciplinary profile, their geographical outreach and their embeddedness in a web of shifting organizational configurations within and beyond the institution.
>
> (Enders et al., 2005: 78)

The second view is essentially pragmatic: 'a university is what it does', and higher education institutions will do many different things in terms of focus and program offerings; the sector will include both public and private higher education institutions (Enders et al., 2005: 90).

A different perspective can be gained by looking outside higher education to the future of work. Here again, many reports adopt a 'scenarios' approach, both suggesting that the future is impossible to predict, and emphasizing the multitude of possible futures that may emerge. A report by PricewaterhouseCoopers (PWC) (2007) is useful for two reasons. First, the report focuses on 'people management' across organizations, which is relevant to the development of professionals; and second, it includes a survey of 3,000 'Millennials'—that is, graduates recruited to PWC from China, the United Kingdom, and the United States who entered work after July 2000, and who were surveyed about their expectations of work. This survey presents a small snapshot of the views of some future professionals who will be working in a sector that has many similarities to the higher education world of the future. The report also provides insight into the nature of professionals, their career motivations, and how these motivations might be developed in relation to the different scenarios.

The PWC report draws attention to three strong themes that were likely to impact on the business context and on people and work. First, business models were likely to change dramatically. Second, people management would become even more challenging as companies grappled with skill shortages, leading people through change, and seeking to create an effective workforce. Third, the human resources function would undergo fundamental change either to become, at one end of the spectrum, central to organizational functioning with a wide remit, or at the other, to be seen as essentially transactional and therefore outsourced, with the core internal function being about identifying and recruiting talent. It is worth noting that the UK higher education sector is currently being alerted to challenges in the development, search, selection, and retention of talented academic faculty (see Universities UK, 2007a), and in an earlier short report by the Higher Education Policy Institute (HEPI) (Archer, 2005) the human resource function in higher education was examined under the title *Mission Critical*.

As with the reports discussed earlier, the PWC authors begin with an analysis of global drivers. This analysis leads to an identification of core dilemmas, many of which are recognizable from the discussion above. However, the interpretation here is focused on the implications for organizations, people, and working environments (see Table 13.2).

The three scenarios that emerge from an analysis of the global drivers and core dilemmas have different implications for the nature of work and the choices open to professionals. In the first scenario (the Blue World), big-company capitalism reigns supreme and corporations are of huge size and scale. They provide the equivalent of the welfare state for employees to ensure that they can retain the best talent. Internally, managed service centers are sophisticated and highly efficient, and 'people metrics' are essential to tracking performance and productivity. The power of large corporations means that, in these cases, all services are laid on for employees. (In smaller enterprises, individuals would need to take care of themselves in terms of educational support, health, and insurance coverage.) Technology is all-pervasive in these globalized corporations, allowing businesses

TABLE 13.2 Global Drivers of Change and the Core Dilemmas Arising

Core dilemmas	Either	Or
Business fragmentation versus corporate integration	The potential breakup of large businesses and the rise of collaborative networks	Corporate integration, where big business becomes still more dominant
Globalization versus reverse globalization	In which the free market prevails and trade barriers disappear	In which protectionist policies begin to rebuild barriers to free movement of goods and people
'Technology controls me' versus 'I control technology'	Where technology enters into almost every aspect of life	Where a longing for the personal touch minimizes the impact of technology on consumers
Collectivism versus individualism	In which the common good prevails over personal preference (such as collective responsibility for the environment over individual interest)	Where individualism (focusing on individual wants) dominates as a response to the infinite choices available to consumers

Source: Adapted from PricewaterhouseCoopers (PWC) (2007).

to refine and individualize their relationships with consumers, employees, and shareholders (PricewaterhouseCoopers, 2007: 7–8).

In the Blue World, people are graded and profiled at 16 and categorized for work suitability in terms of capability and individual preferences. The top talent is highly prized and fought over. University education is managed by the company according to the organizational career path chosen by the individual. At the top level, employees take far greater control of their careers, with senior executives having their own agents to represent them and find the best roles and deals. Lower-level employees also take more active charge of their careers, and are demanding about the circumstances in which they choose to invest their human capital. Those outside the corporate sphere find employment choices limited to smaller companies that cannot provide the same level of development and financial benefits.

In the second scenario (the Green World), consumers and employees force change on companies, pushing them toward greater social responsibility. In this case, because of the strength of lobby groups, companies must be quick to react to consumer concerns, and clarity about products and services is essential. Companies exercise greater control over their supply chains, and rigid contractual obligations are in place. Audit processes assess ethical and environmental responsibilities and responses, and reputations and brands can rise and fall on the basis of green and wider ethical credentials. Businesses operate in a highly regulated world (PricewaterhouseCoopers, 2007: 12–13).

A common belief in the Green World is that employees choose employers who appear to match their beliefs and values. The reality is that the talent pool for the brightest and the best remains competitive, and while Corporate Social Responsibilities (CSR) rankings are a factor, the overall incentive package remains all-important. Incentives, however, include paid secondments to work for social projects and needy causes, which has become a popular trend. In the Green World, organizations have adopted a more holistic approach to developing people, including personal development and measuring the impact they have on the wider world. This has resulted in more employee engagement and longer job tenure within an organization.

In the third scenario (the Orange World), global businesses fragment and 'localism' prevails. Technology has a different impact, facilitating a high-tech business model in which networks prosper in place of large companies. Trade barriers come down to create a truly free market economy; there is a global network of linked, but much smaller, communities; and supply chains are built from complex, organic associations of specialist providers, varying greatly from region to region and market to market. Looser, less tightly regulated clusters of companies are seen to work more effectively. Other functions are picked up on a task-by-task basis. In the Orange World, individuals are responsible for their own development. People are more likely to see themselves as members of a particular skill or professional network than as an employee of a particular company. Individuals rely on achieving high scores in public rating scales of their past performance in order to get the next contract. Specialization is highly prized, and individuals seek to develop the most sought-after specialist skills to command the biggest reward package.

These three scenarios provide further insights into the future working contexts for professionals. They also suggest how certain kinds of environment may be shaped to attract professionals with different career motivations. Since higher education both employs and trains professionals, it is worth capturing some key elements of these different worlds (see Table 13.3).

What might be the implications of these different working and developmental contexts for higher education institutions and higher education professionals themselves? First, it is important to remember that 'one size will not fit all'. There are market opportunities available in a sector of diverse institutions for the multi-professional organizations that higher education institutions have become. Any one of the three scenarios might serve to differentiate an institution from its neighbors or competitors; equally, they may coexist within large and 'comprehensive' universities at faculty, unit, or divisional levels. In most cases it is also likely that different individuals, based on a range of personal and professional circumstances, including age, gender, ethnicity, as well as social and educational backgrounds and political beliefs, will align themselves more clearly with one scenario than with another (and that such alignments may change over a professional life cycle). This has implications for the shaping of career paths and reward packages for all staff; as in other kinds of organizations and sectors, the implications of these scenarios for the work and development of human resources (HR) professionals are of critical importance.

TABLE 13.3 Key Elements That May Impact on Professionals, Their Development, and Working Environments

Key element	Impact on professionals	Impact on development	Working environments
Tailored and comprehensive career opportunities attract performance-driven talent	• Strong competition and performance ethic • Corporate loyalty required	• Wide-ranging opportunities • Organizationally led at start • Senior professionals control their 'brand'	• Large-scale corporations • Performance metrics determine success
Ethical credentials and 'holistic benefits' attract talent	• Lifestyle, work, and values coincide	• Mix of professional, social and personal development opportunities	• Strongly regulated • Consumer and media influence • Measurement of social as well as professional impact
Specialization reaps high rewards	• Individual and specialist skills are key • Professional networks important	• Individual responsibility • Public ratings of performance influence development choices	• Networks prosper • Strong cross-boundary links • Loose regulation • Diverse markets

Source: Adapted from PricewaterhouseCoopers (PWC) (2007).

At this stage it is worth pausing to consider whether there are any threads that might connect these 'scenarios' and their component parts (as they seek to describe potential changes in work and career development contexts) with real changes in the working contexts of academic faculty. One study into the changes affecting the academic professoriate in six countries (Brazil, Denmark, Mexico, Peru, Russia, South Africa) offers interesting insights (Stromquist et al., 2007). The studies point to the massive expansion of higher education across all countries, with an emerging differentiation between institutions and concomitant differential conditions for the professoriate. The professoriate, the researchers find, is affected by new norms and practices derived from educational expansion, privatization, and other values and events associated with globalization. As a consequence, the professoriate faces a range of tensions (or dilemmas) between:

- keeping strong professional identities and having mostly part-time employment;
- reaching gender and racial equality and moving toward increasing efficiency to develop more competitive institutions;
- improving teaching and increasing teaching loads;
- engaging in more research activities and handling more administrative duties;
- developing local knowledge and engaging in more internationalization strategies.

The balance between these different dimensions varies by country, but also in relation to differences between the private and public sectors of higher education, between for-profit and non-profit, elite and non-elite, religious and secular institutions. Other factors that affect all types of institutions include shifts in professional autonomy and accountability, with a diminishing of self-regulation and a growth in external mechanisms of control (as well as an increase in market and competitive pressures). Although the tensions and dilemmas described here tend to be more operational than those described in the PWC scenarios, many of the drivers are the same, and some of the consequences for professionals are similar. In particular, the researchers draw attention to growing 'differentiation' between institutions, and 'segmentation' within the professoriate, because of differing market and employment conditions. These features echo some of the key elements of "borderlessness" identified earlier, and take us now into the domain of 'professions' and 'professional practice'.

Borderless Professions and Professionals

Traditionally, professional practice is defined and configured within the boundaries of 'a profession'. The hallmarks of a profession include specified standards of practice and behavior, specialized training, qualifications and apprenticeship, and membership of a professional association. Professions are, to an extent, spread across a continuum from 'hard professions' to 'soft professions'. In the former, professional bodies have statutory power; curricula, training, and qualifications are tightly specified and controlled; and practice is strongly regulated. Medicine and dentistry would be classic examples of such 'hard' professions. At the other end of the continuum, definitions of a 'profession' are much looser and less precise; there may be many developmental routes to becoming a practitioner, standards may not be sharply defined, and practice may be either semi-regulated or unregulated. An example of a non-statutory profession with less rigid boundaries might be marketing or student services.

At the hard end of the spectrum, standards and regulations are increasingly international, or even global (engineering standards are international, accountancy standards are global, for example). At the other end of the spectrum, standards may vary a great deal across countries and regions, so that professional practice in one country may be much more tightly defined than in another. Some branches of psychology or disciplines allied to medicine (such as podiatry or physiotherapy) are examples. In the modern world, professions have multiplied as knowledge has expanded and new disciplines have emerged. Burton Clark, for example, noted how by the mid-1990s, biological sciences had fragmented and recombined into new disciplines, how economics had created multiple subfields, and how psychology had become twenty or more specialisms, some with large national and international associations (1998: 130–131).

In the twenty-first century, such fragmentation and reconfiguration has continued, but with an added phenomenon of 'interdisciplinarity' and 'inter-professionalism'. Interdisciplinarity is encouraged both because it offers the possibility of gaining different perspectives on a common issue, and because inter-disciplinary working and insights can lead to the development of new knowledge and new disciplines. Interprofessional practice involves bringing different specialisms to bear on a common problem; the particular skills or insights of each specialism are important in their own right, but there is also the potential for the outcomes to be greater than the sum of the parts. As with interdisciplinarity, interprofessional practice has the potential to grow new knowledge or skills. This has happened, for example, in nursing, as new categories of nursing professionals have added aspects of medicine or pharmacy to their portfolio of skills.

If one adds technological developments to epistemological advances, then further levels of convergence (and divergence) occur. For example, analytical techniques in history and archaeology have been transformed by developments in technology, and in many aspects of media studies and the performing arts, technological developments have grown new disciplines and new professional qualifications. Technological, combined with epistemological, developments have created a need for new disciplinary skills—as well as knowledge and under-standing—and have often shifted or blurred the boundaries of what is defined as an 'art' or a 'science'. Technology also facilitates 'unbundling' and 'disintermediation', so that professional practice can be split into different skill sets, activities, or services, undertaken by different practitioners (or providers). It may also reduce the need for human intervention or skills, so that practice can become automated and delivered through new channels.

In these examples it is clear that many of the phenomena that are affecting organizations and sectors also have an impact on the nature of professions and the training and work of professionals. The elements identified in Table 13.1 are all visible. Professions are both converging and reconfiguring their boundaries, and professional associations are coupling through interlocking networks and collaborative activities across geographical and conceptual boundaries. One example from higher education is the growth and development of quality assurance (QA) within nations, at agency and institutional levels. From a handful of national agencies in the early 1990s, there are now more than fifty national agencies across the world.

New networks and professional associations have also developed regionally and internationally; for example, the European Network of Quality Agencies (ENQA) and the International Network of Quality Assurance Agencies in Higher Education (INQAAHE). The former has developed European standards through which to regulate the work of agencies, while the latter is involved in training, capacity building, and the development of new knowledge about the conceptualization and practice of quality assurance. Across countries, professionalization of quality assurance practice has featured both increasing regulation (typically within national boundaries) and pressures for deregulation across countries to permit the export of higher education from one country to another. Commercial opportunities have also developed as new professional quality assurance services are offered in the marketplace, branded in distinctive ways. When reviewing and observing the practice of quality assurance in higher education across the world, it is difficult not to conclude that the picture is now complex, competitive, and dynamic. The practice and profession of quality assurance (QA) are definitely "borderless".

There are other terms that have been used to describe recent changes to professional practice and the work of professionals, as well as shifts in professional identities. These include hybrid professionals with "blended" capabilities (Whitchurch, 2008). The term "blended" is also applied to learning to mean a combination of human and technological delivery of teaching. This meaning of "blended" is also apt in the context of professional skills and capabilities. The concept of hybridity implies a combination of different skills (and identities), and this is a useful descriptor for professions (and professionals) where convergence of skills across professional boundaries has occurred. Once again the sharp distinctions of the past, such as 'academic' and 'administrative' functions, are no longer as clear or as separate as they were. Both in the exercise of particular roles and in the development of professional practice, the skills and knowledge associated with each have converged, requiring new knowledge and skill sets (such as systems thinking and project management) and the development of new specialist fields (such as educational technology or knowledge management).

The academic profession has not been immune to these drivers of change, nor to the consequences of change for work practices and professional identities, as Stromquist et al. (2007) attest on the basis of their findings from six country studies. These authors highlight a shift in identity from academic faculty to "knowledge workers" (and, for those individuals in part-time or hourly-paid employment, as "just-in-time knowledge workers"). The role of the professoriate as intellectuals and, particularly, as "public intellectuals" they see as under particular threat as the nature of the university as a site for social contestation, critical thinking, and academic freedom is challenged by a range of converging forces.

Scott (2006), in a separate analysis of the academic profession in a knowledge society, identifies three main changes affecting academic practice. First, the development of mass higher education systems and the growing demand for all kinds of "knowledge workers" mean that research, scholarship, and university teaching have become mass occupations (rather than niche occupations staffed by small and selected cadres of experts). Second, connections between research and teaching have become much less straightforward. Both have become more professional and 'managed', and this has tended to split them apart, leaving academic faculty either to pursue multiple careers or to choose between different career directions. As Scott points out (ibid.: 24), "they [academic faculty] are not only researchers, but are also research managers and research entrepreneurs; they are not only teachers, but also course designers, quality managers and (even) sales and marketing people." The third change identified by Scott is changes in universities themselves, as they have become much more complex and multi-functional. These institutions are also embedded in more extended and differentiated higher education systems. However, none of these boundaries is static; 'mission differentiation', 'mission stretch', and 'mission volatility' are all visible as institutional leadership seeks to position the university or college within a dynamic environment.

Developments such as these bring consequences for individuals and their careers, for working practices, and for organizations in their efforts to grow capacity and capability, succession-plan, and attract and retain talent. At a human level, many mid-career and senior-level professionals are finding their skills inadequate or their roles squeezed (as elements of one role are coupled with another, previously separate role). An example from universities is the role of pro-vice-chancellor, where the range of portfolios and associated skills is changing rapidly from academic capabilities to management capabilities and, most recently, business and commercial capabilities. At the same time, other roles are affected, for example, the traditional role of university secretary and registrar. In some cases this role has been split into different functions across the boundaries of governance, finance, academic regulation, and corporate services (but still within the boundary of 'professional support services'). In other cases the disaggregated functions have crossed traditional academic and administrative boundaries, so that a pro-vice-chancellor (resources) has taken up an expanded role at the expense of the secretary's and registrar's role.

The role of vice-chancellor is also changing, with new skills, knowledge, networks, and capacities required. Levels of interaction between universities and their communities and regions have increased to such an extent that a large part of the role (in many regions and cities) involves skills of negotiation, chairmanship, and engagement with widely diverse individuals, groups, organizations, and sectors. For others, international linkages are critical, requiring political and intercultural sensitivity, and collaborative leadership across international consortia and networks. The importance of funding and of political priorities for universities adds fundraising, financial expertise, and political skills as further key aspects of a skills portfolio for vice-chancellors. This expansion of responsibilities and skills is also leading, in some universities, to a separation of roles (for example, between president and provost, or vice-chancellor and deputy vice-chancellor). In other cases, there is an implicit or explicit reconceptualization of the individual vice-chancellor's role into an expanded domain—'the Chief Executive Officer's (CEO's) Office'—where several roles and functions contribute (in a blended way) to the exercise of academic, executive, business, political, and community leadership. These changes in role, function, and identity at the vice-chancellor level reflect the expanding role of universities in society, and the increasing levels of inter-connectivity of teaching and research across organizations, sectors, regions, and countries.

Examining the changes and choices for new generations of academic faculty is, of course, as important (and arguably more so) as focusing on changes at more senior levels, since these are of fundamental importance for the future of the university. As Scott comments, the changes can produce bewildering, as well as intoxicating, effects:

Young scholars and researchers now encounter an environment with more emphasis on markets, a dwindling sense of the public interest (and a weakened sense of a public ethic), the erosion of professional norms and structures, a mass and multi-tasking occupation, and much more complex (but also more volatile) "home" institutions.

(2006: 24)

While shifts in identity and changes in roles and skills are occurring within professional groupings, changes are also creating a potential for movement of professionals across types of profession within organizations, across sectors, and across geographical borders. The convergence and reconfiguration of roles across traditional academic and administrative boundaries is made much richer, more varied, and more complex when seen in the context of increasing porosity between sectors. As universities have expanded their roles, activities, and budgets, they have also adopted or adapted the practices of other sectors, and this makes them more attractive to professionals from other sectors. The crossing of boundaries from other sectors into higher education is visible in finance, human resources, marketing, research management, and enterprise, for example. There are also professionals who exercise hybrid roles across sector boundaries (as many academic faculty in the UK National Health Service (NHS) have done for decades). International joint appointments, as well as the movement of academic pro-fessionals across national boundaries, are a further feature of 'coupling' and of "blended" or hybrid roles. Finally, it is also possible for professionals from other sectors such as industry and commerce, or for professionals with different academic or administrative career backgrounds, to cross over, and perhaps ultimately to colonize previously 'bounded' roles or specialisms. This has happened within the role of pro-vice-chancellor (with administrators appointed to an academic role, such as pro-vice-chancellor, student experience) and among vice-chancellors, with appointment of individuals drawn from business, industry, or government circles.

The examples above illustrate the diversity, complexity, and dynamism (some might argue volatility and uncertainty) in the world of professions and professionals. Many elements of borderlessness are visible at these levels, in addition to organizational and environmental levels. So what implications arise for the development of professionals and professional practice?

Borderless Professionals and Their Development

Building Developmental Capacity at Organizational Level

The PricewaterhouseCoopers (PWC) report cited earlier (PricewaterhouseCoopers, 2007) highlights a number of important factors of relevance to development at an organizational level. First, the institutional approach to development is likely to differ across organizations by virtue of their size, the scope and scale of their operations, the markets in which they operate, and the culture and style of organization that their leaders wish to promote. Where differentiation of mission, positioning, and reputation are important, approaches to development may be seen as a source of competitive advantage and part of the visible branding of the institution. Given the demographic profile of the United Kingdom over the next decades, attracting and retaining talent will be of critical importance, and provision of tailored professional development opportunities an attractive selling point. Given the need for regular updating of skills in light of rapidly changing professional practice and a competitive, performance-driven environment, individual professionals will also demand the developmental provision needed to differentiate themselves and their teams. A corporate-driven approach to development, combined with tailored opportunities for individuals and groups, reflects the Blue World of the PWC report.

A second point that arises from the PWC report is the importance of choice for individuals. Modes of working, working environments, and the nature of work itself may all be subject to the lifestyle and stage-of-life choices of individuals. Those belonging to the new generation of professionals (the 'Millennials') are used in exercising individual choice; individual lifestyles are important to them, and technology makes it far more feasible to design work contexts around the choices of individuals. This will pose significant challenges for human resource departments as they exist in institutions today, but may make the difference between institutional survival or decline in the future. Development opportunities in this context may need to be highly tailored once again, but also wide-ranging in terms of variety and type of opportunity. Conventional generic programs for cohorts at a particular level may become a thing of the past. Instead, developmental opportunities may include volunteering, overseas secondment, or time out for personal development through challenging projects and activities. Individual choices around values and lifestyles are part of the Green World, and will be as relevant to universities in the future as they are to companies and consultancies.

The Orange World highlights a different set of issues. Here, developmental opportunities are not necessarily led and organized by large organizations; they are driven by individuals who may be self-employed portfolio workers, or employed in smaller organizations. The skills and capabilities of individuals are as critical as in the Blue World, but it is in the specific interest of professionals to ensure that each working assignment is itself a development opportunity and an opportunity to build new networks. Development opportunities and the capabilities acquired are part of an individual's personal 'brand', and the networks with which they are connected are part of how they find work, join projects, and grow new communities of practice. To attract these professionals, universities and colleges will need to offer interesting assignments, networking opportunities, creative colleagues, and flexible employment conditions. The work of Richard Florida (2002) offers insights into the interests and aspirations of this "creative class". Any employment contract with these professionals cannot be based on the 'parent–child' models of the past. Instead, contracts must be built around a partnership of shared interests where developmental opportunities are part of the deal struck between the parties. Once again this scenario is likely to create significant challenges for the typical bureaucratically structured human resources department, and institutions' views of employer–employee relationships that prevail in many higher education institutions today. The notion of national pay bargaining and associated practices also has no place in an Orange World.

The Nature of Developmental Opportunities

Higher education has followed other sectors in developing more tailored and individualized development opportunities than in the past. While cohort learning, open programs, and collective training schemes still exist—and have their place— they have been complemented, and in some cases replaced, by a proliferation of individual development routes such as one-to-one coaching, 360-degree personal reviews, and self-assessment diagnostics combined with tailored skills development and mentoring. Small-group work in the form of Action Learning or group work in communities of practice is also prevalent, both within professional groups and across professions and sectors.

There has also been a proliferation of 'crossing the boundaries' developmental opportunities as other contexts have been used for development. Music, drama, art, travel, and international and cross-sector contexts are often the focus for the delivery of developmental experiences. Developmental opportunities have also been conceptualized in different ways. Challenging experiences—at a personal, physical, and emotional level—have become much more important, both at senior levels and as part of professional formation by means of challenging work assignments and projects. There has also been greater effort made to blend development more closely with the realities of work and lived experience, and to blend action with reflection and feedback on impact and performance in order to build self-insight as much as new skills and capabilities. Finally, there is evidence in some of the best forms of development of convergence between real-time problem solving and individual and collective learning. One example is the successful "Common Purpose" initiative in UK cities, which brings together diverse professionals to address community problems, learning from the actions taken and the challenges arising.

The challenge for the future will be to continue to develop a wide range of development opportunities, taking advantage of the opportunities that technology provides. Given the changing nature of higher education, cross-sector development and transnational development opportunities are likely to be of increasing importance, as will be the requirement to tailor development to the needs of individuals (and groups), with their varied circumstances and aspirations. The accessibility of knowledge, and the choices of training and development routes available, will also challenge existing practice. Furthermore, just as the employment of professionals could evolve into a partnership with a balance of interests, so development and training could (and arguably should) be reconceptualized in terms of co-design and shared learning. Old-fashioned hierarchies of experts and amateurs, masters and apprentices may finally be laid to rest.

Developing Professional Capabilities at an Individual Level

The concept of a "borderless professional" and the context of "borderless education" suggest a need to develop a range of professional capabilities that are not always evident among today's professionals. ICT skills will be ubiquitous, as will be the need to demonstrate capabilities through regular and sharp forms of performance assessment, clarity about track records, and open forms of performance 'display' (or personal branding). Networking skills, negotiating skills, intercultural sensitivity, and political capabilities will be at a premium. In addition, sophisticated business acumen, as well as detailed (in some cases) and wide-ranging knowledge (in others) of practices and innovations across sectors and professional communities, will be important differentiating factors for individuals. Cross-boundary projects, sometimes multilayered and multidimensional, will require sophisticated project and program management skills and teamwork skills, while complex organizational arrangements that cross sector and country boundaries will require in-depth legal knowledge and financial and business skills.

Interpersonal skills and communication remain important but are likely to have added dimensions such as facility in foreign languages, and familiarity with the languages and discourse of other sectors, for both verbal and written communications. At the other end of the spectrum the level of organizational knowledge and understanding (and organizational 'nous') will require strong conceptual and intellectual abilities and a level of professional education that is only beginning to be evident among higher education practitioners, whatever their background. 'Professionalism' and professional practice will increasingly imply the acquisition of new professional qualifications and continuing professional development in fields that are still in their infancy (such as Master's of Business Administration degrees (MBAs) in higher education management and leadership).

Existing professions such as human resources, marketing, and finance will both increase and extend their levels of specialism to embrace new areas; and there is likely to be an increasing need for cross-fertilization and cross-boundary working in multiprofessional teams. Those with the strongest levels of cross-functional knowledge and understanding and intercultural skills will be most in demand, and there may be further differentiating features based on work experience, for example, "borderless local professionals" and "cosmopolitan borderless professionals". Leading and coordinating relationships, performance, and contributions across these diverse individuals and professional practitioners will be a demanding and highly skilled activity.

Arguably, one of the most important capabilities at an individual level (as well as within organizations, as Hamel (2007) suggests) is "creativity". In a rapidly changing and competitive environment, many reports point to the need for constant innovation. The ability to challenge the status quo, to develop new scenarios, to create new ways of conceptualizing practice, and new ways of working and organizing professional practice, will again be significant differentiating features for individuals and groups. In developmental terms, even more exposure to the concepts and practices of creative disciplines—as well as opportunities to be creative at work—may be needed for the future. It is no longer desirable or acceptable, for economic as well as social, psychological, and health reasons, for individuals to be trapped in tedious, boring, or tightly demarcated roles.

Conclusion

This chapter has ranged widely in a quest to explore the kinds of environments in which professionals will practice, the changes that will affect the nature of professions themselves, and the professionals who work within and across professional boundaries. Professional roles are already in a state of flux, with many varieties and choices available to individuals—as well as tensions and dilemmas—as they progress through their careers. The concept of "borderless education" captures many of the key features of a changing professional environment; and the concept of "borderless professionals" also has value in identifying the kinds of capabilities, experiences, and aspirations that are likely to characterize the professionals of the future.

While the design and delivery of professional development have changed in recent decades to become more varied, creative, and responsive to individual needs, both aspects will need to go much further in this direction. Tailored and individualized development will become a demand as well as a requirement if talented individuals are to be attracted to institutions, projects, and professional networks. Development may also become a matter of 'brand' and reputation, with institutions vying for the attention of talented professionals in a competitive market, where offering particularly challenging and stimulating developmental opportunities may provide the key to recruiting and retaining key individuals and groups. Those who can design exciting and significant developmental opportunities will be in high demand—and will be professionals in their own right—with new qualifications and standards evolving to meet the needs of new cadres of "borderless professionals".

References

Archer, W. (2005) *Mission Critical? Modernising Human Resource Management in Higher Education.* Oxford: Higher Education Policy Institute.

Chatham House Forum (1998) *Open Horizons: Three Scenarios for 2020.* London: Royal Institution of International Affairs.

Clark, B. (1998) *Creating Entrepreneurial Universities: Organizational Pathways of Transformation.* Oxford: IAU Press and Pergamon/Elsevier Science.

Committee of Vice-Chancellors and Principals (CVCP) (2000) *The Business of Borderless Education: UK Perspectives.* London: CVCP (now Universities UK).

Cunningham, S., Tapsall, S., Ryan, Y., Stedman, L., Bagdon, K., and Flew, T. (1998) *New Media and Borderless Education: A Review of the Convergence between Global Media Networks and Higher Education Provision.* Canberra: Department of Employment, Education, Training and Youth Affairs.

Cunningham, S., Tapsall, S., Ryan, Y., Stedman, L., Bagdon, K., and Flew, T. (2000) *The Business of Borderless Education.* Canberra: Department of Employment, Education, Training and Youth Affairs.

Department of Trade and Industry (DTI) (1999) *Work in the Knowledge-Driven Economy.* London: DTI.

Enders, J., File, J., Huisman, J., and Westerheijden, D. (eds.) (2005) *The European Higher Education and Research Landscape 2020: Scenarios and Strategic Debates.* Twente, the Netherlands: Centre for Higher Education Policy Studies (CHEPS).

Florida, R. (2002) *The Rise of the Creative Class.* New York: Basic Books.

Gibbons, M., Limoges, C., Nowotny, H., Schwartzman, S., and Scott, P. (1994) *The New Production of Knowledge: The Dynamics of Science and Research in Contemporary Societies.* Buckingham, UK: SRHE/Open University Press.

Hamel, G. (2007) *The Future of Management.* Boston: Harvard University Press.

PricewaterhouseCoopers (PWC) (2007) *Managing Tomorrow's People: The Future of Work 2020.* London: PricewaterhouseCoopers. Online, available at: www.pwc.co.uk/pdf/managing_tomorrows.pdf (accessed January 13, 2009).

Scott, P. (2006) "The Academic Profession in a Knowledge Society." In *The Formative Years of Scholars,* ed. U. Teichler. London: Portland Press (for the Academia Europeaea–Wenner-Gren International Series).

Stromquist, N., Gil-Anton, M., Balbachevsky, E., Obakeng Mabokela, R., Smolentseva, A., and Colatrella, C. (2007) "The Academic Profession in the Globalization Age: Key Trends, Challenges and Possibilities." In *Higher Education in the New Century: Global Challenges and Innovative Ideas,* ed. P. Altbach and P. McGill. Peterson, MA: Boston College; Rotterdam: Sense Publishers.

Universities UK (UUK) (2007a) *Talent Wars: The International Market for Academic Staff.* Policy Briefing. London: Universities UK.

Universities UK (UUK) (2007b) *Universities UK—Strategic Foresight Project.* Interim Report. London: Universities UK.

Universities UK (UUK) (2008) *The Future Size and Shape of the Higher Education Sector in the UK: Threats and Opportunities.* London: Universities UK.

Vincent-Lancrin, S. (2004) "Building Futures Scenarios for Universities and Higher Education: An International Approach." *Policy Futures in Education* 2 (2): 245–263.

Whitchurch, C. (2008) *Professional Managers in UK Higher Education: Preparing for Complex Futures.* Final Report. London: Leadership Foundation for Higher Education.

14

The Challenges of a Diversifying Workforce

CELIA WHITCHURCH

Introduction

This volume draws on the contributions of twelve international researchers and practitioners to review the diversification of institutional communities, current thinking about roles and identities in higher education, and examples of innovation and good practice. This final chapter reflects back on these contributions to review common issues and problems, and different approaches that may be adopted in providing opportunities and environments that are attractive to talented staff, at the same time acknowledging local, national, and institutional constraints. It suggests that key challenges arise from diversifying staff profiles, changing staff expectations and aspirations, new forms of recognition and reward, the dispersal of management and leadership activity, and the emergence of more fluid, 'amoeba'-like institutions. A further challenge arises from the fact that these changes are occurring concurrently, so that formal, organizational structures and processes continue to coexist with the emergence of lateral relationships and networks.

However, although considerable attention has been paid in the literature to a diversifying student body, and environments in which this has occurred, consideration of a diversifying workforce, and the challenges that this presents, has been more muted. On the one hand, there may have been a reluctance to focus on this because, as noted in Chapters 2 and 10, the concept of 'management', let alone that of 'human resource management', is subject to significant contestation in academic contexts. On the other hand, there would appear to be a need to do so, because research suggests (Whitchurch, 2008) that both academic faculty and professional staff are likely to experience greater anxiety about managing people than about managing budgets or resource allocation.

It is a truism, indeed almost a cliché, to say that staff are an institution's most valuable resource. At the heart of that resource are academic faculty. Around this central core, however, as described by Rhoades in Chapter 3, is a broader professional community that incorporates people working in generalist and specialist functions, as well as in fields as diverse as information services, teaching and learning, academic practice, institutional research, enterprise, and staff development. In common with academic faculty, many of these people also have loyalties to their own professional and disciplinary communities, with associated bodies of literature, associations, and conferences. They are likely to have areas of interest that overlap with those of academic colleagues, and are able to provide additional spaces for academic activity via networks and partnerships that expand opportunities in relation to, for instance, student participation, business development, and research consultancy.

At the same time, as shown by Usherwood in Chapter 4, traditions of academic collegiality may give rise to a mismatch between the questioning and critique associated with knowledge creation in the academic sphere, and more conservative approaches to the development of organizational structures, processes, or practices. This may be exacerbated by what has been seen as the 'professionalization' of management, which is no longer conducted solely by rotating part-time and fixed-term academic managers in roles such as head of department, dean, or pro-vice-chancellor. They have been joined in contemporary institutions by people who may have an academic background but who decide to become full-time higher education managers at senior management team level, as well as by specialist professionals in areas such as marketing, research services, quality, finance, and human resources. Many of the latter have prior experience in other sectors that they bring with them, whereas up until the 1990s it was still possible, in the United Kingdom at least, to find, for instance, 'personnel officers' with a generalist background and no professional qualifications. For all these kinds of reasons, there remains in many higher education locales "a highly resilient anti-management culture—even amongst managers" (Archer, 2005: 5).

This leads to the question as to how 'people management' might occur in higher education, whether universities are indeed 'different' from other knowledge-intensive organizations, and whether practices from other sectors might be adopted by, or adapted to, them. Universities are often major local and regional employers, and also operate in global markets, so it is unlikely that they will be immune to external, cross-fertilizing influences. There are also reputational issues that arise from comparisons with other local and international employers, not only with respect to remuneration, but in relation to conditions of service and work–life flexibility.

A Diversifying Institutional Community

It has long been recognized that the relationship of academic faculty with their discipline is likely to be stronger than their relationship with their institution (for instance, Henkel, 2000; Becher and Trowler, 2001). However, the range of backgrounds and allegiances of contemporary staff has been less well observed. This is evidenced by, for instance:

- A changing disciplinary base, including the incorporation of practice-based disciplines, as in the health field, staffed by individuals whose career trajectories are likely to have included significant periods as practitioners and teachers, but who may have come to research more recently. Their professional identities, therefore, will have been formed initially outside higher education, creating the possibility of not only a dual but a triple allegiance, to their professional body, to their subject discipline, and to their institution. Furthermore, their research is likely to involve significant collaboration with external partners in other settings, such as clinical or social care and, therefore, to have a strong "Mode 2" orientation (Gibbons et al., 1994).

- A greater 'casualization' of the workforce, arising from the increased use of part-time and short-term contracts. As noted by Rhoades in Chapter 3 and Gappa in Chapter 12, the majority of faculty members in the United States are now in non-tenured positions. Oba, in Chapter 6, notes that in Japan too, following legislation, there has been a rapid rise of staff employed on a fixed-term basis since 1998.

- Increasing numbers of staff, particularly those on contracts, are putting together their own portfolios of activity, incorporating elements that include teaching as well as various forms of research and development and/or consultancy. Furthermore, the concept of the 'internal consultant' appears to be gaining currency, whereby people move from project to project and are paid on a project-by-project basis, with or without an institutional retainer.

- A general trend away from an assumed consistency between academic posts, even in the same discipline. While in countries such as France, Germany, and Japan, recruitment processes have in the past been based on a national selection of eligible candidates for posts that were generic, Musselin describes in Chapter 8 how contemporary recruitment is increasingly conducted locally by institutions, with greater specificity in relation to, for instance, programs to be taught and research to be conducted.

- Moves toward more learner-centered and client-oriented services, involving the recruitment of professional staff who are able to work closely with academic tutors in meeting a range of 'student life' needs in relation to areas such as welfare, careers, learning support, and counseling (Whitchurch, 2008).

Within a single institution, therefore, there may exist individuals who perceive themselves as having different professional identities, with different concepts of, for instance, academic autonomy, what constitutes applied research, relationships with students, and pedagogy. This may even occur *within* practitioner-oriented fields that are externally accredited, such as engineering, medicine, the law, nursing, and health visiting. Different program teams may wish, because of their traditions and/or clientele, to have different criteria and procedures for both recruitment and progression. This can create operational and policy complexities, which have to be managed at unit, department, and institutional levels, for instance, in relation to workload models and promotion criteria.

The situation is made more complex by the fact that a blurring of boundaries between functional groupings is also occurring, as described by Whitchurch (2008), and by Middlehurst in Chapter 13. This is illustrated, for instance, in academic support centers dealing with a range of academic and pastoral functions. As shown by Oba in Chapter 6, while the work that takes place in such centers may be innovative and pathfinding, individuals can also be vulnerable to perceptions that they belong neither to 'academic' nor to 'professional' domains of activity, unless they are able to develop new forms of space and identity. This in turn creates challenges in relation to career recognition and development. The opportunity to pursue new forms of activity is likely to depend on the availability of development opportunities such as training programs, mentoring and coaching schemes, secondments or exchanges, and also on recognition by senior and line managers of the potential contribution of staff in roles that move beyond commonly understood boundaries.

Changing Aspirations and Expectations of Individuals and Institutions

There is a significant literature that reflects on the durability of academic identities around traditional values of autonomy and academic freedom. Henkel, in Chapter 1, suggests that insofar as the academic community adapts to pressure for change, external or internal, such adaptation is likely to be based on informed judgments of both the reasons for and likely implications of such change. The higher education sector, in common with other sectors, is not only subject to the 'push' of government policy or market opportunities. There are also 'pull' factors caused by societal change, such as approaches of younger generations to work, and a desire for more flexible working patterns, creative opportunities, and portfolio careers (Strauss and Howe, 1991; McCrindle, 2008; Florida, 2002; PricewaterhouseCoopers, 2007). Such factors also generate change from within higher education sectors and institutions. This is likely to be particularly significant in countries where the average age of teaching staff is falling, as in the United Kingdom, where it continues to fall from 42.5 in 2006 (Watson, 2006).

As noted by Usherwood in Chapter 4, flexibility with respect to lifestyles has become a critical issue for those belonging to the 'Millennial' generation, who tend to value autonomy, choice, and work–life balance as part of the employment 'package'. Career pathways may be sought, therefore, that allow options to be kept open, for instance, via secondments and consultancy opportunities. These may coexist with the traditional pathways pursued by other, more senior, cohorts. In this type of environment, experience counts for less than awareness of current issues: "[U]nwillingness to go by precedents and suspicion against accumulated experience . . . are now seen as the precepts of effectiveness and productivity. You are as good as your successes; but you are only as good as your *last* successful project" (Bauman, 2005: 44).

Thus, younger staff do not necessarily anticipate a career for life, with clearly defined transition points, and wish to acquire experience and qualifications that will be distinctive. Significant variables in relation to expectations and aspirations may also arise from both discipline and type of institution. In the United Kingdom a National Framework Agreement (Universities and Colleges Employers Association (UCEA), 2003) aimed to achieve equity in rewarding work of equal value, and has enabled institutions to develop parallel career tracks for different 'families' of roles, as described by Strike in Chapter 5. These career tracks can be singular (teaching or research) or multiple (a traditional balance of teaching, research, and third-leg), or be represented as a "career climbing frame" in which individuals may move laterally between, and gain credit for, teaching, research, consultancy, and other forms of activity over an extended time period, thus providing the possibility of multi-choice career pathways.

Diffusion of Management and Leadership Responsibilities

A trend toward devolved management (Bolden et al., 2008), particularly in large institutions with a well-developed "periphery" (Clark, 1998), has resulted in more individuals having 'people' responsibilities, whether as heads of academic or functional departments, or as team or project leaders. Furthermore, there is a tendency for management and leadership skills to be required at an earlier stage in people's careers, so that they are not confined to the most senior levels of staff, and 'management' is no longer something that is undertaken solely by a minority of people. It may also occur laterally among peers, so that one person may be leading a team in one setting but be 'managed' by another member of that team in another setting. In such conditions there may be a "cascade" effect (Whitchurch, 2008: 26) whereby 'management' capacity, including self-management, is spread laterally across an institution. It therefore becomes integral to the work of a range of people, including rank-and-file academic faculty, who may be managing a program module or research group.

In order for institutional (and even national) policy to be interpreted at local level, and to be influenced by successful practice, understandings of changing expectations and aspirations are likely to be required not only at senior levels, but also among teaching, research, and project teams. Program leaders and principal investigators are likely to encounter 'people' challenges as part of their day-to-day responsibilities, for instance, in relation to demands for flexible working alongside heavier teaching loads. Addressing such challenges may result in solutions that are tailored to local circumstances, but can also be shared with, and adapted to, other locales.

The spread of distributed management and leadership models is likely to encourage adaptiveness in relation to external requirements, such as the demands of regulatory bodies; obligations arising from institutional strategy, for instance, in relation to workloads; and local innovation, for instance, in relation to new forms of learning as applied to a specific disciplinary field. Since it is often not possible to change or adapt structures sufficiently quickly, 'management' may be a question of being creative with existing mechanisms, and/or bringing local practice and formal frameworks into accommodation. In this situation, 'management' and 'leadership' might be seen more as a joint enterprise among colleagues. It may also be that understandings of professionalism drawn from sets of competencies and behaviors will be increasingly complemented by ideas about generic 'people' skills and that, reflecting Middlehurst's comment in Chapter 13, "[o]ld-fashioned hierarchies of experts and amateurs, masters and apprentices may . . . be laid to rest."

Recognition and Reward Systems

As Strike notes in Chapter 5, it can no longer be assumed that all will pursue traditional career paths, which confer positional status as well as providing clearly defined reward structures, and in which, despite national and local initiatives, priority tends to be given to rewarding research, often because it is easier to measure than teaching. In the United Kingdom, full economic costing initiatives highlight the diversity of individual contributions. Some individuals may wish to pursue a research career, moving from one position to another in research officer-type roles. Others may focus on teaching, or professional practice, or the development of teaching and learning in their field, while others may work on broadly based projects such as widening participation, or the enhancement of the student experience. This increasing spread of activity impacts on the career paths that might be available to a widening range of staff. In the United Kingdom it has been recognized that this raises issues about reward structures, and the Higher Education Academy is in the process of developing a broader range of promotion criteria to assist institutions with comparability issues. It remains to be seen how the provision of more flexible career pathways, for both academic faculty and professional staff, is impacting on career patterns and opportunities.

In the meantime, however, as public funding shrinks, other forms of recognition are emerging to meet specific circumstances, including, for instance:

- An increase in the use of titles such as director of teaching and learning, together with discretionary responsibility allowances at school or faculty level, which provide a sense of recognition and status for people who may not be able to achieve immediate promotion to the next rung on the ladder, while offering them an addition to their curriculum vitae and portfolio. This type of initiative would be more likely to occur at local level, and to have medium-term implications.
- The opportunity to self-invest for the long term, for instance, via mentoring, sabbaticals, and tailored development opportunities. Middlehurst, in Chapter 13, offers a scenario in which staff take responsibility for their own development using professional networks. This type of scenario is likely to be attractive to people for whom "[n]etworking skills, negotiating skills, intercultural sensitivity and political capabilities will be at a premium." Assisting people to invest in their own long-term development and growth, via what Middlehurst terms "co-design and shared learning", may be recognized increasingly as a key element of reward systems, particularly subsequent to the global economic downturn that began in around 2008. As is suggested by Usherwood in Chapter 4, such self-investment opportunities are likely to have a particular appeal for those belonging to the 'Millennial' generation, who are less likely to be attracted solely by the status conferred by a title.

Institutional Adaptation

Greater flexibility in institutional responses to individual expectations and aspirations raises questions as to how institutions might articulate this via their organizational shape and regulatory frameworks. While there may be pressure for clarity and specificity in relation to, for instance, workloads or criteria for promotion, a degree of 'fuzziness' may also be beneficial in dealing with individual circumstances, such as career breaks for family or other reasons. The construction of people-oriented frameworks, therefore, is increasingly likely to be informed by a degree of pragmatism in trying to achieve optimal solutions.

Alongside roles that encompass a balance of teaching, research, and 'third leg' or administrative activity, some roles are becoming more specialized, focusing on, for instance, new modes of learning, while others are coalescing in what were previously seen as discrete activities. Observing this phenomenon in relation to library and information services, Law (Chapter 11) points to "the paradox of an increase in 'professionalism' but a loss of public need for the core skills of the profession." In some countries, such as the United Kingdom, the Netherlands, and Australia, this can create a dissonance between formal positionings in which specialist professional staff are categorized for employment purposes as 'non-academic' even while their work increasingly interdigitates with that of academic colleagues. By contrast, in the United States, for instance, "professional library staff enjoy tenured positions and are seen as much more analogous to academic faculty."

Middlehurst, in Chapter 13, develops the concept of "borderless professionals" who are comfortable operating in global contexts, crossing boundaries of time and space, between knowledge providers in and outside higher education, and between learning modes. Such developments are likely to encourage institutions to become increasingly recombinant and 'amoeba'-like, and to reshape and re-form, partly as a result of people joining and leaving from external environments to meet specific agendas. As is shown by Smit and Nyamapfene in Chapter 7, in countries where rapid change is occurring, as in South Africa, where there is potential for discontinuity between expectations and what might be achieved in practice, policymakers may also be challenged in building in appropriate flexibility that will allow individuals to 'grow' within an evolving system.

Continuity and Change

From the chapters of this volume it would appear that, notwithstanding the specifics of individual systems and institutions, forces for both continuity and change continue to coexist in higher education. Challenges will remain, therefore, from the inherent tensions traditionally associated with institutional "complexity" (Barnett, 2000) including, for instance:

- allegiance to a discipline through which it is anticipated an academic reputation will be built versus becoming a 'good citizen' at institutional level;

- arising from this, "idealism" versus "pragmatism" in achieving progression in an academic career (Henkel, 2000);
- endeavors to attract research grant income versus institutional pressure to cover indirect as well as direct costs (and to reject funding that does not offer this);
- reward structures that may or may not incentivize academic faculty via, for instance, return of overhead income to fund conference attendance;
- increased functional specialization alongside the emergence of team and project working;
- the balance of research and teaching activity, particularly with the introduction of workload models (Barrett and Barrett, 2007);
- making the case for promotion on the basis of teaching, as well as research, activity.

Additional complexities arising from diversification include:

- multiple institutional agendas, for instance, in relation to professional education and new forms of applied research, alongside traditional teaching and research in mainstream disciplines;
- less commonality around professional understandings and histories;
- a broadening base of institutional activity, interest groups, and networks;
- interest groups that may compete with as well as rely on each other;
- less clarity about the boundaries between such groups;
- higher levels of political activity with respect to goals, and means of achieving them;
- new influences exerted by external agendas and collaborations.

This diversification carries with it the potential for extension and enhancement of academic and institutional activity through, for instance, external links and partnerships, at the same time as higher levels of risk from an increasing spread of activities, interests, and stakeholders. All this raises the game for those in universities with 'people' responsibilities in their endeavors to engage and motivate their colleagues.

Conclusion

Many of these changes are happening in parallel, producing multiple frames in which day-to-day activity occurs. While formal organization charts, hierarchies, and line management relationships continue to exist, these are likely to be overlaid with lateral forms of working. Structures and processes may lag behind practice as individuals make their own decisions about their futures. Institutions may, therefore, wish to consider how they might, through local initiatives, increase awareness among their staff of opportunities that exist to influence these structures and processes. On the one hand, the diversification of the workforce has the potential to add value both in relation to the lateral reach of staff inside and outside the university, and in relation to the experience available at different levels of disciplinary and institutional hierarchies. On the other hand, as noted above, this can increase the potential for risk, not least because of a multiplication of interest groups who may create additional synergy, but may also pull in different directions.

These effects are likely to be compounded by the global economic downturn. At the time of writing there is evidence of a freeze on faculty salaries and early retirement schemes in the United States (Smith, 2009), at the same time as calls for government to undertake "sustained, systematic investment" (Rhoades, 2009) in higher education, not only as part of a stimulus for economic recovery, but also to encourage "social innovation" and "[expand] the capacity of our intellectual capital." However, the current signs are that, despite increased demand for student places as a result of the downturn, governments have so far been unwilling to absorb the additional costs. At the same time, tuition fees in private institutions in the United States have risen (Gill, 2009). Even if additional public investment takes place in one form or another, pressures on the higher education workforce, including casualization involving part-time and fixed-term labor, seem likely to persist as institutions seek the flexibility to deal with increasingly uncertain levels of funding. This will in turn engender renewed focus by managers, and those involved in their professional development, on issues around motivations, rewards, and incentives, and the means by which individual aspirations might be met.

Fixed understandings about identities and careers are, therefore, likely to be increasingly difficult to sustain and, as suggested by Usherwood in Chapter 4, it is "impossible to build 'a great place to work' by having a single set of standards." Thus, to quote Law (Chapter 11): "Personal and softer skills are perhaps more valued by interview panels than are specific professional competences, if only because the life-span of such . . . competences can be measured in months rather than decades." The facilitation of individual contributions is likely to involve 'people policies' that bring formal processes and unwritten understandings into accommodation. Such adjustments do not need to be abrupt or radical, and may be incorporated at local level into day-to-day working. The challenge will be to use tensions that may arise with institutional structures and processes in ways that are creative and productive for those on the ground.

It is suggested that addressing these challenges is likely to involve:

- playing to strength while recognizing areas of need;
- offering flexible and bespoke solutions;
- paying attention to lateral communication and networking;
- considerations vis-à-vis the equity of the overall employment 'package';
- adopting enabling frameworks that motivate autonomous professionals in plural environments;
- balancing the rights of individuals as employees with associated obligations and freedoms, for instance, in workload models;
- relating increased self-reliance by individuals to institutional direction;
- modulating perceptions of dualities between, for instance, individual expectations and aspirations, and those of policymakers (whether government or institution based);

- a broadening out of thinking about possibilities for career and professional development.

Finally, the fact that addressing these challenges is likely to involve resource-intensive work and effort should not be underestimated. This process, however, may itself create value if portfolios of good practice that are both innovative and workable can be constructed and shared within and between national higher education systems. It is hoped that this volume may contribute to such a process, and begin to provide a response to the call for "ideas about how universities dedicated to public service could be managed and governed in future" (Deem et al., 2007: 187), in ways that meet the needs and aspirations of a diversifying range of academic faculty and professional staff.

References

Archer, W. (2005) *Mission Critical? Modernising Human Resource Management in Higher Education.* Oxford: Higher Education Policy Institute.

Barnett, R. (2000) *Realizing the University in an Age of Supercomplexity.* Buckingham, UK: Open University/SRHE.

Barrett, L. and Barrett, P. (2007) *The Management of Academic Workloads.* London: Leadership Foundation for Higher Education. Online, available at: www.lfhe.ac.uk/publications/research.html (accessed April 21, 2009).

Bauman, Z. (2005) "The Liquid-Modern Challenges to Education." In *Values in Higher Education,* ed. S. Robinson and C. Katulushi. Vale of Glamorgan, UK: Aureus Publishing.

Becher, T. and Trowler, P. (2001) *Academic Tribes and Territories: Intellectual Enquiry and the Culture of Disciplines.* Buckingham, UK: SRHE/Open University Press.

Bolden, R., Petrov, G., and Gosling, J. (2008) *Developing Collective Leadership in Higher Education.* London: Leadership Foundation for Higher Education. Online, available at: www.lfhe.ac.uk/publications/research.html (accessed April 21, 2009).

Clark, B. (1998) *Creating Entrepreneurial Universities: Organizational Pathways of Transformation.* Paris: International Association of Universities Press and Elsevier Science.

Deem, R., Hillyard, S., and Reed, M. (2007) *Knowledge, Higher Education, and the New Managerialism: The Changing Management of UK Universities.* Oxford: Oxford University Press.

Florida, R. (2002) *The Rise of the Creative Class.* New York: Basic Books.

Gibbons, M., Limoges, C., Nowotny, H., Schwartzman, S., Scott, P., and Trow, M. (1994) *The New Production of Knowledge: The Dynamics of Science and Research in Contemporary Societies.* London: Sage.

Gill, J. (2009) "Applicants Are Denied Shelter from the Storm." *Times Higher Education* (February 5).

Henkel, M. (2000) *Academic Identities and Policy Change in Higher Education.* London: Jessica Kingsley.

McCrindle, M. (2008) "The ABC of XYZ: Generational Diversity at Work." Online, available at: www.quayappointments.com.au/email/040213/images/generational_diversity_t_work.pdf (accessed April 21, 2009).

PricewaterhouseCoopers (PWC) (2007) *Managing Tomorrow's People: The Future of Work 2020.* London: PricewaterhouseCoopers. Online, available at: www.pwc.co.uk/pdf/managing_tomorrows.pdf (accessed April 21, 2009).

Rhoades, G. (2009) Open Letter to the President and Members of Congress. Online, available at: www.aaup.org/AAUP/about/gensec/feb09open+let.htm (accessed April 7, 2009).

Smith, H. (2009) "The Midas Touch Eludes Harvard." *Guardian* (March 10).

Strauss, W. and Howe, N. (1991) *Generations: The History of America's Future, 1584 to 2069.* New York: William Morrow.

Universities and Colleges Employers Association (UCEA) (2003) *Framework Agreement for the Modernisation of Pay Structures*. Online, available at: www.ucea.ac.uk/en/New_JNCHES/Framework_Agreement_.cfm (accessed April 21, 2009).

Watson, D. (2006) "Whatever Happened to the Student Experience?" *Academy Exchange* 4 (Summer): 9–11.

Whitchurch, C. (2008) *Professional Managers in UK Higher Education: Preparing for Complex Futures*. Final Report. London: Leadership Foundation for Higher Education. Online, available at: www.lfhe.ac.uk/publications/research.html (accessed April 21, 2009).

Index